History Plays of Shakespeare

A Revaluation

Second, Revised and Enlarged Edition

History Plays of Shakespeare

A Revaluation

Second, Revised and Enlarged Edition

Jonathan S. Shaw

ATLANTIC

PUBLISHERS & DISTRIBUTORS (P) LTD

Published by
ATLANTIC
PUBLISHERS & DISTRIBUTORS (P) LTD
7/22, Ansari Road, Darya Ganj,
New Delhi-110002
Phones : +91-11-40775252, 23273880, 23275880, 23280451
Fax : +91-11-23285873
Web : www.atlanticbooks.com
E-mail : orders@atlanticbooks.com

Branch Office
5, Nallathambi Street, Wallajah Road,
Chennai-600002
Phones : +91-44-64611085, 32413319
E-mail : chennai@atlanticbooks.com

ISBN 978-81-269-1354-1

Printed in India at Nice Printing Press, A-33/3A, Site-IV, Industrial Area, Sahibabad, Ghaziabad, U.P.

Dedication

To the memory of my father
Valentine Payne Shaw
for my initiation into
Shakespeare's Plays.
To my life partner
Hannah
for immeasurable patience,
and to my
students
far and wide
for invaluable inspiration

Acknowledgements

The real begetters of this book are Prof. S.C. Sen Gupta, (author of *Shakespeare's History Plays*) Head of the Dept. of English, Jadavpur University, and Prof. R.K. Sinha, Head of the Dept. of English, Patna University. While Prof. Sinha with his inspiring lectures, created abiding fascination for Bolingbroke, Prince Hal, Hostpur and Falstaff, Prof. Sen Gupta channelised that fascination to explore the treatment of history by Shakespeare. On account of indifferent health he could not accept the responsibility to provide informal assistance.

The study was formally supervised by Prof. R.C. Prasad, author of the highly acclaimed research, *Early English Travellers to India*. I am deeply indebted to him for constant encouragement, meticulous supervison and many valuable suggestions.

My heartfelt thanks are due also to my sister, Joyce Shaw, lecturer, Arvind Mahila College, for patiently going through the typescript.

I acknowledge my gratitude to the library staffs of the British Council Library, Calcutta and Patna, of the National Library, Calcutta, of the University Libraries of Mumbai, Patna, and Bhagalpur, for the courteous and painstaking service rendered by them.

It is humanly impossible to read all that has been written on Shakespeare or consciously to remember all that one has read and made one's own. Although my debt to scholars whom I have known only in their books is apparent on every page that

I have written and in the bibliography, yet I feel that I have hardly been able to record all my obligations. I take this opportunity to express my indebtedness to the following books in particular—Prof. Bullough's *Narrative and Dramatic Sources of Shakespeare*, Vols. III and IV, L.C. Knights' *Further Explorations,* and Wilbur Sanders' *The Dramatist and the Received Idea.*

J.S. Shaw

Preface

In the *Svarga-Arohanika Parva* of the *Mahabharata,* there is a verse describing that greatest of the Indian epics: "As the sacred ocean and the snow-clad mountains are both regarded as mines of precious gems, so is this *Mahabharata.*" With equal truth the description can well be used for Shakespeare. He too is like an ocean or a mountain full of precious gems. The words of Juliet ring in our ears:

> My bounty is boundless as the sea,
> ...the more I give to thee,
> The more I have for both are infinite.

The store of gems is so inexhaustible, the bounty so boundless, that the customary 'another-book-on-Shakespeare' apology becomes idle.

Indeed, few subjects, if any, have accumulated so vast and astonishing a body of scholarship as the study of Shakespeare's plays. Paradoxically, however, it is the ever-increasing bulk of Shakespeare criticism which in turn necessitates further additions—in some cases to carry on and elaborate a point of view, while in others to clear the dust (even gold or silver dust). The ideal aim of criticism is to view the object as it really is. But in the case of a great poet like Shakespeare this is impossible. The plays written by him about the English Kings were unfortunately christened as Histories. "What's there in a name?" says our poet. Nevertheless, this name, to a great extent, has been responsible for the treatment meted out to these plays. It has been customary to look upon the Histories as works of national glorification or political treatises. The modern historical approach to Shakespeare relates the plays to Elizabethan concepts of degree and order, and to the politics of the time. The poet is generally considered as the unofficial spokesman for the Tudor establishment. It must be admitted that this politico-moral approach created a fresh interest in the History Plays in the early forties of the last century. But it has far outlived its utility. The repeated emphasis on the political import and attempts to place these plays in the frame of their time have done more harm than good. It is time we take these plays out of such frame and give them their due beside the Comedies and the Tragedies of our author. This is possible only if we recognize the universal and the eternal in the plays. "The play's the thing", says Hamlet,

> Wherein I'll catch the conscience of the King.

And so says Shakespeare. He catches the conscience of King John, of King Henry V, of King Richard III, of all his kings. But he also catches the conscience of a murderer, a scrivener, a soldier, a Faulconbridge, a Falstaff. In the process he catches our own conscience too. But, first, we must rid ourselves of all preconceived notions about Tudor politico-moral doctrines and must submit ourselves to the thing, that is, the play. This is the point of view from which the History Plays are studied here.

In keeping with this point of view, which seeks to emphasize the universal, an attempt is also made to consider these plays in the light of the Indian concept of *rasas* (sentiments) and types of characters. The works of Shakespeare, the greatest dramatist of the world, transcend time and space, and as such they can be fruitfully studied in the light of Indian dramaturgy. A detailed study of Shakespeare's drama in this light should be taken up separately. It is hoped that the meagre hints given here of, for instance, the possibility of looking upon *Richard II* as a play of the *karuna rasa* (pathetic sentiment) or upon *Richard III* as a play of the *bibhatsa rasa* (odious sentiment), of considering Bolingbroke as a *pratinayaka* (counter-hero) and Faulconbridge as a *pithamarda* would make the plays more easily accessible to Indian readers and Sanskrit scholars. It should also lead to further and more scholarly work in this direction. In Sanskrit, the History Play was never recognized as a genre, although some of the dramatists did write of historical subjects. Bhavabhuti, for example, wrote semi-historical plays. It is, however, in the plays of Vishakhadatta that we come close to historical drama. His *Mudraksasa,* in particular, can be well placed beside Shakespeare's *Henry V*. The widespread truism that Kalidasa was the Shakespeare of India does not work—at least not in the realm of History Plays. If the former wrote any truly historical plays they are lost to us. In fact, the whole of Sanskrit drama, despite its richness in other respects, has nothing to offer comparable to Shakespeare's History Plays.

In the discussion which follows, only six plays of the 'Histories' group, namely *Richard III, King John, Richard II, Henry IV Parts I and II* and *Henry V*, are included. Thus, in limiting the study, I have followed Lily B. Campbell. Controversies regarding the authorship of *Henry VIII* as well as *Henry VI* plays still persist and their inclusion prejudices our approach to the History Plays. A detailed account of all this is furnished in Chapter 3. A perusal of the chapters dealing with the six plays would make it plain that the viewpoint pursued by me is so amply illustrated by these plays as to make the omission of *Henry VI* trilogy and of *Henry VIII* of little consequence.

The first two chapters dealing with the background serve, among other things, to throw light on the distortions caused by the so-called historical approach to Shakespeare.

Sonnet 84 contains certain lines which remind the reader of the never-withering greatness of Shakespeare, and are pertinent to any study of the supreme poet:

> Who is it that says most which can say more
> Than this rich praise—that you alone are you?
> In whose confine immured is the store
> Which should example where your equal grew?
> Lean penury within that pen doth dwell
> That to his subject lends not some small glory;
> But he that writes of you, if he can tell
> That you are you, so dignifies his story.

He is he, and none other like him. He is he, no less in Histories than in Comedies and Tragedies. This is what I believe and have tried to demonstrate. I would consider my labour amply rewarded if the study introduces the reader to even one or two of the precious gems from that inexhaustible ocean, Shakespeare. The great Indian dramaturgist, Dhananjaya, in an ironical statement pays his homage to him who says that from dramas, which distil joy, the gain is only knowledge, as in the case of *itihasa* (history) and the like. He pays his homage to him, for he has averted his face from what is delightful (*tasmai namah svaduparanmukhaya*). How long shall we keep our faces averted from what is delightful in the Histories of Shakespeare?

Quotations from the History Plays, except *King John*, have been taken from the Cambridge edition of Dover Wilson. In case of *King John*, the New Arden edition of E.A.J. Honigmann has been used. Citations from all other works of Shakespeare are from Peter Alexander's edition of *The Complete Works*. The Bible quotations, except where otherwise mentioned, are from the authorized version.

The book attempts to throw light on the History Plays of Shakespeare from literary perspective. It will be useful to the students and teachers of English literature particularly Shakespearean drama and researchers in this field.

J.S. Shaw

Contents

NON OBEST VIRTVTI SORS

The Background (1): Tudor Historiography

1

"Every true history is contemporary history", says Croce.[1] The historical perspective is constantly changing, and one can look at the past only through the spectacles of the present.[2] Till the nineteenth century the emphasis had been on facts,[3] but today all important historians, even though they may not go as far as Croce and Collingwood, seem to agree that historical writing is "not immune from change".[4] It is the historical milieu of an age which largely determines its outlook on life in general. The historian's outlook, in turn, is bound to colour his vision of the past. Referring to the Medieval historian's outlook, Prof. Sen Gupta dubs it 'singularly unhistorical'.[5] Certainly, 'unhistorical' is not the correct word, for after all the Medieval historians and thinkers looked at the past from their own historical perspective, but what Sen Gupta contends is that the Medieval historians judged all events from the point of view of the omnipresence and omnipotence of God and, thus, made history subserve theology. The Jewish and Zoroastrian prophets looked upon history as "the masterful and progressive execution, on the narrow stage of this world, of a divine plan which is revealed to us in this fragmentary glimpse".[6] Jeremiah, for instance, writing of Judah in the sixth century B.C., says:

> I looked to the earth, and lo chaos,
> To the heavens, their light was gone.
> I looked to the hills, and they quivered,
> All the heights were shuddering.
> I looked and behold there was no man!
> All the fowls of the heaven were fled.
> I looked to the gardens, lo desert,

All the townships were destroyed.
Before the face of Jehovah
The glow of his anger.[7]

In other words, though apparently everything might appear chaotic, yet God remains behind the scene. He is the Potter,[8] having complete authority over all men as well as nations. All authority derives from Him, and He may, for some unknown divine purpose, lend it even to the wicked:

> I have made the earth, the man and the beast that are upon the face of the earth, by my great power and my stretched out arm and I give it unto whom it seemeth right unto me. And now I have given all these lands into the hand of Nebuchadnezzar, the King of Babylon, my servant.[9]

In keeping with such views, the Medieval historian regards God as the first (and almost the only) cause. This provides him with a ready explanation for every event which is traced to the will of God. Like Jeremiah, St. Augustine firmly believes that God controls the kingdoms of men:

> He (I say) having left neither heaven, nor earth, nor angel, nor man, no nor the most base and contemptible creature, neither the bird's feather nor the herb's flower, nor the tree's leaf, without the true harmony of their parts, and peaceful concord of composition; it is no way credible, that He would leave the kingdoms of men, and their bondages and freedoms loose and uncomprised in the laws of His eternal Providence.[10]

and explains the rise of the Roman empire as well as its sack by Marius as the ordinance of God.[11]

As a sharp contrast to this, let us note what Tolstoy has to say about the destructive Napoleonic wars:

> If history had retained the conception of the ancients it would have said that God, to reward or punish His people, gave Napoleon power and directed His will to the fulfilment of the divine ends, and that reply would have been clear and complete. One might believe or disbelieve in the divine significance of Napoleon, but

> for anyone believing in it there would have been nothing unintelligible in the history of that period, nor would there have been any contradictions.
>
> But modern history cannot give that reply. Science does not admit the conception of the ancients as to the direct participation of the Diety in human affairs, and therefore, history ought to give other answers.[12]

This clearly underlines the transition from the Medieval to the Modern approach to history. To the Medieval historian, the role played by man appears, at best, to be confined to secondary causes and contingent happenings, and as such is of little significance. "Man", says St. Thomas Aquinas, "is directed to his ultimate end by the notion of the first cause, and to his proximate end by the notion of subordinate movers, as the soldier is directed to victory by the high command, and to his tactical dispositions by the regimental commander."[13] By 'subordinate movers', St. Thomas means human actions as well as the movements of Fortune with its ceaselessly revolving wheel.[14] Next to Providence, Fortune is the most important factor in the eyes of the Medievals. Essentially changeable as she is, her chief function is to bring men down. Chapman perhaps exaggerates her role, when he remarks that she is 'supreme arbitress of human destiny'. Nevertheless, she plays an important role and, "nowhere was she more powerful than in the courts of Kings".[15] Hence, medieval view of Kings and history is naturally influenced by the image of Fortune. Dante provides an example in his *Divine Comedy*. Fortune is 'a general minister':

> Set over this world's glory and found delight,
> From time to time those vain goods to transfer
> From people to people, and from class to class,
> Beyond cunning of mortals to deter.
> Hence the empire from that to this must pass,
> In wax and wane obeying her decree
> Which lurketh like a snake hid in the grass.
> She is past your wit to understand; but she
> Provideth, judgeth, governeth her own,
> As the other Gods do theirs in their degree.
> To her mutations is no respite known.

Necessity in her forbiddeth pause:

Thus comes he oft who is raised or overthrown.[16]

In Boccacio too, this is the central idea. The goddess Fortune is pictured as blind—blind to virtue and merit alike. She knows only ceaseless movement. Her wheel keeps moving always. As with Providence so with Fortune, man is absolutely helpless, a mere puppet. The result is that, whether due to their strong belief in the omnipresence and omnipotence of God and (or) their concept of Fortune's wheel, the Medieval historians are constrained to attach very little value to human will. They have, therefore, as Hale points out, "generally neglected to inform their readers in the ordinary means of carriage in human affairs, and thereby maimed their narrations".[17]

Undoubtedly, though the Medieval notions of history persist to a considerable extent in the sixteenth century, with the Renaissance, "man was restored to the centre of the universe".[18] The image of Providence, ordaining all human affairs as well as of Fortune pulling the high-ups down, is still there, but with Humanism man's role acquires a far greater significance than was hitherto assigned by the Medieval historians and thinkers. This is the essential difference, as noted by various critics,[19] between Lydgate's *Fall of Princes* and the Tudor *Mirror for Magistrates.* The result is that human motivation is recognised as an element as important as Providence and Fortune. Whereas for the Medievals, only Providence and Fortune constitute the moving forces of history, and man rather than playing is played upon by these forces[20] for the Elizabethans, the moving forces of history are Providence, Fortune, and human character.[21] Hence, as Prof. Sen Gupta observes, though Tudor historiography had its roots in medieval thought and could not totally get rid of its medieval heritage, yet its outlook was essentially humanist and largely free from the dominance of theology. It tried to explain human affairs in a human way, keeping the first cause, as far as possible in the background.[22]

The first indications of this vital shift of emphasis from the theological to the humanist outlook in historiography are to be noticed in the *Chronicles* of the fourteenth century French historian, Froissart, translated into English by Lord Berners during the reign of Henry VIII. Tillyard, though deploring the lack of what he calls "the more philosophical and moralised way of looking at history", has rightly drawn attention to the psychological element in Froissart's chronicles.[23] The very fact that Froissart gives precedence to the psychological element or—to borrow a beautiful expression from Tillyard—'the mental springs of action' over other things, goes to prove that he is more interested in man, his motives and actions. As a simple instance, one may look at his concluding remarks on Richard II's fall:

> .... For I saw, and so did all the world, Richard of Bordeaux twenty two year King of England, and after the crown returned to the house of Lancaster, and that was when King Henry was King, which he had never been if Richard of Bordeaux had dealt amiably with him; for the Londoners made him King because they had pity on him and his children.[24]

The moral, if any, is practical and worldly. Richard is deposed, because he has antagonised the Londoners. There is no talk of his grandfather's sin visiting on him, or of his own sin in getting his uncle, Gloucester, murdered. Even Edward Hall, the spokesman of the Tudor philosophy of history, admits the relevance of human motives. Let us, for instance, examine his account of the events leading to the murder of the Duke of Clarence, the brother of King Edward IV:

> In the xvij yere of Kyng Edward, there fel a sparcle of privy malice, betweene the King and his brother the duke of Clarence whether it rose of older grudges before time passed, or were it newly kyndeled and set a fyre by the Quene, or her blond which were ever mistrusting and prively barkynge at the Kynges lignage or were he desirous to reigne after his brother.... The fame was that the King or the Quene, or bothe sore troubled with a folysh Prophesye, and by reason thereof began to stomacke & grevously to grudge against the duke. The effect of which was after King Edward should reigne, one whose first letter of hys name shoulde be a G.... The

> King much greved and troubled with hys brothers dayly querimonye,...caused hym to be apprehended, and cast into the Towre, where he beyng taken and adjudged for a Traytor, was prively drouned in a But of Malvesey.[25]

Although there is a reference to the extrahuman agency of a prophecy relating to the letter G, yet the emphasis is clearly on human motives: personal grudge, mistrust, 'querimonye'. It may be pointed out that the account given by Hall is vague and that it lacks the neat, bold lines of a historical narrative. Nevertheless, it is clear that in Hall's view what led to the imprisonment and tragic death of Clarence was neither Providence nor Fortune; it was one or perhaps a number of the purely human motives mentioned in the extract. For another instance, one may look at Holinshed's account of Mortimer's imprisonment by Glendower and the question of his ransom:

> The King was not hastie to purchase the deliverance of the earle March, bicause his title to the crowne was well inough knowen, and therefore suffered him to remaine in miserable prison, wishing both the said earle, and all other of his linage out of this life, with God and his saincts in heaven, so they had beene out of the wale, for then all had been well inough as he thought.[26]

Again, personal motive is attributed to Bolingbroke's action or, rather, inaction—a guilty conscience, a weak title. His refusal to ransom Mortimer is plainly due to political expedience. In this as well as in the earlier passage, history is seen from the point of view of cause and effect. According to the Medieval outlook, since all things are governed by the First Cause, there is little sense in exploring the secondary cause, that is human will and human motives. The situation is completely reversed during the Renaissance owing to the impact of Humanism. In fine, as Hale observes, there is "a steady tendency to play down the irrational, the 'marvel' element in their narratives"[27] and simultaneously a growing interest in causation, a serious endeavour on their part "to trace the cause of an effect before throwing in their hands and invoking God, Fortune, or the Spirit of the Times".[28] The extent to which man's free and rational choice is recognised, is evident from the fact that even the theological thinker of the time, Richard Hooker, admits of and puts considerable stress on human will. Underlining the difference between man and other creatures. Hooker observes:

> ...amongst creatures in this world, only Man's observation of the Law of his Nature is Righteousness, only Man's transgression Sin. And the reason of this is the difference in his manner of observing or transgressing the Law of his Nature. He doth not otherwise than voluntarily the one or the other.[29]

Human action, a product of man's free will is, Hooker tells us further, subject to reward or punishment on its merit, not as a result of the capricious ways of Fortune: "Now rewards and punishments do always presuppose something willingly done well or ill."[30] But this is not all. There are situations which may be beyond man's control. Hooker takes those diverse human situations also into account which to a great extent regulate human will:

> What we do against our wills, or constrainedly, we are not properly said to do it, because the motive cause of doing it is not in ourselves, but carrieth us, as if the wind should drive a feather in the air, we no whit furthering that whereby we are driven. In such cases therefore the evil which is done moveth compassion; men are pitied for it, as being rather miserable in such respect than culpable. Some things are likewise done by man, though not through outward force and impulsion, though not against, yet without their wills; as in alienation of mind, or any the like inevitable utter absence of wit and judgment. For which cause, no one did ever think the hurtful actions of furious men and innocents to be punishable. Again, some things we do neither against nor without, and yet not simply and merely with our wills, but with our wills in such sort moved, that albeit there be no impossibility but that we might, nevertheless we are not so easily able to do otherwise.[31]

Three things strike us in Hooker's outlook. First, man, no longer a puppet, has become the chief participant with an independent will and diverse motives. Second, his will though independent is conditioned by particular human situations which cannot be separated from his motives and actions. It must be noted specifically that the conditioning factors are not Providence or Fortune but inevitable human circumstances of which man is a part. Third, the role of God is no longer seen to be that of the chief player. Instead, He has receded to the sidelines as an observer and umpire, the distributor of rewards or punishments. The approach is still fundamentally moral—and the moral becomes more relevant, more immediate[32]—but it is not theological as the medieval approach had been.

The tone is moral in Machiavelli, too, for he "yearns for an unattainable society of good and pure men".[33] For the first time propounding the conception of pure politics, he brings about a dissension between politics and ethics.[34] Nevertheless, by stressing what men actually do rather than what they ought to do, Machiavelli shares with Hooker and others of the Age a growing concern for man and his motives. It is from this point of view that Croce associates him with the Reformation:

> Nicolo Machiavelli is considered a pure expression of the Italian Renaissance; but he should also be connected in some way with the movement of the Reformation, with that general need, which asserted itself in his time, in Italy and elsewhere, to know man and to study the problem of the soul.[35]

From all the above examples it becomes clear that with the Renaissance, history becomes man-centred, and we may conclude with Collingwood that "a return was made to a humanistic view of history based on that of the ancients".[36] However, the providential view does not disappear altogether. It persists particularly in the form of the cyclical theory of sin and retribution. As demonstrated by L.B. Campbell, the theory itself is based on three Biblical texts: *Romans* xii. 19, *Numbers* xiv-18 and *Matthew* xviii,[37] though in fact it goes back to the ancient Greeks. As Elliott-Binns points out, it is rooted in the tendency manifest in the ancient world to look at the group, particularly the family or clan, rather than the individual, as the unit.[38] Hardyng's verse chronicle, first published by Richard Grafton in 1543, provides an example of the theory:

> For when Henry the fourth first was crowned
> Many a wyseman, sayd then full commenly
> The third heyre should not joyse but be uncrouned
> And deposed of all regalitee
>
> To this reason they dyd their wittes applye,
> Of evill gotten good, the third should not enjoyse
> Of longe agone, it hath been a commen voyce.[39]

Precisely the same view that the third heir of an usurper is foredoomed, is also expressed by Grafton in prose:

> Other there be that ascribe his (Henry the Sixth's) infortunitie, only to the stroke and punishment of God, affirming that the Kingdome which Henry the fourth his Grand-father wrongfully got, and unjustly possessed against King Richard the seconde and his heyres, could not by very devine justice, long continue in that injurious stocke: And that therefore God by his divine providence, punished the offence of the Grandfather, in the sonnes sonne.[40]

Later, the sin-retribution cyclical theory is reiterated by Raleigh in his Preface to *The History of the World,* where he connects the cruelty of Edward III with the fall of Richard II, the treason of Henry IV with the tragic fate of Henry VI, and the acts of Henry VII with the end of the Tudor dynasty in Elizabeth.[41]

It is thus apparent that, side by side with the humanistic view of history, the belief in the cyclical theory was widespread during the sixteenth century. An inevitable outcome of the former was the stress on accurate scholarship and authenticity of facts. Lord Berners defines history as "the light of truth, the mistress of the life human, the president of remembrance and the messenger of antiquity,[42] and Froissart himself also declares that his intent as well as that of John Le Bel, his source—"the true chronicles sometime compiled by the right reverend discreet and sage master John Le Bel"—has been to follow the truth as near as possible.[43] Polydore Vergil expresses the view even more forcefully, when he terms history as "a full rehearsall and declaration of things don, not a gesse or a divination", "the only unique, certaine and faithfull witness of time and things".[44] However, as modern historians have convincingly shown "there is no objective historical truth",[45] and for the Renaissance historians it was particularly difficult to devote themselves to objective truth. Trying to analyse the actions and motives of their subjects, they were, more often than not, swayed by personal motives. This was but natural at a time when many of them enjoyed the patronage of the kings and wrote at their behest, when there existed partisan interests and traditions like Roman Catholic and Protestant, English and French, and when powerful monarchs themselves were interested in the propagation of certain ideas about history. To a great extent, history tended to become "the vehicle of propaganda".[46]

The varying accounts of King John and King Richard II amply illustrate the point. While in the eyes of the Protestant writers, John was a martyr, in the eyes of the Roman Catholic writers, he was a heretic. Since *A Myrroure for Magistrates* is strongly pro-Lancastrian, Richard's ghost recounts in it all his misdeeds:

> I am a Kyng that ruled all by lust,
>
> That forced not of vertue, ryght, or lawe,

and goes on to conclude: "Thus lawles life to lawles death ey drawees"[47]—a picture so dark and dismal that it hardly leaves any ground for pity. On the other hand, the French Chroniclers, John Creton in his *Histoire du Roy d' Angleterre Richard II* and the anonymous writer of the *Chronicue de La Traison et Mort de Richart Deux Roy Dengleterre* present Richard as a saintly martyr and are hostile to Bolingbroke.[48] The reasons are apparent. First, the French writers felt a sort of kinship with Richard on account of his French wife. Second, both were in some ways personally attached to him. The writer of the *Traison* belonged to Queen Isabella's entourage, while Creton, formerly in the service of the French King, came to England in 1399 and accompanied Richard on his Irish campaign.[49] As an example of this strongly pro-Richard line, one may look at the description of the King's Lament at Flint Castle as narrated in the *Traison*:

> No mortal man can recount or conceive the great distress of the King and his companions, nor their complaints, sorrows, and lamentations that night at Flint Castle, expecting nothing less than to be beheaded on the morrow.[50]

The above examples demonstrate how greatly the historians' attitudes were coloured by personal attachments and predilections. The greatest single factor responsible for affecting the outlook thus was, however, the Tudor Myth. According to Bullough, the main purpose of historical writing in England was "to support the Tudor regime".[51] Too sweeping a generalisation perhaps, but this was the official Tudor attitude no doubt.

We have noted above the prevalent belief in the cyclical theory of sin and retribution. A politically conscious King like Henry VII could not have been unaware of the grave threat the belief posed to his lineage. Hence, with a view to countering the threat and securing the allegiance of the English nation not only to himself but also to his descendants, he looked for some mythical-philosophical basis for his title—a basis which could be stronger than mere strong possession. Thus, came the Tudor Myth, according to which the Tudors were commissioned by God to bring peace and prosperity to the realm through their reign. It was supported by two 'divine' indications. First, Henry VII's marriage, a purely political marriage, was given out as providential in order to bring to an end the long and terrible Wars of the Roses. Second, Henry VII claimed direct descent from the last British King, Cadwallader and, taking the clue from the old Arthurian legends, wanted to create the impression that he and his heirs were the reincarnations of King Arthur.

Poloydore Vergil, the Italian historian, who undertook the writing of his *Anglica Historia* at the behest of Henry VII, was the man meant for this. Following the official Tudor line, he imposes a pattern on recent English history stretching from Richard II to Henry VII. The fact that he imposes no such pattern on earlier history reflects his prejudice. The pattern is based on the cyclical theory of history which must have been there in the minds of the people. However, though presenting the Tudor Myth and incorporating it into the pattern of history,

Polydore Vergil is "far from dramatising and hallowing it".[52] He is no drum-beater, and on a number of important issues, he shows his independent outlook. He discounts the popular *Brut* legend about the Trojan origin of the British, criticizes a number of the existing English customs and attacks the 'national xenophobia' of the English as well as the French. In all this, he gives evidence of a critical attitude new to the historical writing of the time and was severely attacked by the passionate Protestant, John Bale for "his Romish lies and Italish beggarys."[53] In his attitude to human actions he displays, like Hooker, a sympathetic understanding of mixed motives and is, therefore, "reasonable and kindly" in his judgment.[54] The result is often a deft balance between the contending forces and characters, between Richard II and Bolingbroke, for instance. The sympathy he shows for Richard is as unexpected as the sympathy shown to Gaunt by Froissart.

It was not Polydore Vergil, but Edward Hall, who really became the mouthpiece of the Tudor official view of history. A staunch supporter of the Reformation and of Henry VIII, he faithfully performs the job of a "royal panegyrist", boldly applying his historical studies to the maintenance of an extreme theory of the royal supremacy.[55] Apparently using Vergil's history for his groundwork, he imposes the moral pattern more pointedly with the specific purpose of vindicating the Tudor claim and warning against dissension. The Medieval historians too looked at history from the point of view of patterns and periods, but the pattern was theological and the outlook universal. The pattern went back to creation and dealt with "the general development of God's purposes for human life".[56] Derived from the *Bible*, it naturally included the fall of man, the redemption through Christ and the Last Judgment. Hall himself makes an oblique reference to it:

> By union of the Godhed to the manhod, manne was joyned to God which before by temptacion of the subtle serpante, was from hym segregate and divided.[57]

but he does this in order to emphasize the idea of a union and to give the colour of "the holy sacrament of Matrimony" to Henry VII's marriage with Elizabeth York. The theme chosen by Hall, as the title itself declares, is: *The Union of the The Two Noble and Illustre famelies of Lancastre and Yorke*—"What profite, what comfort, what joy suceded in the realme of England by the union of the forenamed two noble families."[58] The idea that Hall repeatedly wants to drive at is not simply the union itself, but the happy outcome of the union: the nation's prosperity under an unending line of Tudor monarchs. By the "moste noble, puissant and mighty issue of the union, political discord is clearly buried and perpetually extinct". Apparently Hall's history is written with an eye on the future, as the real object of the Tudor myth was to wash away from people's mind the lurking fear that the cyclical pattern might recur and England might relapse into civil strife again. Hall borrows the moral pattern from Polydore Vergil, dramatizes it and makes it subserve the Tudor Myth. The moral pattern beginning with the deposition of Richard II naturally includes the Wars of the Roses and thus affords Hall with excellent opportunity of highlighting the great value of the union, seen against the dark background of dissension: "as by discord greate thynges decaie and fall to ruine, so the same by concord be revived and erected".[59] This is the meeting ground of Tudor Historiography and political philosophy. While hallowing the Tudor Myth. Hall links it not only with the moral pattern but also with the political doctrine of order.[60]

As mentioned at the outset, with the advent of Renaissance and the New Learning, the outlook on history also undergoes a vital change from theological to humanistic and secular. Human actions are treated in a human way with emphasis on human will and motives. This opens the door for dramatization of history. However, the medieval view of history is not wholly extinct and often divine causation is added to human actions. An interesting offshoot is the cyclical theory of human sin and divine retribution. One by-product of the theory of causation is the demand for an objective and faithful scrutiny of facts. Strict objective treatment is, however, almost impossible in history and all the more so during the age under discussion. When the subject is recent national history, usually the approach tends to become blatantly partisan and prejudiced. The Tudor Myth fostered by Henry VII and propagated by Edward Hall is a case in point. In a comprehensive way, it incorporates the cyclical theory as well as the politico-moral doctrine of order.

These were, then, some of the most significant ways in which the Tudor Age looked at history and, needless to say, these being part of the Elizabethan background, were bound to influence the average Elizabethan (Shakespeare's included) notion of history one way or the other.

NOTES

1. B. Croce, *History—Its Theory and Practice* (1916), *vide* P. Gardiner (ed.) *Theories of History* (Illinois: The Free Press, 1960, I ed., 1959), p. 227.
2. *Vide* R.G. Collingwood, *The Idea of History* (Oxford University Press, 1963), especially the unpublished note, quoted by the editor, p. xii.
3. *Vide* E.H. Carr, *What is History?* (London: Macmillan, 1962), pp. 1 *et seq.*
4. A.R. Myers, 'Richard III and Historical Tradition', *History,* Vol. 53, No. 178, June 1968 (Oxford: The Historical Association), p. 181. Carr calls it "an unending dialogue between the present and the past." *op. cit.,* pp. 24 and 116.
5. S.C. Sen Gupta, *Shakespeare's Historical Plays* (London: Oxford University Press, 1964), p. 12.
6. Arnold Toynbee, 'My View of History' extract from his *Civilization on Trial* in Gardiner, *op. cit.,* p. 209. Toynbee contrasts this view of history with the 'cyclic view' of history, held by Ancient Greeks and Indians.
7. *Jeremiah* IV, 23-26, *Holy Bible*, vide L.E. Elliott-Binns, *Jeremiah* (London: S.C.M. Press, 1941), pp. 120 *et seq.*
8. *Ibid.*, xviii, 1-10.
9. *Ibid.,* xvii 5 ff. Quoted by Elliott Binns, p. 122.
10. *The City of God* (trans.), J. Healey (London: J.M. Dent, N. York: E.P. Dulton, 1942), Book V, Ch. II, p. 218.
11. *Ibid.,* Book V, Ch. 3, pp. 218 *et seq* and Book II, Ch. 23, p. 89.
12. L. Tolstoy, *War and Peace* (trans.) Louise and Aylmer Maude (Oxford University Press, 1933), Vol. III, p. 491.
13. *The Works of St. Thomas Aquinas: Philosophical Texts* (ed.), Gilby (London: 1956), p. 66.
14. Illustration of the wheel of Fortune on the first page. Please also see R.A. Fraser, *Shakespeare's Poetics in Relation to King Lear* (London: Routledge and Kegan Paul, 1962), pp. 46 *et seq* and 69. Lydgate calls Fortune the 'double fals goddesse (Sic), *vide* Sen Gupta, *op. cit.,* p. 14.

15. R. Chapman, 'The Wheel of Fortune' in *Shakespeare's Historical Plays,* in *The Review of English Studies,* Vol. I, New Series No. 1, 1950, pp. 1 *et seq.*
16. Dante's *Inferno* (trans.), Laurence Binyon (London: Macmillan, 1933), Canto VII, 78-90.
17. J.R. Hale, *The Evolution of British Historiography: From Bacon to Namier* (London, 1967), p. 12.
18. M. Reese, *The Cease of Majesty* (London: Edward Arnold, 1961), p. 8.
19. *Ibid.,* pp. 15 *et seq* and Sen Gupta, *op. cit.,* p. 15.
20. Hale says, it was as it were, "God played the game, while man watched and learned" *op. cit.,* p. 9.
21. W.D. Briggs (ed.), *Marlowe's Edward II* (London: David Nutt, 1914), Int. pp. xcv *et seq.* Tillyard, *The Elizabethan World Picture* (London: Chatto and Windus, 1967), p. 48.
22. Sen Gupta, *op. cit.,* p. 14.
23. *History Plays,* p. 26.
24. G.C. Macaulay (ed.), *The Chronicles of Froissart* (tr.). Lord Berners (London: Macmillan, 1913), Ch. CCXLV (CCXLIX), p. 473.
25. Edward Hall. *The Union of the two noble and illustre families of Lancastre and Yorke* (1548) from G. Bullough, (ed.), *Narrative and Dramatic Sources of Shakespeare* (London: Routledge, N.Y. Columbia University Press, 1960) (CCXXIXV), Vol. III, pp. 249 *et seq.*
26. R. Holinshed, *The Third Volume of Chronicles* (1587 ed.), [520/1/48] Bullough (ed.), *Narrative and Dramatic Sources,* Vol. IV, p. 182.
27. Hale, *op. cit.,* p. 10.
28. *Ibid.,* p. 12.
29. R. Hooker, *The Laws of Ecclesiastical Polity. Bk.I,* Ch. ix, 1, from Rev. J. Keble (ed.), *The Works of Mr. Richard Hooker* (7th ed. Oxford: Clarendon Press, 1888), Vol. I, p. 237.
30. *Ibid.,* Ch. ix, 2, p. 238.
31. *Ibid.,* pp. 237 *et seq.* If one were to illustrate the three types from Shakespeare: (1) Hamlet, Othello, Brutus, (2) Lear, Glocester, Corlolanus, (3) Macbeth, Edward IV, Bolingbroke.
32. As Ribner remarks: "There was in this an important Renaissance assumption: that man had some measure of control over his own destiny, that by his reason and strength he might determine political success or failure." Ribner, *The Eng. Hist. Play in the Age of Shakespeare* (Princeton, New Jersey: Princeton University Press, 1957), p. 18.
33. Benedetto Croce, *Politics and Morals* (tr.), S.J. Castiglione (London: George Allen, 1946), p. 45.

34. Chapter II *infra.*
35. Croce, *op. cit.,* pp. 4 *et seq.*
36. Collingwood, *op. cit.,* p. 57.
37. L.B. Campbell, *Shakespeare's Histories* (San Marino: Huntington, 1963), pp. 121 *et seq.*
38. Elliott-Binns, *op. cit.,* pp. 39 *et seq.*
39. *Vide* Campbell, *op. cit.,* p. 58.
40. Grafton, *Chronicle at Large,* II, 691.
41. G.E. Hadow (ed.), *Sir W. Raleigh Selections from His Writings* (Oxford: Clarendon Press, 1927), p. 44.
42. Preface to *The Chronicles of Froissart* (trans.), Berners, *op. cit.,* p. xxix.
43. *Ibid.,* Chap. I, pp. 1 *et seq.*
44. *Vide* Bullough, *op. cit.,* Vol. III, p. 8.
45. G. Clark, *The New Cambridge Modern History* (1957), I, xxv. *Vide* E.H. Carr, *What is History?* (London: Macmillan, 1962), p. 2.
46. H. Butterfield, *The Englishman and His History* (Cambridge University Press, 1944), p. 16.
47. A. *Myrroure,* 'Richard II' lines 31-2 and 117. *Vide* Bullough (ed.), *op. cit.,* Vol. III, pp. 420 and 422.
48. *Ibid.,* pp. 370 *et seq.*
49. *Ibid.*
50. *Ibid.,* p. 432 extract from Benjamin Williams (ed. and trans.), the *Traison* (Eng. Hist. Soc. 1846).
51. Bullough, 'The Uses of History' in J. Sutherland and J. Hurstfield (ed.), *Shakespeare's World* (London: Edward Arnold, 1964), p. 96.
52. Tillyard, *History Plays,* p. 45.
53. *Vide* Bullough, *op. cit.,* Vol. III, p. 8.
54. Tillyard, *History Plays,* p. 34.
55. Campbell, *op. cit.,* pp. 68 *et seq.*
56. Collingwood, *op. cit.,* p. 49.
57. *The Union,* 'The General Theme' (ed.), Bullough, *op. cit.,* Vol. III, p. 17.
58. *Ibid.,* p. 17.
59. *Ibid.*
60. For a discussion of the doctrine and other related issues, see Chapter II *infra.*

The Background (2): Political Cross-Currents

2

The preceding chapter, though purporting to be a review of the sixteenth century historiography, touches upon certain aspects of Tudor political thinking. It has been pointed out there how the historian, Edward Hall in particular, is interested in expounding political theories like national unity and royal absolutism. In fact, in Tudor England the two ideas—of nationalism and royalism—are inseparable. With the end of the Wars of the Roses the power of the feudal barons is also broken. The logical outcome is the growth of national unity on the one hand, and of royal power on the other. The King simply becomes the focal point of the spirit of nationalism. And what is true of England is also true of almost all Europe. "It was", as G.B. Adams says, "a new and stormy age on which Europe as a whole was then entering, the transition in political history from medieval to modern times."[1] Along with the emergence of modern nations also emerges absolute monarchy and, by the beginning of the sixteenth century, it has already become, or is rapidly becoming, the prevailing type of government in western Europe.[2]

The strange fact that Henry VII, with "hardly a shadow of hereditary title"[3] succeeded in establishing a new dynasty and in gradually acquiring more and more power, is explained by the country's realisation of the need for a strong rule. As Ribner has pointed out, "England chose to set aside strict hereditary right in favor of centralized absolutism and order."[4] The Tudor Myth propaganda, which, as shown in the previous chapter, played so vital a role in determining the Tudor outlook on history, is an example of how national feelings were blended with monarchical interests. By reviving the myth of King Arthur and the glory of the Britons, it fed the national pride of the English on the one side and strengthened the Tudor title on the other. It would not be incorrect to say that while nationalism fed on the myth of the ancient glory and what went along with it, the promise of the revival of the same glory in the near future, absolute royalism fed on the rising tide of nationalism itself. A number of other factors too contributed to the revival of absolute monarchy in England. With the rise of nationalism also began the era of international rivalry and struggle for the domination of Europe.[5] For England it meant constant threat from Spain and France. The shadow of foreign invasions which lingered till the Elizabethan period, gave new impetus to nationalism and, put further stress on the need for a strong sovereign, solidly backed by the people. With the advent of Reformation, 'the danger became far more acute'.[6] A country threatened by her powerful neighbours as well as by domestic religious quarrels, a country horrified at the thought of the recent War of the Roses, could brook no challenge to her unity and the established government. Moreover, the new English nationalist state with the king as the fountain-head of all political power had to claim "a divine origin as the embodiment of God's will on earth".[7] The same practical necessity which had resulted in the formulation of the Tudor Myth also led to the revival of the divine right of kings. The idea in itself was by no means novel and had been there ever since St. Paul,[8] but it was the sixteenth century political situation which gave a new force to it.

Now, the concept of the divine right goes hand in hand with the denunciation of rebellion in any form. It incorporates the doctrine of passive obedience and proclaims 'the iniquity of rebellion'.[9] A classic example is the *Book of Homilies*, containing *sermon of obedience, or An Exhortation concerning good order and obedience to Rulers and Magistrates* (1547) and *Homily Against Disobedience and Wilful Rebellion* (1574). As Tillyard observes, "Far from being pieces of abstract theology, relatively timeless, the Church Homilies were largely written, as occasion arose, to meet a present need."[10] For instance, the *Homily Against Disobedience* was added to the already existing Homilies in the wake of the Northern Rebellion of 1569. But apart from such specific purposes, the general purpose of these Homilies in the sixteenth century was to support the divine right of kings as well as to preach the doctrine of passive disobedience, "the two fundamental articles of the Tudor state religion".[11] What is more, the Homilies also gave expression to a conception of the world pattern in order to emphasize the significant role of the king and the prime need for obeying him.

> Almightie God hath created and appoyncted all thynges in heaven, yearth, and waters, in a moste excellent and perfect ordre. In heaven he hath appoyncted distincte orders and states of Archangelles and Angelles. In the yearth he hath assigned Kyngs, princes, with other gournors under them, all in good and necessarie ordre.

And it goes on to enumerate the analogies on different planes, the hierarchies which maintain law and order:

> For where there is no right ordre, there reigneth all abuse, carnall libertie, enormitie, synne, and Babilonical confusion. Take awaie Kynges, Princes, Rulers, Magistrates, Judges, and such states of God's ordre, no man shall ride or go by the high way unrobbed, no man shall slepe in his awne house or bed unkilled, no man shall kepe his wife, children and possessions in quietnesse, all thynges shall be common, and there muste nedes folowe all mischief and utter destruction, bothe of soules, bodies, goodes and common wealthes.[12]

In Thomas Elyot's famous book, *The Governour*, we come across another similar exposition of order. It is 'ordre', he says:

> whiche in thinges as wel naturall as supernaturall hath euer had suche a preominence, that thereby the incomprehensible maiestie of god, as it were by a bright leme of a torche or candel, is declared to the blynde inhabitantes of this worlde. More our take away ordre from all thynges what shulde then remayne? Certes nothynge finally, except some man wolde imagine eftsones Chaos: whiche of some is expounde a confuse mixture. Also where there is any lacke of ordre nedes

> must be perpetuall conflicte: and in thynges subiecte to Nature nothynge of hym selfe onely may be norisshed; but whan he hath distroyed that where with he dothe participate by the ordre of his creation, he hym self of necessite muste than perisshe, whereof ensuethe uniuersall dissolution.[13]

Thus, "in the state, as in the universe and in the world of living creatures, Nature's order is manifested in a hierarchy";[14] and at the head of this hierarchy in the state is the King. This idea of an ordered universe arranged in a fixed system of hierarchies,[15] was inherited by the Middle Ages from "an amalgam of Plato and the *Old Testament*",[16] and handed down to the Renaissance. However, though based on theology, it was by no means theocentric.[17] In sixteenth century England it provided the moral, philosophical basis to royal absolutism. Hence, the doctrine of universal order, which in the Middle Ages had served the purpose of highlighting a Christian concept of God and his creation, now served the purpose of highlighting the Tudor concept of the King and his state. The King derived his power directly from God (especially after the break from Rome in 1570) and was responsible to Him alone. There being none to judge his conduct, the subjects were to practise passive obedience even in the case of a bad ruler.[18] Tudor absolutism was, in this way, "couched in religious terms, but it actually grew out of the stern necessity of practical politics",[19] and the Homilies are only one example of this amalgam of current political thought and religious philosophy. Actually there was a flood of such doctrinaire literature.[20]

However, the very fact that the doctrines of royal absolutism and universal order were so often and with such earnestness repeatedly voiced, leads one to conclude that many Englishmen must have been strongly opposed to them. Like all orthodoxy these too had their challengers.[21] The challenge came not from one quarter; it came from Copernicus, who questioned the cosmological order; from Montaigne, who questioned the natural order; from Machiavelli, who questioned the political order.[22] It came also from devout Christians, Catholics as well as Puritans, who questioned the royal prerogative in matters religious.[23] It came also from a number of factors that affected living conditions of the day: social, economic, political, particularly during the last decade of Queen Elizabeth's reign.

The old established Ptolemaic system which had placed the earth at the centre of the universe and which formed the astronomical basis of the popular concept of order, though not forsaken until the publication of Galileo's *Siderius Nuncius* in 1610 was clearly open to doubts ever since 'De revolutionibus' of Copernicus was published in 1543. The Copernican system "was well known as a hypothesis by the English reading public before the end of the sixteenth century[24] through popular handbooks[25] like Thomas Digges' *Perfect Description of the Celestial Orbs* (1576). Girdano Bruno, an ardent follower of Copernicus, had been in England in the early 1580's and had come in contact with distinguished Englishmen like Sir Philip Sidney.[26] Later in 1611, after Galileo's discoveries, Donne was to immortalize the effect of these scientific findings on the traditional concept of the universe:

> And new philosophy calls all in doubt,
> The element of fire is quite put out;
> The sun is lost, and th' earth, and no man's wit,
> Can well direct him where to look for it...
> 'Tis all in pieces, all coherence gone.[27]

But what affected the orthodox concept of established order even more devastatingly was Montaigne's[28] famous essay, *Aplogy for Raimond Sebond* which introduced his translation of Sabonde's *Natural Theology*. The title is 'intentionally misleading', and the essay is actually 'an attack on Christian beliefs in general'.[29] While Sebonde's book is typical of the orthodox optimism about man's place in nature, Montaigne sets out to prove the 'insignificance of man'[30] and the feebleness' of his Reason—'so infirm and so blind that nothing, however clear and easy, is clear enough for her'—whose 'jurisdiction and mediation' are disclaimed by all subjects equally and Nature in general.[31] Thus, exploding the myth of man's reason, by virtue of which he had been placed 'in the traditional cosmic setting between the angels and the beasts,[32] Montaigne strikes at the root of the entire structure of natural hierarchy:

> Let him explain to me by the force of his reason, on what foundation he has built those great advantages he thinks he has over the other creatures. What has induced him to believe that wonderful motion of the heavenly vault, the eternal light of those torches rolling so proudly over his head, the awe-inspiring agitations of that infinite sea, were established, and endure through so many centuries, for his service and convenience?[33]

Making an elaborate comparison between man and different animals, he comes to the conclusion that man, in many respects inferior, is in no wise superior to them. "Shackled and entangled, he is subjected to the same obligation as the other creatures of his order, and is of a very mediocre condition without any real and essential prerogative and preeminence."[34] Thus, this heavenly creature whom we call man[35] who was supposed to far excel all other creatures and to have been appointed by God to rule on the earth,[36] is thrown out of his central position and, shown as a miserable and puny creature by Montaigne.[37]

That the Elizabethans in general, and Shakespeare in particular, were familiar with Montaigne is beyond question. A juxtaposition of Gonzalo's speech:

> I'th' commonwealth I would by contraries
> Execute all things; for no kind of traffic
> Would I admit; no name of magistrate;
> Letters should not be known; riches, poverty,
> And use of service none; contract, succession,
> Bourn, bound of land, tilth, vineyard, none;
> No use of metal, corn, or wine, or oil;
> No occupation; all men idle, all;
> And women too, but innocent and pure;
> No sovereignty....
> All things in common nature should produce
> Without sweat or endeavour. Treason, felony,
> Sword, pike, knife, gun, or need of any engine,
> Would I not have; but nature should bring forth,

Of it own kind, all foison, all abundance,
To feed my innocent people. (*The Tempest*, II. i. 141 ff.)

beside the following shows Shakespeare's indebtedness to the author of the famous *Essais*:

> I am sorie, Lycargus and Plato had it not: for me seemeth that what in those nations we see by experience, doth not only exceed all the pictures wherewith licentious Poesie hath proudly imbellished the golden age, and all her quaint inventions to faine a happy condition of man, but also the conception and desire of Philosophy. They could not imagine a genuite so pure and simple as we see it by experience; nor ever beleeve our societie might be maintained with so little art and humane combination. It is a nation, would I answer Plato, that hath no kinde of traffike, no knowledge of letters, no intelligence of numbers, no name of Magistrate, nor of povertie; no contracts, no successions, no partitions, no occupation but idle; no respect of kindred, but common, no apparell but naturall, no manuring of lands, no use of wine, corne, or mettle. The very words that import lying, falsehood, treason, dissimulations, covetousness, envie, detraction and pardon, were never heard of amongst them. How dissonant would hee finde his imaginarie commonwealth from this perfection?
>
> *Hos natura modos primum dedit.*
>
> Nature at first uprise,
> These manners did devise.[38]

A comparison of the excerpts cited above would make it plain that the similarity is not just a coincidence. The British Museum copy of the *Essays of Montaigne*, translated by Florio, having the autograph, *Willam Shakspere*,[39] is another proof of Shakespeare's familiarity with Montaigne. It may, indeed, be pointed out that the first English translation of Montaigne came out in 1603 and as such Montaigne might have influenced *Hamlet* and *The Tempest* but is irrelevant to the History Plays. But Florio was contemporary and perhaps a friend of Shakespeare's,[40] and the chances of the latter going through the translation in manuscript as indeed of chatting with Florio about Montaigne's philosophy over 'a cup of sack' cannot be discounted.

As mentioned above, the political order or the 'body politic' was a part of the inherited concept of the universe.[41] The King, who represented the Heavenly King and ruled over the Kings of the earthly creatures, could not be conceived of without the highest of morals. His commonwealth was unimaginable without a picture of complete harmony. Machiavelli, however, living in early sixteenth century Italy, noticed a picture altogether different:

> Cruelty and murder had become normal agencies of government; good faith and trustfulness had become childish scruples to which an enlightened man would hardly give lip-service; force and craft had become the keys to success; profligacy and debanchery had become too frequent to need comment; and selfishness naked and unadorned, need only succeed in order to supply its own justification.[42]

All that Machiavelli did was to express "the actual and existing assumptions, on which the scramble of competition was carried out among Italian princes". He saw clearly in the Italy of his day that "the restraints of law and custom had broken down", and he gave it a theoretic expression.[43] The net result is that he becomes the first thinker to divorce politics from ethics. The state, which had been represented as the mirror of universal order, essentially moral, now becomes a morally isolated thing.[44] He discovers the necessity for and the autonomy of politics—politics beyond moral good or evil.[45] Referring to the universally recognised moral virtues, Machiavelli observes:

> ...it is well to seem merciful, faithful, humane, sincere, religious, and also to be so; but you must have the mind so disposed that when it is needful to be otherwise you may be able to change to the opposite qualities. And it must be understood that a prince, and especially a new prince, cannot observe all those things which are considered good in men, being often obliged, in order to maintain the state, to act against faith, against charity,

> against humanity, and against religion. And, therefore, he must have a mind disposed to adapt itself according to the wind, and as the variations of fortune dictate, and, as I said before, not deviate from what is good, if possible, but be able to do evil if constrained.[46]

Thus, the conception of the Law of Nature, governing the various domains of creation, including the body politic, is quite alien to Machiavelli. The only law is expediency and the only measuring rod is success itself. As Copernicus had upset man's relation to his universe, plucking the earth out of the central position it had occupied for ages—so Machiavelli upset his relations to the state, substituting expediency for justice in political action.[47] The impact of Machiavelli on the sixteenth century and subsequent political thought can hardly be exaggerated. "It would be impossible", says Figgis, "to gain any adequate notion of the intellectual forces, that made up the mind of the average European statesman from 1600 to 1800 if we altogether omitted a consideration of the influence of Machiavelli."[48] But what is true of the statesmen is also true of the thinkers and litterateurs, and what is true of the period 1600-1800 is equally true of the second half of the sixteenth century. The two fold impact on thinkers and statesmen reflects only further the dichotomy between theory and practice that had existed already in Italy as well as in England. "Philosophers have been well high unanimous in condemning *The Prince,* and statesmen in practising its precepts."[49] Quite naturally Machiavelli outraged the orthodox sixteenth century sensibilities. The Jesuits burnt his effigy, the Protestants considered him responsible for the massacre of St. Bartholomew; he was put on the Index[50] immediately after the formation of that list; was referred to no fewer than 395 times in Elizabethan drama as the embodiment of human villainy.[51] "But Charles V studied it (*The Prince*) carefully, Catherine de Medici brought it to France, Henry III and Henry IV of France had it with them at their death, Richelieu admired it. William of Orange kept it under his pillow as if to memorize it by osmosis."[52] Despite his devotion to Platonic idealism and the *Faerie Queene*, Spenser used Machiavelli as his guide[53] when dealing with practical politics as Secretary to the Earl of Gray and writing his *View of the Present State of Ireland*; Raleigh, despite his belief in the moral pattern expressed in the *History of the World*, showed the impact of Machiavelli in his *Maxims of State* and in real life, and Bacon conceded that "our thanks are due to Machiavelli and similar writers, who have openly and without dissimulation, shown us what men are accustomed to do, not what they ought to do".[54] A popular poem entitled, 'Churchyard's Charity' by Thomas Churchyard, published in 1595, bears witness to the great impact of Machiavelli on Elizabethan Englishmen:

> Fine Machiavel, is now from Florence flown.
> To England where, his welcome is too great;
> His busy books, are here so read and known
> That charity, thereby hath lost her meat.[55]

Actually, the doctrines of Machiavelli, despite the strong reaction they provoked, had all along been there in use in the sphere of practical politics, long before he was born or his books were published.[56] By giving a theoretical basis to the tactics of practical politics already in vogue, Machiavelli not only questioned the validity of the traditional assumptions of Natural Law and the Divine Right, but also made the sixteenth century conscious of the discrepancy between what men 'ought to do' (or profess) and what they actually do, particularly in the sphere of politics. To say that the doctrines of Machiavelli "lie outside the main sixteenth century interests",[57] is an evasion. In fact, to borrow the words of Wilbur Sanders:

> Machiavelli, whether read or not, whether distorted by popular fancy or judiciously pondered by the wise, represents one of the central facts of Elizabethan culture .... Machiavelli, and the kind of mind he represented, was the radical yeast in the traditional loaf.[58]

It is significant to note that Machiavelli also supported royal absolutism, but in him royalism was devoid of divinity. The King was the secular head; and, rather than carrying out the Law of Nature, had to give his own law to the state.

But, while Machiavelli stressed the essentially secular nature of politics, it was precisely a protest against this that led the strongly religious minded to attack royal absolutism and passive obedience. With the Reformation, new and complicated situations were bound to crop up. The King's confession could often be at variance with that of his subjects or a section of them. In an age of religious intolerance it meant persecution. Under the circumstances, "it was only by some claim to a right of insurrection"[59] that the persecuted religious sect could hope to survive. To fight religious persecution, "a new doctrine, a doctrine of a divine right of rebellion"[60] was proclaimed by Catholics and Protestants alike.

Both Luther and Calvin had advocated non-resistance, but later situations compelled their followers to depart from this line of thought. In Germany after the issue of the Interim in May 1548, it became impossible for the German Protestants to go on believing in the doctrine of non-resistance. Obstinately refusing to accept the Interim, the city of Magdeburg produced the first formal enunciation of the theory of rightful forcible resistance by Orthodox Protestants in the form of a treatise entitled, *Bekentnnis unterricht und Vermanung der Pfarrherrn und Perdiger der Christlichen Kirchen zu Magdeburg in 1550.*[61] The writers of *Bekentnnis* not merely justify forcible resistance for the sake of 'true religion', but consider it obligatory for its followers. In cases of injustice to the subjects also resistance is justified, though not considered obligatory. With the failure of the Interim and the victory of Lutheranism in Germany, the doctrine became superfluous there, but it gained ground elsewhere.

In England and Scotland, for example, similar situation produced similar results during the time of Mary Stuart and, the doctrine was voiced by the Marian exiles like John Ponet, John Knox, Christopher Goodman, George Buchanan, etc. Ponet's *A Shorte Treatise of Politicke Power* (1556), reprinted in England in 1642, is considered one of the earliest expositions of the doctrine of tyrannicide. The very questions, which Ponet attempts to answer, reflect upon the raging controversies of the sixteenth century Europe. To take a few examples:

> In what things and how far subjects are bound to obey their Princes and Governours? Whether it be lawful to depose an evil Governour and kill a Tyrant?[62]

For Tudor England, however, as a direct influence John Knox and the Scottish Calvinists are more significant. "The course of the Scotch Reformation" remarks Figgis, "from the beginning to the deposition of Mary Stuart, and right on through the Bishop's wars to the Revolution, affords, perhaps, the most complete and consistent expression of the duty of rebellion, alike in theory and practice, which we possess outside ultramontane pamphleteering".[63] Knox and his followers adhered to Calvin's Genevan ideal of state organisation, but broke away from his doctrine of submission to the existing powers, and argued that it was the duty of the subjects to realize the ideal by force.[64] The doctrine of just rebellion for the cause of the right religion is expounded most fully by Knox in his *Appelation* (1558), which is actually an appeal for revolt against idolatorous rulers. He illustrated the point by reference to Mary Tudor. "I fear not", says Knox—

> to affirm that it had been the duty of the Nobility, judges, Rulers and People of England, not only to have resisted and againstanded Marie, that Jezebel, but also to have punished her to the death.[65]

The same year (1558) also saw the publication of Christopher Goodman's treatise, *How Superior Powers Ought to be Obeyed*, in which "the subserviency of political to ecclesiastical considerations is yet more violently proclaimed".[66] Goodman was one of the English refugees who had lent their support to Knox at Frankfurt. He had also a hand in the production of the Geneva Bible.[67] His book shows that the English exiles had the same feelings as the Scottish. Like Knox, he too supports the theory of rebellion and justifies Wyatt's insurrection in favour of Elizabeth.[68] Yet another work written to justify the deposition of Mary Stuart was *De Jure Regni Apud Scotos* (1578) by George Buchanan. Born in Scotland in 1506, Buchanan spent most of his life in France,[69] and it was there that he wrote his short but important treatise, *De Jure*. He uses two arguments: historical and theoretical in support of checks on sovereign authority. According to the first, there had always been such checks in every nation. Secondly, Buchanan expounds a theory of original contract, which is employed in one form or the other by almost all the anti-monarchical writers till Rousseau.[70]

In France the Puritan opposition to absolutism was developed into a conscious philosophical system by the Huguenotes as a sequel to the massacre of St. Bartholomew. As Armstrong observes:

> Social gases hitherto cooped up found vent, and new forces were brought into activity. The Huguenot party, ...began to cast about for a permanent basis of resistance, for a philosophical justification of rebellion.[71]

It was under such circumstances in France, that the reformed religion engaged in a 'life-and-death struggle'[72] propounded the doctrine of tyrannicide. *The Vindiciae*[73] which expresses the doctrine most systematically, has been variously attributed to Hubert Languet and Philip Du Plessis Mornay. Both were close friends of Sir Philip Sidney, and the work was soon widely known in England,[74] though it was translated much later in 1648. Like Ponet's work, it also deals with the fundamental questions of contemporary politics: (1) Are the subjects obliged to obey a prince if he commands against the law of God?, (2) Is it lawful to resist a prince who nullifies the law of God?, (3) How far is it lawful to resist a prince, who is oppressing or destroying the state? and (4) Can neighbouring princes lawfully aid the subjects of other princes?[75] The author of the *Vindiciae* postulates a double contract: first, between God and the people, including the King; second, between the people and the King. The real sovereign are the people: as a vassal may forfeit has fief, so a King, if he neglects God and deserts to His enemies, forfeits his kingdom.[76] Thus, like *Bekentinnis* and Knox, the *Vindiciae* goes on to argue that it is lawful, even obligatory on the people to resist a renegade king.[77]

The *Franco-Gallia* of Francois Hotman published in 1573 at Geneva was, unlike the *Vindiciae,* 'strictly political or juristic'. Hotman sketched the constitutional history of France with the object of establishing that except for the period of

Roman rule, sovereignty in France always rested with the people, and was expressed through some representative body like the States General.[78]

It was precisely at this time that in England too, ironical though it is the Puritan protest reached its peak during the reign of the Protestant Queen Elizabeth. This is evident from the religious controversies that continued during the reign, especially after 1570, and the executions of numerous Puritans, notably of Henry Barrow and John Penry in 1593. Though the Elizabethan Puritans did not subscribe to Knox's theory of rebellion, yet they did pose a challenge to the doctrine of royal absolutism. Compared to the large body of Puritan protest against Tudor absolutism, the Catholic protest was 'never very strong'.[79] Nevertheless, the devout Catholics of England never subscribed to the doctrine of Royal absolutism. Sir Thomas More's life and works illustrate this. Refusing to accept the authority of the King as the head of the Church in place of the Pope, committed to the Tower and beheaded, he died a true Catholic, firm in his conviction to the last. In his *Apology*, he argues that the scriptures have been preserved and are known through the Church and, therefore, the authority of the Church cannot be denied without endangering the sanctity of the Scriptures themselves:

> There is like surety and like certain knowledge of the word of God unwritten as there is of the word of God written, sith ye know neither the tone or the tother to be the word of God but by the tradition of the Church.[80]

Like More, Cardinal Pole, Cardinal Allen, Nicholas Sanders, John Feckenham, Thomas Harding, etc. also challenged the notion of royal supremacy.[81] The belief of the Catholics in the Church universal itself implied a denial of the fundamental Tudor contention of royal absolutism and nationalism. Besides, in 1570, the Queen had been excommunicated and the Catholics absolved of their duty of allegiance by Pope Pius V. It appeared that in the event of a foreign invasion, the Catholics might not support the Queen.[82] Though later developments proved such fears to have been unfounded, yet it is apparent from the Gunpowder Plot, hatched by the Catholics immediately after

James I came to the throne, that a section of the Catholic population was not only opposed to the notion of royal absolutism, but was also prepared to take up arms against the 'anointed' king. The truth is that the religious question was highly controversial and sensitive, and that the Catholic opposition, though not so strong as the Puritan, is no less significant.

It is not surprising that "Most of the better known writers passed through trials of faith", as Harrison remarks and demonstrates.[83] It would be naive to imagine that these writers, particularly Shakespeare, remained untouched by the religious controversy of the time—the clash between the Crown and the Church, between the official and the private religion, the concept of the Divine Right of Kings and of tyrannicide, the traditional belief in a God-ordained order and religious persecution.

In socio-economic matters also all was not right with the Tudor world to go on believing in the inherited concepts unperturbed. Though the old convention "of arranging men in grades or classes distinguished clearly and properly from one another"[84] still persisted, yet in practice these classes were no longer closed compartments:

> ...Elizabethans were more ready for social change than we have sometimes been inclined to recognize. It is true that they sometimes spoke of the different classes as though they were clearly defined and had the divisions permanently drawn; but in fact, the reverse was the case. There was a great deal of social mobility; and men were easily accepted into a new class....
>
> Practice was far more flexible than theory; and it was the *arrivistes* who proclaimed most loudly the splendours of title, rank and tradition, and who most feared its decline.

Thus, Hurstfield.[85] In the nursing age of free-trade enterprise and mercantile system, the old social hierarchy, an essential part of the universe-hierarchy, could not remain what it had been. "The tendency of economic forces throughout the period was to break up the sharply defined estates of the Middle Ages and substitute for them that infinite individual differentiation which characterises modern England, and still more the United States."[86] The social hierarchy was no doubt there, but the process of its disintegration had already set in. Encouraged by Calvin to look upon material success as a sign of God's favour, men worked hard and rose to wealth and status in this 'fairly mobile society', where 'the workaday virtues brought their rewards'.[87] This naturally threatened the inherited structure of the society and its degrees. Reaction was inevitable. Even if one agrees with C.H. Wilson that the theme of the poet and the philosopher was the same as that of the legislators, their common aim being to hold social change in check, to prevent encroachment of class upon class, to keep a watchful eye on technical innovations that might have social repercussions; in short, to stabilize and preserve the existing social order,[88] it proves inversely that these changes were historical facts and a threat to the existing social order.

But there was another threat, and a more dangerous one, caused by 'the marvellous commercial expansion'.[89] With the coming up of commercial centres in the towns, there was fierce animosity between town and country,[90] and between the neighbouring towns themselves—Stratford and Coventry, Leicester and Ashby.[91] There was also rivalry for monopoly of trade amongst courtiers[92] and amongst the newly formed companies.[93] With the inflow of precious metals from the Indies, the common Englishman, particularly the wage-earner, found his money shrinking every day. Inflation, rise in prices, confiscation and debasement of the coin were inevitable. These economic conditions frequently called for poor laws and fixation of prices.[94] Whether one agrees with Cunningham or not that a 'social anarchy' was produced under the Tudor regime,[95] it is apparent that the old order was in the process of disintegration. Sir Thomas More's *Utopia*, modelled on Plato's *Republic*, highlights the economic maladjustment of the capitalistic Tudor society in which the dictum was to 'buy them abroad very cheap, and afterwards sell them again exceeding dear'.[96] More deplores the lack of equity and justice and pities the lot of the common labourers and artisans.[97] At the root of the evil he discovers private property:

> ...where possessions be private, where money beareth all the stroke, it is hard and almost impossible that there the weal public may justly be governed and prosperously flourish.[98]

Hythloday's *Utopia* is the ideal communistic nowhere land, where private ownership is completely abolished. Ben Jonson's *The Divell is an Ass* also brings to light the typical abuses of the acquisitive society with characters like Meercraft, the Projector, one of whose projects is to serve the whole state with toothpicks:

> To have all Tooth-picks brought unto an office.
> There seal'd; and such as counterfait "hem mulcted.
> And last, for venting 'hem, to have a booke
> Printed, to teach their use, which every childe
> Shall have throughout the kingdome, that can read,
> And learne to picke his teeth by. (IV. ii. 46-51)[99]

The picture of unemployment and misery that one comes across in *Henry VIII*:

> The Clothiers all, not able to maintain
> The many to them 'longing, have put off
> The spinsters, carders, fullers, weavers, who,
> Unfit for other life, compell'd by hunger
> And lack of other means, in desperate manner
> Daring th' event to th' teeth, are all in uproar,
> And danger serves among them. (*Henry VIII*, I. ii. 31-37)

was not sheer fancy of the poet, and whether Shakespeare wrote these lines or not, he could not have been blind to the actual living conditions of the time, just as he could not have been unaware of the traditional concepts of order and royal absolutism.

The political situation itself was no less insecure and uncertain. As Reese points out, 'it is particularly misleading' to think of the last fifteen years of the reign as a period of calm. New chain of dangers and frustrations came up after the Armada and Mary's execution.[100] The questions suspended so long raise their heads again. In the Parliament of 1593, for instance, Peter Wentworth, supported by Richard Stephens, Sir Henry Bromley and William Walshe sought to introduce a bill entailing the succession to the crown, with the result that Wentworth and Bromley were sent to the Tower, Stephens and Walshe to the Fleet.[101] On September 5, 1595, the Queen entered on her Grand Climacteric (the ninth of the fatal astrological periods of seven years), and there was a general anxiety in the air. This is evident from the publication of a book called *Polimanteia* from Cambridge, a book directed against frivolous and foolish conjectures,[102] as also from the Bishop of St. David's Sermon, delivered on April 9, 1596, before her majesty, on numbers and the Grand Climacteric.[103] In the Parliament of 1601, the Queen faced 'an open challenge to her prerogative'[104] over the question of monopolies. 'She saw that she must stoop to conquer' and 'the prerogative was saved at the expense of the patentees'.[105]

Earlier the same year had witnessed another threat to her authority by Essex and his followers. Robert Devereux, the Earl of Essex, had been a hot favourite with the Queen till the mismanagement of the Irish campaign in 1599. In 1587, "She was fifty three, and he was not yet twenty: a dangerous concatenation of ages."[106] But, what is more, she was suspicious and quick-tempered, he was ambitious and dangerously popular.[107] He was a rival of Walter Raleigh as a courtier, and of Robert Cecil for the leadership of the Government.[108] After his ignominious return from Ireland, he was committed to the Lord Keeper's custody and was asked to explain his conduct of the Irish campaign. Though released after a short while and allowed to return to the court, he could not be restored to the Queen's favour. In October 1600, the lease of the sweet wines, the most lucrative source of Essex's income, lapsed and the Queen refused to renew it.[109] The effect upon Essex was appaling: he became like one possessed.[110] Letters were sent by him to James VI of Scotland, who responded with a letter of encouragement to the Earl.[111] Meanwhile all manner of discontented politicians, gallants and unemployed captains and Puritan divines as well as Catholics who were later associated with the Gunpowder Plot, 'flocked to the house of Essex'.[112]

Reports reached the Government and Essex was summoned to appear before the Council.[113] In desperation and without further preparation, he led his followers, including the Earl of Southampton, into the city.[114] "Being entered into London he began to cry out, 'For the Queen; For the Queen: A plot is laid for my life'."[115] It was expected that the citizens would join him—and on this depended the success of the treason—but, though sympathizing with him, the Londoners, not even the meanest among them, would take up arms for him.[116] As a result, the rebellion ended in fiasco. Essex and his men were forced to surrender,[117] proclaimed traitors[118] and tried.[119] Essex was executed[120] as were his close associates like Sir Christopher Blount. Southampton, Shakespeare's patron, too was sentenced to death, but was lucky to suffer only imprisonment in the Tower.[121]

It is apparent that 'the Government had never been in any danger'[122] during the Essex rising. Nevertheless, 'for more than three years the fortunes of Essex caused continuous excitement'.[123] He was the centre and focus of national feeling. Despite all his failures, in the eyes of his contemporaries, the victor of Cadiz remained 'a fascinating and imposing character', 'a champion of social justice',[124] and even after his ignomnous fall, ballades, bewailing his tragedy as well as satirizing his enemies—Cecil, Burghley and Walter Raleigh—appeared.[125]

The above survey—though inadequate—makes it evident that a concept of order, inherited from Plato and the Middle Ages as well as the threats to it from various quarters—social, economic, religious, philosophic, scientific and political—were inherent in the Elizabethan background. Rightly, therefore, does A. Nicoll call 'extensive inconsistency' a prime symbol of the Age—an age in which 'conflicts, contraries, dominate in thought and in action'.[126] Spencer considers this phenomenon most 'propitious' for the flourishing of great tragic drama.[127] So was it for the flourishing of great historical drama, for, as Bevington points out, in it the impulse for debate and criticism was no less present than that for official propaganda.[128]

NOTES

1. G.B. Adams (rev.), R.L. Schuyler, *Constitutional History of England* (London: Jonathan Cape, 1960), Chap. X, p. 240.
2. G.H. Sabine, *A History of Political Theory* (London: G.G. Harrap, 3rd ed. 1957), Part III, Chapter XVII, p. 287.
3. *Ibid.*
4. I. Ribner, *The English History Play in the Age of Shakespeare* (Princeton: Princeton University Press, 1957), p. 310.
5. Adams, *op. cit.*, pp. 241 *et seq.*
6. *Ibid.*, p. 242.
7. Ribner, *op. cit.*, p. 310.
8. *Romans,* XIII.
9. J.N. Figgis, *The Divine Right of Kings* (Cambridge University Press, 1922, I ed., 1896), p. 88.
10. E.M.W. Tillyard, *Shakespeare's History Plays* (Harmondsworth Middlesex: Penguine, 1962, I ed., 1944), p. 65.
11. A. Hart, *Shakespeare and the Homilies* (Melbourne: Melbourne University Press in association with O.U.P., 1934), p. 17.
12. Homily, *Sermon of Obedience,* vide Tillyard. *op. cit.*, p. 19.
13. Sir Thomas Elyot, *The Governour* (1531) modern ed. with an Introduction by Foster Watson (London: J.M. Dent, 1907), Book I, p. 3. Shakespeare's debt to the passage for the famous Degree-speech of Ulysses (Troilus and Cressida, I, iii, 85 ff.) is apparent.
14. T. Spencer, *Shakespeare and the Nature of Man* (Lowell Lectures, 1942, New York: Macmillan; Cambridge University Press, 1945), p. 15.
15. Tillyard, *The Elizabethan World Picture* (London: Chatto and Windus, 1967), p. 3.

    Also M.D.H. Parker, *The Slave of Life: A Study of Shakespeare and the Idea of Justice* (London: Chatto and Windus, 1955), pp. 20 *et seq.*
16. Tillyard, *The Elizabethan World Picture,* p. 2.
17. Tillyard, however, holds the opposite view: "One can say dogmatically that it was still solidly theocentric". *Vide ibid.*, p. 2.
18. *Homily Against Disobedience, Vide* Hart, *op. cit.*, p. 30.
19. Ribner, *op. cit.*, p. 309.
20. To mention a few: 1. William Tyndale, *Obedience of a Christian Man* (1528). 2. Stephen Gardiner, *D Vera Obedientia Oratio* (1535), translated the same year into English. 3. Thomas Cranmer, *Sermon on Rebellion* (1549). 4. John Cheke, *The Hurt of Sedicion howe grevous it is to a Communewelth* (1549) included in the 1587 ed. of Holinshed. 5. John Jewel, Bishop of Salisbury, *Apologia Ecclesiae*

Anglicanae (1562, 1564, 1581, 1591, 1599). 6. William Cecil, *The Execution of Justice in England.* 7. Thomas Bilson, *True Difference Between Christian Subjection and Unchristian Rebellion* (1585). 8. Richard Hooker, *The Law of Ecclesiastical Polity* (1594). For a comprehensive list see Ribner, *op. cit.*, pp. 311 *et seq.*

21. *Ibid.*, p. 309.
22. Spencer, *op. cit.*, p. 29.
23. Ribner, *op. cit.*, pp. 314 *et seq.*

    And Joel Hurstifield, 'The Elizabethan People in the Age of Shakespeare' in Sutherland and Hurstfield (ed.), *Shakespeare's World* (London: Edward Arnold, 1964), pp. 39 *et seq.*
24. Spencer, *op. cit.*, p. 30.
25. One may agree with Tillyard that in spite of a wide knowledge of Copernicus's theories through these handbooks 'the ordinary educated Elizabethan' continued to think of the Universe as 'geocentric'. (See his *Elizabethan World Picture*, p. 34.) But what about Shakespeare whom, in another context, he places 'among the select few'? See his *Shakespeare's History Plays*, pp. 59, 64.
26. Spencer, *op. cit.*, p. 32.
27. John Donne, *An Anatomie of the World, The First Anniversary*, 11. 205 ff.
28. M.B.H. Parker, The *Slave of Life* (London: Chatto, 1955), pp. 30 *et seq.*
29. *The Essays of Montaigne* (trans.), E.J. Trechmann (Int.), J.M. Robertson (London, New York, Toronto: Humphrey Millford, Oxford University Press, 1942), Vol. I, p. 428 *n.*
30. *Ibid.*, p. 439.
31. *Ibid.*, p. 440.
32. Tillyard, *The Elizabethan World Picture,* p. 1.
33. Montaigne, *op. cit.*, p. 441.
34. *Ibid.*, p. 451.
35. Romei, *Courtier's Academy* (1546, translated into English in 1598), p. 16. Spencer, *op. cit.*, p. 4.
36. Thomas Starkey, *A Dialogue Between Cardinal Pole and Thomas Lupset* (1598), quoted by Spencer, *op. cit.*, p. 14.
37. Montaigne, *op. cit.*, p. 441.
38. Florio's *Essayes of Montaigne* First Borke. Ch. XXX. quoted by A.E. Baker, *A Shakespeare Commentary,* Part I (New York: Fredrick Ungar, 1957), pp. 174 *et seq.*

    In Trechmann's Translation the passage occurs in Book I, Chap. 31, p. 206.

39. Attention first drawn to it by Sir Fredrick Madden's pamphlet in 1838. *Vide* J.M. Robertson, *Montaigne and Shakespeare* (London: Adam, Charles Black 1909, I ed., 1897), p. 32.
40. Though according to Robertson, there are no clear traces of Montaigne in Shakespeare before Hamlet, yet "It is very likely that he knew Florio, being intimate with Jonson, who was Florio's friend and admirer; and the translation, long on the stocks, must have been discussed in his hearing." *Ibid.*, p. 161. He also draws attention to echoes of Montaigne in 2. *Henry IV and Henry V. Ibid.*, pp. 83, 112, et 114. A.L. Attwater, 'Shakespeare's Sources' in Granville-Barker & G.B. Harrison (ed.), *A Companion to Shakespeare Studies* (Cambridge University Press, 1959), p. 238.
41. *Supra*, pp. 22 *et seq.*
42. Sabine, *op. cit.*, p. 290.
43. J.N. Figgis, *Studies of Political Thought from Genson to Grotius* 1414-1625 (Cambridge University Press, 1931), pp. 73 et 77.
44. J.W. Allen, *A History of Political Thought in the Sixteenth Century* (London: Methuen; New York: Barnes & Noble; University Paperbacks, 1961), p. 477.
45. B. Croce, *Politics and Morals* (London: George Allen, 1946), p. 45.
46. N. Machiavelli, *The Prince* (trans.), Luigi Ricci (revised), E.R.P. Vincent (London: Oxford University Press, 1949, I ed., 1935), p. 79.
47. Parker, *op. cit.*, pp. 21 *et seq.*
48. Figgis, *From Gerson to Grotius*, p. 72.
49. Will Durant, *The Renaissance* (N. York: Simon & Schuster, 1953), Chapter XIX, p. 564.
50. *Index Librorum Prohibitorum.*
51. Spencer, *op. cit.*, p. 44.
52. Will Durant, *op. cit.*, p. 564.
53. Tillyard, *Shakespeare's History Plays, op. cit.*, p. 22.
54. F. Bacon, *De augmenis scientiarum*, VII, 2.
55. G.B. Harrison, *Elizabethan Journals* (London: Routledge & K. Paul, 1955), II, pp. 68 and 345 *n.*
56. "The age was aware of Machiavellianism before it was aware of Machiavelli", says Spivack. B. Spivack, *Shakespeare and the Allegory of Evil* (N. York: Columbia University Press, 1958), p. 376.
57. Tillyard, *Shakespeare's History Plays*, p. 21.
58. W. Sanders, *The Dramatist and the Received Idea* (Cambridge University Press, 1968), p. 62.
59. Figgis, *op. cit.*, p. 122.
60. Allen, *op. cit.*, p. 103.
61. *Ibid.*, pp. 104 *et seq.*

62. Ponet, *A Short Treatise,...* Chapter IV and VI quoted by Allen, *op. cit.,* p. 118.
63. *Op. cit.,* p. 127.
64. Allen, *op. cit.,* pp. 107 *et seq.*
65. *Appellation* in D. Laing (ed.), *Works,* IV, p. 501. *Vide* Allen, *op. cit.,* p. 113.
66. Figgis, *op. cit.,* p. 127.
67. Allen, *op. cit.,* p. 117 and Ribner, *op. cit.,* p. 316.
68. Figgis, *op. cit.,* p. 127.
69. Ribner, *op. cit.,* p. 317.
70. Figgis, *op. cit.,* pp. 128 *et seq.*
71. E. Armstrong, 'Political Theory of the Huguenotes' in *The English Historical Review,* Vol. IV, No. XIII, Jan. 1889, Reprint, 1962, p. 16.
72. *Ibid.,* p. 17.
73. Mod. ed. by H.J. Laski, *A Defence of Liberty Against Tyrants* (London, 1924).
74. Armstrong, *op. cit.,* pp. 39 *et seq* and Ribner, *op. cit.,* p. 317.
75. *Vide,* Sabine, *op. cit.,* pp. 322 *et seq.*
76. Armstrong, *op. cit.,* p. 30.
77. *Ibid.,* p. 30.
78. Allen, *op. cit.,* p. 310.
79. Ribner, *op. cit.,* p. 314.
80. *Apology,* vide Allen, *op. cit.,* p. 201.
81. Cardinal Allen for example observed that royal supremacy "is a thing most monstrous and unnatural, the very gap to bring any realm to the thraldom of all sects". *A True Sincere and Modest Defence of English Catholiques* (1584), p. 7. *Vide ibid.,* p. 202.
82. G.B. Harrison, "The National Background" in H.G. Barker and G.B. Harrison (ed.), *A Companion to Shakespeare Studies* (Cambridge University Press, 1962), p. 174.
83. *Ibid.,* p. 175.
84. H.O. Meredith, *Economic History of England* (London: Isaac Pitman & Sons, 2nd ed., 1930), p. 85.

    The Proclamation of 1959, regulating the apparel to be worn by different classes, Quoted in V. Hall, Jr., *Renaissance Literary Criticism* (Glocester, Massachutes: Peter Smith, 1959), p. 184.
85. *Op. cit.,* pp. 36 *et seq.*
86. Meredith, *op. cit.,* p. 85.
87. C.H. Wilson, "Trade, Society and the State", in E.E. Rich and C.H. Wilson (eds.), *The Cambridge Economic History of Europe* (Cambridge University Press, 1967), Vol. IV, p. 489.

88. *Ibid.*, pp. 539 *et seq.* Wilson quotes the degree speech of Ulysses (*Troilus & Cressida*) to illustrate the point. A.L. Rowse, *The England of Elizabeth* (London: Macmillan, 1961), p. 532. Rowse also quotes the degree speech. After referring to the Elizabethan insistence and the necessity of it, is so much evidence of the abounding energies contained within it.
89. W. Cunningham, *The Growth of English Industry and Commerce During the Early and Middle Ages* (Cambridge, 1927, I ed., 1882), pp. 483 *et seq*, especially p. 489.
90. George Unwin, "Shakespeare's England" in R.H. Tawney (ed.), *Studies in Economic History: The Collected Papers of George Unwin* (London: Frank Cass, N. York: Augustus, M. Kelley, 1966), p. 315.
91. *Ibid.*, pp. 305 *et seq.*
92. *Ibid.*, p. 326.
93. *Ibid.*, p. 327.
94. *Ibid.*, p. 309 and Cunningham, *op. cit.*, pp. 488 *et seq.*
95. *Ibid.*, p. 489.
96. Sir Thomas More, *The Utopia* (trans.), R. Robinson (London: Macmillan, 1952), Bk. I, p. 30.
97. *Ibid.*, Bk. II, pp. 143 *et seq.*
98. *Ibid.*, Bk. I, pp. 52 *et seq.*
99. Herford and Simpson (ed.), *Ben Jonson* (Oxford: Clarendon Press, 1938), Vol. VI, p. 232.
100. M.M. Reese, *The Cease of Majesty* (London: Edward Arnold, 1961), p. 21. Churchill, however, seems to hold the opposite view; "With 1588 the crisis of the reign was past". W. Churchill, *A History of the English Speaking Peoples,* Vol. II, *The New World* (London: Cassel & Co., 1956), Chapter X, "Gloriana", p. 106.
101. A.F. Pollard, 'From the Accession of Edward VI to the Death of Elizabeth (1547-1603), *The Political History of England* (ed.), W. Hunt and R.L. Poole (London: Longmans, Green & Co., 1915), Vol. VI, Ch. XXIV, p. 463.
102. *Vide* G.B. Harrison (Ed.), *The Elizabethan Journals* (London; Routledge & K. Paul, 1955), *A Second Elizabethan Journal,* 1595-98, pp. 69, 245.
103. *Ibid.*, pp. 86 *et seq.*
104. Hurstfield, *op. cit.*, p. 44.
105. Pollard, *op. cit.*, p. 475.
106. Lytton Strachey, *Elizabeth & Essex* (London: Chatto and Windus, 1948), p. 5.
107. See the advice given to Essex by one of his followers on 4th October, 1596. *Vide* G.B. Harrison (ed.), *Elizabethan Journals, A Second Eliz.*

Journal (London: Routledge and Kegan Paul, 1955), I Pd. 1931, pp. 139 *et seq*.

108. Pollard, *op. cit.*, p. 471 and Hurstfield, *op. cit.*, p. 44.

Also Strachey, *op. cit.*, p. 207—To his dismay, Cecil was appointed the Master of Wards, for which Essex was contending.

109. Strachey, *ibid.*, pp. 231 *et seq*.

110. *Ibid.*, p. 232.

111. *Ibid.*, p. 234.

112. Harrison, "The National Background" in Barker and Harrison (ed.), *A Companion to Shakespeare Studies* (Cambridge Univ. Press, 1962), p. 179, and Pollard, *op. cit.*, p. 471.

113. *Ibid.*, p. 471.

114. *Ibid.*, p. 471; Harrison, *A Companion*, p. 180.

115. G.B. Harrison (ed.), *The Elizabethan Journals, A Last Elizabethan Journal* (Routledge and Kegan Paul, 1955), 8 Feb., 1601, p. 146.

116. *Ibid.*, p. 146 and Strachey, *op. cit.*, p. 239.

117. *A Last Elizabethan Journal*, 8 Feb., 1601, p. 148.

"So at 10 of the clock at night, all the noblemen came forth, and falling upon their knees, delivered their swords upto the Lord Admiral."

118. *Ibid.*, 9 Feb., 1601, pp. 149 *et seq*.

119. *Ibid.*, 19-21 Feb., 1601, pp. 155 *et seq*.

120. *Ibid.*, 25 Feb., 1601, pp. 162 *et seq*.

121. Pollard, *op. cit.*, p. 472 and Strachey, *op. cit.*, p. 264.

122. Strachey, *ibid.*, p. 242.

123. Harrison, *A Companion*, pp. 180 *et seq*.

124. Quennell, *Shakespeare the Poet and His Background* (London: Weidenfeld and Nicolson, 1963), 255.

125. *Ibid.*, p. 246.

126. A. Nicoll, *The Elizabethans* (Cambridge University Press, 1957), p. 1. M.D.H. Parker, *The Slave of Life* (London: Chatto and Windus, 1955), p. 15. Commenting on the picture of harmony, one finds in Tillyard's *The Elizabethan World Picture*, Parker remarks: "What the curiously constituted class of Elizabethan *litterati* achieved was perhaps not so much a harmony as a poise..., an equlibrium at once steady and insecure."

127. Spencer, *op. cit.*, p. 50.

128. David Bevington, *Tudor Drama and Politics* (Cambridge, Massachusetts: Harvard University Press, 1968), p. 25.

A CATALOGVE

of the feuerall Comedies, Histories, and Tragedies contained in this Volume.

COMEDIES.

HISTORIES.

TRAGEDIES.

Introduction to Shakespeare's History Plays

3

The contents of the First Folio edition (1623) of Shakespeare's works are divided into three clearly demarcated groups, namely Comedies, Histories, and Tragedies.[1] In Quarto publications, however, the terms History and Tragedy are used without much distinction. *Richard II* and *Richard III* are termed tragedies, while *King Lear* and *Troilus and Cressida* are called histories and *Hamlet* is labelled as a 'Tragicall Historie'.[2] This implies that originally *King Lear* and *Troilus and Cressida* were viewed by the playwright himself, or at least by those associated with their production,[3] not as tragedies, but as History Plays. On the other hand, it also implies that while *Henry IV* and *Henry V* were considered Histories, *Richard II* and *Richard III* were not.

On what authority or principle, then, did Heminge and Condell, the First Folio editors, make alterations in the Quarto-titles and classified these ten plays as 'Histories', distinct from Comedies and Tragedies? The question is dealt with by Lily Campbell in her book, *Shakespeare's 'Histories'*:

> When Shakespeare's editors arranged his plays in the First Folio, they grouped them into Comedies, Histories, and Tragedies, putting the ten plays dealing with English history, and only those, into the *Histories* classification. The way of this arrangement implies definition. What was a history play in the thinking of the editors?[4]

Unfortunately, however, she sidetracks the main issue, and instead of telling what a history play was in the thinking of the editors, she rather tells what it is in the thinking of various critics and of herself.[5] The 'why' remains unanswered.

Viewing the question from Shakespeare's rather than the editors' point of view—"Did Shakespeare himself want to make a separate genre of his historical plays?"[6] Prof. Sen Gupta advances a number of arguments in support of the classification. "Heminge and Condell", he says, "may have had the support of Shakespeare himself."[7] However, the First Folio edition came out in 1623, seven years after the death of Shakespeare, and there is no evidence whatsoever to suggest that he had anything to do even with its tentative planning or that he personally held such a view regarding the ten plays. Indeed, whatever evidence is available, is to the contrary.[8]

The other arguments advanced by Sen Gupta take into account the principles of the classification. To sum up his arguments, the History Plays are based on "authentic history"[9] unlike *King Lear* and *Cymbeline*; in them Shakespeare does not take such liberties as in *King Lear* and *Macbeth*, and in them the historical background, unlike that in the Roman plays, has a great significance.[10] That there is some thing in these points can hardly be denied, but that the critic is working out a process of elimination is also quite patent. Coleridge, working out a more or less similar process, put the case thus: "In order that a drama may be properly historical, it is necessary that it should be the history of the people to whom it is addressed."[11] This is to say that historical drama deals only with national history, and if we interpret "the history of the people to whom it is addressed" rather strictly and narrowly, we are close to Prof. Wade-Gery's observation.

> In *Richard II*, and in *Richard III*, Shakespeare is something of a historian: these plays deal with the start and finish of a war which had directly created the world in which the poet lived. The *Iliad* does not: rather (as I have suggested) it resembles *Macbeth*. In *Macbeth*, Shakespeare has no concern with the results of the event....[12]

It is, however, doubtful (whether) Shakespeare himself or Heminge and Condell could ever make such subtle distinctions. The question of the treatment of the historical material is, nevertheless, significant. According to Coleridge,

> The distinction does not depend on the mere quantity of historical events in the play compared with the fictions; for there is as much history in *Macbeth* as in *Richard* but in the relation of the history to the plot. In the purely historical plays, the history forms the plot: in the mixed, it directs it; in the rest, as *Macbeth*, *Hamlet*, *Cymbeline*, *Lear*, it subserves it.[13]

The need for moulding the imagination in accordance with the historical material acts as a rein on the playwright when he is writing a history play. Baker mentions this repeatedly as a "distasteful exaction", which Shakespeare could not meet successfully.[14] "Their sense of historical fact kept them", says Baker, referring to the Elizabethan playwrights in general, "from handling this material with the perfect freedom which marked their use of all other sources."[15] In other words, History Plays call for a close fidelity to historical facts. This may well be taken as a distinguishing feature of the genre. It easily eliminates on the one hand, plays like *George a Greene* and *James IV*, which are appropriately termed "quasi-historical will-o'-the-wisps" by Tucker Brooke,[16] on the other the serious tragedies of Shakespeare like *King Lear*, *Hamlet*, and *Macbeth*. All the same, however, it is difficult to believe that Heminge and Condell made a scrutiny of Shakespeare's sources, their authenticity, and the dramatist's treatment of the material and that they made the classification only after this assiduous scrutiny. The truth is that almost all such definitions and descriptions of the History Plays have a negative approach, seeking to vindicate the First Folio classification by eliminating from the History class on this excuse or that all possible intruders like *Macbeth*, *King Lear*, *Cymbeline* and the Roman Plays. In a sense the descriptions are in different ways tailored to the Folio grouping. This, however, must not leave the impression in our mind that all Shakespearean scholars and critics have accepted the grouping unreservedly. "The Folio classification", says Greg, "into Comedies, Histories, and Tragedies, though generally followed...is not perfect."[17] Wilson Knight considers *Cymbeline* mainly as a historical play.[18] Harbage includes the Roman plays as well as *Troilus and Cressida* among the Histories.[19] Tillyard accepts the conventional classification, yet considers *Macbeth* as "the epilogue of the Histories' at the same time that it is the last of the great tragedies.[20] Charlton thinks that "*Julius Caesar* is a history play in exactly the same sense as are *Henry IV* and *Henry V*."[21] Tucker Brooke's concept of a History Play is wide enough to include Shakespeare's Roman plays as well as *Macbeth*,[22] while Clifford Leech considers only *King John*, *Richard III* and *Richard II* as Histories, labelling the rest—*Henry VI*, *Henry IV*, *Henry V* and *Henry VIII*—as Chronicles.[23]

The last two critics look at the History Plays largely from the point of view of form. According to Brooke, it is "the irregularities of structure and tone which mark the class as a whole for separate discussion",[24] for:

> The species as a whole was a plebeian growth, fostered by unpolished and irregular stage conditions, bound to few if any of the rules of art, and often seeking applause solely by motley spectacular effect.[25]

This criterion, namely the looseness of structure had been noted long ago by Dr. Johnson too: "His histories, being neither tragedies nor comedies are not subject to any of their laws."[26] However, all the History Plays do not share this characteristic and, as admitted by Brooke himself, plays like *Richard III*, and *Richard II* accord wholly or almost wholly "with the strictest rules of tragedy".[27] Charlton also feels that in these two plays tragedy is "the essential substance of the drama", history is only "the accidental form".[28] He subdivides the "Histories" into three groups—Chronicle Play (*Henry VI*), Historical Tragedy (*Richard II*, *Richard III*) and History Play proper (*Henry IV*, *Henry V* and *Julius Caesar*). *King John*, according to him, is neither a chronicle play nor a tragedy, nor a history play; it is a chronical play leaning to tragedy.[29]

That Shakespeare himself set little store by strict conventional classification is evident from his practice of mixing the two classical forms, tragedy and comedy, as also from the following speech of Polonius:

> The best actors in the world, either for tragedy, comedy, history, pastoral, pastoral-comical, tragical-comical-historical-pastoral. *(Hamlet,* Act II, Sc. ii, 392 ff.)

In fact, as Prof. Ludowyk observes, "Shakespeare's forms are generally mixed forms. This is the virtue they derived from being popular drama."[30] The observation though meant for Shakespearean drama in general, is particularly applicable to the History plays. Nicholas Rowe said that these are really tragedies "with a run or mixture of Comedy amongst 'em".[31] In our times, G.L. Evans considers the blending of forms as the special feature of *Henry IV*,[32] and Ribner thinks it "wrong to separate the History Plays from the mainstream of tragedy".[33] Thus, it becomes clear that a history play "cannot be defined by its differentia as a form".[34] In all probability, as Dr. Johnson points out, "The players, who in their edition divided our author's works into comedies, histories, and tragedies, seem not to have distinguished the three kinds by any very exact or definite ideas."[35]

Whether owing to happy chance or some personal whim Heminge and Condell decided to confine the Histories to plays dealing with better known and more authentic chapters of English history. Of the ten plays included by them under the 'Histories' section, four are of doubtful origin. Back in 1850, James Spedding and Samuel Hickson, working independently, advanced the theory of Shakespeare-Fletcher collaboration[36] in *Henry VIII*. Spedding through his verse-test attributed only a meagre share to Shakespeare: Act I. Scenes i and ii; Act II. Scenes iii and iv; and parts of Act III. Scene ii and Act V. Scene i.[37] Rev. F.G. Fleay[38] through metrical-tests, discovering more rhymes in Fletcher and more Alexandrines in Shakespeare as well as Furnivall[39] through 'stopt-line test', pointing out the greater number of 'unstopt' lines in Shakespeare, further confirmed Spedding's division. In the present century, though Peter Alexander[40] and Wilson Knight[41] have argued for Shakespeare's sole authorship of the play, yet the view is far from established. Tillyard as well as Spurgeon refuses to believe that it was entirely a work of Shakespeare's,[42] and more recently A.C. Partridge[43] and Marco Mincoff[44] have reasserted the Spedding-Hickson thesis with greater cogency.

Uncertainty—though comparatively less—prevails regarding the authorship of the *Henry VI* plays also. Malone's theory that

1 Henry VI except the Talbot-scenes, was not by Shakespeare and that in *2 Henry VI* and *3 Henry VI* Shakespeare was only revising the Contention plays[45] generally accepted during the nineteenth century, though challenged in the present century by various critics,[46] is not wholly discredited.[47] In 1876, Jane Lee asserted that *The Contention* and *The True Tragedy* were by Marlowe and Greene[48] respectively, and that they were altered into *2 Henry VI* and *3 Henry VI* by Shakespeare probably with the help of Marlowe.[49] In the ensuing discussions, Furnivall confirmed the finding largely on the basis of the frequency of animal similes and metaphors[50] and remarked: "Every fresh time I read 2 and *3 Henry VI*, the less share in them am I inclined to set down to Shakespeare, though I cannot shut him out of them".[51]

More recently Dover Wilson has argued that Greene "plotted Parts II and III, and I believe that he plotted Part I also".[52] He suggests the names of Nashe 'and possibly' Peele as the other collaborators in the original writing and that of Shakespeare as the reviser.[53] In a detailed comparative study of *The Contention* and *2 Henry* VI, Charles Tyler Prouty has rejected as 'a new orthodoxy'.[54] Peter Alexander's theory that *The Contention* and *Richard Duke of York* are pirated versions of *2* and *3 Henry VI* and has argued afresh the case for revision by Shakespeare.[55]

There are yet other history plays with which Shakespeare's name has, rightly or wrongly, been associated, namely, *Sir John Oldcastle*, *Thomas Lord Cromwell*, *The Famous Victories of Henry V*, *Sir Thomas More* and *Edward III*.[56] It is, however, in the case of only *Sir Thomas More* and *Edward III* that evidence weighs rather heavy in favour of at least part authorship by Shakespeare.[57] Since appearance in 1923 of *Shakespeare's Hand in the Play of Sir Thomas More*,[58] which contained powerful and varied arguments by a number of competent critics like Pollard, Greg, E.M. Thompson, J.D. Wilson and R.W. Chambers, critical opinion has generally favoured Shakespearean authorship of a part of *Sir Thomas More*. Caroline Spurgeon by drawing attention to the presence of Shakespearean imagery in part of the play, has lent further support to the view.[59] "The Shakespearean authorship of this scene", as Kenneth Muir observes, "is now generally accepted".[60] And at least some editors include the play, or part of it, along with the other works of Shakespeare.[61] R.C. Bald, making a survey of the whole debate in 1949, concluded that despite some details seeming "less convincing than they did twenty years ago, the essential case remains intact" and, with every advance in our knowledge of the Elizabethans, "the argument by elimination for Shakespeare's authorship of the Addition becomes stronger".[62]

Since 1760, when Capell claimed that *Edward III* was written by Shakespeare,[63] its authorship has remained open to debate. Chambers thinks that the Countess scenes as well as Act IV, Scene iv might have been by Shakespeare.[64] Alfred Hart makes out a scientific case on the basis of vocabulary tests, for Shakespeare's hand in it.[65] In a "Reconsideration of *Edward III*", Kenneth Muir applies a number of tests and takes into account both sides of the argument, concluding that here, as in *Pericles,* Shakespeare "was hastily revising a play by another dramatist, certain scenes being entirely rewritten and the remainder being left with comparatively few alterations".[66]

There is as much or as little justification for the inclusion of these two plays as for that of *Henry VIII* and *Henry VI* plays in the canon. Indeed, it is queer that modern critics, while discussing the Histories of Shakespeare, exclude *Sir Thomas More* and *Edward III* altogether, and though not quite sure about the sole authorship of *Henry VIII* and *Henry VI* plays, generally refuse to exclude them.[67] The entire question regarding the authenticity or otherwise of the six plays and the justification for their inclusion in toto or in parts, stands in need of fresh investigation. Since such an investigation falls beyond the scope of the present study, it has been deemed more reasonable to leave out all such plays the origin of which continues to be debatable. The present study, therefore, confines itself only to such plays of the 'Histories' group regarding the authorship of which there prevails near unanimity, namely *Richard III*, *King John*, *Richard II*, *1* and *2 Henry IV*, and *Henry V*.

The explanation for the usual inclusion of the controversial *Henry VI* and *Henry VIII* in discussions of Shakespeare's

History Plays lies in the predilections of the critics in the light of which they are prone to view their theme. "While the editors' design", remarks Greg, referring to the inclusion of *Henry VIII* and the exclusion of *Pericles* and *The Two Noble Kinsmen* in the First Folio, "was to exclude any play they knew not to be substantially Shakespeare's, they made an exception of *Henry VIII* in order to round off the series of Histories".[68] That a similar desire on the part of the critics has led to the inclusion of *Henry VI,* plays and *Henry VIII* becomes apparent when we examine the theme of the Histories.

What is their theme? The obvious answer would be 'English History'.[69] This is the factor shared by Shakespeare's 'Histories' with a number of History Plays (or Chronicle Plays), written during the time. These History Plays in general, which drew their material from the English Chronicles, provided historical narratives to the contemporaries. They were the common man's history. In Ben Jonson's *The Divell Is An Asse*, we come across a testimony to this:

> *FIT*.... But Thomas of Woodstocke,
> I'm sure, was *Duke*, and he was made away,
> At *Calice*, as *Duke Humphrey* was at *Bury*;
> And *Richard* the third, you know what end he came too.
> *MER*. By my 'faith, you are cunning i' the *Chronicle, Sir.*
> *FIT*. No, I confesse I ha 't from the *Play-bookes.*
> And think they are more *authentique.*
> *ING*. That's sure, Sir. (Act II. Sc. iv. 8-14)

Thomas Heywood, in his defence of the theatre, laid especial emphasis on this very aspect of the History Plays:

> Playes have made the ignorant more apprehensive, taught the unlearned the knowledge of many famous histories, instructed such as cannot reade in the discovery of all our English Chronicles; and what man have you now of that weake capacity that cannot discourse of any notable thing recorded even from William the Conquerour, nay, from the landing of Brute, untill this day?[70]

An interesting instance of such historical knowledge acquired from the theatre is provided in Iter Boreale, a poem by Bishop Corbet. The host, 'full of ale and history', is giving a vivid description of the battle of Bosworth:

> Why, he could tell
> The inch where Richmond stood, where Richard fell:
> Besides what of his knowledge he could say.
> He had authenticke notice from the Play;
> Which I might guesse, by's mustring up the ghosts,
> And policyes, not incident to hosts;
> But chiefly by that one perspicuous thing,
> Where he mistook a player for a King.
> For when he would have sayd, King Richard dyed.
> And call'd—A horse! a horse! he, Burbidge cry'de.[71]

Thus, history for its own sake was one of the recognized themes of the history plays. "The dramatist", says Briggs, "catered to the desire of the people for historical information, and in return the uneducated accepted him as an historical authority."[72]

The revival of interest in the past history of the nation was partly a by-product of the growth of Nationalism during the sixteenth century. It was truly an age of discoveries. While the sailors discovered distant lands, the historians discovered the past of the country, and the poets the innermost recesses in the soul of man. The curiosity in the past of the country was largely a patriotic urge to exult in the past glories of England, to commemorate the national heroes.

> Feared by their breed, and famous by their birth,
> Renowned for their deeds.... (*Richard II.* II. i. 52-53)

More than the chronicles themselves, it were the Chronicle plays which satisfied this urge. As Thomas Nashe[73] argued in defence of the Chronicle plays, they revived "our fore-fathers' valient acts (that have line (*sic*) long buried in rustic brasse and worme-eaten books)". They raised the dead heroes "from the Grave of oblivion". As examples of such heroes, he made especial mention of Talbot and Henry V.

> How would it have ioyed brave Talbot (the terror of the French) to thinke that after he had byne Two hundred

> years in his Tombe, he should triumphe againe on the stage, and have his bones new embalmed with tears of ten thousand spectators at least (at severall times) who, in the Tragedian that represents his person, imagine they behold him fresh bleeding.[74]
>
> .... What a glorious thing it is to have Henrie the fifth represented on the stage, leading the French King prisoner, and forcing both him and the Dolphin to sweare fealty....[75]

It has often enough been observed that the years immediately following the Armada were the heyday of the English Chronicle Play, which was an offshoot of the growing spirit of patriotism.[76] Nationalism had, thus, generally been recognized as the theme of all English History Plays, including those by Shakespeare. George Baker, echoing Nashe, asserted that the chief purpose of Chronicle Plays was to exhibit the famous historical figures.[77] The figure that stands in the brightest light cast by this nationalistic interpretation of the 'Histories', is that of England itself. In the beginning of the last century, Schlegel had drawn attention to the epic-reach of the 'Histories'. "It is, as it were", he remarked, referring to the ten plays together, "an historical heroic poem in the dramatic form, of which the separate plays constitute the rhapsodies".[78] *King John* and *Henry VIII*, the two plays which by virtue of their historial distance, do not fall easily in line with the rest of the History Plays, were termed by him the Prologue and Epilogue to the great poem on English history.[79] It must, however, be borne in mind that Schlegel looked at the ten plays as one single work from the point of view of structure and not from that of the national spirit. The epic idea was inherent in the very arrangement of the 'Histories' by Heminge and Condell and the question whether the plays are 'Epic or Drama'? continues to be a debatable one to this day.[80] In fact, as would be seen below,[81] Schlegel had a very balanced approach to the Historical Plays and he anticipated nearly all modern trends in the criticism of these plays. Yet, however, all this is quite conveniently forgotten and Schlegel is often looked upon as the father of the nationalistic approach to Shakespeare's Histories. Carlyle, misquoting him uses perhaps for the first time the words 'National Epic' and links the plays with patriotism. Making particular reference to the battle of Agincourt in *Henry V*, he remarks:

> There is a noble Patriotism in it, far other than the 'indifference' you sometimes hear ascribed to Shakespeare. A true English heart breathes, calm and strong, through the whole business; not boisterous, protrusive; all the better for that.[82]

It was, however, the historian, Marriott, who, while asserting most forcefully the theme of nationalism in the History Plays of Shakespeare, was to plead for the recognition of England, as the unnamed hero of all these plays. "England", he says, "though not, as in Bishop Bale's *Kinge Johane*, named in the list of characters, was the hero of everyone of the Chronicle Plays."[83]

The fact, as repeatedly admitted by Marriott himself, that he was writing under the dark shadows of the First World War[84] just as Wilson Knight was to do two decades after during the crisis of the Second War[85] must not be lost sight of. In an hour of crisis, the English have always turned to Shakespeare's Historical Plays as to the *Bible*. In a theatrical survey of the Histories, Sprague has recently drawn attention to the revival of their popularity in the eighteenth century and even to the insertion of patriotic martial speeches in the productions of the time. This, as he points out, was occasioned by a fresh wave of patriotism in the wake of the war with France.[86]

It is, therefore, clearly wrong to dismiss the nationalistic approach to the Histories as merely characteristic of the last century as Harold Jenkins does. "For an age", he says referring to the nineteenth century, "of industrial and commercial progress, of growing nationalisms and imperialist expansions, the most obvious thing about Shakespeare's History Plays was their expression of a national spirit."[87] A cursory glance back at the critics mentioned above, makes it evident that the nationalistic approach to Shakespeare's History Plays is at the same time more antique and more recent than Jenkins imagines. Generalisations are always dangerous, if however, a *raison d' état* is to be sought for the emphasis on the nationalistic aspect of the 'Histories', it is to be found in national crises, recurring from time to time. This does not explain, of course, the attitude of critics like Baker, Brooke and Schelling, who were all writing in the beginning of the present century and were associated with American Universities.

The nationalistic approach to Shakespeare's History Plays, which persisted till the twenties of the twentieth century, has more recently been discredited. Tillyard strikes at what he calls "a hard-dying habit of putting down the vogue of the English Chronicle Plays to the Spanish Armada". Taking the cue presumably from Schelling, he gives greater credit to the publication in 1587 of Holinshed's Chronicle for the growth of the English Chronicle Play.[88] Lily Campbell, whose work is almost contemporary with Tillyard's is more categorical in refuting the nationalistic theory and deserves to be quoted in extenso:

> But the descriptions of the history play as essentially the expression of the great patriotic ardor which centred about the victory of 1588, as resulting from the "triumphant exhilaration" of the Armada year, as exhibiting "exuberant nationalism", and as being "jubilant in pride of country and of race", ignore, strangely enough, the fact that with the exception of *Henry V* and perhaps *Henry VIII*, Shakespeare's plays were written, not about the admirable rulers of England and their times, but rather about those rulers who had sowed the wind and reaped the whirlwind.... Surely, the implied definition of patriotism, limiting it to its prideful and jubilant aspects is too narrow to cover Shakespeare's loyal, but searching study of England's past.[89]

It was apparently and especially with an eye on the works of Tillyard and Lily Campbell that Derek Traversi was to observe sometime later:

> The increased volume of work which has recently been devoted to Shakespeare's series of English history plays, has not been without its uses. In particular it has served to bring these works decisively out of the sphere of patriotic common-place to which they had often been

> consigned by relating them firmly to the political conceptions of the Elizabethan period.[90]

Admittedly, this shift of emphasis from the national to the political, which takes place round the late thirties and early forties, is significant, but it would be wrong to consider the political approach as entirely new. As already noted in Chapter I, in the sixteenth century political philosophy was often incorporated in historical writings.[91] If, as seen above,[92] the Chronicle Plays themselves were looked upon as authentic history in popular form, it was inevitable to look for political ideologies also in them. So Heywood, in the very passage already quoted, after laying emphasis on the patriotic aspect of the History Plays, goes on to underline their politico-moral purpose:

> ...because playes are writ with this ayme, and carryed with this methode, to teach their subjects obedience to their King, to shew the people the untimely ends of such as have moved tumults, commotions, and insurrections, to present them with the flourishing estate of such as live in obedience, exhorting them to allegeance, dehorting them from all trayterous and fellonious stratagems.[93]

It is evident that Heywood recognizes politics, besides national history as the theme of these plays. Again, in the middle of the nineteenth century, the German critic, Gervinus emphasizes politics as the essence of Shakespeare's Histories. Referring to these plays, he observes:

> The poet here passes into a distinctly opposite sphere. Hitherto we have seen him in the range of private life and of personal existence, insinuating himself into the internal history of single individuals, or occupied with the productions of their brain. Here, in this series of historical plays, he enters the wide outward sphere of public life; he is occupied with states and histories, and is stirred by thoughts political and national, and not merely by moral ideas and psychological truths.[94]

How closely Gervinus anticipates the 'new critics', would be apparent from a look at the following two extracts from

Lily Campbell's *Shakespeare's Histories* and M.M. Reese's *The Cease of Majesty*:

> ...it is to this distinction between private and public morals that we must look for the distinction between tragedy and history. Tragedy is concerned with the doings of men which in philosophy are discussed under *ethics*; history with the doings of men which in philosophy are discussed under *politics*.[95]
>
> But the distinguishing quality of the English Histories is that here, and here alone, political virtue is the only standard of reference. The characters exist in a single dimension and are judged solely by the Dramatist's overriding conception of the welfare of society.[96]

The difficulty, however, is that it would be impossible to arrive at any singie unchallenged Elizabethan conception of political virtue or public morals. For, as already observed in Chapter II, the conventional doctrines of order, royal absolutism as well as the new threats to them in the form of just rebellion and tyrannicide, went hand in hand during the time. Hence, the approach to Shakespeare's History Plays via politics has led criticism into two blind alleys in opposite directions.

As Richard Simpson demonstrated nearly a century ago, the raging political controversies of the time were reflected in Elizabethan drama. "Dramas were part of the machinery of political propagandism"[97] and the stage had become "a bear-garden of angry controversy".[98] Viewing Shakespeare in the light of the political controversies, Simpson regarded him as a spokesman of the doctrine of rebellion, and drawing parallels with contemporary political events, endeavoured to prove that the real theme of the 'Histories' consisted of the current politics of Shakespeare's life-time viewed from the angle of the opposition (to the throne). Seen in this light, Henry VI and Richard II become 'the stock examples of weak princes ruined by their favourites and ministers'[99] the favourites in the Elizabethan context being Leceister and Cecil,[100] and *Henry V* becomes 'a poem of victory, a glorification of war' incorporating the policy pursued by Essex and his followers.[101]

In the twenties of the present century, Richard Simpson's thesis was zealously reasserted by a group of American critics, Edith Rickert, Evangelia H. Waller and Evelyn M. Albright. All these critics, and a little later Robert B. Sharpe, emphasized the polemical nature of Elizabethan drama, and identifying Shakespeare's cause with that of Essex, considered the criticism of the Government policies and the voicing of the opposition grievances as the covert theme of his History Plays.[102] More recently, Peter Quennell has asserted: "the historical plays were evidently calculated to interest Essex and Southampton and their friends".[103]

The above approach—which may be termed Essexian—has its origin in three well-known facts of history: Shakespeare's patron, the Earl of Southampton's closeness to Essex;[104] the staging of *Richard II* on the eve of the Essex rebellion in 1601;[105] and the reported conversation of the Queen with William Lambarde, the antiquary, on August 4, 1601.[106] But the apparent logical conclusion that Shakespeare's interests were one with the Essex faction and his intention in the History Plays was to justify rebellion against a weak and inefficient monarch, remains open to question, when one considers that the playwright as well as the players were perhaps completely exonerated from the charge of rebellion[107] and that *Richard II* was written at least six years in advance of the Essex rebellion.

The other outcome of relating Shakespeare's 'Histories' to Elizabethan politics, has been the orthodox theory. The politico-moral purpose of giving a warning against insurrections and of inculcating allegiance, which was stressed by Thomas Heywood,[108] is claimed by many to be the chief substance of the History Plays of Shakespeare. Dr. Johnson had complained that unfortunately Shakespeare "is so much more careful to please than to instruct, that he seems to write without any moral purpose".[109] But about a century later, the German critic, Hermann Ulrici, claimed for Shakespeare a deeply ethical view of life, which coincided with leading Christian ideas.[110] The orthodox theory also interprets the History Plays as the works of a devout Christian who believed in the divine authority of the

King and who had heard over and over again the sermons against insurrection.

But even before Ulrici, Schlegel had hinted at the specific political moral of the 'Histories':

> But this series of dramas is intended as the vehicle of a much higher and much more general instruction; it furnishes examples of the political course of the world, applicable to all times. This mirror of kings should be the manual of young princes; from it they may learn the intrinsic dignity of their hereditary vocation, but they will also learn from it the difficulties of their situation, the dangers of usurpation, the inevitable fall of tyranny, which buries itself under its attempts to obtain a firmer foundation; lastly the ruinous consequences of the weaknesses, errors, and crimes of kings, for whole nations and many subsequent generations.[111]

Such general political instructions were perhaps too general for the taste of the 'new critics',[112] and so they have narrowed it down to the Elizabethan concepts of Order, Degree, and Harmony. But we have already noted in the preceding chapter that these hallowed concepts, inherited from the Medieval Age, served mainly the purpose of strengthening the monarch's hand and the nation's solidarity. We have also noted that royalism was a natural corollary to nationalism during the Renaissance. Hence, it is not at all surprising—despite what Tillyard, Campbell and Traversi maintain[113]—to come across hints of the political theme in the writings of those critics who were chiefly concerned with nationalism. Thus, in Tucker Brooke's classification, the plays which especially distinguish 'Elizabethan history play as a dramatic species' are put under the following head:

> Fourth. Plays *par excellence* of national feeling or national philosophy, where the normal interest in *dramatis personae* is more or less absorbed either in the expression of patriotic sentiment or in the interpretation of problems of government and statecraft.[114]

This implies that patriotism and politics were inseparable as themes. And Marriott, though maintaining that Shakespeare "espoused no party; he was no slavish adherent of any political doctrine; he uttered no shibboleths",[115] yet declares him to be a plain believer in true kingship and hierarchy.[116] In an article written some years later, Marriott again emphasizes Shakespeare's faith in "order and degree; national unity; social solidarity and selfless patriotism".[117] Introducing the Histories, Charles Whibley admits that the History Plays in general were "fashioned for the glory of England and the delight of the people".[118] Shakespeare also "flattered the taste of his contemporaries".[119] And without discrediting the spirit of nationalism, Whibley goes on to assert the orthodox political ideologies as the theme of Shakespeare's History Plays:

> Look where you will in his histories, and you will discover indications of Shakespeare's political opinions. He was, before all things, a champion of tradition, a friend of the established order. He had as devout belief in the divine right of kings to rule as in the plain duty of subjects to obey.... "Degree" was for him what "subordination" was for Dr. Johnson.[120]

Thus, apparently for the critics upto the first three decades of the present century there was no dichotomy between nationalism and royalism (which by its very nature included concepts of hierarchy). In fact, to them as to the Elizabethan historian, the two appeared to a great extent to be complementary. The shift in the critical outlook referred to above[121] is, therefore, not a radical change, but rather a shift of stress from the national to the political, from patriotic sentiments to political ideologies of order and royal absolutism.

This orthodox political theory, supposedly opposed to the earlier nationalistic theory, emerged in the early forties, and it continues to be the most popular theory concerning the History Plays of Shakespeare. In methodology, it is indebted to the Essexian theory, while in ideology it owes largely to the nationalistic one. The nationalistic theory was enunciated under the shadow of the First World War; the orthodox order theory comes up similarly under that of the Second World War. History repeats itself, but this time it repeated itself rather too soon. Hardly twenty years had elapsed in peace and security when Britain was again exposed to another grave—perhaps graver—crisis. Criticism too repeats itself, but is couched in a different language, dressed in a different guise.

Two separate scholarly 'finds' also helped provide criticism with the bases for such a different guise. First, the growing conviction regarding Shakespeare's debt to the Chronicle of Edward Hall. In the Second Chapter, we have already examined the 'moral pattern' imposed on history by Hall, and the political purpose behind this pattern.[122] In 1923, the historian C.L. Kingsford in the course of his lectures on fifteenth century England, devoted a lecture to 'fifteenth-century History in Shakespeare's Plays' and therein emphasized the significance of Hall's prejudices in lending a unity of conception to history, which, according to him, appealed to historians and poets alike and culminated in the concept of dramatic unity which underlies the cycle of Shakespeare's 'Histories'.[123] With further emphasis in the thirties by critics like Edleen Begg, Lucille King, W.G. Zeeveld, etc. it became customary to interpret Shakespeare's cycle of plays according to the pattern imposed on history by Hall.[124] The theme of Hall's Chronicle, as we know was the happy outcome of 'the union' and the dangers of dissension. Hence, the recognition of Shakespeare's debt to the official Tudor Historian Hall has naturally led to the attribution of the orthodox viewpoint to Shakespeare.

Second, in the thirties of the present century there appeared two important works of scholarly investigation into the Elizabethan background, which were bound to have far-reaching impact on the historical approach to Shakespeare. Alfred Hart in 1934 drew attention for the first time to the Tudor Homilies and their influence[125] on Shakespeare; and in 1936, Arthur Lovejoy similarly highlighted the doctrine of the chain of being[126] current in the Elizabethan Age. Hart tried to demonstrate that the dramatist got the views on divine right and the mutual relation of monarch and subjects from the official book of Sermons.[127] Hart's thesis appears quite credible, and was as such warmly accepted by the critics interested in the orthodox theory. Lovejoy's work provided an impressive philosophical framework to their theory.[128]

The orthodox political theory is too well-known to need any introduction. It should suffice to say that it considers Order, Degree, royal absolutism, and support for the establishment to be the specific theme of Shakespeare's Histories. It substitutes a rational philosophy based on the doctrine of order for sheer national sentiments. Tillyard, Dover Wilson and Lily Campbell have been the chief exponents of the theory, but the point made by them is perhaps best illustrated by Wilson Knight's *The Olive and The Sword.*[129] With the avowed object of extracting contemporary meanings out of Shakespeare's Histories, Wilson Knight declares:

> His historical plays are mainly studies of internal disorder during the centuries leading to the England of Elizabeth. Shakespeare's thinking functions continually in terms of order.... The issues troubling Europe today are here in embryo; and the desire for world order which fabricated the League of Nations is an expansion of a desire pulsing throughout Shakespeare.[130]

It would not do simply to lay aside Knight's work as lying outside the domain of literary criticism—"less a study of the histories than an exploitation of them to provide a 'gospel' for Britain at war".[131] Of course, Knight had extra-literary motive in preparing the lectures, but might it not be that a similar motive lay—though below the conscious level—behind the works of Tillyard and Dover Wilson too?

Perhaps we can understand the orthodox order theory of these critics better if we remember the work of Arnold Toynbee,[132] which provides an exact parallel in the field of history. Toynbee's concept of history as 'challenge-and-response', which incorporates a faith in Divine Will and human suffering, is well-known. Coming after Spengler,[133] who had noted the signs of the decline of the western civilization and predicted its doom, and living under the shadow of the great wars, Toynbee seeks to—and indeed, claims to—discover a meaningful pattern in history. He has himself acknowledged that he came by his idea of history under the impact of the spectacle of war:

> The general war of 1914 overtook me expounding Thucydides to Balliol undergraduates reading for *Literae*

> *Humaniores*, and then suddenly my understanding was illuminated. The experience that we were having in our world now had been experienced by Thucydides in his world already.[134]

The idea of history that he develops out of this illumination is stated thus:

> While civilizations rise and fall and, in falling, give rise to others, some purposeful enterprise, higher than theirs, may all the time be making headway, and, in a divine plan, the learning that comes through the suffering caused by the failures of civilizations may be the sovereign means of progress.[135]

It cannot be denied that his *A Study of History* has been the most influential single work on history in recent times. Moreover, it had especial meaning for his generation.[136] As Pieter Geyl puts it:

> A generation only just recovering from the terrible experiences of the war and already anxious about the future is reading the work in the hope of finding in its pages the answer to its perplexities. It is indeed the author's claim to discover for us, in the at first sight chaotic and confusing spectacle of human history, a pattern, a rhythm.[137]

Like Toynbee, the Shakespearean critics too come under the impact of the catastrophic wars (as perhaps also under the impact of Spengler's gloomy picture) and they too look for some definite meaning in history. Happily for them, in the Tudor background they come across the degree-order-doctrine.

Having thus examined the external bases of the orthodox theory, let us turn to its internal basis. By the very nature of their material, Shakespeare's Histories cannot be easily reconciled with order-theme. The order theory relating to them, therefore, is exposed to the same objections that were made against the nationalistic theory by Lily Campbell.[138] Tillyard admits that rather than victory abroad and order at home, mostly unsuccessful war abroad, civil war and fear of disorder at home, form their subject.[139] However, drawing analogy between Shakespeare's History Plays and Spenser's *Faerie Queene*, he suggests that the apparent picture of disorder is a part of the 'total doctrine' of order: "Behind disorder is some sort of order or 'degree' on earth, and that order has its counterpart in heaven".[140] Shakespeare, in other words, presented his thesis through antithesis. Once the idea of order is accepted as basic to Shakespeare, it is not difficult to find a text for it. There is no dearth in Shakespeare's plays of speeches, proclaiming the established order, but by far the best exposition comes from the mouth of Ulysses in *Troilus and Cressida*:

> The heavens themselves, the planets, and this centre
> observe degree, priority, and place,[141]

and no wonder the speech has been quoted innumerable times in support of the orthodox theory.[142] 'But', as Theodore Spencer reminds us in his analysis of the speech in the dramatic context: "What we see on the stage is a complete violation of the whole traditional belief. Instead of order we have anarchy, instead of degree there is violent personal rivalry."[143] It is unfortunate that the large body of critical writing on the History Plays in the present century has generally overlooked such apparent contradictions in the plays themselves as well as the contradictions—referred to in the previous chapter—inherent in the age. Historical criticism, with its zeal to relate the plays to their background and to applaud Shakespeare as a political thinker, has too often led to the interpretation of the plays as political treatises. Admittedly, there have been occasional dissensions and shifts of emphases at times from the conception of order to the image of the ideal ruler, as in the works of Una Ellis-Fermor[144] and M.M. Reese.[145] Nevertheless the general tendency has been to view the History Plays as incorporating the orthodox Elizabethan beliefs.[146] The warning given by Derek Traversi:

> There is very real risk that erudition, in relating these plays to their period, may end by obscuring their true individuality, the personal contribution by which they live as works of art.[147]

has perhaps come too late to be heeded. The apprehension voiced by him has come true. As Reese tells us, "due to the recent emphasis on Elizabethan order and degree Shakespeare's political thinking is reduced to a mere formula".[148] Ribner also, while admitting Shakespeare's belief in the orthodox conception, remarks:

> Too great a concentration upon these traditional ideas, however, and too great an attempt to see Shakespeare's history plays entirely in the light of them, has tended to obscure other elements in the plays.[149]

This has naturally had the effect of reducing these plays to political treatises and of equating Shakespearean history with science. As demonstrated above, it had its origin in the modern preoccupation with war and other disintegrating forces. If history ought to have meaning and pattern, it follows that such meaning can be deduced from the historical writings of our greatest poet. However, even if we condescend to agree that history has meaning, there is a world of difference, reminds Walsh, between 'meaning in history'[150] and 'the meaning of history'. While the former is to look for the meaning of some events of history, the latter is to look for the total meaning of the historical process. It not only brings history close to science but also to ethics. "To say that history 'makes sense'", observes Walsh, "or is meaningful as a whole is, often at any rate, to say that we can feel morally satisfied when we contemplate it. To assert that history fails to make sense is conversely to proclaim that it offends our moral susceptibilities".[151] In a way, Toynbee's theory performs the same function, which the Christian conception of history performed in the Middle Ages and the official Tudor version of history did in the sixteenth century.

The fact is that history is not yet a science and never will be, for one cannot shut the subjective element completely out of it. To comprehend the true nature of history we must go back to Spengler, who, borrowing the words from Geothe, said that history is the 'thing-becoming' and not the 'thing-become'.[152] History can be captured perhaps only in moments,[153] and while we may look for meanings of various actions and events of history, any attempt to seek 'the meaning' of history is bound to meet with failure. "I do not believe", says Geyl, "that at any time it will be possible to reduce the past to so rigid a pattern as to enable us to forecast the future."[154] While nature is to be handled scientifically, History must be handled poetically.[155] Despite all the facts that may be available to the historian, he can only imagine the past, and he has to imagine not merely the events, but also the men behind the events, and not only the men, but also their thoughts and feelings. This is precisely what Shakespeare does in his History Plays. What he gives, therefore, in these plays is, to borrow an expression from Collingwood, an imaginative 're-enactment' of the past.[156] As a result of this, the Histories provide the very substance of history, which is the same as the substance of life itself.

We have noted the Renaissance stress on human motivation and on man as the prime force of history. MacCallum tells us that Shakespeare's interest lies chiefly in the career of individuals,[157] and Charlton observes that he grasps history in the Carlylean way as a product of individuals.[158] To a great extent this is true, for imaginative re-enactment is possible only by re-living with the agents of history. But who are these agents of history? A Richard, a Henry, a John, a Caesar, a Brutus? Yes, but there are also the commoners, the soldiers, the gardeners, the executioners, the superstitious Welshmen, the unpredictable citizens and Shakespeare does not forget them. Unlike Carlyle's, Shakespeare's concept of history is man-centred, not hero-centred. What makes the Agincourt scenes so moving is not just the hair-raising trumpet speech of Henry V, but the doubts and apprehensions of a Bates and a Williams. What is more, even his heroes are again and again brought to the level of common men,[159] subject to the same human passions and emotions, which govern all. He presents the historical persons in their entirety, with all the complexity, all the contradictions which an ordinary mortal is prone to. He anticipates Tolstoy and succeeds alike—though the task is enormously more difficult in drama—in giving a comprehensive picture of the historical events. Moreover, to recognize the human agency is also to recognize the relevance of political ideologies, but only to the extent that such ideologies affect the man involved in the drama of history. Each of the characters may have his theory of life or the body politic, and "the matter of a play may be chockfull of more or less explicit systems of thought."[160] Indeed, it cannot be denied that Shakespeare's history plays deal with 'concepts of power, authority, honour, order and freedom',[161] and we cannot simply shut our eyes to them, saying that "Shakespeare is an artist and as such he has no politics".[162] We would do well always to remember Shakespeare's 'negative capability' and his 'philosophic impartiality'.[163]

Indeed, it is these which enable him to recreate the conflicting ideologies in the Elizabethan Age. All such ideas of naturally find expression in the historical drama. Consequently, as Prof. Sen Gupta has amply demonstrated, one political idea seemingly espoused in this or that play is contradicted in another.[164] Rossiter[165] and Empson[166] have rightly drawn attention to the equivocations and ambiguities in these plays. The traditional conception of Order, Degree, *etcetera* is too black and white, too doctrinaire and narrowly moral for Shakespeare. And the same thing can be said of the earlier nationalistic or Essexian theories regarding these plays. Shakespeare does not offer any "predetermined pattern of ideas"[167] in them. He holds no brief either for or against Divine Right, Rebellion or such other topical issues. And why should he? To look for a valid system of religious or political ideas in an artist is to look for turnips on a rose tree.[168] The ideas become meaningful in drama, as in life, only when they are 'emotionalized'.[169] The ideas which we come across in the History Plays are indispensable parts of history, but they are not abstractions: they are emotionalized. They derive their essential meaning from the men who live them and the events which interact upon them. In the supreme artist there is a constant "refusal to allow the abstract and general to obscure the personal and specific".[170] While presenting the history of the nation, Shakespeare does not remain satisfied with the chronicle of events, nor is he interested in homiletic harping on doctrines; he tries, rather, to depict the throes of history by unfolding the inner history of the historical personages. The important question is not what the characters believe, but to what tasks and techniques in life do their beliefs lead them, and how far do these beliefs help or hinder them in their public achievements as well as private relationships.[171] It is not enough to say that Shakespeare's characters are not his mouthpieces, nor is it enough to stress the aesthetic objectivity of the artist. He displays an awareness of the essentially enigmatic nature of man, no less in the Histories than in his tragedies and comedies. While the characters reflect certain beliefs, these beliefs themselves are exposed to the tests of experience, and no character in him as no man in real life, whether hero or saint, King or rebel, ever acts with unmixed motives, no character remains static. The facts are—by and large—those supplied by the chroniclers, the ideologies are those professed by the political, religious thinkers and practised by the statesmen as well as the populace of the time, but Shakespeare transcends them alike and absorbs us rather in the emotional content of the drama. It is thus that he "metamorphoses the dry lines of the history (as well as—one may add—of political ideologies) into human documents, quickens them into human figures".[172] He anticipates Spengler's and Collingwood's conception of history rather than Toynbee's.

We have noted above the Renaissance emphasis on human will as well as the persistence of the Medieval belief in Providence and Fortune.[173] One of the enigmas of life as well as of history is linked with the question of man's free will versus inevitability.[174] In the final analysis it remains insoluble. There can be no simple answer to the question whether man moves the wheel of history or history moves the wheel of his life. Shakespeare dramatises the interaction of man and the various forces of history. The greatness of his realism consists in his awareness of the extent to which people are involved in history,[175] for willingly or unwillingly involved they are. They may be ladders to the throne, like Buckingham or Northumberland, or even base instruments, like Hubert, Exton and the executioners. They may be like the scrivener in *Richard III* and like the London citizens and gardeners in *Richard II*, bearing witness to the events, or like the Nyms, Pistols, Bardolphs and Falstaffs biding their time for the new reign. They may be like the common soldiers wishing to be away from Agincourt and doubting the justness of the war, or they may be the kings and princes, the rebels and nobles vaingloriously imagining that they are making history.

NOTES

1. See illustration facing page 42.
2. *Vide* E.K. Chambers, *William Shakespeare* (Oxford: Clarendon Press, 1930), Vol. I, pp. 294-95, 348-49, 408, 438, 463-64. See illustrations of the title pages of *Richard III, Richard II* and *Hamlet* (good Quarto editions).
3. Since Pollard established the authenticity of the Good Quartos as distinguished from the Bad Quartos, it is generally accepted that the former were published at the instance of Shakespeare and (or) his company. *Vide* A.W. Pollard, *Shakespeare Folios and Quartos: A Study in the Bibliography of Shakespeare's Plays* (London: Methuen, 1909), *passim,* esp. Chapter III.

   Also his *Shakespeare's Fight with the Pirates and the Problems of the Transmission of His Text* (Cambridge University Press, 1920), *passim.* W.W. Greg, *The Editorial Problem in Shakespeare* (Oxford: Clarendon Press, 1962), pp. 1-18, esp. p. 17.

   C.H. Herford, *A Sketch of Recent Shakespearean Investigation, 1893-1923* (London: Blackie & Son), pp. 16 *et seq.*
4. L.B. Campbell, *Shakespeare's 'Histories'* (Sen Marino, California, The Huntington Library, 1963), p. 8.
5. *Ibid.,* pp. 8 *et seq.*
6. S.C. Sen Gupta, *Shakespeare's Historical Plays* (London: Oxford University Press, 1964), p. 1.
7. *Ibid.,* p. 2.
8. If one considers the titles of the Good Quartos, mentioned above, as such.
9. F.P. Wilson poses the pertinent question: "Who is to be the judge of what is or is not authentic?" in his *Shakespearian and Other Studies* (ed.), Helen Gardner (Oxford: Clarendon Press, 1969), p. 3.
10. Sen Gupta, *op. cit.,* pp. 2 *et seq.*
11. Vide Campbell, *op. cit.,* p. 9.
12. Vide P. Alexander's *Shakespeare* (London: Oxford University Press and ELBS, 1965), p. 164.
13. *Op. cit.,* pp. 164 *et seq. Vide* Campbell, *op. cit.,* p. 9.
14. G.P. Baker, *The Development of Shakespeare as a Dramatist* (N.Y.: Macmillan, 1923), Chap. IV, pp. 142 *et seq,* esp. p. 180.
15. *Ibid.,* p. 161.
16. C.F.T. Brooke, *The Tudor Drama* (London: Archon Books, 1964), p. 297.
17. W.W. Greg, *op. cit.,* p. 15. *n.* 2.
18. G.W. Knight, *The Crown of Life* (London: Mithuen, Univ. Paperbacks, 1966), p. 129.

19. A. Harbage, *As They Liked It* (New York: Harper Torchbooks, 1961), pp. 123 *et seq.*
20. E.M.W. Tillyard, *Shakespeare's History Plays* (Harmondsworth, Middlesex: Penguin, 1962), p. 315.
21. H.B. Charlton, *Shakespeare: Politics and Politicians* (The English Association Pamphlet No. 72, April, 1929), p. 19.
22. T. Brooke, *op. cit.*, pp. 329 *et seq* and 336 *et seq.*
23. C. Leech, *Shakespeare The Chronicles* (Published for the British Council and the National League by Longmans, Green & Co., 1962), p. 11.
24. Brooke, *op. cit.*, p. 298.
25. *Ibid.*, p. 301.
26. Dr. Johnson, Preface to Shakespeare, *Vide* W. Raleigh (ed.), *Johnson on Shakespeare* (London: Oxford University Press, 1946), p. 24.

    M.W. MacCallum, *Shakespeare's Roman Plays and Their Background* (London: Macmillan, 1935), pp. 74 *et seq.*
27. Brooke, *op. cit.*, p. 297.
28. Charlton, *op. cit.*, p. 7.
29. *Ibid.*, pp. 7 *et seq.*
30. E.F.C. Ludowyk, *Understanding Shakespeare* (Cambridge University Press, 1964), p. 69.
31. Quoted by F.P. Wilson, *op. cit.*, p. 1.
32. G.L. Evans, The Comical-Tragical-Historical Method: Henry IV. Chapter VII in J.R. Brown and B. Harris (ed.), *Early Shakespeare,* Stratford Studies 3 (London: Edward Arnold, 1967), pp. 145 *et seq.*
33. I. Ribner, *Patterns in Shakespearean Tragedy* (London: Methuen, 1962), p. 36.

    Also in *The English History Play in the Age of Shakespeare* (Princeton, New Jersey: Princeton University Press, 1957), pp. 28 *et seq.*
34. G.P. Baker, *op. cit.*, p. 142.
35. Dr. Johnson, *op. cit.*, p. 17.

    F.P. Wilson, *op. cit.*, p. 2. "Heminge and Condell...were not making subtle distinctions between the kinds of drama. The arrangement was dictated by its obvious convenience, a convenience of subject-matter."
36. J. Spedding, "On the Several Shares of Shakespeare and Fletcher in the play of Henry VIII,' originally printed in *The Gentleman's Magazine,* Aug., 1850, pp. 115-23, with the title 'who wrote Henry VIII?' reprint in *New Shakespeare Society Transactions* (1874), Appendix to part I, pp. 1-18. S. Hickson's view confirming Spedding's findings, first printed in *Notes and Queries,* I, Series, ii, 198, No. 43, Aug. 24, 1850: reprint in N.S.S.T. (1874), pp. 18-20.

37. *Ibid.*, p. 14.
38. *Ibid.*, p. 23.
39. *Ibid.*, p. 24.
40. P. Alexander, *English Studies* (1939), pp. 85-120 cf. John Munro (ed.), *The London Shakespeare,* Vol. IV (London: Eyre and Spollinvoode, 1958), Int. p. 1146. P. Alexander, *Introductions to Shakespeare* (London and Glasgow: Collins, 1964), pp. 83 *et seq.*
41. G.W. Knight, *The Crown of Life* (London: Methuen, Univ. Paperbacks, 1966), pp. 258 *et seq.*
42. Tillyard, *op. cit.* Preface, p. viii. C. Spurgeon, "Shakespeare's Iterative Imagery" in P. Alexander (ed.), *Studies in Shakespeare* (London: Oxford University Press, 1964), p. 190.
43. A.C. Partridge, *The Problem of 'Henry VIII' Reopened* (Camb., Bowes & Bowes, 1949), cf.
44. M. Mincoff, '*Henry VIII* and Fletcher', *Sh Q*. xii, Summer 1961, No. 3, pp. 239-60.
45. E. Malone, *A Dissertation on the Three Parts of Henry VI* reprint in Boswell's edition of Malone's *Shakespeare* (1821) cf. in A.S. Cairncross (ed.), 2 *Henry VI* (N. Arden. Lond: Methuen), xviii, pp. xvi *et seq.* E.K. Chambers, *Shakespearean Gleanings* (Oxford University Press, 1944), 'The Disintegration of Shakespeare', p. 3.
46. Notably by P. Alexander. See his *Shakespeare's Henry VI and Richard III* (Cambridge University Press, 1929), *passim.*
47. A Fresh defence of Malone's view has been attempted by J.D. Wilson in 'Malone and the Upstart Crow', *Sh. Sy.* 4 (1951).
48. J. Lee, 'On the Authorship of the Second and Third Parts of *Henry VI* and Their Originals', *New Shakespeare Society Transactions,* (1875-76) Chapter X, p. 236.
49. *Ibid.*, p. 263.
50. *Ibid.*, pp. 280 *et seq.*
51. *Ibid.*, pp. 283 *et seq.*
52. D. Wilson (ed.), *Henry VI. Part I* (The New Shakespeare, Cambridge University Press, 1952), Int. p. xxxi.
53. *Ibid., passim,* especially the table of *1 Henry VI* on p. XL and the Int. to *Henry VI Parts II and III, Henry VI, Part II* (The New Shakespeare, Camb. University Press, 1952), *passim,* esp. p. xxviii.
54. C.T. Prouty, *The Contention and Shakespeare's & Henry VI* (New Haven: Yale University Press, 1954), p. 2.
55. *Ibid., passim,* esp. pp. 107 *et seq.*
56. The first two were included in the Third Folio (1664), cf. K. Miur, *Shakespeare as Collaborator* (London: Methuen, 1960), pp. 2 *et seq.*

    And S.M. Pitcher tries to make a case for Shakespeare's authorship of *The Famous Victories.* See his '*The Case for Shakespeare's Authorship of 'The Famous Victories*' (London: Alvin Redman, 1962).

57. Greg also thinks only these two history plays outside the canon worth considering. See his *The Shakespeare First Folio Its Bibliographical and Textual History* (Oxford University Press, 1955). Note A, p. 99.
58. A.W. Pollard (ed.), *Vide* J. Munro (ed.), *op. cit.*, Vol. IV, pp. 1257 *et seq*.
59. *RES* vi, 1930, pp. 257-70. cf. *Ibid.*, p. 1258.
60. *Op. cit.*, p. 8.— 'this scene' refers to the insurrection scene.
61. H. Farjeon (ed.), *The Complete Works of Wm. Shakespeare* (London: The Nonesuch Press, 1958), Vol. III, pp. 1385-1459.

    J. Munro (ed.), *op. cit.*, pp. 1269-78.—contains only the parts supposedly written by Shakespeare, i.e. Sc. vi and Part of Sc. viii.
62. R.C. Bald, *The Bk of Sir T. More and Its Problems*', *Shakespeare Survey* (Camb. University Press, 1949), p. 59.
63. K. Muir, 'A Reconsideration of *Edward III*', *Sh Survey* 6 (Camb. University Press, 1953), p. 39.
64. E.K. Chambers, *William Shakespeare* (Oxford: Clarendon Press, 1930), Vol. I, p. 516.
65. A. Hart, *Shakespeare and the Homilies* (Melbourne: Melbourne University Press, 1934), 219 *et seq*.
66. K. Muir, *op. cit.*, p. 47.
67. As an exception, L.B. Campbell excludes both *Henry VIII* and the *Henry VI* plays on precisely the same ground that they are excluded by the present author. Campbell, *op. cit.*, p. 120.
68. Greg. *The Shakespeare First Folio*, p. 77. In the footnote he adds that the same desire might account for the inclusion of *1 Henry VI.*

    Also see his *Editorial Problem*, pp. 19 *et seq*.
69. Tillyard, *op. cit.*, p. 147.
70. *Apology for Actors*, p. 52. *vide* W.D. Briggs, *Marlowe's Edward II* (London: David Nutt, 1914), Int., p. Liii.
71. *Vide ibid.*, p. Liv.
72. *Ibid.*, p. Lv.
73. R.B. Mckerrow (ed.), *The Works of T. Nashe*, Vol. I, *Pierce Pennilesse*, F. 3 (London: Sidgwick and Jackson, MCMX), p. 212.
74. *Ibid.*
75. *Ibid.*, p. 213.
76. "Between 1588 and 1598 the Chronicle play was the most popular kind of play in England", says G.P. Baker, *op. cit.*, p. 145.

    Also H.B. Charlton, *op. cit.*, p. 8.

    C.F. Tucker Brooke, *op. cit.*, p. 299.

J.A.R. Marriott, *English History in Shakespeare* (N. York: E.P. Dutton, 1918), p. 3.

F.E. Schelling, *The English Chronicle Play* (N. York: Macmillan, 1902), pp. 30 *et seq*. Though admitting their origin in patriotism, Schelling, instead of linking them directly with the Armada, links them rather with the historical writings of the time. In this, he anticipates Tillyard. See Tillyard, *op. cit.*, p. 100.

77. *Op. cit.*, p. 162.
78. A.W. Schlegel, *Dramatic Art & Literature* (Tr.), John Black (London: Henry G. Bohn 1861), p. 419.
79. *Ibid.*, p. 422.
80. R. David, 'Shakespeare's History Plays—Epic or Drama? *Sh. Survey* 6 (ed.), A. Nicoll (Camb. University Press, 1953), pp. 129 *et seq.*
81. See pp. 57 *infra.*
82. Carlyle, *On Heroes, Hero-Worship, and the Heroic in History,* Lecture IIII, 'The Hero as Poet', delivered 12th May 1840. From D.N. Smith (ed.), *Shakes. Criticism 1623-1840* (London: O.U.P., 1961), pp. 366 *et seq.*
83. *Op. cit.*, p. 30.
84. *Ibid.*, pp. 2 *et seq*, esp. p. 8.
85. G. Wilson Knight, *The Olive and the Sword* (originally composed in 1940), pp. 60 *infra.*
86. A.C. Sprague, *Shakespeare's Histories: Plays for the Stage* (London: "The Society for Theatre Research. 1964), pp. 2-3.
87. Shakespeare's History Plays: 1900-1951', *Sh. Survey,* Vol. 6 (Camb. University Press, 1953), p. 1.
88. *Op. cit.*, p. 100.
89. *Op. cit.*, p. 11.
90. *'Henry IV-Part I' Scrutiny XV*, No. 1 (Dec. 1947). Reissued (Camb. University Press, 1963), p. 24.
91. See especially p. 13 *supra.*
92. *Ibid.*
93. *Vide* Briggs, *op. cit.*, p. liv.
94. G.G. Gervinus, *Shakespeare Commentaries,* 1850 (Tr.), F.E. Bunnett (London: Smith, Elder & Co., 1875), p. 248.
95. Campbell, *op. cit.*, p. 17.
96. M.M. Reese, *The Cease of Majesty* (London: Edward Arnold, 1961), p. 163.
97. R. Simpson, "The Political Use of the Stage in Shakespeare's Time", *New Shakespeare Society Transactions 1874* (London: Trubner & Co.), No. 1, Paper IX, p. 371.

98. *Ibid.*, p. 374.
99. *Ibid.*, Paper XII, 'Shakespeare's Polities', p. 440.
100. *Ibid.*, Paper X, 'The Politics of Shakespeare's History Plays', pp. 406 *et seq.*
101. *Ibid.*, p. 418.
102. D. Bevington, *Tudor Drama and Politics* (Harvard, 1968), p. 2.
103. P. Quennell, *Shakespeare* (London, 1963), p. 196. However, unlike Simpson and others, he does not try to distinguish in his works 'a deep political intelligence', p. 201.
104. Chapter II, *supra.*

    G.P.V. Akrigg, *Shakespeare and the Earl of Southampton* (London: Hamish Hamilton, 1968), *passim,* for the relations especially p. 185; and the interpretation of *The Phoenix & the Turtle* in this light, pp. 252 *et seq,* Shakespeare looking back on the Essex group, of which Southampton and himself had been a part, sees a brilliant and gifted company of friends overwhelmed with disaster: 'Truth & Beauty buried be.'

    And P. Quennell, *op. cit.,* p. 250. "But Shakespeare had been Southampton's man and through Southampton, presumably, had entered Essex's charmed circle."
105. Chambers, W. *Shakespeare,* I, pp. 353 *et seq* and P. Ure, Int. to *R II* (New Arden, 5th ed., 1961), pp. lvii *et seq.*
106. The Queen's sensitivity to the analogy commonly drawn between herself and King Richard II is amply illustrated by her ironic remark to William Lambarde: "I am Richard II know ye not that."—P. Ure, *op. cit.,* p. lix.
107. *Ibid.,* p. lviii.
108. *Ibid.,* p. 60.
109. *Op. cit.,* pp. 20 *et seq.*
110. *Shakespeare's Dramatic Art* (trans.), L.D. Schmitz (London: George Bell, 1889-90), 2 Vols. *passim.*
111. A.W. Schlegel, *op. cit.,* pp. 419 *et seq.*
112. Tillyard, D. Wilson, L. Campbell, etc.
113. *Ibid.,* pp. 51 *et seq.*
114. *Op. cit.,* p. 303.
115. *Op. cit.,* p. 30.
116. *Ibid.,* pp. 27 *et seq.*
117. 'Shakespeare and Politics' (*Cornhill,* new series, LXIII, 1927), cf. *Sh. Sy,* Vol. 6, p. 6.
118. *The Works of Shakespeare,* Vol. II, *Histories* (London: Macmillan, 1925), Int., p. xi.
119. *Ibid.,* p. xii.

120. *Ibid.*, p. xliii.
121. Pages 51 *et seq supra,* particularly the quotation from Traversl, ixx.
122. Chapter II, p. 19 *supra.*
123. C.L. Kingsford, *Prejudice and Promise in Fifteenth Century England* (London: Frank Cass, 1962), p. 3.
124. *Vide* Jenkins, *op. cit.*, p. 7.

    Edleen Begg, 'Shakespeare's Debt to Hall and Holinshed in *Richard III*', *Studies in Philology,* xxxii (1935); Lucille King, 'The Use of Hall's Chronicles in Folio and Quarto Texts of *Henry* VI', *Philological Quarterly,* xiii (1934) and 'Text Sources of the Folio and Quarto Henry VI', *PMLA,* LI (1936); W.G. Zeeveld, 'The Influence of Hall on Shakespeare's English Historical Plays', *ELH,* III (1936).
125. *Shakespeare and the Homilies* (Melbourne University Press, 1934).
126. *The Great Chain of Being* (Mass.: Cambridge, 1936).
127. *Op. cit., passim.*
128. Tillyard's acknowledgment of debt to both, *op. cit.*, pp. 18 *et seq.*
129. Initially written in 1940, presented in various forms (lecture recitals and broadcasts) in 1941 (London: Oxford University Press, Sept. 1944).
130. *Ibid.*, pp. 4 *et seq.*
131. Jenkins, *op. cit.*, p. 9.
132. *A Study of History* (London: Oxford University Press), in 12 volumes of which volumes I to VI appeared in the thirties, I-III (1934), IV-VI (1939).
133. *The Decline of the West,* 2 Vols. first published in German, Vol. I (1918), Vol. II (1922) in Eng., Vol. I (1926) and Vol. II (1928).
134. 'My View of History', extract from his *Civilization on Trial* in P. Gardiner (ed.), *Theories of History* (Illionis: The Free Press, 1959), p. 205.

    'The Disintegration of Civilizations', extract from his *A Study of History* in *ibid.*, pp. 204 *et seq.*
135. 'My View of History', *ibid.*, p. 210.
136. That is, the generation of Dover Wilson, Wilson Knight, Tillyard and Lily Campbell.
137. Geyl, in the course of a debate with Toynbee, broadcast on the B.B.C. on Jan. 4 and March 7, 1948—'Can We Know the Pattern of the Past?' *Vide* Gardiner, *op. cit.*, p. 308.
138. Quoted above on p. 53.
139. *Op. cit.*, p. 7.
140. *Ibid.*, p. 8. This again reminds of Toynbee. *supra.*
141. *Troilus and Cressida,* I, iii, 85 ff.

142. Marriott, *op. cit.*, pp. 128 *et seq.*

G. Wilson Knight, *op. cit.*, pp. 46 *et seq.*—"That slow working out of a stable system from chaos and conflict dramatised in the historical plays is here given its phil." (47). H. Craig, *The Enchanted Glass* (N.Y.: O.U.P., 1936), p. 73.—"The idea of stability in gradation...is fundamental to Shakespeare's political and most of his social thinking." T. Spencer, *Sh & the Nature of Man* (Lowel Lectures, 1942, N.Y.: Macmillan, Camb. University Press, 1945), pp. 21 *et seq*. Tillyard, *op. cit.*, pp.16 *et seq.*

143. Spencer, *op. cit.*, p. 112.

144. Una. Ellis-Fermor, 'Shakespeare's Political Plays' in *The Frontiers of Drama* (London: Methuen, 1964), pp. 34-35.

145. M.M. Reese, *The Cease of Majesty* (London: Edward Arnold, 1961).

146. E.M. Waith (ed.), *Shakespeare the Histories Twentieth Century Views* (Englewood Cliffs, New Jersey: Prentice Hall, 1965), Int. pp. 7 *et seq.*

147. D. Traversi, *Shakespeare From Richard II to Henry V* (London: Hollis and Carter, 1957), p. 1.

148. Reese, *op. cit.*, Preface, p. vii.

149. Ribner, *The English History Play in the Age of Shakespeare,* (Princeton, N. Jersey: Princeton University Press, 1957), p. 158.

150. W.H. Walsh, '"Meaning" in History', *Vide* Gardiner, *op.cit.*, pp. 296-307 especially p. 302.

Toynbee and, before him, Marx and Comte have tried to make sense of history and have given us general laws of the historical process.

151. *Ibid.*, p. 302.

152. 'The World-as-History', extract from *The Decline of the West, Vide* Gardiner, *op. cit.*, p. 197.

153. 'Physiognomic, that is, *history* captured in a moment'. *Ibid.*, p. 199.

154. *Ibid.*, p. 315.

155. Spengler, *ibid.*, p. 198.

156. R.G. Collingwood, *The Idea of History* (Oxford: Clarendon Press, 1946).

Gardiner, *op. cit.*, p. 253.

157. MacCallum, *Roman Plays and Their Background* (London: Macmillan, 1935), Ch. II, *passim.*

158. H.B. Charlton, *op. cit.*, p. 24.

159. Tolstoy, distinguishing the work of art from history remarks: "For an historian considering the achievement of a certain aim, there are heroes; for the artist treating of man's relation to all sides of life there cannot and should not be heroes, but there should be men." 'Some words about *War and Peace',* Louise and Aylmer Maude (trans.), *War and Peace* (Oxford University Press, 1933), Vol. III, p. 541.

160. Charlton, *op. cit.,* p. 6.
161. L.C. Knights, *'Shakespeare's Politics: With Some Reflections on the Nature of Tradition'. Further Explorations* (London: Chatto and Windus, 1965), p. 32; and Bevington, *op. cit.,* p. 25.
162. Jean-Louis Barrault, 'Shakespeare and the French' in Oswald Lewinter (ed.), *Shakespeare in Europe* (Penguin Shakespeare Library, 1970), p. 353.
163. K. Muir, 'Shakespeare and Politics' in A. Kettle (ed.), *Shakespeare in a Changing World* (London: Lawrence and Wishart, 1964), pp. 78, 82.
164. Sen Gupta, *op. cit.,* pp. 20 *et seq.*
165. A.P. Rossiter, 'The Dialectic of the Histories', *Angel With Horns* (ed.), G. Storey (London: Longmans, 1962), pp. 40-64.
166. W. Empson, 'Falstaff and Mr. Dover Wilson', *Kenyon Review* (Spring, 1953), *Vide* G.K. Hunter (ed.), *Henry IV, Parts I and II* Casebook Series (London: Macmillan, 1970), pp. 135-54.
167. Knights, *op. cit.,* p. 14.
168. Charlton, *op. cit.,* p. 4.
169. A.H. Johnson, *Whitehead's Philosophy of Civilization* (New York: Dover Publications, Inc. 1962, I ed., 1958), p. 27.
170. Knights, *op. cit.,* p. 14.
171. The expression is borrowed from L.A. Cormican, Review of *The Enchanted Glass* in *Scrutiny,* xvii. No. 4, March 1951, p. 355, Cormican is talking of the Elizabethans' beliefs and their use in literature.
172. Baker, *op. cit.,* p. 170.
173. Chapter I, pp. 3 *et seq. supra.*
174. Tolstoy, *War and Peace* (tr.), Louise and Aylmer Maude (London: Oxford University Press, 1933), Vol. III, p. 518 *et seq.* and Isaiah Berlin, *Historical Inevitability* (1954), extract in Gardiner, *op. cit.,* pp. 320-29.
175. Jan Kott, *Shakespeare Our Contemporary* (London: Metheun, 1967), p. 17.

Richard III

4

It is a commonplace of criticism to view *Richard III* as the final play of the so-called first tetralogy and to interpret it in the light of the curtain speech of Richmond (V. v. 18-41). Seen in this light the play becomes a moral history, with a rigid providential (or rather Tudor) pattern of retributive justice. "The main business of the play", observes Tillyard, "is to complete the national tetralogy and to display the working out of God's plan to restore England to prosperity."[1] In course of his discussion of the play, he also talks of Shakespeare's 'official self' and goes on to reassert that "the play's main end is to show the working out of God's will in England's history".[2] This provides a striking instance of the orthodox approach to Shakespeare's Histories. It buries the real Shakespeare and by raising the intimidating ghost of his 'official self', prevents us from appreciating the more lasting and deeper values of the play. If we concentrate on the text itself, without trying to press it into the service of generality and without losing sight of the dramatic context of the episodes as well as the speeches, it is unlikely that we would arrive at such naive optimistic Christian concept of history.[3] In fact, what Shakespeare displays most powerfully in this drama, as in his other great dramas, is the 'constant inversions of meaning'.[4] It is a play of the *bibhatsa rasa* (the odious sentiment) and its protagonist, Richard III, is a *dhiroddhata nayaka*.

In the understanding of the play, a great deal hinges upon the understanding of Richard himself and his character clearly illustrates the inversions of meaning. He is a Machiavellian careerist, the new man of the Renaissance like Tamburlaine, who knows that the world belongs to the strong and the wise. But as the tyrant, the devil-king, he is also the scourge of God.[5] Moulton, who considers Nemesis as the recurrent pattern of the play, observes that the various Nemesis Actions receive an impetus from contact with Richard.[6] This poses the pertinent question: who is then morally responsible for the inhuman crime—Nemesis or Richard? Or to put it differently, God or man? What is Shakespeare's purpose: to prevent conventional moral judgments, Tudor myth and Christian feelings from compromising the almost unbounded admiration that he excites for the prowess of his Marlovian hero, or to prevent this admiration from compromising the moral judgments, Tudor myth and Christian feelings? There can be no simple answer as there can be no simple answer to the questions raised, for instance, by Margaret's curses. She terms herself 'a prophetess' and she is treated as 'the chief exponent of the philosophy of Providence in the play'.[7] Indeed, she does foretell almost all the events of the play, but before breathing her curses, she has herself doubted the viability of curses:

> Did York's dread curse prevail so much with heaven
> That Henry's death, my lovely Edward's death,
> Their kingdom's loss, my woeful banishment,
> Should all but answer for that peevish brat?
> Can curses pierce the clouds and enter heaven?
>
> (I. iii. 191-95)

and each of her curses springs out of personal malice and unappeased rancour. To take the curses at their face-value amounts to forgetting that Providence itself becomes an instrument of faction in the scene. To say the least, "her raucous demands for justice shock us, and the execution of that justice horrifies us". Nevertheless—we may agree with Lily Campbell—"they contribute to the pattern of the play".[8] They lend a retributive pattern of unity to the seemingly never-ending sequence of horrible crimes. But is this all? Are they not meant to itch the conscience of all those present?

> My hair doth stand an end to hear her curses.

Says Hastings.

> And so doth mine: (I. iii. 304-05)

Adds Rivers. Even the strong unscrupulous Richard is not entirely unmoved, for, the curse which Margaret pronounces against him, he tries to shift to her by anticipating her and closing the santence with her name:

Q. Margaret Thou slander of thy heavy mother's womb:
Thou loathed issue of thy father's loins!
Thou rag of honour: thou detested—
Gloucester Margaret (I. iii. 231-34)

The only character who remains composed throughout the scene is Bukingham. His platitude:

curses never pass
The lips of those that breathe them in the air.
(I. iii. 285-86)

is reassuring, but the fact remains that he is the only one left out of the compass of Margaret's dreadful curses.

To view the play as a moral history, extolling the Tudor political doctrines is a simplification, and simplifications hardly ever work when we are face to face with a great work of art. *Richard III* dramatizes 'the discrepancy between the moral order and the order of practical behaviour',[9] the interaction between man's will and his conscience. Though an early play, and presumably the first History written by Shakespeare, it is replete with complexities and demands the same critical awareness, the same liberal imagination, which are demanded by his maturer works.

Richard III has a symmetrical construction. It both begins and ends with a set speech.[10] The opening soliloquy by Richard—at least the first thirteen lines of it (I. i. 1-13)—bears close resemblance to the curtain speech of Richmond already referred to. Both are speeches of triumph spoken after the defeat of adversaries, for 'Now' in the above soliloquy refers to the time after the battle of Tewkesbury. In Richard's soliloquy there is a description of peace, actually established after the battle of Tewkesbury, while in Richmond's speech, there is a projected vision of peace and it is remarkable to note that in both cases occurs the image of smooth face:

Grim-visaged war hath *smoothed* his wrinkled front;
(I. i. 9)

> Enrich the time to come with *smooth-faced* peace, (V. v. 33)

Moreover, in both cases the road from the battlefield leads to 'a lady's chamber',[11] and this adds a rather strong and unsavoury spice of irony to Richmond's proposed matrimony of policy with Elizabeth York. Another such matrimony of policy takes place between the victor of Agincourt and the French Princes and we know what comes out of its promise of "a boy, half French, half English, that shall go to Constantinople and take the Turk by the beard?"[12]

The second part of Richard's soliloquy (ll. 14-15)[13] abruptly changes the topic of 'glorious summer' and introduces the character of the villain-hero:

> But I, that am not shaped for sportive tricks
> Nor made to court an amorous looking glass: (ll. 14-15)

This provides the basis for a psychological explanation of the diabolic nature of Richard. The description of the physical deformity of Richard is derived from More's *Life of Richard III*, as incorporated by Hall and Holinshed:

> Richard duke of Gloucester the third sonne (of which I must moste entreate) was in witte and courage egall with the other Edward and George, but in beautee and liniamentes of nature far underneth bothe, for he was litle of stature, eivill featured of limnes, croke backed, the left shulder muche higher than the righte, harde favoured of visage, such as in estates is called a warlike visage, and emonge commen persones a crabbed face.... he came into the worlde the fete forwarded, as menne, bee borne outwarde, and as the fame ranne, not untothed: whether that men of hatred reported above the truthe, or that nature chaunged his course in his beginnynge, whiche in his life many thynges unnaturally committed, this I leve to God his judgemente.[14]

Shakespeare accepts the description without any misgivings about the veracity of the report and uses it in two ways to enrich the character of Richard. On the one hand, he incorporates the above suggestion that the unnatural form of Richard from the very hour of his birth was perfectly in keeping with the deeds performed by him in later life; on the other hand, he allows Richard to reverse the suggestion and to hold out that his deeds, howsoever gruesome, are in keeping with the unnatural form given to him by God. The prophetic words of Henry VI[15] at the point of death:

> Teeth hadst thou in thy head when thou wast born,
> To signify thou cam'st to bite the world;
>
> (*3 Henry VI*. V. vi. 53-54)

as well as Richard's own assertion a few lines later:

> The midwife wonder'd; and the women cried
> 'O, Jesus bless us, he is born with teeth!
> 'And so I was, which plainly signified
> That I should snarl, and bite, and play the dog.
>
> (3 *Henry VI*. V. vi. 74-77)

provide examples of the first. As we find in the above speech of Richard, the idea is developed into the symbolic image of dog. The second idea—Richard's self-justification—follows on the heels of the first:

> Then, since the heavens have shap'd my body so,
> Let hell make crook'd my mind to answer it.
> I have no brother, I am like no brother;
> And this word 'love', which grey beards call divine,
> Be resident in men like one another
> And not in me! I am myself alone.
>
> (*3 Henry VI*. V. vi. 78-83)

The two ideas occur again in the second part of the opening soliloquy already referred to above. Richard, after accepting the legend about his birth and giving a sardonic account of his own deformity, instead of indulging in self-pity, sheds light on the psychological roots of his misanthropy. He appears to declare, as Freud puts it: "Nature has done me a grievous wrong in denying me the beauty of form which wins human love. Life owes me reparation for this, and I will see that I get it.... I may do wrong myself, since wrong has been done to me."[16] Clemen, however, disagreeing, thinks that "to view Richard's choice of evil as 'compensation' ignoring both his freedom of will and his subsequent guilt, is to view the play from an alien standpoint".[17]

In fact, the whole debate regarding Richard's free will is irrelevant and though it does not absolve Richard of responsibility for his misdeeds, the psychological justification nevertheless remains valid for the character itself. Rather than being alien to Elizabethan thought, Richard's argument appears to enliven Bacon's views on the deformity of men:

> Deformed persons are commonly even with Nature. For as Nature hath done ill by them; so doe they by Nature: Being for the most part (as the Scripture saith) *void of Naturall Affection*; And so they have their Revenge of Nature.[18]

In his deformity Richard is Caliban-like, and this is one of the few points on which he differs sharply from Macbeth. Despite this self-confessed deformity, however, there is in him—unlike Richard II—no allowance to self-pity and the physical deformity is transformed into a mental asset. "But surely the Richard of Shakespeare", says Charles Lamb, while criticizing Cooke's presentation of Colley Cibber's version of *Richard III*:

> mingles in these allusions a perpetual reference to his own powers and capacities, by which he is enabled to surmount these petty objections; and the joy of a defect conquered, or turned into an advantage, is one cause of these very allusions, and of the satisfaction with which his mind recurs to them. These allusions themselves are made in an ironical and good humoured spirit of exaggeration....[19]

Lamb makes particular note of the 'self-congratulating soliloquy', spoken after the successful wooing of Anne, which recounts the tale of his wrongs to her and goes on to exult in his, what appears to have been an unlooked for victory over God, virtue, and nature:

> And will she yet abase her eyes on me, ...
> On me, whose all not equals Edward's moiety?
> On me, that halts and am misshapen thus?

My dukedom to a beggarly denier,
I do mistake my person all this while:
Upon my life, she finds, although I cannot,
Myself to be a marv'llous proper man.
I'll be at charges for a looking-glass,
And entertain a score or two of tailors,
To study fashions to adorn my body:
Since I am crept in favour with myself,
I will maintain it with some little cost.
But first I'll turn yon fellow in his grave;
And then return lamenting to my love.
Shine out, fair sun, till I have bought a glass,
That I may see my shadow as I pass.

(I. ii. 246, 248-63)

This soliloquy is linked closely in undertones with the previous two soliloquies, but at the same time it reveals new facets in the personality of the speaker. The same Crookback, who considered himself incapable of 'sportive tricks', of courting the looking glass, of wanting love's majesty to strut before a wanton ambling nymph, has just now indulged though out of policy in sportive tricks to the extent of offering his bare bosom for sacrifice and strutted before an angry cursing nymph of a widow and is now willing to pay for a looking glass. He appears to be losing his two favourite delights of descanting on his own deformity and spying his shadow in the sun. Howsoever insincere Richard might have been in his wooing, the very fact that he, the self-centred egoist, the outcast from human society, has succeeded in winning the heart of a lady, seems to affect him in a strange way. He begins to like himself and only wishes the sun not to set till he buys a glass for himself, which may imply that he wishes Edward to live on till Richard is reconciled with himself, God and nature. This, however, is not to be, for Richard would first 'turn yon fellow in his grave', and there is a long line of such 'yon fellows' to be disposed of. The result is that Richard never finds time to buy the looking glass. All human love proceeds from self-love, and towards the end of the play it becomes apparent that Richard, the megalomaniac, devoid of love for his fellow-men, is equally devoid of love for himself. It is wrong to say that in his case 'the sin of self-love' turns to 'self-hate'.[20] The misanthrope hates all mankind, including himself:

> Richard loves Richard; That is, *I am I.*
> Is there a murderer here? No—Yes, *I* am:
> Then fly. What, from *myself*? Great reason why—
> Lest *I* revenge. *Myself* upon *myself*?
> Alack, *I* love *myself.* For any good
> That *I myself* have done unto *myself*?
> O, No! Alas, *I* rather hate *myself*
> For hateful deeds committed by *myself*! (V. iii. 183-90)

He suffers from *melancholia*. He is like no one else ('I am I') and is incapable of any truck—except intrigues—with all those he comes across. Even a cursory glance at his speeches, reveals the overwhelming predominance of 'I's', 'me's' and 'my's', emphasizing his complete isolation. In the eight lines quoted above, for instance, '*I*', and '*myself*' occur fifteen times, besides *Richard*, which occurs twice. The Kings of Shakespeare commonly use the plural form of the pronoun, and it is striking that Richard throughout, both before and after his accession to the throne, goes on using the first person singular.[21] There can be no doubt that this complete isolation, the sense of being cut off from all human relations, is the essence of all villainy in Shakespeare,[22] but in Richard's case it is closely linked with his hump. While on the one hand, the hump and the misshapen form of Richard, help us to identify him with the conventional figure of Vice, they also generate a kind of inverted pride in him.[23] For, "if despite being inferior in form and shape,"[24] and his having "the gift of seeing himself as others see him",[25] he does not suffer from any apparent inferiority complex, that is because of his intellectual superiority over others and his pride in the same.

It is thus that Shakespeare has succeeded in humanizing Richard unlike Aaron (or Richmond) and in making him 'more than the stock villain-hero of Senecan revenge drama' or the Vice of the Morality Play. 'As a symbol of evil, Richard might have been a wooden, lifeless figure' like Richmond himself, 'but Shakespeare has created in him the illusion of an intriguing individuality.'[26] Once we accept this reality and rid ourselves of the view that the character is conceived intellectually, rather than emotionally like the latter villains of Shakespeare,[27] we may be in a position to appreciate certain basic questions of human predicament posed by the play. It may be wrong on the part of Richard to look upon "his deformity as putting him beyond the verge of all that is human, as setting the seal on his depravity"[28] or as giving him any plausible excuse for his determined devilry[29] and revenge upon nature,[30] but the questions that keep us haunting all the while are an unfair distribution of assets by nature and the limits to which human will is subject. To accept the symbolical implication of Richard's birth and deformity is to accept predestination, which makes short work of the free will of man. On the other hand, to accept the explanation offered by Richard is to recognize the seemingly ultimate freedom of human will, despite the initial drawback inherited at birth. Bardolph cannot change his face,[31] so also Richard cannot change his gait and smooth his hump, but if these traits make him an outcast from human community and deprive him of all human affection, he is, in fact, left with very little choice. As Purdom says, Richard is "a protagonist with a problem". But his problem is not the political one "to secure the throne and keep himself there";[32] it is, rather, the tragic problem 'to be or not to be' with the hump. When we meet him he has already made the tragic choice 'to be', and to secure the throne is only a part of it. Marriott complains that there is "No gradual evolution of character, no subtle revelation."[33] This is but inevitable as the choice has already been made long back and Shakespeare only lets his villain-hero ruminate over the choice emphasizing its justness. This, however, in no way interferes with our appreciation of the play. "His character does not grow upon us", says Dowden:

> "from the first it is complete. We are not curious to discover what Richard is, as we are curious to come into presence of the soul of Hamlet. We are in no doubt about Richard; but it yields us a strong sensation to observe him in various circumstances and situations; we are roused and animated by the presence of almost

> superhuman energy and power, even though that power and that energy be malign.[34]

It is superhuman energy and power, combined with an equally superhuman intellect and a strong sense of humour, that win respect and admiration for him, despite his ugliness of appearance as well as action. For him 'to be' means, and is only possible by, an exercise of what Dowden calls 'daemonic energy of will'. "The same cause", he says, "which produces tempest and shipwreck produces Richard; he is a fierce elemental power raging through the world, but this elemental power is concentrated in a human will."[35]

The classic example of the exercise of Richard's daemonic will is the wooing of Anne. Towards the end of the first scene, he already announces his determination to marry Anne, after the exit of Clarence and Edward from the scene:

> For then I'll marry Warwick's youngest daughter.
> (I. i. 153)

In the next scene follows the fantastic wooing. As Bullough notes: "There was no basis in the chronicles for this scene except that Richard actually married Anne."[36] The scene is not only an invention, but in its presentation Shakespeare takes gross liberties with history as well as credibility.[37] Anne's marriage to the assassin of her husband and father-in-law was in itself 'a mystery which challenged the dramatist's skill'.[38] Shakespeare could very well have ignored the incident, for 'the secret close intent'—the political purpose of the marriage is never brought to light, and plays no part in the development of the plot or the furtherance of Richard's ambition. Instead, Shakespeare chooses to add to the mystery by making his Richard woo the bereaved Anne in the very presence of the freshly bleeding corpse of Henry VI. Bullough has suggested a parallel with the wooing of Megora by Lycus in Seneca's *Hercules Furens* and with the wooing of Princess Elizabeth by Richard in Thomas Legge's *Richardus Tertius*.[39] It may be that the latter work in particular suggested to Shakespeare the idea of his villain-hero in the role of what Anne Righter calls 'an impassioned lover',[40] but in both *Richardus Tertius* and *Hercules*

Furens, the tyrant-wooer fails in breaking the will of the injured woman. On the other hand, with all odds against him, Shakespeare's Richard goes on "to win her! all the world to nothing!" It is the most spectacular[41] of his many triumphs:

> With curses in her mouth, tears in her eyes,
> The bleeding witness of my hatred by;
> Having God, her conscience, and these bars against me,
> And I no friends to back my suit at all,
> But the plain devil and dissembling looks,
>
> (I. ii. 232-36)

There can be no doubt that the situation itself is outrageous[42] to say the least, and that Richard's success, in changing bitter hatred to willing submission, strains the limits of credibility. Coleridge could not believe that the part was written by Shakespeare,[43] and Henry James certainly had such scenes in mind when he labelled the play as "a loose, straddling romance", "a hurly-burly".[44] In fact, however, although the scene has generally suffered on the stage,[45] it is meant to be a perfect *coup de theatre*. It begins with the spitting on the face of the wooer and ends with the passing on of the engagement ring by him. In his suit the plea that Richard takes for having killed Anne's husband and his father is her own beauty itself and thus he makes her already a partner in his villainy:

> Is not the causer of the timeless deaths
> Of these Plantagenets, Henry and Edward,
> As blameful as the executioner?
> *Anne*—Thou wast the cause of that most accurs'd effect.
> *Glo.*— Your beauty was the cause of that effect;
> Your beauty, that did haunt me in my sleep
> To undertake the death of all the world,
> So I might live one hour in your sweet bosom.
>
> (I. ii. 117-24)

The theatrical gesture of offering his breast to the naked sword is again accompanied with similar emphasis on the same idea.

> Nay, do no pause; for I did kill King Henry,
> But 'twas thy beauty that provoked me.

Nay, now dispatch; 'twas I that stabbed young Edward,
But 'twas thy heavenly face that set me on.

(I. ii. 179-82)

Significantly enough the excuse taken here—though in jest—is a reiteration of the general excuse taken by Richard for his villainy. Richard's own deformity does not sanction his villainy, nor does Anne's beauty sanction his killing of King Henry and Prince Edward. In both cases, it is God's gift—ugliness or beauty—which is blamed for subsequent human action.

In Anne's own words, Richard is a 'dissembler' (l. 184) (an irresistible actor, says Righter[46])—a characteristic he shares with the Kings of Shakespeare in general and with Henry V in particular. The two wooings, perhaps meant to demonstrate Richard's power over his victims, are melodramatic to the extreme and appear to be exercises in hypnotism. They are emblamatic reminders of the serpent's tempting of the first woman and are sad commentaries on the frailty of woman. "If...we wish to find a mood of cynicism concerning women in Shakespeare, we should have no difficulty in making out a case for *Richard III*", says Sisson.[47] Just as Anne's beauty does not sanction the brutalities of a Richard, so it does not sanction the subduing of her own conscience. But this is exactly what happens with the rhythmic reminders of her beauty:

But 'twas thy beauty....
But 'twas thy heavenly face...

And overpowered, 'she falls the sword'. She is already won, and in response to Richard's final gesture of sacrifice:

Take up the sword again, or take up me. (l. 183)

She in effect takes him up, when she says:

"Arise, dissembler." (l. 184)

Only a moment ago she had been cursing the self-same man in the most bitter terms:

O cursed be the hand that made these holes!
Cursed the blood that let this blood from hence!
Cursed the heart that had the heart to do it!

(I. ii. 14-16)

and, ironically enough, cursing herself:

If ever he have wife, let her be made
More miserable by the life of him
Than I am by my young lord's death and thee!
(I. ii. 26-28)

'Shallow-changing woman!' (to borrow the words used by Richard for Queen Elizabeth). The portrayal of Anne more than confirms *Catullus LXX*:

There is no one, none.
Says my mistress, whom she'ld rather
Wed than me, no, not if Jove
Himself should woo her—
  Says—but a woman's words
  Spoken to her hungry lover
  Should be writ on wind, or in a
  Swirling river.[48]

Palmer has rightly drawn attention to the nature of Richard's exultation after Anne's tame submission. His success is not so much against a woman, it is against human nature itself, against God and conscience. It "vindicates his whole philosophy of life"[49]—the philosophy of evil. And Richard is 'almost completely evil'[50] no doubt, but the potency of his evil rests at least partially, upon the moral impotence of an Anne, the moral cowardice of a Brakenbury, the moral laxity of an Edward, the folly of a Hastings,[51] the blindness of a Clarence, and the gullibility of the citizens.

In the concluding part of the opening soliloquy, Richard has already outlined his future course of action, a Senecan device:

Plots have I laid, inductions dangerous,
By drunken prophecies, libels and dreams,
To set my brother Clarence and the King
In deadly hate the one against the other:
And if King Edward be as true and just
As I am subtle, false and treacherous,
This day should Clarence closely be mewed up,

About a prophecy, which says that G
Of Edward's heirs the murderer shall be.

(I. i. 32-40)

and has reiterated the same in the subsequent soliloquies (I. i. 117-20, 145-50). The first on the list of those who stand in his way, Clarence is already under detention,[52] when the play opens. In his account of the plots leading to Clarence's murder, Shakespeare, discarding the ambiguities of the Chronicles,[53] closely follows *The Mirror*. Hall, though referring to the prophecy regarding the letter G, does not appear convinced that this was precisely the factor which led to the undoing of Clarence. Simultaneously he refers to a number of factors, which might be held responsible for it.[54] All such circumstances, which possibly led to the doom of Clarence are present in Shakespeare but they are present in the baroque style, not in the rococo. They form the various mechanizations deployed by Richard to hurl 'plain Clarence' into the malmsey-butt. It is Richard who has sparkled the fire of 'privy-malice' between the two elder brothers[55] it is Richard who convinces Clarence of the Queen's complicity in the matter (I. i. 62-65). It is Richard, who charges the Queen's kindred with barking at the King's lineage (I. iii); it is Richard who has spread the false prophecy regarding the letter G.[56] Dover Wilson has rightly drawn attention to the following lines in *The Mirror*:

A prophecy was found, which sayd a G,
Of Edwardes children should destruccion be.
Me to be G, because my name was George
My brother thought, and therefore did me hate.
But woe be to the wicked heads that forge
Such doubtful dreames to brede unkinde debate.[57]

which find a clear echo in Richard's: "Plots have I laid" speech. But whereas *The Mirror* only says that the prophecy was forged by 'wicked heads', Shakespeare leaves no ambiguity about the 'wicked heads' and shows Richard as forging it. The treatment of the Clarence-plot thus provides an illustration of the oft-noted fact that "All that is done in the play proceeds from Richard."[58] By the end of Act I, Scene iii, where Richard is despatching the two murderers, the scene is already laid out for—to use a modern term—the liquidation of Clarence.

The various sources provide only a hint regarding the manner in which Clarence was done away with: drowned in a butt of Malmesey.[59] Out of this meagre hint, Shakespeare produces one of the most moving scenes ever written. In *Henry VI, Part 3,* Clarence is no better than Richard, but in the present play, he appears in a different light and succeeds in drawing our sympathy despite all his past follies, as no other character does. This is largely through the poetic rendering of his dreadful dream, which, as noted by Dover Wilson, belongs to a special class of after-life-vision poems, drawing their inspiration from the sixth book of the *Aeneid* and Dante's *Inferno*; and draws in particular upon Sackville's *Induction.*[60] It is wrong to say that the 'extraordinary beauty' and 'vividness' of the poetry makes us see a much nobler person 'than Clarence actually is' and that he becomes a symbol of fear, conscience, and retribution.[61] The Clarence we meet here is different from the Clarence of history or the Clarence of *3 Henry VI*, and it is not for nothing that Richard himself has warned the murderers in the previous scene not to let him plead:

> For Clarence is well spoken, and perhaps
> May move your hearts to pity, if you mark him.
> (I. iii. 348-49)

He moves our hearts to pity.

In fact, Clarence's dream looks forward structurally as well as thematically to Richard's on the eve of the battle and, like the latter, has been used by Shakespeare to humanize history. It is through such scenes that our writer "not only dramatizes history; but dramatizes psychology, gives us large slices of it; and in them we find ourselves".[62] Both Clarence and Richard have been hard-boiled criminals and before their deaths confront the ghosts of those killed or betrayed by them. Each has suspended his conscience during his life-time, each is forced to realize before his final hour like the two murderers of Clarence—howsoever, fleeting the realization might be in the case of Richard and that of the first murderer—"that the operation of conscience does not fall entirely under the jurisdiction of a man's conscious will"; that "around the finite, temporal action, laps a whole sea of infinite and impalpable scruple;...there is too much one does not and cannot know".[63] And yet how different is the reaction of the two brothers to the itching of conscience! Clarence is altogether broken by the assault of conscience and would feign pass another such night even though it might buy him 'a world of happy days'. In this sense he is truly reborn 'a Christian faithful man'. Edith Sitwell has compared the end of Clarence with that of Richard II, sacrificial victims both, who attain beauty and purity in death.[65] Struck by the shadows from the other side the world, Clarence is moved to penitence. Washed by true penitence unlike that of Bolingbroke or Henry V, he makes his final confession and is already prepared to die:

> Ah, Keeper, Keeper, I have done these things,
> That now give evidence against my soul,
> For Edward's sake, and see how he requits me!
> O God: if my deep prayers cannot appease thee,
> But thou wilt be avenged on my misdeeds,
> Yet execute thy wrath in me alone!
> O, Spare my guiltless wife and my poor children!
>
> (I. iv. 66-72)

"Clarence is murdered", remarks Lily Campbell, "before an Elizabethan audience that knew his last prayer had not been answered, for the destruction of his wife and children by Henry VII and Henry VIII, who feared their possible claims to the throne, was an oft-told tale."[66] If this be so, how much deeper must have been the pathos of Clarence's death and how bitter the irony of God's justice!

It is significant, however, to note that whereas Clarence's thoughts go out to his wife and children, Richard's recoil to himself:

> Richard loves Richard; that is, I am I. (V. iii. 183)[67]

whereas Clarence accepts the verdict of conscience, Richard, despite admitting to Ratcliffe:

> By the apostle Paul, shadows to-night

Have struck more terror to the soul of Richard
Than can the substance of ten thousand soldiers
Armed in proof, and led by shallow Richmond.
(V. iii. 216-19)

remains unyielding to the end, within the fortress of egotism and armed to the teeth with Machiavellian politics of amoral practicality. Instead of submitting to the assault of conscience, he, therefore, endeavours to rebuke it:

O coward conscience, how dost thou afflict me!
(V. iii. 179)

There follows self-introspection and, Richard, waging a bitter struggle for existance against the 'coward conscience', is momentarily turned into a Hamlet, hopping like a flea—to borrow Sanders' expression—from one antithesis to another.[68]

I am a villain: yet I lie, I am not.
Fool, of thyself speak well: fool, do not flatter.
(V. iii. 191-92)

It is true that conscience, with 'a thousand several tongues' appears to get better of his egotism and Machiavellian amorality, it is true that the choric curse of the ghosts—'despair and die'—appears already bearing fruit and, Richard stands dangerously on the brink of despair and death:

I shall despair. ...
And if I die, (V. iii. 200-01)

but this is a temporary phase and even in this moment of mental weakness (or moral awareness), Richard in sharp contrast to Richard II, thinks rather of the practical aspects of the battle than of the damnation of his soul:

O Ratcliffe, I have dreamed a fearful dream!
What thinkest thou, will all our friends prove true?
(ll. 212-13)

'Tis not yet near day. Come, go with me;
Under our tents I'll play the eaves-dropper,
To hear if any mean to shrink from me.
(ll. 220-22)

By the time we meet him next just before his battle with Richmond commences, he has already won his battle royal against conscience and has regained his former agility as well as self-confidence. "No actor" wrote Bernard Shaw in 1903 to Forbes-Robertson, "has ever done the curious recovery by Richard of his old gaiety of heart in the excitement of the battle.... He is again the ecstatic prince of mischief of the 'Shine out, fair sun, till I have bought a glass' phase...."[69]

But the fair sun, no longer at Richard's beck and call, refuses to shine at Bosworth and, it is as if 'the shadow from that hell governed arm' has literally 'blotted out the sun'.[70] The darkness thus caused may be interpreted symbolically and, as a supernatural omen:

> The Sun will not be seen to-day;
> The sky doth frown and lour upon our army.
>
> (V. iii. 281-82)

Richard's own words testify this, but in the same breath, he defies and explains away the supernatural augury:

> Not shine to-day; Why, what is that to me
> More than to Richmond? for the self same heaven
> That frowns on me looks sadly upon him.

To Richard the providential order remains a 'delusion' like conscience. He finally goes into the battle "under a heaven void of omens and cleared of all watching presences, the 'babbling dreams' of uneasy conscience consigned to oblivion":[71]

> Conscience is but a sword that cowards use,
> Devised at first to keep the strong in awe:
> Our strong arms be our conscience, swords our law.
> March on, join bravely, let us to it pell-mell;
> If not to heaven, then hand in hand to hell.
>
> (V. iii. 309-13)

Shaw discovers 'all Nietzsche' in the first three lines and finds the last two lines 'delicious' 'after all the pious twaddle of Richmond'[72] and no wonder, for at Bosworth Richard comes near Shaw's conception of the Superman. A thousand hearts are great within his bosom[73] and as Catesby reports: he 'enacts more wonders than a man'.[74]

Earlier in the Clarence-scene, the Second Murderer has already made 'an anatomy of conscience',[75] which voices in rather more comprehensive terms Richard's whole philosophy of life.

> I'll not meddle with it: it makes a man a coward: a man cannot steal, but it accuseth him; a man cannot swear, but it checks him, a man cannot lie with his neighbour's wife, but it detects him: 'tis a blushing shamefaced spirit that mutinies in a man's bosom; it fills a man full of obstacles. It made me once restore a purse of gold, that (by chance) I found; it beggars any man that keeps it: it is turned out of towns and cities for a dangerous thing; and every man that means to live well endeavours to trust to himself and live without it. (I. iv. 133-44)

"If Richard be the flower of his age", says Palmer, "the murderers of Clarence are weeds of the soil from which it sprang...they run true to the society that bred them."[76] But it is not enough to say this; the two murderers in fact are minor figures duplicating the brothers, Richard and Clarence. The second murderer, though expounding the Machiavellian philosophy of Richard, lacks the heart to remain true to it and breaks down, like Clarence, at the assault of conscience. The first murderer, on the other hand, is 'strong-framed' like Richard, and conscience, though itching his elbow, 'cannot prevail with' him.[77] The equation of Clarence and Richard with the hired assassins[78] is deliberate and pointed as the equation of Henry V with common soldiers or of Lear with poor Tom:

Cla.— In God's name, what art thou?
1 *Mur.*— A man, as you are.
Cla.— But not, as I am, royal.
2 *Mur.*— Nor you, as we are, loyal. (I. iv. 163-66)
Cla.— Which of you, if you were a prince's son,
Being pent from liberty, as I am now,
If two such murderers as yourselves came to you,
Would not entreat for life?
Even so I beg
As you would beg, were you in my distress.
(I. iv. 257-61)

But in both passages Clarence represents the royal family and this confirms the view that the two murderers, apparently similar and yet essentially contrasted, highlight the opposite stands taken by the two royal brothers on the eternal question of conscience. Richard and Clarence, the first and the second murderer, are in fact archetypal figures who recall to our minds the two thieves crucified along with Christ—one railing, the other penitent.[79] Though diabolic and superhuman, Richard is no anti-Christ[80] just as Richmond is no Christ. Richard is only the first thief railing at Christ. Like Marlowe's Machiavellians, he has ranged himself knowingly and deliberately against God,— 'God's enemy' as Richmond labels him (V. iii. 252-53) —for he believes in the natural order as against the providential order. "Richard is the prince of Punches: he delights Man by provoking God, and dies unrepentant and game to the last."[81] Undoubtedly, it can be asserted that his last hour, like Clarence's last hour, is the finest of all. He makes "adherence to his philosophy of chance a kind of moral duty, demonstrating to the world that he has the courage of his Epicurean convictions."[82] Note his angry retort to Catesby's suggestion to withdraw:

Catesby.— Withdraw my lord; I'll help you to a horse.
K. Richard.— Slave, I have set my life upon a cast,
And I will stand the hazard of the die...
A horse! a horse! my kingdom for a horse!
(V. iv. 8-13)

In *The True Tragedie*, Richard is in a desperate state and lacks any firm conviction. The above situation is depicted thus in it:

King.—A horse, a horse, a fresh horse.

Page.—A (*h*) flie my Lord, and save your life.

King.—Flie villaine, look I as the I would flie, no first shall this dull and sencelesse ball of earth receive my bodie cold and void of sence, you watry heavens rowle on my gloomy day, and darksome cloudes close up my cheerfull sownde, downe is thy sunne Richard, never to shine againe, the birdes whose feathers should adorne my head, hovers aloft and dares not come in sight, yet faint not man, for this

> day if Fortune will, shall make thee King possest with quiet Crown, if Fates deny, this ground must be my grave, yet golden thoughts that reached for a Crowne, danted before by Fortunes cruell spight, are come as comforts to my drooping heart, and bids me keepe my Crowne and die a King. These are my last, what more I have to say, ile make report among the dammed soules.[83]

Hall also depicts the desperate suicidal attitude of Richard in more or less similar terms:

> and when the losse of the battayle was imminent and apparante, they brought to hym a swyfte and a light horse to convey hym away. He which was not ignorant of the grudge & yll will that the common poeple bare toward him, casting awaye all hope of fortunate success & happy chaunce to come, answered (as men saye) that on that daye he woulde make an end of all battailes or els ther finish his lyfe.[84]

Shakespeare's Richard, unlike his counterpart in the sources, never suffers—once he has stifled his conscience—from a drooping heart, never becomes a pitiable figure as is some times made on the stage.[85] Even Macbeth begins to falter and wishes to avoid the last cup at Dunsinane:

> They have tied me to a stake, I cannot fly,
> But bear-like must fight the course.[86]

When informed by Macduff of his premature birth, he even refuses to fight, and it is only at the thought of the humiliation in defeat that he finally resolves to go through it:

> I will not yield,
> To kiss the ground before young Malcom's feet
> And to be baited with the rabble's curse.
> Though Birnam wood be come to Dunsinane,
> And thou oppos'd, being of no woman born,
> Yet I will try the last.[87]

Macbeth had been fortified with superstitions engendered by the prophecies of the witches, and it is natural for him to despair, when the two impossible conditions of his defeat and death stand fulfilled. Richard's defiance of God and man rests on a surer ground, the Epicurean philosophy he has been living by. But for a brief moment after the dream it has never forsaken him and has never let him down. He is drunk with success and, brimming with confidence to face a Richmond, 'never trained up in arms' (V. iii. 272) he puts his philosophy to the final test. Cassius also was an Epicurean, but could not remain uneffected by omens and was against the gamble of setting everything upon one cast.[88] Richard combines in him the Epicurean philosophy of Cassius with the stoic fortitude of Brutus. He is not a tragic hero in the conventional sense, for, as Purdom puts it: "He seeks evil, and fails through the accident of battle."[89] He kills five shadows of Richmond instead of the real Richmond and at the most critical hour his throne is lost for the timely supply of a horse.[90] At least this is what Richard himself believes. Perhaps, as Sanders holds, Richmond's ultimate victory is a part of the play's ambivalence.[91]

However, since Shakespeare is looked upon as the spokesman of the orthodox Tudor doctrine of order, Richard is not allowed generally to come up as a living character. Too often is he treated as a bare symbol—the Vice of the Morality Plays,[92] the Elizabethan tyrant,[93] the scourge of God,[94] the mastermind behind the Grand Mechanism of history, and so on and so forth. He becomes a melodramatic figure, a pantomime. One reason for looking at the play as an allegory and at Richard as an abstraction is the extra-weightage given to Richmond's curtain speech,[96] the other is the frequent comparison of Richard with Macbeth. Contrasting the two villain-heroes. Reese notices a lack of moral concern in Richard and his universe and consequently of tragic power.[97] Perhaps, as he goes on to remark, no other character in Shakespeare is so one-dimensional as Richard.[98] "The corruption has gathered into one place" says Leggatt.[99]

That Richard is completely evil can hardly be denied. Indeed, he is so completely wedded to the doctrine of evil that he appears more a monster than a man. This idea of evil in Richard is powerfully reinforced through the use of "a continuous and insistent animal symbolism".[100] No doubt, animal imagery is used in *Henry VI* plays too, but there it hardly serves individual characterization as it does in *Richard III*. Exploiting the legend that Richard was born with teeth, Shakespeare makes the image of a biting venom-toothed dog suggest his character. In *3 Henry VI* the image is already employed by Richard himself.[101] The image keeps recurring throughout *Richard III*. Margaret warns Buckingham of 'yonder dog':

> Look when he fawns, he bites: and when he bites,
> His venom tooth will rankle to the death:
>
> (I. iii. 289-91)

He is 'a hell hound', that hath crept forth from the kennel of his mother's womb (IV. iv. 47-48). Besides this repulsive dog image, other equally repulsive animal images are also used to suggest the deformed body as well as mind of Richard. He is a 'bottled spider', a 'poisonous hunch-backed toad' (I. iii. 242, 246), 'a boar' (III. ii. 10, 28-33; IV. v. 2, V. ii. 7-10). Through such forceful and recurring images we feel Richard's presence even when he is off the stage.[102] A striking instance is the following advice of Elizabeth to Dorset:

> Death and destruction dogs thee at thy heels...,
> Go, hie thee, hie thee from this slaughter-house,
>
> (IV. i. 40, 44)

Richard is death and destruction and, of course, 'the dog'. With his cold-blooded off-with-his heads, he has converted the whole of England into a veritable slaughter-house. Never for a moment are we allowed to forget that he is an embodiment of evil, a dangerous threat to everyone around. However, in painting Richard thus, Shakespeare has merely accepted the saga regarding the person, prevalent during his time. For in the light of the threats to the Tudor regime and the weak title of Henry VII, it was necessary to blacken Richard's character to the utmost.[103] "By the end of the sixteenth century the facts of his real appearance, character, and deeds had been buried under a great mound of tradition. He had become the archetypal tyrant king, incarnate evil enthroned."[104] However, while accepting the Tudor tradition of Richard and giving immortality to it, Shakespeare also tries to explore it imaginatively and psychologically. His Richard is a queer mixture of the Senecan Villain-hero, the Vice of the Moralities, Marlovian machiavel and a die-hard Epicurean;[105] and yet he transcends each of them and retains his individuality as a man. It is unfair to Shakespeare to hold that Richard changes from a credible human being till the third act into a symbol of sheer denial and diabolism,[106] unfair to compare the play with *Punch and Judy* and to admire Richard as the 'prince of Punches'.[107]

In our century which has seen the two world wars and the more recent atrocities of Vietnam and Bangladesh, perhaps it ought to be easier to accept the monstrous in Richard as human after all. No wonder that parallel has often been drawn between Richard and Hitler.[108] Commenting on the following lines from the first wooing scene:

> *Anne.*—Villain, thou know'st no law of God nor man.
> No beast so fierce but knows some touch of pity.
>
> *Glo.*— But I know none, and therefore am no beast.
> (I. ii. 70-72)

Kott observes that the action takes place on earth, the cruellest of planets, and among men, who are more cruel than beasts.[109] The following plainspeaking by Nietzsche on man's sadism, highlights the monstrous in a Richard:

> For man is the cruellest animal. At tragedies, bull-fights, and crucifixions hath he hitherto been happiest on earth; and when he invented his hell, behold, that was his heaven on earth.[110]

There is no doubt that Anne's comment on Richard "thou hast made the happy earth thy hell"[111] is apt; but, ironically, it is an unhappy earth for man in general and for the 'lump of foul deformity'[112] in particular. By making it hell, he finds his heaven.

Richard is 'the catastrophic evil',[113] as Brockbank puts it and yet as a theatrical creation, he remains 'a force to be reckoned with'.[114] The role has attracted the greatest actors[115] in subsequent ages and the play holds the stage, not because of Richmond or Margaret but because of the charming crookback. It would be injudicious to dismiss him as an elemental force of nature,[116] and it is not sufficient to say that he is 'reptilian alike in his cunning and his charm'[117] or that 'where we can never approve, we may nevertheless admire'.[118] Referring to the enigmatic charm of Richard, Purdom remarks:

> It is the poetical spirit with which Shakespeare endows him that gives him a deceitful romantic charm,.... Yet a protagonist cannot invite an audience to participate in villainy, for to do that would make the drama an instrument of evil.[119]

It is a stroke of Shakespeare's genius to have made the arch-villain so superbly bewitching, and the best comment on the process of such an enigmatic Creation comes from Shakespeare himself:

> Or whether doth my mind, being crown'd with you,
> Drink up the monarch's plague, this flattery?
> Or whether shall I say, mine eye saith true,
> And that your love taught it this alchemy,
> To make of monsters and things indigest
> Such cherubins as your sweet self resemble,
> Creating every bad a perfect best
> As fast as objects to his beams assemble?
> O, 'tis the first; 'tis flatt'ry in my seeing,
> And my great mind most kingly drinks it up;
> Mine eye well knows what with his gust is greeing,
> And to his palate doth prepare the cup.
> If it be poison'd, 'tis the lesser sin
> That mine eye loves it and doth first begin.
>
> (Sonnet 114)

"There is a risk", says Wilson Knight, "in 'creating every bad a perfect best'; and a glory too, as the actor of Richard III, Iago, or Caliban well knows."[120] The risk is that though we may deplore the actions of such villains as Richard and Iago, morally, "we are in danger of being more interested in Iago than in Othello".[121] In *Richard III,* the apprehension comes true, for as admitted even by Tillyard, Richard's character, like Satan's in *Paradise Lost*, has been the main attraction of the play.[122]

It could not have been so if Shakespeare had conceived of Richard as a mere abstraction nor if he had lacked a complete emotional understanding of the character.[123] In fact, he "could see the unity, the harmony, the essential being of men of all sorts",[124] even of a Richard, an Iago or a Macbeth. We have already seen how without changing the outlines of the Tudor tradition of Richard, Shakespeare succeeds in breathing life into it and exploring the essential being of the man through the various vicissitudes of his life. But the secret of the lasting charm of Richard lies only partly in the noble poetry and the 'myriad-minded' genius of Shakespeare. Besides the main objection of Purdom that a protagonist cannot invite an audience to participate in villainy still remains unanswered, especially when we remember that part of Richard's charm rests on taking the audience into confidence. The quotations from Nietzsche and Kott given above[125] provide a clue to this. For a proper understanding and appreciation of a creation like Richard, we must not dismiss him simply as a tyrant or evil incarnate, or admire his cunning and histrionics, rather we must look within and admit our own 'worst fantasies'.[126] Part of the play's success and of the character's spell rest upon the potential evil in ourselves. The worst of the potential evils is to evade one's conscience. How easy it is to send one's conscience to sleep with a Brakenbury:

> I will not reason what is meant hereby,
> Because I will be guiltless from the meaning.
>
> (I. iv. 94-95)

or with a Lord Cardinal:

> My Lord, you shall o'er-rule my mind for once.
>
> (III. i. 57)

Almost equally worse an evil is to subdue one's consciousness. The three citizens on their way to the justices, voice their apprehensions. The third is the wisest. He understands the explosive nature of the political situation. He can see behind the mask of Richard's hypocrasies with a clearer sight than his superiors can:

> O, full of danger is the Duke of Gloucester;
>
> (II. iii. 27)

But even the third, after giving evidence of his foresight and understanding, says: "But leave it all to God" (II. iv. 45). Thus, the citizens subdue their consciousness and, like 'tongueless blocks', like 'dumb statuas or breathing stones' keep staring at each other (III. vii) when Buckingham pleads with them for electing Richard as their King. They are conscientious enough not to lend their voice to the cry, 'God save King Richard'. Nevertheless not being conscious enough they allow themselves to be duped and led like dumb cattle.

By far the best comment on Brakenburies, Cardinals, and citizens, on Richard's world—and on ours—comes from a scrivener in a scene which might easily be cut in a production of the play. The scene itself—the shortest in the play—is a pure invention of the poet and beautifully illustrates how Shakespeare can illuminate the dark alleys of history. The sources only state that the proclamation indicting Hastings, written in a fair set hand, was issued within two hours of his execution. This caused amazement to the people. A schoolmaster remarked: "here is a gaye goodly cast, foule cast awaye for hast", and a merchant observed that it was written "by inspiracyon and prophesye".[127] Out of these hints, Shakespeare imagines the scrivener, who has been at the job since 'yesternight', hours before any charge was brought against Hastings. Now when he has finished his arduous task he soliloquizes and moralises:

> Here's a good world the while! Who is so gross,
> That cannot see this palpable device?
> Yet who's so bold, but says he sees it not?
> Bad is the world; and all will come to nought,
> When such ill dealing must be seen in thought.
>
> (III. vi. 10-13)

But the scrivener exaggerates. Some are not conscious enough—like Clarence, Hastings and the citizens—to see the device; while others are not conscientious enough to speak and act. Thus, as if by tacit consent they let the hound fawn and bite.

NOTES

1. E.M.W. Tillyard, *Shakespeare's History Plays* (Penguin, 1962), p. 199.
2. *Ibid.*, p. 208.
3. A.P. Rossiter, *Angel With Horns* (ed.), G. Storey (London: Longmans, Green, 1962), p. 21.
4. *Ibid.*
5. L.B. Campbell, *Shakespeare's 'Histories'* (San Marino: Huntington, 1965), pp. 313 *et seq.*
6. Quoted by J.D. Wilson, Introduction to *Richard III* (The New Shakespeare, Cambridge University Press, 1968), p. xlii.
7. Sanders, *The Dramatist and the Received Idea* (Cambridge University Press, 1968), p. 94.
8. *Op. cit.*, p. 316.

   For the first part of the statement see also the quotation from W.J. Birch's *An Inquiry into the Religion and Philosophy of Shakespeare* in Sanders, *loc. cit.*
9. Jan Kott, *Shakespeare Our Contemporary* (tr.), B. Taborski (London: Methuen, 1967), p. 28.
10. Clemen's analysis of the set speech in his *English Tragedy Before Shakespeare* (London: Methuen, 1961), *passim.*
11. Not only l. 12 in the above speech, but also the following in the next soliloquy by Richard:

    For then I'll marry Warwick's youngest daughter.
    What though I killed her husband and her father?
    The readiest way to make the wench amends
    Is to become her husband and her father:
    The which will I; not all so much for love
    As for another secret close intent
    By marrying her which I must reach unto. (I. i. 153-59)

    ——foreshadow the politic marriage of Richmond.
12. *Henry V*, V. ii. 216-18.
13. According to the division of the soliloquy made by W. Clemen in his *A Commentary on Shakespeare's Richard III* (London: Methuen, 1968) (tr.), J. Bonheim, pp. 3 *et seq.*
14. G. Bullough, ed. *Narrative and Dramatic Sources of Shakespeare* (London: Routledge; New York: Columbia University Press, 1960), III, p. 253.
15. The speeches from *3 Henry VI*, which follow have no bearing on the controversy regarding the authorship of that play. They are cited because they appear agreeable to Shakespeare's conception of the character.
16. *Vide* W. Clemen, *Commentary*, p. 7.

17. *Ibid.* D.S. Berkley, 'Determined in *Richard III,* I. i. 30', *Sh.Q.*, XIV (1963), pp. 483 *et seq.*
18. Bacon, Essay 44, 'Of Deformity.'—the Scripture reference is to *Romans,* I, 31, *The Bible.*
19. *Vide* J.D. Wilson (ed.), *Richard III* (The New Shakespeare, Cambridge University Press, 1968), pp. xxxviii *et seq.*
20. Paul Haeffner. *A Critical Commentary on Shakespeare's Richard III* (London: Macmillan, 1966), p. 21.
21. See also the analysis of I. i. 14 ff. by Theodore Weiss, *The Breath of Clowns and Kings* (London: Chatto and Windus, 1971), p. 161.
22. Stauffer, *Shakespeare's World of Images* (Bloomington: Indiana University Press, 1966), p. 27.

    "Richard's isolation might almost be said to be the isolation of one who has become the consciousness of his time", remarks J.F. Danby, *Shakespeare's Doctrine of Nature* (London: Faber and Faber, 1968), p. 60.
23. J. Palmer, *Political and Comic Characters of Shakespeare* (London: Macmillan, 1962), p. 71.
24. Coleridge, quoted by Haeffner, *op. cit.*, p. 38.
25. E.E. Stoll, *Shakespeare Studies* (N.Y.: Fredrick Ungar, 1960), p. 346.
26. I. Ribner, *Patterns in Shakespearean Tragedy* (London: Methuen, 1960), p. 23.
27. Stauffer, *op. cit.,* p. 26.
28. Stoll, *op. cit.,* p. 347.
29. Freud's interpretation quoted on p. 80 *supra.*
30. Bacon's views on deformity quoted on p. 81 *supra.*
31. *1 Henry IV.* III. iii. 23.
32. C.B. Purdom, *What Happens in Shakespeare* (London: John Baker, 1963), pp. 70 *et seq.*
33. J.A.R. Marriott, *English History in Shakespeare* (New York: E.P. Dutton, 1918), p. 210.
34. E. Dowden, *Shakespeare: A Critical Study of His Mind and Art* (London: Routledge, 1957), p. 182.
35. *Ibid.*

    F.E. Schelling's description of Richard causing wonder and admiration like "an avalanche or an irresistible stream of molten lava" in his *The English Chronicle Play* (New York: Macmillan, 1902), p. 93.
36. *Op. cit.,* Vol. III, p. 236.
37. S.C. Sen Gupta; *Shakespeare's Historical Plays* (London: Oxford University Press, 1964), pp. 91 *et seq.*
38. Bullough, *loc. cit.*

39. *Ibid.*, pp. 306 *et seq.*
40. A. Righter, *Shakespeare and the Idea of the Play* (London: Chatto and Windus, 1964), p. 98.
41. *Ibid.*
42. Palmer, *op. cit.*, p. 82.
43. Quoted in *ibid.*, p. 81.
44. Quoted in A.C. Sprague, *Shakespeare's Histories* (London: Society for Theatre Research, 1964), pp. 137 *et seq.*
45. Lamb's remarks quoted by D. Wilson, *op. cit.*, p. xxxviii and Wilson's own comment in footnote.
46. Righter, *op. cit.*, pp. 97 *et seq.*
47. C.J. Sisson, 'The Mythical Sorrows of Shakespeare' in *Studies in Shakespeare,* ed. by P. Alexander (London: Oxford University Press, 1964), p. 27.
48. *Catullus LXX* (tr.), RC. Trevelyan, *Vide Poetry Review,* Vol. 62, No. 2 (Summer, 1971), p. 179.
49. Palmer, *op. cit.*, p. 84.
50. Stauffer, *op. cit*, p. 26. Also Ribner, *op. cit.*, p. 24.
51. Sanders, *op. cit.*, p. 87.
52. Palmer, *op. cit.*, p. 78.
53. Sen Gupta, *op. cit.*, p. 90.
54. *The Union,* ccxxixv, *vide* p. 4 *supra.*
55. The last part of the opening soliloquy, esp. ll. 34-35.
56. *See supra.*
57. *The Mirror,* 'Clarence', M. 181-86, *vide* D. Wilson, *op. cit.*, p. xxv.
58. Dowden, *op. cit.*, p. 182 and Marriott, *op. cit.*, pp. 210 *et seq.*
59. E. Hall, *The Union,* ccxxixv, *vide* Bullough, *op. cit.*, p. 250 and *The Mirror,* ll. 369-71. *Vide ibid.*, p. 305.
60. D. Wilson, *op. cit.*, pp. xxvli *et seq.*—convincing parallels with the *induction* are drawn by Wilson.
61. Haeffner, *op. cit.*, pp. 40 *et. seq.*
62. Jan Kott, *op. cit.*, p. 15.
63. Sanders, *op. cit.*, p. 80.
64. I. iv. 2-7.
65. E. Sitwell, *A Notebook on William Shakespeare* (London: Macmillan 1962), p. 163.
66. Campbell, *op. cit.*, p. 314.
67. See *Supra.*
68. Sanders, *op. cit.*, p. 107.
69. Quoted by Palmer, *op. cit.*, p. 115.
70. Sitwell, *op. cit.*, p. 173.

71. Sanders, *op. cit.,* pp. 92 *et seq.*
72. Shaw, *op. cit., vide* Palmer, *op. cit.,* pp. 115 et *seq.*
73. V. iii. 347.
74. V. iv. 2.
75. B.Ifor Evans, *The Language of Shakespeare's Plays* (London: Methuen, University, Paperbacks, 1965), p. 50.
76. *Op. cit.,* p. 80.
77. I. iv. 150.
78. Kott's observations on it in *op. cit.,* p. 27.
79. *St. Luke,* xxiii; 39-43, *Holy Bible.*
80. As made out by critics e.g. T.F. Driver, *The Sense of History in Greek and Shakespearean Drama* (New York: Columbia, 1961), p. 100 and W.A. Armstrong, 'The Eliz. concept of the Tyrant' in *Review of English Studies,* Vol. 22, No. 87 (July, 1946), p. 180.
81. Shaw, Review of Sir Henry Irving's *Richard III,* Lyceum Theatre, 19 December, 1896, *The Saturday Review* (26 December 1896), from *Our Theatres in the Nineties by Bernard Shaw* (London: Constable, 1932), Vol. II, p. 285.
82. Samders, *op. cit.,* p. 93.
83. *The True Tragedie,* Sc. xix, 1985-2000. *Vide* Bullough, *op. cit.,* p. 341.
84. *The Union, ibid.,* p. 298.
85. In Colley Cibber's version and Laurence Olivier's film for e.g. see comments by Spragne, *op. cit.,* p. 127.
86. *Macbeth,* V. vii. 1-2.
87. *Ibid.,* V. viii. 27-32.
88. *Vide Julius Caesar,* V. i. 73-88.
89. Purdom, *op. cit.,* p. 71.
90. Sen Gupta, *op. cit.,* p. 43.
91. *Op. cit.,* p. 92.
92. B. Spivack, *Shakespeare and the Allegory of Evil* (New York: Columbia University Press, 1958), pp. 394 *et seq.*
93. Armstrong, *op. cit., passim.*
94. Tillyard, *op. cit.,* p. 208.
95. Kott, *op. cit.,* p. 35.
96. Page 86 *supra.*
97. Reese, *op. cit.,* p. 223.
98. *Ibid.,* p. 224.
99. Leggatt, A. *Shakespeare's Political Drama* (London and N. York, 1988), p. 52.

100. C. Spurgeon, *Shakespeare's Imagery* (Cambridge: University Press, 1965), p. 232.
101. *3 Henry VI, V,* vi, 74-77.
102. W. Clemen, *The Development of Shakespeare's Imagery* (London: Methuen, 1959), p. 51.
103. A.R. Myers, *'Richard III and Historical Tradition'* in *History,* Vol. 53, No. 178 (June, 1968), p. 182.
104. *Ibid.,* p. 184.
105. Sanders says, though in a different context: "Shakespeare is at that creatively frustrating stage of his career when he has more philosophic souls on his shelves than he has dramatic bodies for them to inhabit", *op. cit.,* p. 109. But Richard III demonstrates that Shakespeare does not need as many dramatic bodies as he has philosophic soul.
106. Tillyard, *op. cit.,* p. 211.
107. G.B. Shaw, quoted on p. 93 *supra.*
108. Palmer, *op. cit.,* p. 65. and G.W. Knight, *Shakespeare and Religion* (London: Routledge and Kegan Paul, 1967), p. 18.
109. Kott, *op. cit.,* p. 36.
110. *Thus Spake Zarathustra* (ed.), Dr Oscar Levy (tr.), Thomas Common (London: George Allen and Unwin; New York: Macmillan, 1923), LVII. The Convalscent, p. 267.
111. I. ii. 51.
112. I. ii. 57.
113. J.P. Brockbank, 'The Frame of Disorder; Henry VI', Chap. IV in *Early Shakespeare* (ed.), J.R. Brown and B. Harris (London: Edward Arnold, 1967), p. 98.
114. Sanders, *op. cit.,* p. 93.
115. Actors like Burbage, Garrick, and Laurence Olivier.
116. See Dowden's remark, quoted on pp. 84 *et seq.*
117. Schelling, *op. cit.,* p. 92.
118. Sanders, *op. cit.,* p. 93.
119. Purdom, *op. cit.,* p. 71.
120. G.W. Knight, *op. cit.,* p. 239.
121. *Ibid.,* p. 288.
122. Tillyard, *op. cit.,* p. 209.
123. As Stauffer thinks, *op. cit.,* p. 26.
124. Knight, *loc. cit.*
125. Page 99 *supra.*
126. Knight, *op. cit.,* p. 18.
127. Hall, *The Union, vide,* Bullough, *op. cit.,* p. 268.

King John

5

If, as noted in the preceding chapter, *Richard III* is a play totally dominated by the villain-hero's personality, the next[1] History Play, *King John*, lacks 'a commanding central figure',[2] a 'focal point'.[3] There are two claimants to the central position; John, the titular hero, and Philip Faulconbridge, the bastard son of Richard Coeur-de-lion. In the plot the Bastard's role is to assist John. According to Indian dramaturgy, he would be called *pithamarda*, such as Makranda in Bhavabhuti's[4] *Maltimadhava*. The *pithamarda* is the chief attendant of the *nayaka* (hero). He assists the *nayaka* and is devoted to him. He is possessed of the qualities of the *nayaka* in a lesser degree. Now Faulconbridge is in every respect the *pithamarda* in the play except that in certain qualities he excels John. This, along with his bluff manner, makes him more impressive than John, and no wonder that some critics consider him the real hero of the play.[5] Adrien Bonjour has argued that the play has two heroes and its structure is balanced with 'a falling curve' in the career of John and 'a rising curve' in that of the Bastard. It presents the 'decline of a hero—rise of a hero'.[6] This is no doubt, the impression we derive from a reading of the play, but it is a superficial impression. In the analysis of the play that follows, an attempt has been made to demonstrate that what appears at first sight as the rise of the Bastard represents, in fact, his moral degeneration. If we analyse the last act of the play closely, we would come to the conclusion that the Bastard is tempted to rule the country in the name of the sick and deserted King John. This is followed by another curve in his character. Though much has been written about the Bastard, this aspect of his character has hitherto gone unnoticed. By accepting this reading of the character, we arrive at a better and clearer understanding of some of his speeches and actions which have remained enigmatic.

Spurgeon and Honigmann have discussed the imagery aspect of the play so well that efforts to expatiate on it now appear unnecessary. However, while pursuing some of the scenes of the play the reader would come across certain images and words which seem to have escaped the notice of earlier writers. An attempt has also been made in the following pages to treat the major recurring images, such as 'hand' and 'eye', in a new way. In the process, fresh light has been thrown on certain minor characters, who are generally neglected, but are of vital importance to the total meaning of the play.

As we approach the play without any predilection, we become aware of its richness and of Shakespeare's growing understanding of the man and his motives. The lack of a dominant central figure, for instance, though apparently a radical change and a drawback when considered in the light of what was achieved in *Richard III*, is in fact, a natural development in the course of Shakespeare's exploration of man. The process of humanizing or, as Danby puts it, 'redeeming the machiavel'[7] that begins in *Richard III* itself is the result of a fundamental contradiction in Shakespeare's own personality, or of his realization that such a contradiction is inherent in human nature. Perhaps, a clue to his creative process is provided by the following sonnet on self-love:

> Sin of self-love possesseth all mine eye,
> And all my soul, and all my every part;
> And for this sin there is no remedy,
> It is so grounded inward in my heart.
> Metninks no face so gracious is as mine,
> No shape so true, no truth of such account,
> And for myself mine own worth do define,
> As I all other in all worths surmount.
> But when my glass shows me myself indeed,
> Beated and chopt with tann'd antiquity,
> Mine own self-love quite contrary I read;
> Self so self-loving were iniquity.

'Tis thee, my self, that for myself I praise,
Painting my age with beauty of thy days.
(Sonnet 62)

We hear both Richard and Faulconbridge pronounce 'I am I'[8] but at some indeterminate point 'I' changes into 'thee'. The poet has touched the depth of self-love and has become conscious of the essential dualism in his own personality. "At this period", remarks O'Connor, "I feel in Shakespeare a duality that is almost neurotic, as though he might quite easily have walked into a room and found himself sitting there."[9] This split in personality transforms Richard III into Richard II[10] on the one hand, and into Henry V on the other. *King John* marks the first phase of the metamorphosis, and here Richard is split into John and Faulconbridge. Just as Faulconbridge is half-way round the circle from Richard III, the 'villain-hero', to Henry V, the 'hero-villain',[11] so is John half-way home to Richard II. Margaret Webster's observation that King John 'falls between two Richards'[12] is truer, therefore, than she herself appears to realize.

John had been a tyrant in history and had particularly been regarded with disapproval by the monastic chroniclers of the Medieval Age because of his opposition to the Pope and heavy exactions from the religious orders.[13] But the Tudor historians with their 'Protestant fervour' and 'adoration of monarchy' sought to glorify him[14] as a Protestant martyr. This reaction against the monastic chroniclers' account of John is clearly underlined in the following words of Holinshed:

> Verilie, whosoever shall consider the course of the historie written of this prince, he shall find, that he hath beene little beholden to the writers of that time in which he lived; for scarselie can they afoord him a good word, except when the trueth inforceth them to come out with it as it were against their willes. The occasion whereof (as some think) was, for that he was no great freend to the clergie....[15]

As against this, Holinshed held that "the man had a princelie heart in him, and wanted nothing but faithful subjects to have assisted him in revenging such wrongs as were doone and offered by the French King and others".[16] John Foxe's *Actes and Monuments of Martyrs*, written in 1563, eulogised John as a martyr of Christ. The two pre-Shakespearean plays on John—Bishop Bale's *King Johan* (1538-60) and the anonymous *The Troublesome Raigne* (1591)—also glorify him and seek to establish his image as the champion of the 'true faith'. In the Epilogue to *King Johan*, Verity, while assuring us of the worth of the king, reflects the reaction against the earlier writers:

> I assure ye fryndes, lete men wryte what they wyll
> Kynge Johan was a man both valeaunt and godlye.
> What though Poydorus reporteth hym very yll
> At the suggestyons of the malicyouse clergye.
> Thynke yow a Romane with the Romanes can not lye?
> (2145-49)[17]

The Troublesome Raigne presents John as David to Solomon,[18] as Moses to Henry VIII, the saviour to come:

> I am not he shall buyld the Lord a house.
> Or roote these Locusts from the face of earth:
> But if my dying heart deceave me not,
> From out these loynes shall spring a kingly braunch
> Whose armes shall reach unto the gates, of *Rome*,
> And with his feete triade downe the strumpets pride,
> That sits upon the chaire of Babylon.[19]

However, the attempt to rehabilitate King John perhaps never quite succeeded[20] and 'the malcontents' of the Elizabethan Age were wont to liken the Queen to him as to Edward II, Richard II and Philopater.[21] Thus, John occupied a peculiar place in Elizabethan historiography, and a proper understanding of the man was impossible.[22]

In choosing a middle course between the two extremes, Shakespeare makes King John an enigma or, to put it differently, in choosing to write about a controversial figure of history like John, Shakespeare finds a proper channel for the dualism he desires to dramatize. He eliminates the crude anti-Catholic bias and refrains from presenting John as the Moses of the Reformation,[23] thus, entirely supressing the political tendency of *The Troublesome Raigne*.[24] The points brought out instead, in his play, are directly connected with the tenure of the crown. The questions raised are whether it is held by hereditary right of the eldest branch, or the eldest male of the family (or by the will of the last king), or by the accident of possession, fortified by the utility of the State. The questions raised further are whether the crown might be forfeited by crimes, and whether such forfeiture might be adjudged and executed by neighbouring sovereigns, or by the State itself, its peers or its people, or by the Pope. For Shakespeare's play is particularly a discussion whether John shall remain King. The grounds of the doubt are not, as in the chronicles, the general villainy of the king, his cruelty, debauchery, effeminacy, falsehood, extravagance, exactions, and general insufficiency, but the defect of his title as against the son of his elder brother. The defect is further aggravated by his supposed murder of that son. The historical quarrel against John as a tyrant is thus changed into a mythical one against him as a usurper.[25] The defect in John's title is highlighted clearly in the first Act of the play. Chatillon, the French emissary, addresses him as 'the borrow'd majesty of England' (I. i. 4) and the message brought by him, directly charges John with usurpation, demanding his abdication in favour of the lawful claimant, Arthur. Even more revealing is Eleanor's cryptic comment a few lines later: "Your strong possession much more than your right" (I. i. 40). The fact that this as well as Chatillon's phrase, 'the borrow'd majesty' is Shakespeare's addition, puts it beyond doubt that he presents John as a usurper from the start and has made 'right versus might' the central theme of the play.[26]

Eleanor's whispers to John are scarcely over when he is called upon to judge over a 'controversy come from the country' (I. i. 44-45). The controversy between Robert Faulconbridge and his bastard brother, though an unhistorical digression, has a direct bearing on the central issue of the play—the usurpation by John. The issue involved is 'primogeniture versus father's will'[27]—the same that is involved in the case of John and Arthur. In the next scene during her sharp exchanges with Constance, Eleanor declares:

I can produce
A will that bars the title of thy son. (II. i. 191-92)

John's claim to the throne rests on Richard's will just as Robert Faulconbridge's does on the will of his father (I. i. 109-15). The issue is more complicated here as it also involves a legitimate son and a bastard. In this respect, the situation bears close resemblance to the scandals set afloat by Richard III regarding Edward's bastardy in order to bar his issues from the throne (*Richard III*. III. vii). In his judgment John ignores the will as well as the illegitimacy of the Bastard, thus rejecting the claim of Robert Faulconbridge. John's own case is much the weaker theoretically, though stronger practically by virtue of strong possession.[28] It is significant that despite John's decree in favour of the bastard first-born, the estate is ultimately inherited by Robert and that the case is finally decided not by John's judgment but by the choice made by the Bastard. (Towards the end of the play, the Bastard would again be called upon to make a choice.) To Eleanor's question:

Wilt thou forsake thy fortune,
Bequeath thy land to him and follow me? (I. i. 148-49)

his reply is an instantaneous 'Yes'. He exults in his bastardy just as Richard III exults in his hump; he disdains the physical features of his fellow creatures, just as Richard disdains their intellect. Not aggrieved with God, nature or his mother for his illegitimacy, he rather congratulates himself and thanks his mother for her faithlessness: "With all my heart I thank thee for my father!" (I. i. 270). Goddard highlights the difference between him and the other bastards in Shakespeare, bastards like Don John, Thersites and Edmund, who consider themselves born outside the law and therefore, entitled to revenge themselves upon nature and society. Faulconbridge on the other hand, considers himself free from customs and conventions, true to the impulses of life. He is the 'son of nature' and prefers 'the truth without worldly possessions and position' to 'worldly possessions and position without the truth'.[29] He would rather be a landless seeker of fortune than possess all the land and lose the honour of being Richard-Coeur-de-Lion's bastard son.

John, on the other hand, like the other rulers in the play, is little better than a landlord[30] and Gaunt's indictment, of Richard II: "Landlord of England art thou now, not King" (*Richard II.* II. i. 113), applies to him as aptly as it does to Richard. At Angiers, he willingly parts with his French provinces in order to retain the crown that he has usurped:

> Then do I give Volquessen, Touraine, Maine,
> Poictiers, and Anjou, these five provinces, (II, i, 527-28).

The latter line, as noted by Malone and others is one of the two lines in *King John*, exactly identical with their counterparts in *The Troublesome Raigne*,[31] yet how different in import they are: In *The Troublesome Raigne*, it is not an offer but a demand and John is reluctant to concede it:

> *Philip.*— Then I demand *Volquesson*, *Torain*, *Main*
> *Poiters* and *Anjou*, these five Provinces,
> Which thou as King of *England* holdst in *Fraunce*:
> Then shall our peace be soone concluded on.
>
> *Bastard.*—No lesse than five such Provinces at once?
>
> *John.*—Mother what shall I do? my brother got these lands
> With much effusion of our English bloud:
> And shall I give it all away at once?
>
> *Q. Elinor.*—*John* give it him, so shalt thou live in peace,
> And keepe the residue sanz jeopardie.[32]

It is clear that this John, unlike Shakespeare's, does not think of the provinces merely as his personal property to be used as convenient tools at his own whim and for his personal security. He thinks of them rather as England's property and England's glory won by English blood.

In both the plays a moment later John also gives away the Dukedom of Brittaine, the Earldom of Richmont and the city of Angiers to Arthur, but again there is a marked difference in the manner he does it. In *The Troublesome Raigne*, Lewis and King Philip speak on behalf of Arthur and the impression we derive is that of John's generosity and genuine desire for lasting peace:

> *Lewes.*— But now King *John* what say you to the Duke?
> Father speak as you may in his behalfe.

Philip.—*K. John*, be good unto thy Nephew here,
And give him somewhat that shall please thee best.
John.—*Arthur*, although thou troublest *Englands* peace,
Yet here I give thee *Brittaine* for thy owne,
Together with the Earledome of *Richmont*
And this rich citie of *Angiers* with all.[33]
(*T.R.* I. iv. 845-51)

King John, on the other hand, portrays King Philip in a conscientious fix, reflecting on the state of Arthur's mother. Neither he nor Lewis pleads for Arthur's cause. John is too forward in his voluntary offer, but he aims rather at stopping the loud exclamations of Constance than at lasting peace (II. i. 544-58). Lewis's description of Constance—'sad and passionate'—Philip's guilty bewilderment, John's politic offer and the wound-cure-imagery, all make Constance the voice of conscience[34] in these early scenes of the play. It is conscience, which has been grievously wounded in this 'mad world', where kings 'break faith upon commodity' and prefer 'a most base and vile-concluded peace' to 'honourable war' (II. i. 561-98). No measure of title or land can heal up the deep wound, and John cherishes a vain hope.

"John explores and exploits his fellow men", observes Honigmann, "he tries to find everyone's price."[35] But no price can buy conscience. With his ad hoc policy of commodity,[36] what he achieves at best is, in the words of Constance,—'painted peace' (III. i. 31). Earlier, the two kings had in the same manner joined in a Machiavellian league against the citizens of Angiers. Indeed, the commodity-speech 'is not gratuitous',[37] but it is ironic to hear it from the mouth of the very person, who had suggested the first 'vile peace' against the innocent citizens of Angiers. In fact, Constance is the one character in the play to cry against commodity.[38] 'Impotent and shrill' as the cry is 'among the unheeding male forces',[39] it symbolises the impotence of conscience among the forces of history. A trifle tedious as her scenes tend to become[40] they suggest the sheer irrelevance of her exclamations against commodity. And yet Act III Scene i gives the impression that her cries (III. i. 33-37) are instantaneously heard, for, as if in answer to her prayer, arrives Pandulph, the Pope's legate, with a demand and a threatening gesture. A subtle, almost imperceptible link conjoins Lady Constance's prayer with all the preceding speeches of the scene, and provides an excellent example of what Sutherland calls 'the moving pattern of Shakespeare's thought', 'his ability to shape long speeches, passages, and even whole scenes in a continuously developing movement'.[41] The developing movement is here directed by the word 'day', which occurs as a refrain in all these speeches.

K. Philip.—'Tis true, fair daughter; and this *blessed day*
Ever in France shall be kept festival.
To solemnize *this day* the glorious sun
Stays in his course and plays the alchemist,
Turning with splendour of his precious eye
The meagre cloddy earth to glittering gold.
The yearly course that brings *this day* about
Shall never see it but a *holy day*.

Const. [Rising]—A *wicked day*, and not a *holy day*!
What hath *this day* deserv'd? What hath it done,
That it in golden letters should be set
Among the high tides in the calender?
Nay, rather turn *this day* out of the week,
This day of shame, oppression, perjury;
Or, if it must stand still, let wives with child
Pray that their burdens may not fall *this day*,
Lest that their hopes prodigiously be cross'd;
But on *this day* let seamen fear no wreck;
No bargains break that are not *this day* made;
This day, all things begun come to ill end,
Yea faith itself to hollow falsehood change!

K. Philip.—By heaven, lady, you shall have no cause
To curse the fair proceedings of *this day:*
(III. i. 75-97) (Italics Mine)

In all, the twenty-two lines of the exchange, contain the word no less than fourteen times, where it is personified like other abstractions in the play,[42] and it changes its complexion from 'blessed' and 'holy' to 'wicked' and 'ungodly'. The recurring idea of this day also suggests the associated image of sun-set, employed by both King Philip and Constance. There is a subtle irony in Philip's contention that the sun stays in his course on purpose to solemnize this day. If the sun stays even for a fraction of a minute, it would disrupt the cosmic order. With the famous Ulysses speech[43] echoing in our ears, we are reminded of the Bastard's words in the previous scene:

> The world, who of itself is peised well,
> Made to run even upon even ground,
> Till this advantage, this vile-drawing bias,
> This sway of motion, this commodity,
> Makes it take head from all indifferency,
> From all direction, purpose, course, intent— (II. i. 575-0)

It is as if, the sun itself, bribed by commodity, stays its course, causing chaos and confusion, solemnizing an unholy alliance and lending a hand with his alchemy at painting peace. On the other hand, seen from the vantage point of Constance's prayer: Let not the hours of this ungodly day clear out the day in peace; but ere sunset. Set armed discord 'twixt these perjur'd kings! (III. i. 109-11)—it appears that the Sun stays its course in order to allow time to Cardinal Pandulph to cause fresh discord between France and England. With Pandulph's mission fulfilled and Constance's prayer answered, the 'day'-refrain is heard again, and significantly enough this time from the mouth of Blanche, who finds herself in the same position in which Constance and Angiers had been. To Lewis's—"Father, to arms!" —she exclaims in puzzled dismay (just as Constance had done when the news of the marriage was first broke to her):

> Upon thy wedding *day*?
> Against the blood that thou hast married?
> What, shall our feast be kept with slaughter'd men?
> Shall braying trumpets and loud churlish drums,
> Clamours of hell, be measures to our pomp?
> (III. i. 300-04)

and when France finally falls from England and war becomes imminent, she cries with bitter irony: "The sun's o'ercast with blood: fair day, adieu!" (III. i. 326). In *The Troublesome Raigne* also the parallel scene begins with a reference to the day:

"*John.* This is the day, the long desired day"[44] but contains nothing to compare with the subtle links and undertones of irony, found in *King John.* Moreover, whereas in *The Troublesome Raigne*, Philip is without a moment's doubt,[45] Shakespeare shows him hanging in doubt and facing a genuine dilemma[46] before he finally breaks his faith with England. He is deeply perplexed and unable to take a decision (III. i. 221). In the same way, in the latter part of the scene, Shakespeare focuses attention on the dilemma of Blanche, who finds herself in as difficult a fix as did the citizens of Angiers a short while ago (III. i. 327-30). And in her case, unlike in that of the citizens, the solution cannot be as simple as to accept might as right. This is in sharp contrast to Blanche's reaction in *The Troublesome Raigne*, the reaction of a newly married bride denied nuptial pleasures and a total unconcern for the complexity of the situation:

> And will your Grace upon your wedding day
> Forsake your Bride and follow dreadfull drums:
> Nay, good my Lord, stay you at home with mee.[47]

The two instances are characteristic of Shakespeare's subtle way of supplementing the source material with 'moral complexity'[48] and his refusal to oversimplify the issues of right versus wrong.[49] The above-noted dilemma of the French King provides appropriate occasion for the expounding of the conception of order by Pandulph:

> All form is formless, order orderless,
> Save what is opposite to England's love. (III. i. 253-54)

A singularly distorted picture. As Kenneth Muir notes, 'the sympathies of the audience are divided', but Pandulph's use of order is rather ironic than 'ambivalent'.[50] And the irony becomes more piquant when we remember the Biblical text—"love ye your enemies"[51]—the French King's desire for 'some gentle order' (III. i. 251), and the fact that the exponent of the above order is a prelate. The dilemma of Philip also provides the occasion for what Ivor John terms the 'glib sophistry' of Pandulph,[52] by the use of which he seeks to convince Philip as well as to justify his inverted concept of honour (III. i. 263-97).

One may or may not agree with Robert Stevenson's thesis that Shakespeare's attitude to the prelates was unsympathetic in general, but there can be no two opinions that *The Troublesome Raigne* leaves "a far kindlier memory of Pandulph", foreshadowing "not so much Shakespeare's sinister cardinal of Milan as he does the Bishop of Carlisle".[53] Indeed, by allowing Pandulph a full presentation of his case unlike *The Troublesome Raigne*, Shakespeare provides a more lethal analysis of Papal pretensions in his play.[54] In Act I. Scene III the pretensions of faith are completely given up by Pandulph. Here, laying aside the Holy father's cassock, he appears as an adept in practical politics, prophesying[55] and planning. Applying general statements of mature political wisdom, he tells Lewis that since John is the usurper he cannot have a minute's rest till the rightful heir Arthur is killed (III. iii. 131-40). The idea that usurpation causes the subduing of man's conscience and inevitably leads to other more grievous crimes which in turn cause his fall is central to Shakespeare's political thinking. It incorporates the current ideas of the fortune's wheel, divine vengeance and order. It illustrates the Machiavellian doctrine of expediency, but looks beyond expediency and present gain; it exemplifies belief in the natural order. The John-Arthur situation, as analysed by Pandulph here, is a neat illustration of the idea and looks forward to Bolingbroke-Richard-complex. When Lewis shrinks from the hazard, Pandulph has a dig at the ignorance of the Dolphin and utters the aphorism, which diagnoses the central malady of the play:

> How green you are and fresh in this old world!
> John lays you plots; the times conspire with you;
> For he that steeps his safety in true blood
> Shall find but bloody safety and untrue. (III. iii. 145-48)

The realisation dawns upon John himself in the hour of crisis and he echoes the very words of Pandulph in a fit of remorse:

> There is no sure foundation set on blood,
> No certain life achiev'd by others' death. (IV. ii. 104-05)

Undoubtedly, the reasons advanced by Pandulph are, as Lewis remarks, 'strong' (III. iii. 182) but they are self-contradictory.

While forecasting the inevitable fall of John owing to his reign's foundation on Arthur's blood, he has been urging Lewis to base his own foundation on the same blood.

It has rightly been noted that in Shakespeare's version the significance of the religious issue is reduced to the minimum, and the Papal legate is made only an instrument of aggression.[56]

In the earlier plays on John, the King-Pope relation is central,[57] but in Shakespeare's play, the Arthur-affair is made central[58] instead. It is not surprising, therefore, that the best scenes of the play revolve round Arthur, and his death forms the climax. The Pandulph-Lewis scene discussed above falls between the murder suggestion and the attempted murder.[59] No other scene in the play has won such warm tributes as the short scene in which John urges Hubert to murder Arthur. Schlegel calls it 'superlatively masterly'[60] and Hazlitt, though he considers it inferior to Hubert-Arthur scene, terms it as 'a master-piece of dramatic skill'.[61] The beauty of the scene lies in the 'dramatization of psychology'.[62] As Schlegel remarks, "the cautious criminal hardly ventures to say to himself what he wishes the other to do" —[63]

> I had a thing to say—
> But I will fit it with some better tune. (III. ii. 25-26)
> I had a thing to say, but let it go: (l. 33)

He wishes it were midnight, he wishes they were in a churchyard, he wishes that Hubert's blood was cold and thick (ll. 40, 43). The imagery employed by him throughout is suggestive of death, though, unlike Richard III, he lacks the easy insouciance to utter the dreaded word. If only he were possessed with the 'iron tongue and brazen mouth' (l. 38) of a Richard how easy had been his task! But since he is not, he wishes Hubert to become inanimate—*sans* tongue, *sans* eyes, *sans* ears (ll. 48-49) —a mere handy tool, which could be used to liquidate Arthur. The kind of language which John tries in vain to adopt and which would have suited his purpose ideally, is later to be adopted by Bolingbroke: 'Have I no friend will rid me of this living fear?'—words which are aided by wishtful looks towards the man intended.[64] Since he does not know Bolingbroke's language, he has to cover an extremely long and circuitous route, and, as Dowden puts it. "He trembles lest he should have said too much; he trembles lest he should not have said enough; at last the nearer fear prevails, and the words, 'death', 'a grave', form themselves upon his lips."[65] In sharp contrast to the style used by John throughout the scene, with superb dramatic skill Shakespeare completes the final communication of the murder-idea in a single line of almost inaudible whispers:

> *K.J.*—Death.
> *Hub.*— My lord?
> *K.J.*— A grave.
> *Hub.*— He shall not live.
> *K.J.*— Enough. (III. ii. 66)

The fact that the word 'death' forms an extrasyllable in the line[66] and introduces a jarring note is all the more significant since it underlines the ugliness and the disharmony implicit in the evil suggestion of death. It is also striking to note that before the dreadful word 'death' forms itself upon the lips of John, it is uttered by Hubert—"Though that my *death* were adjunct to my act"(57)—and this appears to give to John the necessary moral (or immoral) courage to whisper it back to Hubert. The speech already referred to is significant for 'night-death-thick blood, day-life-fresh blood contrasts',[67] but this is not all. Its echoes can be heard distinctly enough in Pandulph-Lewis scene and Hubert-Arthur scene. The image of warm blood, which 'runs tickling up and down the veins' anticipates Pandulph's 'warm life plays in that infant's veins'—(III. iv. 132), and seen in that context it becomes a personification of natural human feelings, which John seeks to subdue. Yet ironical as it is, the strings touched repeatedly by him throughout the scene are the strings of love and gratitude. The same sentiments recur in Arthur-Hubert scene. If John succeeds in subduing the natural human instincts of Hubert with crafty protestations of love and gratitude, Arthur succeeds in reviving them with his innocent prattle of love and gratitude (IV. i. esp. ll. 23-24 and 31). It would be wrong to hold that Arthur's love and 'winning innocence'[68] are diplomatic like John's, and Shakespeare makes his Arthur forestall such a notion:

Nay, you may think my love was crafty love,
And call it cunning: do, and if you will. (IV. i. 53-54)

The contrast between John's cunning and crafty love on the one hand and Arthur's innocence and genuine love on the other is obvious, and Hubert should be able to discriminate between the two. If, despite this, Hubert finds it difficult to neglect his avowed duty, it is because of *commodity* which has cooled his blood and replaced his natural instincts with *iron*. In the blinding scene *iron* is the instrument to be employed by Hubert for the gruesome act just as Hubert himself is the instrument employed by John. By repeatedly drawing pointed attention to *iron*[69] and by personifying it, Shakespeare completes the equation:

Are you more stubborn-hard than hammer'd *iron*?
(IV. i. 67)

Lo, by my troth, the instrument is cold. (IV. i. 103)

Tyrell, Buckingam, the two murderers of Clarence, Mowbray, Exton, the executioners employed by Macbeth, are also instruments, but none of them achieves the archetypal stature of Hubert. In both the scene of encitement and the blinding he appears to bear the shears of destiny. John as well as Arthur, the tiger as well as the lamb is beholden to him as to a presiding deity and the way they keep chanting his name repeatedly is suggestive of a sacred ritual:

K. Jn.—Come hither, *Hubert.* O my gentle *Hubert,*
(III. ii. 19)

K. Jn.—Good *Hubert, Hubert, Hubert,*
(III. ii. 59)

Arth.—For heaven sake, *Hubert,* let me not be bound!
Nay, hear me, *Hubert,* drive these men away,
(IV. i. 78-79)

Arth.—Let me not hold my tongue, let me not, *Hubert!*
Or, *Hubert,* if you will, cut out my tongue,
(IV. i. 100-01)

John utters the name eight times in about fortysix lines of his speech, Arthur utters it fifteen times in about ninetyfour lines spoken by him. Finally Hubert himself joins the chant, assuring Arthur:

That *Hubert*, for the wealth of all the world,
Will not offend thee. (IV. i. 130-31)

Hubert, thus unable to resist the despairing cry of the helpless child, becomes an enlarged version of the second Murderer in *Richard III.*[70] W.P. Ker has justly paid a glowing tribute to this scene and drawn attention to the universal human feelings dramatized herein.[71] It is out of such stuff that Shakespeare goes on to build the great murder scene in *Macbeth*.

Attention has also been drawn to the contrast between eyes and hands, the former symbolising right and the latter might,[72] but right or conscience is symbolised by tongue and ears also. As noted above, in the earlier scenes Constance apears as the voice of Conscience and in the murder-incitement-scene, John, shuns ears as well as eyes, sound as well as sight.[73] In the blinding scene itself Hubert tries his utmost to avoid the 'innocent prate' (IV. i. 25) of Arthur: "go to, hold your tongue" (IV. i. 97). To which Arthur's reply:

Hubert, the utterrance of a brace of tongues
Must needs want pleading for a pair of eyes:
Let me not hold my tongue, let me not, Hubert;
(IV. i. 98-100)

further confirms the eye-tongue-ear-association. On the other hand, Hubert being employed by John as an instrument becomes the hand. It is hardly surprising therefore, that the word 'hand' occurs repeatedly in the scenes immediately following the Hubert-Arthur scene. The dialogue between King John and Hubert in Act IV, Scene ii is, according to Lily Campbell, "totally out of character and inconsistent with the story of King John as told in the Chronicle", and might be in essence a dialogue that took place in fact between Queen Elizabeth and Secretary Davison.[74] Nevertheless, it is beautifully incorported in the structure of the play and Dr. Johnson was just in his appreciation of it.[75] John's attempt to act Bolingbroke and put the total blame on the instrument—"Thy *hand* hath murd'red him:" (IV. ii. 205), boomerangs against himself. Symbolically Hubert is the hand—John's own hand, as he is quick to remind the King: "Here is your *hand* and seal for what I did" (l. 215).

Unable to contradict and argue, John fears the Final Judgment; when his own hand and seal would bear witness to his crime (ll. 216-18). Yet, in desperate bid to shift the blame, he goes on to slander nature in Hubert's form:

Hadst not thou been by,
A fellow by the hand of nature mark'd,
Quoted and sign'd to do a deed of shame,
This murder had not come into my mind; (ll. 220-23)

The equation between John's 'hand and seal' on the one hand, and nature's hand on the other, is interesting as is the journey of the hand-image from Hubert to nature. Not Hubert, but John is the fellow, marked by the hand of nature, and the instigation scene has already made it clear enough that it is John who serpent-like puts the idea of murder into the mind of Hubert. The audience who have witnessed this and who are all along aware that Arthur is alive and that, despite John's command, Hubert's hand has shrunk from the bloody deed, can hardly miss the irony in the above lines of John.

In Act IV Scene iii, when the dead body of Arthur is discovered, the hand-image reappears powerfully:

Bast.—It is a damned and a bloody work;
The graceless action of a heavy *hand,*
If that it be the work of any *hand.*
Sal.—If that it be the work of any *hand*!
We had a kind of light what would ensue:
It is the shameful work of Hubert's *hand,*
(IV. iii. 57-62)

If it is the work of any hand, apparently the hand is Hubert's, but the Nobles recognize that Hubert himself is only 'the practice and the purpose of the King' in other words, the hand employed by the King.

Spurgeon says that John "is always pictured as a *portion* of a body only, which seems in some way to create of him something especially sinister and horrible".[76] This is so largely because the parts of the body repeatedly used as images portraying him are lower limbs: hand and foot. In Act III Scene i after the ignominious treaty, when the two Kings stand hand in hand, the hand image aptly occupies the central place, for here two mights have stifled the right, but even here it is John who is suggested through the image of hand (ll. 118 and 187). In Act III, Scene iv, while forecasting the murder of Arthur, Pandulph again applies to John: 'bloody fingers' ends' (l. 168). The other image used (though less frequently) to suggest the character of John is foot. In the incitement scene, already discussed above, John tells Hubert of his fear of Arthur in the following words: "And wheresoe'er this *foot* of mine doth tread" (III. ii. 62). After Arthur's death when the nobles revolt and, burning with righteous indignation, refuse to return to the King, the foot image reappears in the speech of their spokesman, Salisbury:

> nor attend the foot
> That leaves the print of blood where'er it walks.
> (IV. iii. 25-26)

In the case of Hubert on the other hand, frequent attention is drawn to his appearance in general and to his eyes in particular. When he enters the prison to perform the bloody deed, his face looks pale and sad to Arthur (IV. i. 11 and 28). A few lines later, in an attempt to waken the mercy of the man, the prince again draws pointed attention to his face (ll. 41-42). This is followed by the Biblical image of a mote in the eye[77] which in a subtle way equates "that most precious sense of man with conscience itself", "O heaven, that there were but a mote in yours" (IV. i. 92). Finally when Arthur succeeds in dissuading Hubert from his 'sworn' purpose, he makes another reference to Hubert's appearance: 'O now you look like Hubert!' (IV. i. 125). To the nobles and to John, however, Hubert appears murderous, but in their descriptions too the face-eye imagery is prominent: "The image of a wicked heinous fault/Lives in his eye;" (IV. ii. 71-72). He is a fellow with 'abhorr'd aspect' (IV. ii. 224) and 'eyes of blood' (IV. ii. 265).

It has been noted by various critics that Shakespeare presents the English nobles in better light than does *The Troublesome Raigne* and that he makes their revolt essentially moral.[78] It is quite in keeping with this that the eye image is used to suggest their conscientious indignation at the supposed crime. John after his second coronation looks forward to their 'cheerful eyes' (IV. ii. 2). Begrudgingly they approve of the 'wasteful and ridiculous excess' (ll. 16, 37-39). But at the news of Arthur's death, they turn away from John and the Bastard describes their indignation in the following words: 'eyes as red as new-enkindled fire' (l. 163). With sharp dramatic irony the image reminds us of 'cheerful eyes' with which the scene opens and of the previous scene, where the fire refuses to burn (IV. i. 106). In the source play the English lords form a part of the Catholic conspiracy. Note the words with which Lewis welcomes them:

> Thanks to you all of this religious league,
> A holy knot of Catholique consent.[79]

and Salisbury himself confirms 'this holy League'.[80] They are represented not only as betraying the motherland but also as betraying God, out to 'please hell' and make havoc of the welfare of their souls.[81] In *King John* on the other hand, Shakespeare shows them in a terrible dilemma (just as he has shown King Philip in a dilemma earlier in the play), "as good men rebelling against an erring monarch for a righteous reason, yet in so doing putting themselves in the wrong".[82] Salisbury himself is grievously aware of this and his speech to Lewis immediately after the league clearly underlines the misgivings of a noble spirit (V. ii. 8-39). Here too the eye image is present in the form of tears and drooping brows.[83] As Bevington remarks, "Rebellion is not a feasible solution for political ills, but the complexity of its impulses can be appreciated."[84] Refusing to oversimplify the issue, Shakespeare justifies the rebellion morally, but condemns it politically as unpatriotic.[85]

Judged by the same standard, the Bastard's reaction to Arthur's death is politically right, but morally wrong. Though he condemns the 'graceless action' in the strongest possible terms,[86] and appears deeply shocked and bewildered for a moment:

> Here's a good world: (IV. iii. 116)
> I am amaz'd, methinks, and lose my way.
> Among the thorns and dangers of this world.
> (IV. iii. 140-41)

he does not waver in his loyalty. This has naturally puzzled the critics and has proved the biggest stumbling block in their appreciation of the character. Middleton Murry, who is most eloquent in his praise of the Bastard, holds that he (the Bastard) "cannot believe that the King would command a murder so devilish".[87] Such an interpretation would be more applicable to *The Troublesome Raigne* than to Shakespeare's *King John.* In the former the Bastard knows that Arthur died of suicide and defends John in unequivocal terms, whereas in the latter he is quite unware of Arthur's suicide and does not condone the crime. After his confession that he has lost his way, the next words he utters are:

> How easy dost thou take all England up
> From forth this morsel of dead royalty:
> The life, the right and truth of all this realm
> Is fled to heaven; (IV. iii. 142-45)

This, in effect, is to crown the dead Prince Arthur.[88] Lines such as these and words like 'wrested pomp' (l. 153) make it manifest that the Bastard recognizes the crime of usurpation committed by John. It cannot be that upto this critical juncture, he had all along been blissfully unware of John's usurpation and Arthur's rightful title.[89] Tillyard's observation, therefore, that "hitherto the Bastard has needed to do no more than serve his master faithfully, 'and that now he is' forced to consider the whole case of Arthur",[90] is far from satisfactory.

The Bastard's dilemma and decision form the crux of the play. He is generally looked upon as the spokesman of the patriotic spirit[91] or of the Tudor doctrine of order,[92] as an early version of the ideal ruler.[93] It is extremely difficult to reconcile this image of the character with his acquiescence in the murder of Arthur. Various critics in an attempt to justify the Bastard's reaction have contrasted John with Richard III. The similarity of situation in the two plays and yet the great dissimilarity in treatment are obvious and have to be explained. Tillyard's explanation is that though bad, John is not a tyrant like Richard III, and it was better to acquiesce in John's rule, hoping for a reformation of the King's heart. Ribner too accepts the logic, but adds two more reasons. The first is historical that the alternative to Richard was Henry Tudor and that to John the French King, supported by the papacy. The second reason, purely thematic, is that Shakespeare makes John a symbol of English nationalism, and in supporting him irrespective of his merits and demerits, Faulconbridge is suporting England.[94] Danby also contrasts the revolt in *Richard III* with that in *King John*, but he notices the difference rather in the approach of the dramatist than in the characters or the historical background:

> The difference is simple—the army marching against Richard is in rightful revolt. The theory justifying it is the classical medieval one that the wicked tyrant may rightly be resisted; the theory of Shakespeare's contemporary Catholic world, of those Calvinists who followed John Knox, and of the 1569 rebellion. The theory in *King John* is the theory of the Homilies: nothing justifies rebellion, no wickedness nor wrongfulnes in the ruler whatsoever.[95]

Danby also compares the Bastard's action with Prince John's treatment of the rebels in *Henry IV, Part Two* and with Albany's supporting Goneril and Regan against Lear and Cordelia. Morality, it would appear, is irrelevant when the peace of *Res Publica* is threatened.[96] Analysing the reaction of the Bastard, Sen Gupta contrasts it with Hector's logic against the war:

> 'Tis mad idolatry,
> To make the service greater than the god,[97]

and remarks that the Bastard proceeds without 'a qualm of conscience to the thousand businesses that are brief in hand'. He is a man of action 'who delights in nothing so much as in riding a storm' and 'has no time either for moral casuistry or for criminal investigation'. In the heat of action he cannot stop 'to pursue a line of thought to its logical extreme'.[98]

However, none of these explanations is fully satisfactory. The comparisons made by Danby are illuminating, but rather than justifying the Bastard's stand, they censor him. Morality (if the word denotes eternal human virtues, like truth and honesty, and not homiletic didacticism), it would appear, is never irrelevant to Shakespeare's vision of life. In the vicissitudes and intricacies of the political scramble, Shakespeare finds a way to test the Bastard also. The choice that he is called upon to make over the corpse of Arthur, is, in fact, a replica of the first choice made by him at the beginning of the play: truth or commodity. There he had chosen truth, here too he recognizes the truth but accomplishes a volte-face and chooses commodity instead. Bevington who thinks that the crux of the play lies in defining "commodity", says that in the case of the Bastard it becomes 'a kind of political morality justifying rightminded expediency'.[99] To treat the character as static and his political morality as fixed is to undermine it. In order to appreciate the play fully, we have to take into account the ambiguities as well as the metamorphoses in the character. Learned critics like Ellis-Fermor and Tillyard have drawn attention to the regal qualities of the Bastard.[100] But it is not enough to recognize these ideal criteria of a successful ruler in the Bastard, we have also to remember that he has a threefold function in the play. He is a symbol, chorus-character as well as a historical figure. Refusal to recognize this led S.L. Bethel to pronounce that the Bastard is hardly a character and keeps shifting his function from scene to scene.[101] As a symbol, he becomes a part of the theme of England. He 'is England', says Bradbrook.[102] "A rudimentry John Bull, a bullwork of England", says Charlton.[103] "His function", according to Murry, "is to embody England, to incorporate the English soul."[104] But it is only in the last Act of the play that the Bastard thus becomes the symbol of England. Until the last Act John, despite all his shortcomings, embodies the spirit of England, but in the final Act he ceases to do so, and it is not an accident that the first scene of this Act opens with John's handing over the crown to the Papal legate and ends with his relinquishing the charge to the Bastard: "Have thou the ordering of this present time" (V. i. 77). The Bastard as noted by Charlton is technically promoted to the middle stage and pushes John into the wings,[105] and so long as we look at the two characters as political symbols we may very well accept Adrien Bonjour's thesis that 'John's career represents a falling curve, the Bastard's career a rising curve', the structure in very simple terms being: 'decline of a hero—rise of a hero'.[106] If we look at the two characters as men, the curves look upside down. The same moral awareness which makes a coward of John and the lack of which makes the Bastard a determined general, ennobles John even in his burning fever and inglorious death. The last lines uttered by him seem to describe graphically not merely the physical effect of the poison but also the spiritual effect of his share in Arthur's death: "The tackle of my heart is crack'd and burn'd" (V. vii. 52). The Bastard, on the other hand, has been finally wooed by commodity, and Shakespeare makes the point so quietly that one may very well miss it. In an unexpected place, at the end of a scene apparently designed to enable the audience to keep pace with the events, where Hubert informs the Bastard, that the King, poisoned by a monk, lies almost speechless attended by Prince Henry and the English Lords, who have 'all come back' and been reconciled with the King, the Bastard says:

> Withhold thine indignation, mighty heaven,
> And tempt us not to bear above our power!
>
> (V. vi. 37-38)

The lines echo St. Paul's words to *The Corinthians*:

> Wherefore let him that thinketh he standeth take heed lest he fall. There hath no temptation taken you but such as is common to man: but God is faithful, who will not suffer you to be tempted above that ye are able; but will with the temptation also make a way to escape, that ye may be able to bear it.[107]

There is an abrupt pause after the two lines and there is no apparent link with what follows. The Bastard tells Hubert that half his forces are drowned in the Lincoln Washes and he himself has had a narrow escape (V. vi. 39-42). In *The Troublesome Raigne* also we are told of the near tragedy, but there the informtion is given direct to King John and without any allusion to heaven's indignation or temptation.[108] It cannot be that Shakespeare introduces the motif of temptation without any purpose. Who has been referred to as being tempted 'above our power'? The King, the subjects, the French, the rebel lords? The reference is, in fact, to the Bastard himself, and the entire speech is in the form of a confession. The Bastard with his deep insight and sharp intelligence discerns a link between the nobles' return and the Lincoln-Washes catastrophe. He had been tempted almost beyond his power to rule the country in the name of the sick and deserted king. The nobles going to the French King had left him alone to prop up the weak and drooping monarch. In *The Troublesome Raigne*, the Bastard makes a strong plea to the Lords and tries to touch every sentiment in them. After telling them that Arthur died of suicide, he goes on in the vein of the Homilies:

> I say tis shame, and worthy all reproofe,
> To wrest such pettie wrongs in tearmes of right,
> Against a King annoynted by the Lord.
> Why *Salsburie*, admit the wrongs are true,
> Yet subjects may not take in hand revenge,
> And rob the heavens of their proper power,
> Where sitteth he to whom revenge belongs.
> And doth a Pope, a Priest, a man of pride
> Give charters for the lives of lawfull Kings?
> Theres not a man that dyes in your beliefe,
> But sels his soule perpetually to payne.
> Ayd Lewes, leave God, kill *John*, please hell,
> Make havock of the welfare of your soules,
> For heere I leave you in the sight of heaven,
> A troupe of traytors, foode for hellish feends;
> If you desist, then follow me as friends,
> If not, then doo your worst as hatefull traytors.[109]

Shakespeare's Bastard, on the other hand, maintains a diplomatic silence in the climactic scene. Though sent by John to woo the Lords back to him, the few words that he does utter are—it seems—rather calculated to irritate them and whip up their indignation. The first words with which he greets them are 'distemper'd lords' (IV. iii. 21) and in his subsequent speeches he endeavours to teach them manners:

> Whate'er you think, good words, I think, were best.
> (l. 28)

> But there is little reason in your grief;
> Therefore 'twere reason you had manners now.
>
> (ll. 30-31)

> 'Tis true, to hurt his master, no man else.
>
> (l. 33)

The irony becomes apparent only if we remember his own bitter contempt for the 'sweet' words and manners of the aristocracy (I. i. 191-205). The pupil has become the teacher now.

Essentially the Bastard belongs to a different class from the Nobles. As Simpson observed, in *King John* the chivalrous old families are on one side, the unscrupulous and blustering upstarts on the other.[110] He defends Hubert against the angry Lords, not because he believes in the innocence of the man,[111] but because in Hubert he recognizes one of his own class. "As a contemporary figure", remarks Bethel, "he links the disorder of an usurper's reign to the subtler social malaise of Elizabethan times, which proceeded from the uncontrolled growth of commercial enterprise and the dissemination of a secular and individualistic philosophy."[112]

When the Lords are going to Edmundsbury to join the French, Shakespeare's Bastard, unlike his counterpart, makes no attempt to stop them. It is only later when they have already joined the enemy camp, that he does make use of the patriotic motif in strong terms:

> And you degenerate, you ingrate revolts,
> You bloody Neroes, ripping up the womb
> Of your dear mother England, blush for shame;
>
> (V. ii. 151-53)

But it is an indictment rather than an appeal. The difference in the situation from that of the Bastard's speech in *The Troublesome Raigne*,[113] entirely changes its meaning. In the desertion of the nobles, the Bastard sees his own chance for further advancement and virtually to govern the realm in the name of John. This, then, is the reason why he connives at what seemed to be the *murder* of Arthur, and decides to 'second a villain and a murderer'.[114] Naturally, therefore, though he talks of Arthur as 'the life, the right and the truth' and vividly foresees the imminent chaos in the realm, he exults at the thought of the 'thousand businesses' that are sure to come to his hand. It is no accident that in the last Act of the play for a brief but momentous spell, he becomes the *de facto* king. He has been tempted by the lure of power and has sinned in thought, though not in action. The loss of John's army in the Wash is not 'an act of criminal stupidity' accredited to him by Shakespeare to prove his utter failure 'in the higher spheres, despite his triumphs as a bully',[115] it is God's way of enabling him to bear the temptation. And in this respect it has the same implication for him as the nobles' return and the unexpected death of John. The second mention of the accident by the Bastard coincides with the death of John and this makes his words ambiguous, investing them with a symbolic import:

> For in a night the best part of my power,
> As I upon advantage did remove,
> Were in the Washes all unwarily
> Devoured by the unexpected flood. (V. vii. 61-64)
>
> *The King dies.*

It is another night. Even as the Bastard was taking advantage of the situation, the best part of his power is gone with the sudden death of John.

In the next speech of the Bastard uttered just after the King's death the crack between the character and the symbol becomes obvious. The first four lines are spoken by a self-conscious loyal servant who has failed his master in some measure:

> Art thou gone so? I do but sty behind
> To do the office for thee of revenge,
> And then my soul shall wait on thee to heaven,
> As it on earth hath been thy servant still.
>
> (V. vii. 70-73)

Perhaps, as Tillyard thinks, there is no insincerity in the words.[116] "He is the king's true servant", observes Bullough, "and Shakespeare goes so far, anticipating Kent at the end of *King Lear* ('I have a journey soon to go'), as to make him suggest that he will shortly follow his master to the grave".[117]

However, we can hardly take him literally. Only a few lines later, we find him offering his services to the new King:

> To whom, with all submission, on my knee
> I do bequeath my faithful services
> And true subjection everlastingly. (V. vii. 103-05)

It is significant that in this final scene, Shakespeare keeps us constantly reminded of the secondary position of Faulconbridge as a royal servant. These repeated protestations of his loyalty, though genuine in themselves, become fully meaningful only against the background of his late temptation. Though for a short spell, Shakespeare allows the Bastard to overshadow the titular hero, leaving the impression that the man whose interests are at stake plays second fiddle to the man who protects those interests,[118] yet at the same time he does not let us forget the fact that the Bastard is essentially the servant and warns us against accepting him as the hero of the play.

The four lines of servile devotion to the dead usurper are, strangely enough, followed by fine patriotic verse of a high order, which could have been spoken by a John of Gaunt or a Henry V (V. vii. 74-80). The speech is in the same key as the curtain speech made a short while later:

> This England never did, nor never shall,
> Lie at the proud foot of a conqueror,
> But when it first did help to wound itself.
> Now these her princes are come home again,
> Come the three corners of the world in arms,
> And we shall shock them! Nought shall make us rue,
> If England to itself do rest but true! (V. vii. 112-18)

'The resounding clarion'[119] of the speech keeps echoing long after one has heard it. Another echo mingles with it—the thunderous applause of the Globe theatre audience. No praise is too high for the speech. Indeed, it is so powerfully moving that it carries us off our feet like a tide so much so that we may very well forget the essential nature of the speaker as well as the central meaning of the play. Goddard thinks that in breaking the Elizabethan custom of giving the final lines of a play to the man of highest rank and allowing the Bastard rather than Prince

Henry to utter them, "Shakespeare clinches the fact that the Bastard is the King of the play." The truth is that the lines are spoken not so much by Faulconbridge, the man, as by Faulconbridge, the symbol of England, and the chorus. The play closes with a choric[120] summing up. The sentiments expressed are in keeping with the symbolic nature of the Bastard's character.

Two contrary views have been expressed regarding the curtain speech. First, it incorporates *the theme* of the play.[121] Second, it is a concession made by Shakespeare for the commonplace of his age, and it has nothing to do with the ethical meaning of the play.[122] By admitting the threefold function of the Bastard in the play, we may be able to accept both the interpretations. The political tugs of war dramatised throughout the play illustrate rather more fully the commodity-speech. In the light of all the vicissitudes of King John's reign, the insouciance of various dramatis personae (including the Bastard himself) on the stage of history, this summing up appears a worn out platitude. Perhaps, despite these final words of the Bastard, the lasting impression we are left with is that of 'a mad world', with commodity as its bias. But this is not all. After having witnessed the political scramble from close quarters and himself having gone through the trials and temptations of faith, the Bastard has come to realise that in this 'mad world', the only positive virtue is unselfish patriotism. Thus, when we look at the curtain speech in the light of the late temptation and deliverance (from evil) of the Bastard, we realise that it is a changed, a regenerate Bastard, who speaks. This Bastard has lately qualified to incorporate in his character the role of the chorus as well as that of the symbol of England. The curtain speech does reflect a current leitmotif: England's fierce nationalism in the Elizabethan age. But to put the case thus is, inadvertantly, to weaken it. For the patriotic sentiments expressed in the speech are as relevant to this second Elizabethan age as they were to the first, and they have as much meaning for Africans or Asians as they had for the British.

NOTES

1. Critics are almost evenly divided in placing *King John* immediately before and immediately after *Richard II* and no one to-day would agree with Schlegel that the play was written perhaps like *Henry VIII* after all the other Histories. *Vide* A.W. Schlegel, *Dramatic Art and Literature* (tr.), J. Black (London: H.G. Bohn, 1861), pp. 422 *et seq.* For twentieth century views on the question, see I.B. John (ed.), *King John* (London: Methuen, 1925), pp. xxviii *et seq.*, E.K. Chambers, *William Shakespeare* (Oxford: Clarendon Press, 1930), Vol. I, p. 366. J.D. Wilson (ed.), *King John* (New Shakespeare, Cambridge University Press, 1954), p. Lvi, J.D. Wilson (ed.), *Richard II* (New Shakespeare, Cambridge University Press, 1968), p. x and E.A.J. Honigmann (ed.), *King John* (London: Methuen, Arden Edition, 1962), pp. XLiii *et seq.*
2. I.B. John, *op. cit.*, p. xxxiii.
3. M. Webster, *Shakespeare To-day* (London: J.M. Dent, 1957), p. 181.
4. A famous Sanskrit dramatist of the early eighth century.
5. Dover Wilson, *King John,* p. xxxix and H.C. Goddard, *The Meaning of Shakespeare* (Chicago and London: Phoenix Book, University of Chicage Press, 1967), I, p. 146.
6. A. Bonjour, 'The Road to Swinstead Abbey', *E.L.H.*, xviii (1951), p. 270.
7. J.F. Danby, *Shakespeare's Doctrine of Nature* (London: Faber, 1968), p. 75.
8. *Richard III,* V. iii. 183 and *King John* I. i. 175.
9. Frank O'Connor, *Shakespeare's Progress* (New York: Collier, 1961), pp. *56 et seq.*
10. *Ibid.*, p. 56.
11. Danby, *op. cit.*, p. 75.
    See also Reese, *The Cease of Majesty* (London: Edward Arnold, 1961), p. 285 and M. Murry, *Shakespeare* (London: Jonathan Cape 1965), p. 156 for the link between Faulconbridge and Henry V.
12. Webster, *op. cit.*, p. 181.
13. G. Bullough (ed.), *Narrative and Dramatic Sources of Shakespeare* (London: Routledge and Kegan Paul; New York: Columbia University Press, 1962), IV, p. 3.
14. H. Butterfield, *The Englishman and His History* (Camb. University Press, 1944), p. 19.
15. *The Third Volume of Chronicles* (196/1/4), *vide* Bullough, *op. cit.*, p. 49.
16. *Ibid.*, p. 49.
17. *Ibid.*, p. 71.

18. R. Simpson, *The Politics of Shakespeare's History Plays,* New Shakespeare Society Transactions (1874), p. 397.
19. *T.R. II,* 1081-87. *Vide* Bullough, *op. cit.,* p. 148.
20. Butterfield, *op. cit.,* pp. 23 *et seq.*
21. R. Simpson, *op. cit.,* p. 405.
22. Reese, *op. cit.,* pp. 264 *et seq.*
23. *Ibid.,* p. 271.
24. Simpson, *op. cit.,* p. 397.
25. *Ibid.,* p. 398.
26. Honigmann, *op. cit.,* Lxiv.
27. Danby, *op. cit.,* pp. 70 *et seq.*
28. It is difficult to agree with Dowden who thinks that neither John's title is just nor his authority strong. See his *Shakespeare: His Mind and Art* (London: Routledge and Kegan Paul, 1957), p. 169.
29. H.C. Goddard, *op. cit.,* pp. 141 *et seq.*

    Walter Pater, *Appreciations* (London: Macmillan, 1889), p. 188.—he represents 'a certain potent natural aristocrcy'.
30. Una Ellis-Fermor, *The Frontiers of Drama* (London: Methuen, University, Paperback, 1964), p. 39.
31. *Vide* Honigmann, *op. cit.,* p. 50 *n.*
32. *The Troublesome Raigne Part I,* 827-36, *Vide* Bullough, *op. cit.,* p. 94.
33. *Ibid.*
34. Reese calls her the last of the women who in the earlier Histories appear as the mouthpieces of conscience, *op. cit.,* pp. 283 *et seq.*
35. *Op. cit.,* p. Lxviii.
36. He is a 'King of Commodity' according to Bullough, *op. cit.,* p. 23.
37. Honigmann, *op. cit.,* p. Lxviii.
38. Marriott, *English History in Shakespeare* (New York: E.P. Dutton, 1918), p. 56.
39. Dowden, *op. cit.,* p. 172.
40. Marriott, *op. cit.,* p. 56.
41. J. Sutherland, 'The Moving Pattern of Shakespeare's Thought', G.I. Duthie (ed.), *Papers Mainly Shakespearean* (Edinburgh: Oliver and Boyd, Aberdeen Univ. Studies, No. 147, 1964), p. 10.
42. C. Spurgeon gives examples of various other abstractions seen as persons in the play. See her *Shakespeare's Imagery* (Cambridge University Press, 1965), pp. 246 *et seq.*
43. *Troilus & Cressida,* I. iii. 85 ff.
44. *T.R.* I, 904, Bullough, *op. cit.*, p. 96.

45. To John's query as to how he would react if John refused to submit to the Pope's pressure, his reply is instant and unhesitant: "What should I say? I must obey the Pope." *T.R.* I, 1014, Bullough, *op. cit.*, p. 99.
46. D. Bevington, *Tudor Drama and Politics* (Camb., Massachusettes: Harvard University Press, 1968), p. 199.
47. *T.R. I*, 1038-40, *vide* Bullough *op. cit.*, p. 100.
48. A Harbage, *As They Liked It* (New York: Harper, 1961), p. 8.
49. Bevington, *op. cit.*, p. 199.
50. K. Muir, 'Shakespeare and Politics', *Shakespeare in A Changing World* (ed.), A. Kettle (London: Lawrence and Wishart, 1964), pp. 67 *et seq.*
51. *St. Luke.* VI. 35 and *St. Matthew*, V. 44.
52. Ivor John, *op. cit.*, p. xxxiv.
53. R. Stevenson, *Shakespeare's Religious Frontier* (The Hague: Martinus Nijhoff, 1958), pp. 10 *et seq* and p. 14.
54. Reese, *op. cit.*, pp. 271 *et seq.*
55. Carlisle and Gaunt also prophesy, but their prophecies are warnings, meant to curve the person from the evil course of action, whereas Pandulph's is encitement, meant to whet Lewis's ambition and spur him to action.
56. Sen Gupta, *Shakespeare's Historical Plays* (London: Oxford University Press, 1964), p. 103.
57. According to Marriott the aspect of King John's reign which appealed most to the Elizabethan dramatists was the King-Papacy relations, *op. cit.*, 35.
58. Sen Gupta, *op. cit.*, p. 102.
59. The *T.R.* lacks this concentration, where the ransacking of the monastries by Philip Faulconbridge intervenes (I. xi).
60. Schlegel, *op. cit.*, p. 423.
61. Hazlitt, *The Round Table Characters of Shakespeare's Plays* (London: J.M. Dent, 1960), p. 307.
62. See p. 104 *supra.*
63. Schegel *op. cit.*, p. 423.
64. *Richard II*, V. iv. 2, 7-9.
65. Dowden, *op. cit.*, p. 170.
66. Whether we accept the above editing of Honigmann or keep 'death' at the end of l. 75, as Ivor John, following Walker has done, the word forms an extra syllable.
67. Noted by Honigmann, *op. cit.*, p. 78 *n.*
68. Schlegel, *op. cit.*, p. 423.

69. The word *iron* occurs five times directly in the short scene besides occurring at least twice indirectly. In the scene of incitement too it is used by John: "*iron* tongue" (III. ii. 48).
70. Chapter IV, *supra.*
71. *Form and Style in English Poetry* (ed.), R.W. Chambers (London: Macmillan, 1928), pp. 248 *et seq.*
72. Honigmann, *op. cit.,* p. lxi.
73. III. ii. 48-51.
74. *Shakespeare's 'Histories'* (San Marine, California: Huntington, 1963), p. 163.
75. W. Raleigh (ed.), *Johnson on Shakespeare* (London: Oxford University Press, 1946), p. 109.
76. Spurgeon, *op. cit.*, p. 248.
77. St. Mathew, VII. 3. and *St. Luke*, VI. 41, *Holy Bible.*
78. Bevington, *op. cit.,* p. 199.
    R. Simpson, *op. cit.,* p. 432, and Ellis-Fermor, *op. cit.,* p. 39.
79. *T.R.,* II, 544-45. *Vide* Bullough, *op. cit.,* p. 134.
80. *T.R.,* II, 562. *Vide ibid.,* p. 134.
81. The Bastard's speech in *T.R.*, quoted on p. 131 *infra.*
82. Bullough, *op. cit.,* p. 21.
83. V. ii. 29—'I must withdraw and weep', and II, 45-54—Lewis's offer to wipe the tears.
84. Bevington, *op. cit.,* p. 199.
85. Simpson, *op. cit.,* p. 432.
86. IV. iii. 57-59 quoted above. Also IV. iii. 120-34.
87. Murry, *op. cit.,* p. 166.
88. M.C. Bradbrook, *Shakespeare the Craftsman,* Clark Lectures, 1968 (London: Chatto, 1969), p. 20.
89. The Commodity Speech, II. i. esp. l. 562 makes it plain that he is not.
90. E.M.W. Tillyard, *Shakespeare's History Plays* (Penguin, 1962), p. 225.
91. G. Brandes, *vide* A New Variorum Edition, *King John* (ed.), H.H. Furness (Philadelphia and London: J.P. Lippincott, 1919), p. 594.
92. Ribner, *op. cit.,* p. 125.
93. Una Ellis-Fermor and Tillyard, see p. 124 *infra.*
94. Ribner, *op. cit.,* pp. 125 *et seq.*
95. Danby, *op. cit.,* p. 78. For a discussion of the two theories see Chapter II *supra.*
96. *Ibid.,* pp. 79 *et seq.*

97. *Troilus* and *Cressida,* II. ii. 56-57; quoted by Sen Gupta, *op. cit.,* p. 105 *n.*
98. Sen Gupta, *op. cit.,* pp. 105 *et seq.*
99. Bevington, *op. cit.,* p. 200.
100. According to Tillyard, the Bastard posseses the strength of the lion, the cunning of the fox and the self-abnegation of the pelican, *op. cit.,* pp. 227 *et seq,* and according to Ellis-Fermor he has tenacity, resourcefulness, and shrewdness, *op. cit.,* p. 39.
101. S.L. Bethel, *Shakespeare and the Popular Dramatic Tradition* (London: King and Staples, 1944), p. 50.
102. Bradbrook, *op. cit.,* p. 20.
103. Charlton, *Shakespeare. Politics* and *Politicians* (Eng. Asso. Pamphlet No. 72, April 1929), p. 11.
104. Murry, *op. cit.,* p. 156.
105. Charlton, *op. cit.,* p. 11.
106. *A. Bonjour loc. cit.*
107. *1 Corinthians,* X, 12-13.
108. *The T.R. II,* 331-38, Bullough, *op. cit.,* p. 141.
109. *The T.R. II,* 461-80, Bullough, *op. cit.,* pp. 131 *et seq.*
110. R. Simpson, *op. cit.,* p. 427.
111. As Goddard thinks, *op. cit.,* p. 146.
112. S.L. Bethel, *op. cit.,* p. 50.
113. Quoted above on p. 154.
114. IV. iii. 102—Bigot's words hold good—though Hubert is no villain, no murderer—in a larger context.
115. As Honigmann, *op. cit.,* p. Lxxii.
116. Tillyard, *op. cit.,* p. 228.
117. Bullough, *op. cit.,* p. 23.
118. Reese, *op. cit.,* p. 261.
119. M. Webster, *op. cit.,* p. 183. Also Goddard: 'It is like the note of a trumpet', *op. cit.,* p. 146.
120. Campbell, *op. cit.,* p. 166.
121. *Ibid.,* p. 126. Goddard, *op. cit.,* p. 146. V.K. Whitaker, *Shakespeare's Use of Learning* (San Marino: Huntington, 1964), p. 124.
122. W. Sanders, *The Dramatist and the Received Idea* (Cambridge University Press, 1968), p. 73.

Richard II

6

Whereas *Richard III* and to some extent, *King John* are plays which give rise to what the Indian dramaturgists would have called the *bibhatsa rasa* (the odious sentiment), *Richard II* especialises in the *Karuna rasa* (the pathetic sentiment). According to Dhananjaya, the tenth century Indian dramaturgist, the essence of the *Karuna rasa* is *soka* (sorrow) and it results from loss of something cherished and from attaining of something undesired. In consequence of it there occur heaving of sighs, drawing of sighs, weeping, paralysis and the like; the transitory states are sleeping, epilepsy, depression, sickness, death, indolence, agitation, despair, stupor, insanity, anxiety and so forth.[1] When we look at *Richard II*, especially at the strange behaviour of King Richard after his return from Ireland, we would come across almost all the attributes of *Karuna*. It is a commonplace of criticism to view Richard as an actor, a poet. This is to undermine the genuine pathetic element in the play. An attempt has, therefore, been made to explain Richard's poetry and alleged acting, which are generally considered gratuitous.

In this play as in *Richard III*, and *King John*, Shakespeare again dramatises the interaction between belief and actual experience. At the same time he also dramatises the tension between abstract ideals and personal motives. Besides, in this play Shakespeare also gives indications of the technique of juxtaposition which he goes on to employ so brilliantly in *1 and 2 Henry IV*. On account of these factors, *Richard II* becomes a very complex play and deserves a kind of close study which is hardly permitted by the nature and scope of the present work.

Nevertheless an attempt has been made in the chapter to examine certain scenes and passages as intimately as possible. If some of the scenes and passages are passed over lightly it is because others have already discussed them brilliantly. The following pages would, it is hoped, demonstrate how Shakespeare invests even seemingly ordinary and trivial details with far-reaching significance.

As noted by various critics, Richard is a weakling. What is more, he is surrounded by a group of parasites like Bushy, Bagot and Green. Dhananjaya would have termed them as *vita* and we may well compare them with Sekharaka in Harshadeva's *Nagananda.* Juxtaposed next to Richard is the practical and strong-willed Bolingbroke, who like Richard III has all the characteristics of a *dhirodhata nayaka.* He is more impressive than Richard perhaps, yet it would be wrong to look upon him as the hero. Though ultimately he succeeds in ousting Richard, yet essentially his role remains that of a *pratinayaka*[2] or counter-hero. One of the chief attractions of *Richard II* is the deft balance maintained by Shakespeare between Richard, the hero and Bolingbroke, the counter-hero. This becomes evident if we examine the opening scenes of the play and take into account the changes introduced by Shakespeare into the source-material.

It has rightly been observed by various critics[3] that Shakespeare begins his *Richard II* at exactly the same point where Edward Hall begins his chronicle: the Bolingbroke-Mowbray quarrel. Undoubtedly, Shakespeare is indebted to Hall for the point of departure, but the wide difference in the origin of the quarrel itself is strangely overlooked. Hall's account, highly favourable to Bolingbroke, presents Mowbray as the accuser, who meanly betrays the confidence shown in him by the former. Bolingbroke, a well-meaning soul, is thus forced by circumstances to challenge Mowbray to combat, in order to defend his honour and prove his innocence:

> affirmying that if the kyng would permit & suffre hym he would prove his acusor untrue, unjust & a false forger of lies & sedicious tales by the stroke of a spere & dent of a swerd.[4]

Holinshed has an altogether different story to tell. While the various nobles, dissatisfied with the king's manners, are still hopeful of his mending himself, Bolingbroke with his accusation of Mowbray precipitates the crisis.

> But all was in vaine, for so it fell out, that in this parlement holden at Shrewsburie, Henrie duke of Hereford accused Thomas Mowbraie duke of Norfolke, of certaine words which he should utter in talke had betwixt them, as they rode togither latelie before betwixt London and Brainford, sounding highlie to the kings dishonor. And for further proofe thereof, he presented a supplication to the king, wherein he appealed to the duke of Norfolke in field of battell, for a traitor, false and disloyall to the king, and enimie unto the realme.[5]

It is evident that Shakespeare's account is nearer to Holinshed's than to Hall's. Bolingbroke in Shakespeare, as in Holinshed, initiates the action and, though much is said about the waves of events carrying him[6] and about the deliberate obscurity maintained by the dramatist as regards his real motive,[7] there is at least one person, who (Shakespeare leaves us in no doubt whatsoever) is aware of the political motive behind 'bold' Bolingbroke's 'boistrous' appeal from the very beginning. And the person is no other than King Richard himself. When he enquires of Gaunt:

> Tell me, moreover, hast thou sounded him,
> If he appeal the Duke on *ancient malice*,
> Or worthily as a *good subject* should,
> On some known ground of *treachery* in him?
>
> (I. i. 8-11) (Italics Mine)

he is already suspicious, if not sure, of the malicious motive behind Bolingbroke's appeal. At the same time, he cannot be unaware of the 'known ground of treachery' in Mowbray, which, as later exposed by Bolingbroke, is the murder of Gloucester. As Wilbur Sanders observes, the issue is extremely complex.[8] When Bolingbroke appeals against Mowbray's treachery, he cannot but be malicious towards the King himself. Though perhaps he is a good kinsman, ready to avenge his uncle's murder, he is hardly a 'good subject' at all. Throughout the opening scene, Richard shows definite awareness of Bolingbroke's political motive. His remark in reply to the greetings of the two rivals: "We thank you both, yet *one* but flatters us" (I. i. 25), is meant clearly enough for Bolingbroke. And, when the latter declares his determination to avenge Gloucester's death, Richard makes the cryptic comment: "How high a pitch his resolution soars!" (I. i. 109). Indeed, Gloucester's death can only be avenged with Richard's:

> Oh my dear friends, the fearfull wrath of heaven
> Sitts heavy on our heads for Woodstocks death
> Blood cryes for blood, & that almightie hand
> Permitts not murder unrevenged to stand;[9]

And Bolingbroke's ambition can only be satisfied with the crown. But it is only Richard who can foresee this 'high pitch' of Bolingbroke's resolution. Not even his father, old Gaunt has an inkling of the indirect crooked ways (*2 Henry IV*. IV. v. 185), adopted by his son to attain the crown. In the context of Bolingbroke's resolve, the implorings of the Duchess of Gloucester in the next scene 'to venge my Gloucester's death' (*Richard II*. I. ii. 36), seem superfluous and Gaunt's self-righteousness (I. ii. 4-6) and God-fearing belief in the divine sanction of kingship (I. ii. 37-41) appear out of place. Yet, the very fact that 'the chronicles provide nothing for this scene'[10] is indicative of the value attached to it by Shakespeare. It would not be an exaggeration to say that such extra-historical scenes, more than any other thing, enrich the historical drama of Shakespeare.

In the portrayal of Gaunt, there is clear departure from history.[11] Perhaps, as Dover Wilson maintains, the sympathetic portrayal might have been suggested by Froissart,[12] or as Rossiter argues, it might have been influenced by the portrait of Thomas of Woodstock, Duke of Gloucester, in the annonymous, *Woodstock*.[13] But in either Froissart or *Woodstock,* there is hardly anything of the Divine Right,[14] of which Gaunt is made such an eloquent spokesman in Shakespeare's *Richard II*. In *Woodstock*, Gaunt, along with York, immediately promises revenge to the Duchess of Gloucester:

Goe to our tents deere sister. Cease your sorrows.
We will revenge our noble brother's wrongs,
& force that wanton Tirant to reveale
The death of his deere uncle, harmles Woodstocke,
So trayterously betrayed.[15]

Shakespeare's Gaunt, on the other hand, has nothing to offer but stock Tudor reply to any suggestion of rebellion, so much so that he appears almost inhuman in dismissing the final appeal of the Duchess:

Duch.—Where then, alas, may I complain myself?

Gaunt.—To God; the widow's champion and defence.
(I. ii. 42-43)

The scene must have been introduced, observes Lily Campbell, 'only to restate the Tudor theory of kingship'.[16] However, in the dramatic context, it may mean more. First, the orthodox concept of kingship stated here and later by King Richard and the Bishop of Carlisle, is already exposed to new threats, as revealed by the opening scene. For as stated above, Bolingbroke's is an indirect challenge to the king's authority. Acclaiming the aptness of the first scene, Campbell draws attention to the significance of the king's role as an administrator of justice. 'And it is as God's justicer that Richard first appears'.[17] Apparently yes, but in fact it is Bolingbroke who has already assumed the role of the justicer:

Which blood, like sacrificing Abel's, cries,
Even from the tongueless caverns of the earth,
To me for justice and rough chastisement:
And by the glorious worth of my descent,
This arm shall do it, or this life be spent. (I. i. 104-08)

It is not simply 'incipient arrogance' and 'personal righteousness',[18] but also the hidden political ambition of the speaker, who aims at replacing God's deputy as the justicer. As stated above, Richard is shrewd enough to recognise this: 'How high a pitch....' (I. i. 109). Wilbur Sanders aptly reminds us, "In scripture it was to Jehovah that Abel's blood cried from the ground"[19] and we have seen, Gaunt in I. ii. 43, advises the

Duchess to take her complaint to 'God, the widow's champion'. Is it not as a 'widow's champion' that Bolingbroke appears?

> O, sit my husband's wrongs on Hereford's spear....
>
> Be Mowbray's sins so heavy in his bosom
> That they may break his foaming courser's back
> (I. ii. 47, 50-51)

In the context of the Abel-Cain imagery and of Gaunt's words, to assume the role of 'widow's champion' is to assume God's own prerogative, which only His substitute, that is, the King could do. Later in Act III. Sc. i and again in Act IV. Sc. i Bolingbroke openly assumes the role of the administrator of justice, even though the deposition has not yet taken place. 'Correction lieth in those hands, which made the fault' (I. ii. 4-5), but it is imparted by those hands which are now making the fault.

One may perhaps concede that Gaunt's 'comments need not be taken as Shakespeare's interpretation of history',[20] but they are comments by a 'time-honoured' statesman, by a father,—comments, which take the wind out of his son's claims. And especially Bolingbroke's pride in his lineage—'the glorious worth of my descent' acquires an ironic pinch. On the other hand, in the light of Bolingbroke's ambition and the action already initiated in the opening scene, Gaunt's aphorisms appear as far removed from reality as some of Richard's own remarks later in the play. Yet it would be wrong to consider Gaunt's words as merely "characteristic of a dying old man who speaks bitterly but cannot act".[21] Of course, he is too old to act, but not given to despair, as the Duchess believes he is: "Call it not patience, Gaunt, it is despair" (I. ii. 29). Gaunt is old, but not yet dying and desperate. It is not that brotherhood finds no spur in him, yet if love does not cause any 'living fire' in his blood, it is not owing to his dotage, but rather to his plain belief in God's justice and the Divine Right of the King. Like York in Act V. Sc. 2, he looks upon himself primarily as a loyal subject rather than as a kinsman. He lives in the world of abstract ideas and is not easily touched by the immediate. Note his cool counsel to Bolingbroke in the next scene (I. iii).

But, as L.C. Knights observes, Shakespeare's realism is fundamentally "a refusal to allow the abstract and general to obscure the personal and specific".[22] Gaunt's beliefs are there, but they are put to the stress of experience—'the personal and specific'. The same beliefs which were firm enough to have successfully withstood the shock of brother 'Woodstock's blood' and piteous 'exclaims' of his widow, are already cracking in Act I Sc. iii, when the sentence of banishment—though Gaunt's tongue giving 'a party-verdict' to it and though lessened from ten years to six 'in regard of me'—is pronounced on his son. Suddenly, as it were, he becomes conscious of the anachronisms inherent in the conception of 'God's deputy' as well as in his own thoughts and feelings. To Richard's good humoured (howsoever insincere): "Why, uncle, thou hast many years to live" (I. iii. 225), his reply (I. iii. 226-32), is not simply the bitter complaint of an old man, waiting for his last 'inch of taper' to be burnt. It draws pointed attention to the limitations of the king's authority. Just a moment ago, half-mockingly, half-languishingly, Bolingbroke had remarked:

> How long a time lies in one little word!
> Four lagging winters and four wanton springs
> End in a word—such is the breath of kings. (I. iii. 213-15)

Now, Gaunt reminds us that the breath of Kings is after all earthly. The powers bestowed on God's substitute are not divine. They are human and essentially of a negative nature. They are capable of more harm than good.[23] They may cause death but are themselves powerless before its sting. How far have we travelled from Gaunt's: "God's is the quarrel" and from the orthodox Tudor stand? And why? Because: "Things sweet to taste prove in digestion sour" (I. iii. 236). Under the stress of circumstances, Gaunt is forced to this realisation: the contradiction between taste and digestion, between a judge and a father.

> You urged me as *a judge*, but I had rather
> You would have bid me argue like *a father*.
> (I. iii. 237-38) (Italics Mine)

Gaunt as a judge, a counsellor loyal to the King, has been a party to the banishment of Bolingbroke, but meanwhile the other Gaunt, the unofficial self of him, has woken up. In the previous scene too the Duchess had attempted—unsuccessfully though—to wake up this very unofficial self in him, by urging him as a brother, as a son (I. ii. 22-28). Now, at last, with Bolingbroke's exile, the father in him has been touched and is struggling to throw off the official gown. The same Gaunt who seemed callous and inhuman to the Duchess's implorings is human after all.

In the case of King Richard and that of Bolingbroke a different process is at work. Unlike Gaunt, neither Bolingbroke nor even Richard begins as an honest believer in the Divine Right. In the opening scenes they are both much alike, crafty politicians and dissemblers. As already noted, the personal feelings, which Gaunt tries to exclude from his deliberations on the Divine Right, are, in fact, active in public life.[24] Gaunt is honest enough to acknowledge them at least in Act I. Scenes iii and iv. But though unacknowledged by Richard and Bolingbroke they appear already in the opening scene itself. One may discern them in Richard's insincere affectations as an impartial judge and a righteous ruler:

> Mowbray, impartial are our eyes and ears,
> Were he my brother, nay, my kingdom's heir,
> As he is but my father's brother's son,
> Now by my sceptre's awe I make a vow,
> Such neighbour nearness to our sacred blood
> Should nothing privilege him.... (I. i. 115-20)

The piquant irony implicit in these words could not have escaped the Elizabethan audience, who must have been familiar with *Woodstock*.[25] It was the 'neighbour nearness' to Richard's blood that cost Gloucester his life and it is the same 'neighbour nearness' that makes Bolingbroke a suspect in his eyes. Moreover, even an audience ignorant of the Gloucester affair can hear strong echoes of 'my father's brother's son' in the very next scene, where the Duchess of Gloucester appeals to Gaunt to take revenge in the name of brotherhood. The elaborate family-tree-imagery used by her to describe 'Edward's seven sons' (I. ii. 9-21) serves as an ironic reminder of Richard's words. Even stronger echoes are heard in Act II. Scene i:

Richard—Wert thou not brother to great Edward's son,...
Gaunt—O, spare me not, my brother Edward's son,
For that I was his father Edward's son; (ll. 121, 124-25)

Wilbur Sanders observes that the first scene leaves us with bewildering assortment of contradictory impressions, not only about the Gloucester affair, but also about Richard's ability personally to fill out the dignity of his office, the sincerity of Mowbray's honour or the significance of Bolingbroke's appeals to his 'descent'.[26] Yes, but such contradictory impressions are not confined to the first scene only, they are a part of a large scheme and the central idea to which they are related is that of justice. The figure of justice is like that of Fortune, blind—blind to human relations, totally objective. This is what makes Gaunt relent his role as a judge. But both Bolingbroke and Richard, without acknowledging their personal motives, are bent upon using 'justice' as a tool.

However, the combat scene (I. iii) does give rise to the expectation that impersonal, impartial justice would design the victor's chivalry (I. i. 203). This is one reason, besides the purely theatrical[27] one and the hope of a 'decent interment' of the confusions of the first scene[28] which makes us as eager for the fight as are the two rivals themselves. The 'dancing tattoo of language', as analysed by Mahood,[29] is refreshing and reveals the keen desire of the contenders to go to fight 'as jocund as to jest' (I. iii. 95).

They do not know, however, that there is another kind of jest[30] in store for them. Just as the charge is sounded and the leopards are to spring at each other, the lion intervenes. We share the disappointment of the two combatants who had girt up their loins. "Policy has supervened upon the 'feast of battle'."[31]

That the two antagonists never actually came to blows was a fact of history which Shakespeare could hardly ignore.[32] But, as is well-known, there are two divergent versions of the encounter given by historians: One by Froissart, the other by Hall and Holinshed. While the former gives a detailed account of the reasons behind Richard's action, Hall and Holinshed leave the reason unstated. For some strange reason, Shakespeare follows the second version. That Froissart directly, or indirectly through Daniel, was one of the sources for *Richard II* has been almost conclusively established by a number of scholars.[33] Even if we suppose—a most unlikely supposition—that Hall-Holinshed version was the only one available to Shakespeare, still undoubtedly, while adopting this version, Shakespeare must have been aware of its obvious disadvantages and to circumvent them, he might well have taken the audience into confidence as he so often does,[34] or he might have let the last scene of the Act, where Richard discloses his personal motives, precede the combat-scene. But he does no such thing and apparently seems to relish the ambiguity of the issue. A question naturally arises: "Is the prevention of the combat a sudden whim or a premeditated move?"[35] Since the critics differ so widely in their answers to it, the question remains an enigma like Bolingbroke's usurpation itself. However, most of the critics seem to be in general agreement that the abrupt freezing of the trial by Richard just before blows were struck reflects above all his love for the dramatic, the ceremonial.[36] They also generally agree that Richard's decision to stop the fight and banish the two knights was a political blunder. Craig, for instance, points out that if Mowbray had won, Bolingbroke would have been silenced. If Bolingbroke had won, the King would have been rid of a follower who, he feared, would betray him and he would have been at least no worse off as regards Bolingbroke. In the decision of the council, which Richard had dictated, he follows the one course of conduct that was sure to do injustice to both appellants. Besides, most cruelly and unnaturally, he inflicts the heavier penalty on Mowbray, who had no ulterior motive and had been honest and faithful to Richard.[37] The answer is that Richard was playing safe. As Craig has analysed above, the elimination of either of the appellants, would have been in the interest of the king. But at the same time, one must bear in mind that the victory of Mowbray would have made him more indispensible to the King, while the victory of Bolingbroke would have made him more ambitious and more popular. Richard did not want to take any risks and so at one stroke of the warder, he attempted to kill both the birds. Palmer[38] is perhaps the first critic to attempt a bold defence of Richard's action. The deeper significance of the scene, according to Palmer lies in the fact that "Richard had decided beforehand to quash the proceedings."[39] He even goes on to suggest that the actor who plays Richard should watch the two champions with a 'twinkle', 'impishly' waiting for his moment. The King's decision is no sudden freak of temperament; it is a sudden flash of genius. The flash comes in the middle of the scene with the leave-taking of the two champions. As Peter Ure remarks, "these leave-takings can hardly have been a prescribed part of the trial ritual"[40] and in Holinshed there is just a brief, bald mention of the leave-takings:

> The sundaie before they should fight, after dinner the duke of Hereford came to the King (being lodged about a quarter of a mile without the towne in a tower that belonged to Sir William Bagot) to take his leave of him. The morrow after, being the daie appointed for the combat, about the spring of the daie, came the duke of Norfolke to the court to take leave likewise of the King.[41]

By making the ceremonious leave-takings a part of the tournament, Shakespeare is not using them to enhance the general dramatic excitement, as Peter Ure would have us believe. There is already too much of dramatic excitement to require any more reinforcement. Instead, Shakespeare uses them in subtle manner, just before the two champions are scheduled to meet, to suggest to the King an alternative procedure, i.e. the banishment of both the appellant and the defendant. And, it is precisely with the following words of Bolingbroke:

> For Mowbray and myself are like two men
> That vow a long and weary pilgrimage,
> Then let us take a ceremonious leave,
> And loving farewell of our several friends. (I. iii. 48-51)

that the idea dawns upon King Richard. The metaphor—'a long and weary pilgrimage'—is singularly inapt to convey the idea of the tournament, which is to be short and swift, welcome and sweet.[42] If the metaphor is to suggest the idea of death,[43] only one of the champions—the 'bird' not the 'falcon'—would be making this pilgrimage. The metaphor acquires some significance only in the light of the later events. "Bolingbroke's figure carries a suggestion of future events of which he is unconscious", says Craig.[44] But the suggestion is meant not only for the audience, it is a suggestion for the characters as well and Richard is shrewd enough to grasp it. Such a course to send both Mowbray and Bolingbroke on a 'long and weary', never-to-return pilgrimage, would suit exactly his political end to be free at once of a foe as well as a friend, whose services in the past could never be adequately rewarded.

Justice is not allowed to take its course, through 'God or Fortune', nor is the *widow's champion* allowed to administer 'justice and rough chastisement'. Richard has regained his royal prerogative as Justicer and is also able to combine it with the role of a peace-maker, in which he had earlier failed. Indeed, as Peter Ure remarks:

> Richard's sudden regaining of the initiative and the submissions which follow it, can be seen as a ruler's stroke: it deflates the quarrelling magnates, and is explicitly justified by that highest of all Elizabethan arguments, the avoidence of civil tumult.[45]

But, in fact, in the name of peace and mercy, the justice that is given is a political compromise. Richard has nearly succeeded in imposing his personal motives on justice. And this is what lies behind his rhetoric on peace, which clearly reflects his insincerity and lack of genuine feeling.[46] We have a sense of what Wilbur Sanders calls 'rhetorical resplendence' masking some 'obscure malady'.[47] After Mowbray has reproached the 'man' Richard:

> A heavy sentence, my most sovereign liege,
> And all unlook'd for from your Highness' mouth.
> A dearer merit, nor so deep a main
> As to be cast forth in the common air,
> Have I deserved at your Higness' hands....
>
> Within my mouth you have engaoled my *tongue*,....

What is thy sentence, then, but speechless death,
Which robs my tongue from breathing native breath?
(I. iii. 154-58, 166, 172-73)

the 'rhetorical resplendence' and the facade of peace give way, and the obscure malady comes to the surface. It is Richard's personal fear, for, as if reminded of the potential danger from Mowbray's *tongue*, in a panic, he extracts from the two banished knights 'an oath of perpetual enmity'[48] (I. iii. 183-90). Similarly the facade of mercy gives way in the next scene. He had been observing Bolingbroke's 'courtship to the common people' and through it his political ambition. He has also observed with some distress Aumerle's behaviour at the time and has his doubts about the latter's loyalty. As such, at the sight of Aumerle, he abruptly changes the topic and, with a touch of irony, enquires:

We did observe. Cousin Aumerle,
How far brought you *high* Hereford on his way?...
And say, what store of parting tears were shed?
(I. iv. 1-2, 5)

It is only when Aumerle declares his loyalty in unequivocal terms, by expressing a desire for adding years to Bolingbroke's banishment (11-19), that Richard opens his mind:

He is our cousin, cousin;[49] but 'tis doubt,
When time shall call him home from banishment, (ll. 21-22)

Confident of Aumerle's loyalty, he goes on with the interrupted conversation:

Ourself, and Bushy, Bagot here, and Green,
Observ'd his courtship to the common people;
(ll. 23 ff.)

"It reveals", Lily Campbell aptly remarks, "jealousy masking as justice, and trickery as mercy."[50] In other words, Shakespeare lets us have a peep at the inner springs of the actions, the human motives lying behind political decisions, at "an offending gap between the public and the private character".[51] The personal and specific refuse to be subdued by the general and abstract.[52] As noted above, Shakespeare does not allow even his 'prophet new inspired' (i.e. Gaunt, II. i. 31) to be above the personal and specific. Strange as it is, the famous patriotic speech of Gaunt, containing the oft quoted lines (II. i. 40 ff.), is meant not for the ears of Richard, but for those of York[53]—and this, when only a moment ago, he has himself stated: "Where words are scarce they are seldom spent in vain" (II. i. 7). What follows on Richard's arrival is more a vent to personal grievances than to public wrongs. There is a beautiful but rather out-of-place use of pun by the man on his death bed, "Old Gaunt indeed, and gaunt in being old" (II. i. 74). Throughout the exchange between Gaunt and Richard it is the personal motif which keeps recurring (II. i. 73-146). To take Gaunt at his words, he is determined to breathe his last in wholesome counsel (II. i. 1-2), though Richard has ignored his 'life's counsel' (II. i. 15), for he hopes that "his death's sad tale may yet undeaf his ear"[54] (l. 16). However, his actual words to Richard bring out the private bitterness of a father, denied the pleasure of his son's looks, the apprehensions of a patriarch regarding his lineage much more forcefully than the public grievance of letting 'this land by lease' (l. 110). Any one can see that the specific charge of leases is more prominent and pointed in the patriotic speech which ends before the arrival of Richard:

> Like to a tenement or pelting form (l. 60)
> With inky blots and rotten parchment bonds. (l. 64)

Richard Simpson relates the charges to "a fiscal oppression and mismanagement which specially pressed upon the poet," and reminds us that Shakespeare's father was a recusant in 1592.[55] Marriott, on the other hand, relates them to the incidents in the anonymous *Woodstock*.[56] In either case, it would appear that the playwright is swayed by extra-dramatic considerations.

It must be admitted that compared with Richard's mind, Bolingbroke's mind and motives are not fully revealed. He maintains a tacit silence over the question of the divinity of the crown.[57] Yet one cannot help agreeing with Coleridge[58] and Hazlitt[59] regarding Bolingbroke's design. "Our uncertainty about his real motives", says Wilbur Sanders, "dates from the very first hint of his return from banishment (II. i. 224 ff.)".[60] In fact, it is precisely from this very point that we become more and more certain about Bolingbroke's purpose. Unlike the sources, Shakespeare does not give any hint that emissaries were sent on behalf of the nobles to Bolingbroke. Instead we are told straightway that Bolingbroke, with eight tall ships and three thousand men of war is near "our northern shore" (II. i. 288). Bolingbroke is "his own carver", cutting out his way (II. iii. 144). It is true that Northumberland offers Ross and Willoughby various inducements to join Bolinghroke:

> If then we shall shake off our slavish yoke,
> Imp out our drooping country's broken wing,
> Redeem from broking pawn the blemish'd crown,
> Wipe off the dust that hides our sceptre's gilt,
> And make high majesty look like itself,
> Away with me...." (II. i. 291 ff.)

Yet it would be wrong to say that "we are in no position to know upon which of these grievances the lords are acting".[61] Indeed, they are acting upon none of these, they are acting rather to forestall "the storm" (l. 264), to save their own skin: "our lives, our children, and our heirs" (l. 245). It is the same scene in which only a few minutes earlier Richard has announced the seizure of Gaunt's estate, against the established norms of feudal rights. Within the space of some twenty odd lines, Shakespeare lets us see York's prophetic warning (ll. 201-06) taking shape. Perhaps, Northumberland, Ross and Willoughby might not deserve the epithet 'well-disposed hearts'; nevertheless, they are goaded into opposition by Richard's wilful act against Time, which engenders in them a sense of personal insecurity. It is clear that these rebel Lords look upon Bolingbroke as their 'hope'[62]: "Even through the hollow eyes of death/I spy life peering",... (ll. 270-71). It is significant to note that just a few lines later Northumberland informs us that Bolingbroke and his forces are waiting only for the departure of Richard for Ireland (II. i. 289). To miss this is to take Bolingbroke and his lieutenant Northumberland at their words that he (Bolingbroke) has come 'but for his own' (III. iii. 196 and II. iii. 148-49). True, as F.P. Wilson[63] points out, Bolingbroke announces his intention of accepting the crown only after it is offered to him by Richard, but this only reveals the consummate machiavel that he is. As such it would certainly be an error to imagine that

"Shakespeare represents him as initially loyal."[64] It is not Shakespeare, but Bolingbroke the skilled actor who represents himself as initially loyal. He "infringes the order of exile", remarks the Italian critic, Alessandro Manzoni, "and returns to England on the pretext of claiming the inheritence which has been taken away from him by an illegal act".[65] The denial of his rights (as Bolingbroke argues with York, II. iii. 113 ff.) does not cause his return. It simply provides him with the much needed excuse for his return. And on his return, while he already acts as a King and while his adherents too behave towards him as if he really were so, he still continues to give out that he has come with an armed band merely to demand his birthright.[66]

Thus, whatever ambiguity (if the term must be used) there appears to be in Bolingbroke's conduct, it is there not because his plans and purposes are wholly withheld from us[67] nor because of "his creator's irresolution",[68] nor even "because ambiguity is for him an instrument of policy",[69] but because of the contradictions between the real and the ostensible in him. For the prospective usurper, not ambiguity, but affectations of loyalty and deliberate concealment of the real motive are the instruments of policy. Bolingbroke's purposes are clear enough to himself, to his close supporters, and to Richard. His is not "the somnambulist powerlust of a Macbeth",[70] and although he does not make any declarations of policy, not even in a soliloquy,[71] scattered hints regarding his purposes are not lacking.

The hope-image, already noted, reappears in Act II. Sc. iii. when we first meet Bolingbroke on his return and is here linked with the sugar imagery. Northumberland, delivers a classic speech of sycophancy, woven with the two threads of sweetness and hope (II. iii. 4-16). The speech ending with a general statement of truth, "And hope to joy is little less in joy/Than hope enjoyed", depicts the rebels' state of mind in general. The hope cherished by Northumberland and company feeds upon the 'sugar' of Bolingbroke, who offers the sweet recipe generously in terms of his fortune and the reward of his accomplices:

> And as my fortune ripens with thy love,
> It shall be still thy true love's recompense.
>
> (II. iii. 48-49)

all my treasury
Is yet but unfelt thanks, which more enriched
Shall be your love and labour's recompense.
(II. iii. 60-62)

Evermore thanks the exchequer of the poor,
Which till my infant fortune comes to years,
Stands for my bounty. (II. iii. 65-67)

It would be absurd to imagine all this if Bolingbroke has not been looking forward to anything beyond 'his own'. What lies at the bottom of such sugar-coated expressions is clearly the tacit assumption of the entire group that Bolingbroke has come to wrest the sceptre and the crown from Richard. Besides, it is unthinkable that while using the word 'fortune'. Shakespeare did not have in mind the wheel of Fortune,[72] which Bolingbroke is shown as mounting at the moment.

The full significance of the hope-sweetness-fortune association is brought home to us in an angry recollection of the Berkeley Castle meeting by the temperamental Hotspur:

Why, what *a candy deal of courtesy*
This fawning greyhound then did proffer me!
Look "when his infant *fortune* came to age"
And "gentle Harry Percy," and "kind cousin"
O, the devil take such cozeners; God forgive me!
(*1. H. IV.* I. iii. 249-53) (Italics Mine)

Cozeners—echoes the Queen's words *cozening Hope* (*R II.* II. ii. 69), *false Hope* (*R II.* II. ii. 72) and the remorseful disillusionment of Hotspur, the late realisation of having been tricked by the calculated usurper, adds a tinge of dramatic irony to the word *beguiled* used by Northumberland in his flaterring speech referred to above.

Palmer who would have us believe that in Bolingbroke "instinctive premeditation is reconciled with an equally instinctive yielding to circumstance", quotes the retrospective words of the dying King (2 *Henry IV.* III. i. 72-74) as final evidence and observes:

He looks back over the troubled years of his reign and, though pregnantly conscious of the 'indirect crook'd

> ways', whereby he had achieved the crown, he nevertheless meditates on the blindness with which he once pursued his infant fortune, and goes on to state explicitly that he had acted throughout undesignedly, as a man thrust on by force of circumstance.[73]

It is interesting to note how in the above analysis, the critic waters down (though pregnantly conscious of the 'indirect crook'd ways') the contrary evidence:

> God knows, my son,
> By what by-paths and indirect crook'd ways
> I met this crown; (*2 H. IV.* IV. v. 184-86)

As a matter of fact, there should hardly be any doubt as to which of the two statements carry greater weight as regards the speaker's past motives. The first speech spoken to the courtiers is a public utterance and a further extension of the diplomatic pretentiousness of Bolingbroke. On the other hand, the second meant only for Prince Hall, is a private confession. Here, if anywhere we might expect Bolingbroke to bare his bosom.

Such implicit indications of Bolingbroke's real purpose, as witnessed in the beginning of Act. II. Sc. iii. are naturally followed by diplomatic pleadings of 'but for his own'. But before the scene ends, Bolingbroke is shown quite explicitly as taking over the royal prerogative:

> Bushy, Bagot, and their complices,
> The caterpillars of the commonwealth,
> Which I have sworn to weed and pluck away,
> (II. iii. 165-67)

The self-proclaimed administrator of justice is back again. When we analyse the caterpillar-weed-plucking imagery in the light of the Garden-scene,[74] it becomes clear that on the allegorical plane at least the determination of the speaker amounts to deposing the gardener-king. When we next meet Bolingbroke, we find him translating his words to action: "Bring forth these men..." (III. i. 1). As pointed out by Reese, the execution of Bushy and Green marks the assumption of sovereignty by Bolingbroke.[75]

It is not surprising, therefore, that the trial of these men bears close resemblance to the Deposition-scene (IV. i.), which is in effect the trial of King Richard. While despatching his enemies, Bolingbroke must attempt a public justification of the action:

> Yet to wash your blood
> From off my hands, here in the view of men,
> I will unfold some causes of your deaths:
>
> (III. i. 5-7)

'The causes of your deaths'—genuine or otherwise—[76] must be publicised, just as the causes of Richard's deposition. Note Northumberland's insistence that Richard must read the cooked up list of his own crimes (IV. i. 223-28). The commons must be satisfied (l. 272)—the commons, not God, nor conscience, nor law.[77] The noble Brutus, too, as shown by Brents Stirling[78] and Adrian Bonjour,[79] is deeply concerned with public opinion. But in an ardent Republican such concern is inevitable and conscientious; in Bolingbroke, on the other hand, "wooing poor craftsmen with the craft of smiles" (I. iv. 28) and leaning heavily on 'men's opinions' (III. i. 26) for personal aggrandisement, are sheer calculated policy. Hence, the irony of the Pilate-image. Bolingbroke, who initially appears as the defender of justice, the 'widow's champion', as Christ himself, turns out to be the executioner of Christ. But, in the Scripture, Pilate allows a mockery of justice by letting himself become an instrument of the public opinion. Bolingbroke and his complices on the other hand, make the public opinion an instrument, while meting out the 'justice' of their taste. The image boomerangs against Bolingbroke with all these ironic implications in the deposition-scene, where Richard makes a forceful use of the Christ-Pilate imagery:

> Though some of you, with Pilate, wash your hands,
> Showing an outward pity; yet you Pilates
> Have here deliver'd me to my sour cross,
> And water cannot wash away your sin. (IV. i. 239-42)

But this is not all. The image dogs Bolingbroke to the very end of the play,[80] where as more public washing of his hand, he declares:

I'll make a voyage to the Holy Land,
To wash this blood from my guilty hand: (V. vi. 49-50)

He still believes in 'expiation on the public level',[81] the washing away of guilt with water—an impossible proposition, but the logical culmination of the off-going-of-his-bonnet to an oyster-wench (I. iv. 31). The sham submissiveness, the hiatus that exists between the heart and the knee of the man, between love and formal courtesy:

York.—Show me thy humble *heart*, and not thy *knee*,
(II. iii. 83)

Richard.—Fair cousin, you debase your princely *knee*,
To make the base earth proud with kissing it:
Me rather had my heart might feel your *love*,
Than my unpleased eye see your *courtesy:*
Up, cousin, up; your *heart* is up, I know,
[Touching his own head] Thus high at least,
although your *knee* be low.
(III. iii. 190-195) *(Italics Mine)*

naturally culminates in sham remorse and ostentious religiosity.

When Richard is looked upon as an actor,[82] it is often forgotten that Bolingbroke too is an actor and a more skilled one at that. The stage image, as referred to by Ludowyk and others,[83] does have its relevance, but more than Richard, it is Bolingbroke who has been play-acting. On the symbolic plane the deposition of Richard, the actor, accompanies the deposition of Richard, the King. That both Richard and Bolingbroke are actors and the latter is the better of the two is apparent from the following words of York:

As in a theatre the eyes of men,
After a well-graced actor leaves the stage,
Are idly bent on him that enters next,
Thinking his prattle to be tedious; (V. ii. 23-26)

The ambiguity and the lack of design that so many critics discern in Bolingbroke are a measure of the success of the well-graced actor. In fact, as Dean has pointed out, the propensity for self-dramatisation shared by both Richard and Bolingbroke reflects 'the theatricalism of politics', but whereas for the former the staging of scenes becomes a deeply personal necessity, for the latter it is a purely political device.[84]

As examined above, Richard appears as a crafty politician like Bolingbroke himself in the first Act of the play. Thus, far he shares self-dramatisation, thus far he uses it as a political device—not beyond. Already in the second Act, when he goes to visit Gaunt at his death-bed, he is unable to sustain his pretentious role as the impartial judge, the preserver of peace, the sympathising kinsman (II. i. 115 ff.). When we next meet him, we find him fondling the earth on his return from Ireland (III. ii. 4-26). It may be granted that the speaker is self-conscious,[85] but the emotions are genuine. There is hardly any ground to suspect acting, especially when we remember the company that is, Aumerle and the Bishop of Carlisle, the two most loyal supporters. Palmer links the speech rightly with other expressions of the patriotic sentiment like Mowbray's lament over his exile and Gaunt's declaration of his love for England, incorporating the 'chorus-theme'[86] in the play. Despite this remark, however, Palmer goes on to analyse what he, in conformity with conventional criticism, calls Richard's self-dramatisation of his tragedy.[87] And this self-dramatisation, according to Palmer, begins precisely at this very point: Richard's return from Ireland—"history pauses and tragedy takes the stage".[88] In fact, history does not pause, but as always with Shakespeare, it is humanised. Tragedy does take the stage, but that is because history takes a tragic turn and that not suddenly.

In his analysis of the play's structure, Peter Ure also recognises a fresh beginning from Act III. Scene ii and labels the phase from this point to Act V. Scene i as Richard's passion.[89] Sen Gupta, on the other hand, looking at it from the point of view of Richard's character, holds that 'here is a sea-change in his attitude to life' after his return from Ireland.[90] It would be nearer truth to say that there is a sea-change in the fortune of Richard and that this inevitably affects his whole attitude. At the time of leaving for the Irish campaign, Richard was at the top of the forture's wheel (*regno*), after his return he finds himself almost at the bottom (*regnavi*). And, as Manzoni observes, it is here

> that the character of this king begins to assume a development so natural and so unexpected. The spectator had already made the acquaintance of this astounding personality and flattered himself that he had fathomed it; but there was in it something secret and profound which had not appeared at all in prosperity and which adversity alone could elicit.[91]

The development is at the same time natural and unexpected, for the ingredients lay hidden there from the first. Richard has been, like Gaunt, a believer in the Divine Right of Kings and this belief when "accompanied by power, showed itself by levity, by impatience with every obstacle, by a thoughtlessness which did not permit it even to suspect that all human power has its judges and its limits".[92] This is evident especially in his treatment of Gaunt and in the emphasis on 'royal' in the speech referred to above in another context.[93] Facing contrary winds on his return, he still holds on to this quasi-religious belief:

> This earth shall have a feeling, and these stones
> Prove armed soldiers, ere her native king
> Shall falter under foul rebellion's arms (III. ii. 24-26)
>
> Not all the water in the rough rude sea
> Can wash the balm off from an anointed king.
> The breath of worldly men cannot depose
> The deputy elected by the Lord, (ll. 54-57)

To dismiss such sentiments simply as 'the jargon of politics' that he, a political amateur, has picked up[94] would not do. Alfred Hart reminds us that the ascription to Richard II as to John, or any of their nobles of a belief in the doctrine of Divine Right of Kings is historically false.[95] The belief was Tudor and the words that Shakespeare puts into the mouth of Richard, the last of the Plantagenets, would not have sounded 'childish'[96] to Elizabethan ears. Shakespeare makes his Richard a plain believer in the doctrine, notwithstanding his vacillations.[97] To have a faith does not preclude the possibility of having a doubt, for, as Peter Ure rightly observes, all faiths are at times held with 'sublime confidence' but at other times have to struggle with facts which seem to contradict them.[98] The alternating moods' of Richard discredit the view that he has been play-acting and reveal the essential Richard. Certainly Richard's convictions are badly out of touch with the political realities—and therein lies the tragic irony—for Shakespeare has already shown us Bolingbroke as the King in the scene just preceding (III. i.) and is about to show Richard as conceding defeat and deposition in the scene just following (III. iii.). As Shakespeare presents it: "The sense of 'divine right' in kings is found to act not so much as a secret of power over others, as of infatuation to themselves."[99] The fact, however, remains that for Richard Divine Right is a passionate faith and it is the loss of this faith more than the political deposition by Bolingbroke which Shakespeare has placed at the centre of Richard's tragedy. To label his deep personal faith as "an all-too-empty trust in Heaven's help for an anointed King", and his subsequent suffering as an "all-too-easy despair"[100] is to miss the deep pathos of the play. The French actor-teacher-critic, Jean-Louis Barrault declared, in the course of a lecture delivered at the Edinburgh festival in 1948 that Shakespeare introduced a new Renaissance hero. "Shakespeare communicates to us", he said,

> the experiences of this hero, and with him we see that paradise has once again been lost and with it faith. Everything is again put into question; men have to endure the test of doubt and live through the drama of belief....[101]

And the heroes specifically put under this category by Barrault are Richard II, Henry VI and Hamlet. In the case of Richard, the highly emphatic reiteration of his faith (Not *all* the water in the rough rude Sea/can wash the balm from an anointed king,) just before its loss, adds to the pathos[102] of his predicament.

Alfred Hart observes that Shakespeare's 'anointed' kings are invariably described as 'sacrosanct and above the law,' yet his wise princes get what obedience they can and know that they will be obeyed only as long as they keep a firm grip on their royal power.[103] (But surely no other king displays such strong belief in his sacrosanctity as does Richard.) Richard, on the other hand, is 'mesmerised' by the bare name of king, and the authority which he should have commanded by force of character, is made over to this name.[104] This is so because he really believes in the name as the faithful believe in God. As God's deputy he even identifies himself with Christ.

Critics have rightly drawn attention to two contradictory traditions regarding Richard's character—Lancastrian and French.[105] While the former found in Hall, Holinshed and *Woodstock*, represents him as foolish, weak, cowardly and moody, the latter, found in Froissart, Daniel, *Traison* and Creton, is sympathetic and presents him in a much better light. The last two named[106] even exalt Richard to the stature of a martyr-king and compare his passion to that of Christ Himself. Bullough opines that in the first half of the play, i.e. upto the second Act, Shakespeare presents the Lancastrian image of Richard and after that the French.[107] The theory is fascinating, though it is also a fantastic oversimplification. Shakespeare does not present his characters in piecemeal. In fact, as Black has pointed out, while inclining to none of the traditions, Shakespeare could reconcile them by portraying Richard as a man, a complex and unusual sort of man, yet completely believable in his kind. "The feat of maintaining the king as a consistent human being while transforming him from a wasteful and tyrannous abuser of power into something near to a martyr is a profound imaginative triumph."[108] As noted above, for the idea itself Shakespeare was indebted to his sources, but he could achieve the extraordinary feat of reconciling contrary impressions only through the breadth of his vision and the touch of his poetry.

Richard II is the most poetic of Shakespeare's History Plays. It is a commonplace of criticism to explain the poetic style of the play in terms of Richard's character and to explain his tragedy in terms of his poetry.[109] The play has, it is said, ornate lyricism because its central character, Richard himself is a poet. And because he is a poet, he lives in a fanciful world of words, divorced from reality, hence his fall. This is a simplification which prevents us from appreciating the play fully. As Madeleine Doran observes, *Richard II* demonstrates 'the perfection of union between character and style which Shakespeare had mastered at that stage of his career'.[110] But the poetry which comes out of the mouth of Richard not only reflects his character, it is also welded to the dramatic need. It is palpably wrong to say that in Richard's portrayal subject and treatment are never fully equated, 'the emotion portrayed has no full formal equivalent'.[111] That it is not so would become apparent if, rather than accepting the usual explanation for Richard's tragedy in terms of his poetry; we try to explain his poetry in terms of his tragedy. To say that Richard luxuriates in feeling, that he is 'gluttonous of emotions',[112] is to undermine his tragedy. No, 'Richard does not bleed in sport'.[113] His best speeches are recited only when he suffers most. His sweetest songs are made out of the saddest thoughts. (A parallel may be drawn with the poetic speeches of Gaunt.) He does not poetise his grief, he cannot, for the grief is too real and too deep for that. To those like Bolingbroke, not believing in the sanctity of the royal breath, it might appear as 'the shadow of your sorrow' (IV. i. 292), but to the suffering soul, 'the grief lies all within' (IV. i. 295), it cannot be given full expression. The emergence of the poet in Richard in Act III. Sc. ii has baffled critics. "How this poetical fantast", complains Sen Gupta, "lay concealed behind the arrogant wastrel of the first two Acts has not been represented in course of the action."[114] He considers this the only enigma about Richard's character and the greatest defect of the drama.[115] But there is a poet hidden in every human breast, awaiting an emotional surcharge. William Bodham Donne had discerned in Richard "a noble kingly nature, awaiting only the purification of sorow to resume its original lustre".[116] When we think of Richard's image in the first two Acts of the play, we hardly find anything to substantiate 'a noble kingly nature' and its 'original lustre', rather we feel inclined to accept Sen Gupta's epithet 'arrogant wastrel'. But the same arrogant wastrel, when 'plume plucked', undergoes 'the purification of sorrow' and becomes a poet. In the process, he also becomes noble and lovable. It is the alloy of sorrow that transforms him into 'the vessel of porcelain'.[117] Ironical though it might appear, it is only by recognising himself as 'the vessel of clay' that Richard is to become 'the vessel of porcelain'. At the crucial moment of his disillusionment with the Divine Right,

Richard realises the hollowness of the crown and utters the philosophy which underlies all the Histories of Shakespeare.[118] On the stage of history, a king is only like an ordinary actor allowed a little time to monarchise. He is after all 'flesh and blood', subject to the same human wants and sentiments as you and I (III. ii. 160-77). "Every man wears but his own skin; the Players are all alike", says Walter Raleigh.[119] It is thus that Shakespeare universalises the tragedy of Richard. "The full shock of political disaster compels Richard", observes Winny, "to acknowledge the emptiness of his grand identity, and to fall back towards the simply human character whose development he has ignored."[120] And the same Richard, the most eloquent spokesman of absolute monarchy and Divine Right, becomes their strongest critic. He has himself realised the hollowness of 'self and vain conceits'. On the spiritual plane, the painful realisation brings about the regeneration of Richard, the man; on the political it comes too late to ensure the regeneration of Richard, the King. Hence, the tragic predicament, the pathetic consciousness of the impending tragedy and of his inability to avoid it. "Oh, hadst thou ever been a king", cries Edward II in a similar situation,

> thy heart
> Pierced deeply with sense of my distress,
> Could not but take compassion of my state;
> Stately and proud, in riches and in train,
> Whilom I was, powerful, and full of pomp.
> But what is he whom rule and empiry
> Have not in life or death made miserable?[121]

In the next scene, when the humble Bolingbroke's ('on both his knees', III. iii. 31) proud emissary, Northumberland, fails to kneel to Richard, as earlier he had failed to use the prefix King to Richard's name, he is sharply pulled up for the lapse (III. iii. 72-88). As Sanders says, now already ceasing to be king, Richard presents for the first time a fully-formed royalty of demeanour and utterance.[122] But after the powerful I-live-with-bread-speech, all utterance, all demeanour, howsoever impressive would be facile. It is not suprising, therefore, that the short encounter which begins with sharp admonition, ironically ends with a submissive pleading.

> With all the gracious utterance thou hast,
> Speak to his gentle hearing kind commends.
>
> (III. iii. 125-26)

The truth is that here, if anywhere in the second half of the play, Richard has been indulging in self-conscious acting. He confesses to Aumerle, immediately on Northumberland's departure:

> We do debase ourselves, cousin, do we not,
> To look so poorly, and to speak so fair? (III. iii. 127-28)

But the kind of sustained acting demanded by the situation and prescribed by Aumerle, "let's fight with gentle words" till a more opportune time (III. iii. 131-32), is typical, not of Richard, but of Bolingbroke. What follows, therefore, is abject surrender to his grief, which makes him half insane and reminds one of Lear. The view commonly held that Richard luxuriates in grief[123] does grave injustice to his character as well as to the play. Shakespeare himself provides the real explanation of the subsequent pathetic poetry uttered by Richard, and this through the words of his most unfeeling enemy, Northumberland:

> Sorrow and grief of heart
> Makes him speak fondly, like a frantic man.
>
> (III. iii. 184-85)

Richard knows plainly enough that he has already lost his kingdom, 'barren and bereft' as he is and though legally still the king, is virtually Bolingbroke's captive.[124] The only thought that now lurks in his mind is whether he would be allowed to die a natural death:

> Most mighty prince, my Lord Northumberland,
> What says *King Bolingbroke*? Will his majesty
> Give Richard leave to live till Richard die?
>
> (III. iii. 172-74)

This is also suggested by the abundance of death images in almost all his speeches in the previous scene.[125] He is in so desperate a state that the only desire, apart from preservation of life, he cherishes is the very human, though essentially childish, desire to have the thing over as quickly as possible, lest the agony is prolonged:[126]

> What you will have, I'll give and willing too,
> For do we must, what force will have us do...
> Set on towards London, cousin, is it so? (III. iii. 206-08)

According to Brents Stirling,[127] thus Richard himself prompts in Bolingbroke the decisive action of deposition, as his later words: "Whither you will, so I were from your sights" (IV. i. 315) prompt the commital to the Tower and the subsequent murder. And Sanders thinks that this substantiates his thesis that Richard is a 'murderee'.[128]

No, Richard's words do not prompt any decision in Bolingbroke's mind. The latter is already decided and does not require any promptings for taking a decision and Richard, who can look through his pretences (How high a pitch his resolution soars! (I. i. 109) 'up cousin up' (III. iii. 194), knows this only too well. His words, therefore, only precipitate the action. He is not a 'murderee'. His predicament is comparable to that of the lamb being drawn to the slaughter house. He can foresee the events as clearly as Bolingbroke has designed. He is the 'wise man' who can see through the schemes of the 'empty man'.[129] If the axe has to fall, would it not be better if it falls sooner? Why prolong the suffering?

The deposition remains a mere formality, but Shakespeare creates a great scene out of it. Before presenting the deposition, he introduces a number of events and situations, which by their implicit as well as explicit critique, enrich the central act of deposition and transfer of power. Such, for instance, is the Garden Scene (III. iv.). In Act IV. Scene i itself where the deposition is staged, Shakespeare allows it to be preceded by the challenge-scene and Carlisle's protest. In the chronicles both the events take place long after the deposition.[130] The challenges with which the scene opens, throw further light on the *de facto* sovereignty of Bolingbroke.[131] Indeed, he even adopts the royal form of address:

When he's return'd,
Against Aumerle *we* will enforce his trial.
(IV. i. 89-90)

Your differences shall all rest under gage,
Till *we* assign you to your days of trial.
(IV. i. 105-06)

Lords, you that here are under *our* arrest,
Procure your sureties for your days of answer.

Little are *we* beholding to your love,
And little looked for at your helping hands.
(IV. i. 158-61) (Italics Mine)

The challenge episode is often seen as a replica of the challenges between Mowbray and Bolingbroke, with which the play opens. "Bolingbroke", says Palmer, "is dealing masterfully with precisely the same political situation which confronted Richard at the beginning of the play."[132] But the similarity between the two situations is only skin-deep. While in Act I. Sc. i the appeal was directed against the king, here the charges are levelled at the instigation of the King-to-be. In both cases, the real target is the same person, Richard, but the situation is completely changed. In the first case, he was holding the strings of justice in his hands, here the strings of justice are closing round him. Dover Wilson points out that one of the purposes of the scene here is "to re-introuduce the issue of Gloucester's death, for his part in which Richard was being justly punished".[133] In fact, it is Bolingbroke's purpose to give a colour of justice to the forthcoming deposition of Richard by recalling the Gloucester-event and in the opening speech itself Bolingbroke lays the charge overtly at Richard's door:

Now, Bagot, freely speak thy mind,
What thou dost know of noble Gloucester's death,
Who wrought it with the king, and who performed
The bloody office of his timeless end. (IV. i. 2-5)

Bagot has apparently made his peace with the usurper. This initially makes us suspect his motives in accusing Aumerle a suspicion which is confirmed when we hear Fitzwater, the other accuser profess:[134]

As I intend to thrive in *this new world*,
Aumerle is guilty of my true appeal.
(IV. i. 78-79) (Italics Mine)

Personal motive comes more clearly to the surface than it did in Mowbray-Bolingbroke conflict, but since the setting is the same—Medieval tournament and knightly honour—by retrospect it also becomes a comment on the first challenges.

Bolingbroke's large gesture of justice and good will even to his old enemy Mowbray—

Repealed he shall be,
And, though mine enemy, restored again
To all his lands and signories:.... (IV. i. 87-89)

further reveals the theatrical nature of the scene, for Mowbray is already dead and as Kreyssig notes, Bolingbroke himself also knows it.[135] In Holinshed, Mowbray is not yet dead, but dies during the course of the year at Venice.[136] In such a made-up atmosphere of theatrical justice and histrionic emotions, Carlisle's protest (ll. 114 ff.) is singularly out of place[137] and hence the more impressive. By deliberately changing the order, Shakespeare has made it the "dramatic prelude to the 'Deposition'".[138] It is tempting to consider the speech as incorporating the moral of the play[139] but Carlisle's warning to Bolingbroke and his accomplices is too simple to be taken for an editorial comment. Like Richard's claim to Divine Right, it characterises the speaker without illuminating Shakespeare's private opinions.[140] As far as it reflects the speaker, it shows him—to borrow the words of Dr. Johnson—"as brave, pious, and venerable".[141] But the fact that Carlisle is too minor a character to be given such a long and significant speech for just self-portrayal (and that too when we are approaching the climax of the play), should make it apparent that the speech has some other purpose as well. While it is prophetic of future events,[142] it also causes a 'moral stimulus'[143] in the audience at the proper juncture. If one can explain the execution of Bushy and Green (III. i) in terms of the weeding away in the commonwealth-garden (III. iv), one cannot explain the arrest of Carlisle in the same manner.

It is only after such oblique comments that Shakespeare allows us a glimpse of the actual Deposition. In Holinshed,

Deposition, publishing of judgment and coronation (which takes place a fortnight after the Deposition) are three separate events. Shakespeare in combining the three, not only telescopes and avoids triplication, but also draws pointed attention simultaneously to Richard's political fall and to the wrong done by Bolingbroke. In Carlisle's speech there is a highly suggestive echo, *thieves* (l. 123), of Richard's words:

> That when the searching eye of heaven is hid,
> Behind the globe, that lights the lower world,
> Then *thieves and robgers* range abroad unseen.
>
> (III. ii. 37-39) (Italics Mine)

As Palmer observes, Bolingbroke is cautious[144] and concedes to Carlisle's objection to the extent that Richard will not be tried in absentia. But who is the thief, Richard or Bolingbroke? And as the sun-image ('the searching eye of heaven') implies not only the king, but also God,[145] we are left morally disturbed as regards the question of justice. Though condemned as weak and as being his own deposer, Richard brings during the trial, serious allegations against his persecutors, both explicitly and implicitly. Sanders has rightly drawn attention to the 'symbolic revenge', in the subtle manner in which he "exposes Bolingbroke's discreet campaign as a one man's brazen attempt to wrest a golden bauble from the grasp of another"[146] through:

> Here, cousin, seize the crown:
> Here, cousin,
> On this side my hand, and on that side, thine....
>
> (IV. i. 181-83)

This is followed by a reminder of the unpredictability of Fortune's wheel, through the imagery of the buckets: one hanging in the air, the other deep down the well. (IV. i. 184-89). The image grows very naturally, as Clemen notes, out of the actual scene on the stage.[147] "This image", says he, "marks the climax of the scene, but at the same time it sums up the whole substance of the play: the tragedy of kingship which demands that the parting king must wane in the same proportion as the new king waxes."[148] Thus, it implies a fair warning to the new king who presently in the state of *regno* (ruling) on Fortnue's wheel, would tomorrow reach the state of *sum sine regno* (cast off) like Richard himself. Bolingbroke, however, with his eyes fixed on the crown, is not in a position to take the hint and it is striking that in the subsequent exchange, all his single line speeches harp on the same string: Richard's resignation of the crown.[149]

Finally, as Richard proceeds to resign—simultaneously to depose himself and to crown Bolingbroke—he makes a mockery of the new king's coronation (IV. i. 4 ff.), for as Walter Pater remarks, "It is as if Shakespeare had in mind some...*inverted rite*."[150] Pater looks at it as a long, 'agonising ceremony'—a ceremony that adds 'the last touch of unkindness to human justice'. While it is an agonising ceremony for Richard, no doubt it is also a mocking ceremony for Bolingbroke. In an attempt to substantiate his thesis that *Richard II* depicts the Medieval way of life, Tillyard remarks, "we are in fact in a world where means matter more than ends, where it is more important to keep strict to the rules of an elaborate game than either to win or to lose it".[151] In no world can one be indifferent to victory or loss. The sensible Richard far from being indifferent to his lot, having lost the political battle, is determined to win the moral one. That precisely is the purpose of the elaborate ceremony in the Deposition Scene.

'The last touch of unkindness' to *justice* is added not by such ceremony, but by Northumberland's pestering that the deposed king read a cooked up confession of his own follies. In Holinshed the articles are actually read over by Richard.[152] Shakespeare's Richard not only avoids this, but goes on instead to condemn the folly of his persecutors: "One heinous article,/ Containing the deposing of a King" (IV. i. 233-34). The allegation is meant not only for Northumberland, but for the whole lot: "all of you" (l. 237). The modification of the washing motif from:

> Not all the water in the rough rude sea
> Can wash the balm off from an anointed king
>
> (III. ii. 54-55)

to "And water cannot wash your sin" (IV. i. 242) through the Pilate-image is significant. Richard has lost the political battle (the balm has been washed away—IV. i. 207), but Bolingbroke is going to lose the moral battle.

With Northumberland's continued pestering that Richard must read the articles for the satisfaction of the commons, we hear after a few lines that Richard is going to read in the mirror: "the very book indeed/Where all my sins are writ, and that's myself" (IV. i. 274-75). The mirror is introduced into the scene not because "Narcissus has reached the supreme moment of his tragedy",[153] but because of its symbolic effect on the moral aspect of the Deposition. The mirror reflects the man and if all the sins of a Richard are writ in it, so are also the sins of a Bolingbroke, a Northumberland, an everybody. When the mirror is dashed and lies cracked in 'a hundred shivers' in the Westminster Hall, it reflects the sins of one and all present there: "all of you, that stand and look upon me" (IV. i. 237). Carlisle has questioned the bonafides of the subjects to judge their king (what subject can give sentence on his king?—IV. i. 121), Richard raises a more fundamental question, the question asked by Christ:

> Judge not, that ye be not judged. For with what judgment ye judge, ye shall be judged: and with what measure ye mete, it shall be measured to you again. And why beholdest thou the mote that is in thy brother's eye, but considerest not the beam that is in thine own eye?[154]

> He that is without sin among you, let him first cast a stone....[155]

The humanisation of the political tragedy continues and it is significant that in the next scene Shakespeare depicts the parting between Richard and his Queen. That the juxtaposition of the scene next to the deposition is deliberate becomes evident from the following words of Richard:

> Doubly divorced! Bad men, you violate
> A twofold marriage—'twixt my crown and me,
> And then betwixt me and my married wife.
> Let me unkiss the oath 'twixt thee and me;
> And yet not so, for with a kiss 'twas made. (V. i. 71-75)

What he attempts here is a vain repetition of inverted ceremony of coronation. On the purely human level, no ceremony of oath or 'unkissing the oath' would do. And, although to the Queen's heart-wringing query:

> And must we be divided? must we part?

Richard replies:

> Ay, hand from hand, my love, and heart from heart
> (V. i. 81-82)

we know that this on a deeper level suggests that though they might be parted 'hand from hand', they cannot be parted 'heart from heart'. And this by inference makes an oblique comment on the shallow relationships of the political world. Hence, the great dramatic significance of the prophetic warning regarding the dangerous relationship of mutual mistrust:

> Northumberland, thou ladder wherewithal
> The mounting Bolingbroke ascends my throne,
> The time shall not be many hours of age
> More than it is, ere foul sin gathering head
> Shall break into corruption. (V. i. 55-59)

Once again, we are reminded of what Kiernan has called Shakespeare's prime interest in 'positive human relationships'.[156] And the idea is followed up further in the subsequent scenes. The kind of climber-ladder relationship described by Richard above is graphically presented again through the fate of Exton. The short scene, depicting Exton's resolve (V. iv.) reverberates with the word, *friend*:

> 'Have I no *friend* will rid me of this living fear' (l. 2)
> Have I no *friend*? quoth he—he spoke it twice (l. 4)
> I am the king's *friend*, and will rid his foe. (l. 11)
> (Italics Mine)

For his labours, however, the 'friend' is not rewarded but coldly discarded: 'They love not *poison* that do poison need' (V. vi. 3).[157] And we are reminded of the moral expressed in the *Civil Wars* by Daniel, which must have influenced Shakespeare:

> The aspirer once attained unto the top
> Cuts off those means by which himself got up.[158]

Juxtaposed to this is another kind of subversion of natural human instincts and relationships presented through the character of York in the second and the third scenes of the Act. It is a pity that the scenes are generally cut in the theatre[159]—a pity that dramatic producers as well as critics have generally failed to see the full significance of the scenes. Nicholas Brooke, highly critical of them, calls them 'the feebly contracted concerns of the Duke of York and his family'.[160] Even Granville-Barker, who defends the scenes, has only this to say that they form 'a swift, excited interlude' between the slow farewell scene and the slow, philosophical death scene.[161] In York's character Shakespeare gives a complete reversal of the character of Gaunt. It has already been noted how under the stress of experience, Gaunt's beliefs are modified and humanised.[162] In the case of York, we find him finally dehumanised in his more strict adherence to his beliefs. According to Middleton Murry, in York "Shakespeare depicts the attitude of the good man, distraught between ideal loyalties and practical necessities".[163] This is how we can perhaps explain the behaviour of York in the earlier acts, not here. The schism here is between political loyalties and personal relationships. As the scene opens, Shakespeare gives a very human and sympathetic picture of York as a warm-hearted, emotional person, who, while narrating a sad tale, has himself broken down to tears[164] ("when weeping made you break the story off" (ll. 2)). He goes on to complete the tale—a highly moving account of deep human suffering—and in the process, draws as much sympathy to himself as he draws pity towards Richard. And then follows the anti-climax:

> But heaven hath a hand in these events,
> To whose high will we bound our calm contents.
> To Bolingbroke are we sworn subjects now.
> Whose state and honour I for aye allow. (V. ii. 37-40)

Taken independently, the explanation might appear quite sound, as suggesting York's loyalty to the divine principle of order in contrast to Carlisle's or Richard's to the Divine Right of a King, but placed as it is in the dramatic context, it becomes rather a manifestation of a queer psychic malfunction in the character. Instinctively York feels pity for the tragic lot of Richard, but subverts human instincts to certain abstract ideals. To explain the events of history in terms of God's will, was a typically

Medieval approach, not Elizabethan and certainly not Shakespearean: Whether 'heaven hath a hand' or not, York certainly had, in these events.

The unnatural denial of human instincts and relationships is carried to the extreme in his pleading against clemency to his own son, Aumerle. In Holinshed also York denounces his son's treachery, but there the denunciation has a personal motive, since York stood security for Aumerle's loyal behaviour.[165] By removing the personal motive, Shakespeare has made York's behaviour more unnatural and inhuman. That the dramatist has the father-son relationship primarily in mind here becomes evident when we remember the opening speech of the third scene:

> Can no man tell me of my unthrifty son? (V. iii. 1)[166]

Kiernan draws attention to the tensions within the Elizabethan family:

> All the strains and tensions of an age of change set up vibrations inside the family, which is indeed the historian's most sensitive seismograph for detecting them. There was much to disturb the harmony of the Elizabethan family: disagreements over religion, politics, morality, and the financial jealousies that always become more obtrusive when 'the time is out of joint'.[167]

York-Aumerle relationship is a depiction of the disagreement over politics disturbing the harmony of the family. The ironies involved in the situation, have been beautifully pointed out by James Winny.[168] As regent, York has acted as treacherously to Richard as Aumerle to the usurper and deserves the punishment himself. Aumerle's continuing loyalty to the true King puts the traitor York to shame. Bolingbroke overlooks the parallel between himself and York as well as between himself and Aumerle.

York's action which reflects the deposition of the humane by the political, naturally wins Bolingbroke's acclaim:

> O loyal father of a treacherous son!
> Thou sheer, immaculate and silver fountain,
> (V. iii. 60-61)

But it is the Duchess (an invention of Shakespeare) who exposes the loss of human values in York: "Love loving not itself none other can" (V. iii. 88). By denying natural human bonds, the character becomes comic[169] and is definitely held to ridicule in his insistence on his boots[170] (V. ii. 75-87). He cares more for the 'cause' than for his son; he cares more for the 'boots' than for the cause.

But human emotions reappear powerfully in the next scene, and Shakespeare chooses a groom of the stable for the purpose. "He visits the captive king in prison, and shames the desertion of the great."[171] York's character bears close resemblance to the behaviour of roan Barbary, which has pained the simple groom so much. In depicting roan Barbary's passive acceptance of the new rider and the change of loyalty, Shakespeare draws upon the following episode in Froissart:

> And as it was enformed me, kynge Rycharde had a grayhounde called Mathe, who alwayes wayted upon the kynge, and wolde kinowe no man els; for whansoever the kynge dyde ryde, he that kept the grayhonde dyde lette hym lose, and he wolde streight rynne to the kynge and fawne upon hym, and leape with his fore fete upon the kynges shulders. And as the kyng and the erle of Derby talked togyder in the courte, the grayhounde, who was wont to lepe upon the kyng, left the kynge and came to the erle of Derby, duke of Lancastre, and made to hym the same frendly countinaunce and chere as he was wonte to do to the kyng.[172]

By changing the 'grayhounde' into Richard's horse, Shakespeare makes the incident more credible; by making the groom report it, he makes it more touching; and by transplanting it in the drama just after the York-episode and before the 'friendly' act of murder by Exton, he uses both the groom and the horse for double-edged ironic commentary.

Richard's world is a world of moral bewilderment. Thoughts are like men and neither thoughts nor men are contented (V. v. 1-6). The word is set against the word. With an unsolved political dilemma,[173] "an intractable dilemma" at its core;[174] it leaves an impression of "moral opacity".[175] The soliloquy has been called a dramatisation of Richard's own 'introverted responses to the tragedy', a review by the actor of his different roles,[176] the final realisation by the artist whose intuitions have not fitted him for the business of his life[177] and a turning towards nihilism.[178] But the strange fact is that, though a soliloquy, it looks outward rather than inward.[179] Richard becomes everyman, his tragedy everyman's tragedy[180] and the poet, identifying himself with Richard, reflects on common human destiny, on 'thoughts tending to ambition' and 'thoughts tending to content', on the intractibility of ideals contending against each other, on the instability of human fortune.

> But whate'er I be,
> Nor I, nor any man that but man is,
> With nothing shall be pleased, till he be eas'd
> With being nothing. (V. v. 38-41)

Truly, as Yeats observes, Shakespeare "meditated as Solomon, not as Bentham (and, one may add not as York or Carlisle or the Gardener)...upon blind ambitions, untoward accidents, and capricious passions, and the world was almost as empty in his eyes as it must be in the eyes of God."[181] The only positive things that survive this nothingness and emerge despite the emptiness of the vision are some instances of positive human relationships and feelings, some signs of genuine love and pity to Man, "a strange brooch in this all-hating world" (V. v. 66).

NOTES

1. Dhananjaya, *The Dasarupa: A Treatise on Hindu Dramaturgy* (tr.), G.C.O. Haas (Delhi: Motilal Banarsidass, 1962), p. 146.
2. In the classical Indian epics, *Ramayana* and *Mahabbharata,* for instance, Ravana and Duryodhana are such *pratinayakas* respectively to Rama and Arjuna. It might, however, be noted that in Indian classical literature the *pratinayaka* was never allowed to come out victorious at the end.
3. See for instance, E.M.W. Tillyard, *Shakespeare's History Plays* (Penguin, 1962), p. 45. and L.B. Campbell, *Shakespeare's Histories* (San Marino, California: Huntington, 1963), pp. 70 and 194.
4. *The Union,* Bullough (ed.), *Narrative and Dramatic Sources of Shakespeare* (London: Routledge and Kegan Paul, N.Y.: Columbia University Press, 1960), Vol. III, p. 384.

5. *The Third Volume of Chronicles (493/1/58). Vide* Bullough, *op. cit.,* p. 388.
6. D. Wilson (ed.), *Richard II,* The New Shakespeare (Cambridge University Press, 1968), p. xx.
7. See W. Sanders, *The Dramatist and the Received Idea* (Cambridge University Press, 1968), Ch. IX, esp. p. 164.
8. *Ibid.,* Ch. IX, *passim,* p. 160.
9. *Woodstock.* V, iv, 2899 ff., *vide* Bullough, *op. cit.,* p. 490.
10. D. Wilson, *op. cit.,* p. 130.
11. As noted by various editors and critics, e.g. P. Ure (ed.), *Richard II* (New Arden, 1961), pp. xxxiv and 16 and L. Campbell, *op. cit.,* p. 196.
12. *Froissart op. cit.,* p. lv.
13. A.P. Rossiter (ed.), *Woodstock,* cf. P. Ure. *op. cit.,* pp. xxxv *et seq.*
14. Though the following lines spoken by Gloucester, may be said to contain certain hints:

    His youth is lead by Flatterers much a stray.
    But hees our Kinge, & gods great deputye
    & if ye hunt to have me second ye
    In any rash attempt against his state,
    Afore my god, Ile nere consent unto it.

    Woodstock IV. ii. 2139-43, vide Bullough, *op. cit.,* p. 484.
15. V. iii. 2718-22, *vide ibid,* p. 489.
16. Campbell, *op. cit.,* p. 197.
17. *Ibid.,* p. 194.
18. W. Sanders, *op. cit.,* p. 159.
19. *Ibid.,* p. 159.
20. S.C. Sen Gupta, *Shakespeare's Historical Plays* (London: Oxford University Press, 1964), p. 116.
21. *Ibid.,* p. 116.
22. L.C. Knights, 'Shakespeare's Politics: With some Reflections on the Nature of Tradition', The Annual Shakes. Lecture of the British Academy, 1957, *Further Explorations* (London: Chatto and Windus, 1965), p. 14.
23. Dr. Johnson aptly comments, "It is matter of very melancholy consideration, that all human advantages confer more power of doing evil than good." Walter Raleigh (ed.), *Johnson on Shakespeare* (London: Oxford University Press, 1946), p. 110.
24. L.C. Knights, 'Personality & Politics in *J. Caesar*', *op. cit.,* p. 42—See his observations related to Brutus.
25. It is difficult to agree with Sanders that Shakespeare's audience was dependent on the playwright for all but the broad outlines of the plot, *op. cit.,* p. 160.

26. *Ibid.*, p. 160.
27. J. Palmer, *Political and Comical Characters of Shakespeare* (London: Macmillan, 1962), p. 130 and P. Ure, *op. cit.*, p. lxiv.
28. W. Sanders, *op. cit.*, p. 160.
29. M.M. Mahood, *Shakespeare's Wordplay* (London: Methuen, 1957), p. 76.
30. Palmer, *op. cit.*, p. 131—'The whole scene is in the nature of a practical joke'.
31. W. Sanders, *op. cit.*, p. 161.
32. P. Ure, *op. cit.*, p. lxv.
33. R.M. Smith, *Froissart and the English Chronicle Play* (New York: Columbia University Press, 1915), pp. 143 *et seq.* M.W. Black, 'The Sources of Shakespeare's *Richard II*', *Joseph Quincy Adams Memorial Studies* (eds.), J.M. McManaway *et al.* (Washington, D.C.: Folger Shakespeare, 1948), pp. 210 *et seq.* and D. Wilson, *op. cit.*, pp. liv *et seq.*
34. Prince Hal's soliloquy in *1 Henry IV*, I, iii.
35. S.C. Sen Gupta, *op. cit.*, p. 119, *n.* 2.
36. Tillyard on the ceremonial nature of the play, *op. cit.*, pp. 245 *et seq.* Sanders, *op. cit.*, p. 161—staged act of state—for there is something inescapably histrionic about Richard's exquisite timing of this *coup*.

    H. Craig, *An Interpretation of Shakespeare* (New York, 1948), p. 128—"he loves the pomp of his office, else he would hardly have suffered Bolingbroke and Mowbray to meet." *Vide* Ure, *op. cit.*, p. lxiv; S.C. Sen Gupta, *op. cit.*, p. 119 *n.* 2. "the episode is an unnecessary theatricality exposing a weakness of Richard's character."

    S.H. Atkins (ed.), *Richard II* (The London Eng. Lit. Series, 1963), p. 16—"Instantly the attention of the great assembly is switched to him, he becomes a central figure in a 'situation', and from what he says and does it is clear that he enjoys it all."
37. H. Craig, *op. cit.*, p. 128.
38. Palmer, *op. cit.*, pp. 130 *et seq.* More recently P. Ure endorses Palmer's views, *op. cit.*, lxvi *et seq.*
39. Palmer, *op. cit.*, p. 131.
40. P. Ure, *op. cit.*, p. 24.
41. Chronicles, III (494/2/41). *Vide* Bullough, *op. cit.*, pp. 391 *et seq.*
42. Note the consequent images: 'falcon's flight against a bird' (ll. 61-62). 'swift like lightning' (l. 79), 'fall like amazing thunder' (l. 81), 'Lo, as at English feasts, so I regreet The daintiest last, to make the end most sweet' (ll. 67-68), 'feast of battle' (l. 92), a captive casting off 'his chains of bondage' and embracing his 'golden uncontrolled enfranchisement' (ll. 88-90).

43. Though in II. i. 154, Richard's 'our pilgrimage must be', is used in the sense of life.
44. H. Craig (ed.), *An Introduction to Shakespeare* (Chicago: Scott, Foresman, 1952), p. 128.
45. P. Ure, *op. cit.,* p. lxv.
46. H.C. Goddard, *The Meaning of Shakespeare* (Chicago and London: The Univ. of Chicago Press, Phoenix Books, 1967), pp. 151 *et seq.*
47. W. Sanders, *op. cit.,* p. 161.
48. *Ibid.,* p. 162.
49. D. Wilson follows the Quarto edition (1597)—*cousin's cousin,* but generally the editors follow the Folio edition—*cousin, cousin.*
50. Lily Campbell, *op. cit.,* p. 198. See also A. Harbage, *As They Liked It* (New York: Harper Torchbooks, 1961), pp. 48 *et seq.*
51. P. Ure, *op. cit.,* p. lxvi.
52. Page 169 *supra.*
53. In fact, the speech is delivered in the spirit of a soliloquy. P. Ure argues that this is so "perhaps because Shakespeare avoided having to show a lack of response on Richard's part that would have prejudiced the beholder too finally against him." *op. cit.,* p. lxvi. W. Sanders remarks: "It is an old man's profession of faith privately confided to another old man". *op. cit.,* p. 191.
54. Though callous, Richard is not much off the mark in his cynical retort: 'Presuming on an ague's privilege' (l. 116).
55. R. Simpson, 'The Politics of Shakespeare's History Plays', *N.S.S.T.*, 1874 (London: Trubner, 1874), p. 408.
56. J.A.R. Marriott, *English History in Shakespeare* (New York: E.P. Dutton, 1918), p. 77.
57. P. Ure, *op. cit.,* p. lxxii.
58. Coleridge, 1818 notes. *Vide* D. Wilson, *op. cit., XX.*
59. Hazlitt calls Bolingbroke, "humble, crafty, bold, and aspiring, encroaching by regular but slow degrees, building power on opinion, and cementing opinion by power." *The Round Table Characters of Shakespeare's Plays* (London: J.M. Dent; New York: E.P. Dutton, 1960), p. 275.
60. W. Sanders, *op. cit.,* p. 164.
61. *Ibid.,* p. 164.
62. The idea is crystallized in the next scene where the dramatist makes a deliberate play upon the word, 'hope':

    Green.—I *hope* the King is not yet shipp'd for Ireland.

    Queen.—Why *hopest* thou so? 'tis better *hope* he is;

    For his designs crave haste, his haste good *hope.*

    Then wherefore dost thou hope he is not shipp'd?

    Green.—That he, our *hope,* might have retir'd his power,

And driven into despair an *enemy's hope.*
Who strongly hath set footing in this land.
The banish'd Bolingbroke repeals himself,
And with uplifted arms is safe arriv'd
At Ravenspurgh. (II. ii. 42-51)

63. F.P. Wilson, *Shakespearian and Other Studies* (ed.), H. Gardner (Oxford: Clarendon Press, 1969), p. 34.
64. *Ibid.,* p. 34 *et. seq.*
65. From the *Letter to Monsieur Chauvet on the Unity of Time and Place in Tragedy,* tr. by F. Rosen, *Shakespeare in Europe* (ed.), Oswald Le Winter (Penguin: Shakespeare Library, 1970), p. 125.
66. A.W. Schlegel, *Dramatic Art and Literature* (tr.), J. Black (London: H.G. Boh, 1861), p. 424.
67. A.C. Sprague, *Sh's Histories: Plays for the State* (London: The Society for Theatre Research, 1964), p. 46.
68. P. Ure, *op. cit.,* p. lxxv.
69. *Ibid.,* p. lxxv.
70. W. Sanders, *op. cit.,* p. 165.
71. Sprague, *op.cit.,* p. 46.
72. R. Chapman, 'The Wheel of Fortune in Shakespeare's Historical Plays', *Rev. of English Studies,* Vol. I, New Series No. 1 (Jan. 1950), pp. 1-7, especially p. 5.
73. Palmer, *op. cit.,* p. 137.
74. III. iv. esp. II, 43-53.
75. M.M. Reese, *The Cease of Majesty* (London: Edward Arnold, 1961), p. 25. Also Palmer, *op. cit.,* p. 150—"in effect an act of sovereignty".
76. W. Sanders, *op. cit.,* p. 169 *et seq.* for a brilliant analysis of the passage.
77. Sanders comments, Northumberland unfurls "that all-too-*familiar* document of the police-state—the prepared confession, drawn up to the specifications of the new regime, not by the accused, but by his accusers...." *Ibid.,* p. 170.
78. B. Stirling, *The Populace in Shakespeare* (New York: Columbia University Press, 1949), p. 29 and 'or else this were a savage spectacle', *PMLA.* LXVI (1951), pp. 769 *et seq.*
79. A. Bonjour, *The Structure of J. Caesar* (Liverpool University Press, 1958), pp. 19 *et seq.*
80. Sanders, *op. cit.,* p. 170.
81. *Ibid.,* p. 170.
82. As an exception, Peter Ure reminds us that Richard is not unlike Brutus or Cassius, who are all conscious of 'bearing a part', their role in life. He is no more an actor than a poet. *Op. cit.,* pp. lxxviii *et seq.*
83. Ludowyk, *op. cit.,* pp. 116 *et seq.*

Anne Righter, *Shakespeare and the Idea of the Play* (London: Chatto and Windus, 1964), p. 116.

84. L.F. Dean, '*Richard II:* the State and the Image of the Theatre', *PMLA,* LXVII (1952), 211-18.
85. L.C. Knights, *Shakespeare: The Histories* (London, 1962), p. 35. cf. Sanders, *op. cit.,* p. 177.
86. Palmer, *op. cit.,* p. 142.
87. *Ibid.,* p. 152.
88. *Ibid.,* p. 151. Contrast I. Ribner, *Patterns in Shakespearian Tragedy* (London: Methuen, 1960), p. 52.—'In *Richard II* history and tragedy are perfectly fused'.
89. P. Ure, *op. cit.,* p. lxii.
90. Sen Gupta, *op. cit.,* p. 120. Bullough, *op. cit.,* p. 379.
91. Manzoni, *op. cit.,* p. 126.
92. *Ibid.*—Manzoni uses the word, 'pride', not Divine Right.
93. II. i. 115-22, esp. II, 118-200.
94. Marriott, *op. cit.,* Chap. III, 'Richard the "Redeless"—the Amateur in Polities', p. 92—The hint that Richard is an amateur politician first comes from the German critic, Kreyssig. Marriott also mentions the German distrust of the amateur and the English love for it.
95. A. Hart, *Shakespeare and the Homilies* (Melbourne: Melbourne University Press, 1934), p. 68.
96. As Sanders calls it, *op. cit.,* p. 187.
97. Sanders takes Richard's vacillations to be a sign of 'psychological malfunction'. *Ibid.,* pp. 187 *et seq.*
98. P. Ure, *op. cit.,* pp. lxxvi *et seq.*
99. W. Pater, 'Shakespeare's English Kings', *Appreciations* (Calcutta: Rupa, 1967), p. 146.
100. Bullough, *op. cit.* Int. p. 379.
101. J.L. Barrault, 'Shakespeare and the French', tr. by Joseph Chiari from *Shakespeare in Europe,* ed. by Oswald LeWinter (Penguin, 1970), p. 355.
102. Pater, *op. cit.,* p. 145.
103. A. Hart, *op. cit.,* p. 67.
104. James Winny, *The Player King: A theme of Shakespeare's Histories* (London: Chatto and Windus, 1968), p. 55.
105. D. Wilson, *op. cit.,* p. lix. Bullough. *op. cit.,* p. 378. Neither Wilson nor Bullough uses the term French, but the sympathetic attitude to Richard is characteristic of the French.
106. M.W. Black has quite plausibly established the case for Shakespeare's familiarity with the two French works and, their impact on *Richard II, op. cit.,* pp. 199-216, esp. pp. 213 *et seq.*

107. Bullough, *op. cit.,* p. 378.

108. Black, *op. cit.,* p. 214. Also D. Wilson, *op. cit.,* p. lix—"Shakespeare's genius succeeded in fusing these originally contradictory conceptions and in composing therefrom the figure of a king who seems to us one of the most living of his characters."
and C.L. Kingsford. *Prejudice and Promise in Fifteenth-Century England,* Ford Lectures, 1923 (London: Frank Cass., 1962), p. 5.

109. B.I. Evans, *The Language of Shakespeare's Plays* (London: Mathuen, 1965), pp. 56 *et seq;* W. Clemen, *The Development of Shakespeare's Imagery* (London: Methuen, 1959), pp. 54 *et seq;* Tillyard, *op. cit.,* pp. 245 *et seq;* Bullough, *op. cit.,* p. 379; R.D. Altick, 'Symphonic Imagery in *Richard II*' *PMLA,* LXII (1947), p. 351. F. Turner, *Shakespeare and the Nature of Time* (Oxford: Clarendon Press, 1971), p. 84.

110. M. Doran, 'Imagery in *Richard II* and in *Henry IV*', *Modern Language Review,* xxxvii, No. 2 (April, 1942), p. 121.

111. F. O'Connor, *Shakespeare's Progress* (New York: Collier Books, 1961), p. 72.

112. Marriott, *op. cit.,* p. 91.

113. P. Ure, *op. cit.,* p. lxxix.

114. Sen Gupta, *op. cit.,* p. 120.

115. *Ibid.,* p. 121.

116. W.B. Donne, *Essays on Drama* (London, 1858), pp. 196-97, cf. Sprague, *op. cit.,* p. 49.

117. W.B. Yeats, 'Richard II and Henry V'. First appeared in *Ideas of Good and Evil,* 1903, from *Discussions of Shakespeare's Histories* ed. by R.J. Dorius (Boston: D.C. Heath, 1964), p. 22.

118. *Henry V.* IV. i. 100 ff.

119. *The History of the World* (ed.), G.E. Hadow (Oxford, Clarendon Press, 1927), p. 56.

120. James Winny, *op. cit.,* p. 55.

121. *Edward II.* IV. vi. 9-15. ed. by M. Merchant (London: Ernest Bann, 1967).

122. Sanders, *op. cit.,* p. 176.

123. *Ibid.,* pp. 176, 178.

124. In Holinshed, he is actually a prisoner at Flint Castle. D. Wilson (ed.) (Richard II Cambridge, 1968) p. 189 and Sen Gupta, *op.cit.,* p. 122.

125. See especially III, ii, 145 ff.

126. Sanders, *op. cit.,* p. 180.

127. B. Stirling, *Unity in Shakespearean Tragedy,* Chap. III, 'Up Cousin Up' (New York: Columbia University Press, 1956), pp. 33 *et seq.*

128. *Op. cit.,* p. 180. See also p. 173.

129. Yeats, *op. cit.*, p. 22.
130. In Holinshed the events take place in the following order: The deposition on 29 Sept. (503/1/53), the challenges on 16 Oct. (511/2/39) and the Bishop's protest on 23 Oct. (512/2/29). See Bullough, *Narrative and Dramatic Sources of Shakespeare* (London), Vol. II, pp. 406 *et seq.*
131. Palmer notices one of the instances, ll. 105-06, *Political and Comic Characters of Shakespeare* (London, 1962), p. 160.
132. *Ibid.*, p. 160.
133. D. Wilson, *op. cit.*, p. 201.
134. Sanders, *op. cit.*, pp. 163 *et seq* for comments on this as well as on Surrey's counter-challenge to the accusers—"As Shakespeare gives us it, there is not much doubt of Surrey's bonafides."
135. *Vide*, D. Wilson, *op. cit.*, p. 203.
136. *Chronicles*, III (511/2/39), Bullough, *op. cit.*, p. 410.
137. Sanders calls him 'old anachronism' representing the old-world order like Gaunt and Mowbray, *op. cit.*, pp. 191 *et seq.*
138. D. Wilson, *op. cit.*, p. 204.
139. As Ludowyk does, see *op. cit.*, pp. 92 *et seq.*
140. Winny, *op. cit.*, p. 78.
141. W. Raleigh (ed.) *Johnson on Shakespeare* (London, 1908), p. 112.
142. D. Wilson, *op. cit.*, p. xxxviii.
143. A. Harbage's discussion of 'moral stimulus' in his *As I Liked It* (New York: Harper Torchbooks, 1961), pp. 3-15.
144. Palmer, *op. cit.*, pp. 161 *et seq.*
145. The Eye of Providence on the title page of Sir Walter Raleigh's *The History of the World* (1614), *vide* R.A. Fraser, *Shakespeare's Poetics* (London: Routledge & Kegan Paul, 1962), Plate VII between pp. 68-69.
146. Sanders, *op. cit.*, p. 170.
147. For the arresting situation Shakespeare was indebted to Froissart; who describes the abdication thus: "Than Kynge Rycharde toke the crown fro his heed with bothe his handes, and set it before hym, and sayd: Fayre cosyn, Henry duke of Lancastre, I gyve and delyver you this crowne...." Froissart (Cap. CCXL). *Vide* Bullough, *op. cit.*, p. 431.
148. W.H. Clemen, *The Development of Shakespeare's Imagery* (London: Mathuen & Co., 1959), pp. 57 *et seq.*
149. R. Chapman, *op. cit.*, pp. 3 *et seq.*
150. W. Pater, *Appreciations* (London), p. 146. Italics mine.
151. E.M.W. Tillyard, *Shakespeare's History Plays* (Penguin), p. 252. For a strong refutal of Tillyard's thesis see P.G. Phialas, 'The Medieval in

Richard II', *Shakespeare Quartery,* XII, No. 3 (Summer, 1961), pp. 305-10. Phialas has rightly pointed out that the action and the comment in the play look to the past for significance, not to the future.

152. Holinshed, III, 504/1/19. *Vide* Bullough, *op. cit.,* p. 406.
153. Palmer, *op. cit.,* p. 165.
154. *St. Matthew,* VII, 1-3. *Holy Bible.*
155. *St. John,* VIII, 7. *Holy Bible.*
156. V.G. Kiernan, 'Human Relationships in Shakespeare', *Shakespeare in A Changing World* (ed.), A. Kettle (London: 1964), pp. 43-64.
157. Northumberland too is such a poison, but compared to Exton, he is a slow poison.
158. Daniel, *Civil Wars,* ii. 15, II, 7-8.
159. A.C. Sprague, *Shakespeare's Histories: Plays for the Stage* (London: Society for Theatre Research, 1964), pp. 41 *et seq.*
160. N. Brooke, *Shakespeare's Early Tragedies* (London, 1968), p. 107.
161. *Vide* Sprague, *op. cit.,* p. 43.
162. *Ibid.,* pp. 146 *et seq supra.*
163. J.M. Murry, *Shakespeare* (London, 1965), p. 146.
164. *Ibid.,* p. 147.
165. Chronicles, III, 515/1/9. *Vide* Bullough, *op. cit.,* p. 412.
166. As noted by Hilda Hulme, the word 'unthrifty' further links the two sons Hal and Aumerle. See her *Explorations in Shakespeare's Language* (London: Longmans, Green, 1962), p. 164.
167. Kiernan, *op. cit.,* p. 54.
168. James Winny, *op. cit.,* pp. 75 *et seq.*
169. Sprague notes that the character has at times been treated as comic in the theatre, e.g. by William Poel, *op. cit.,* pp. 40 *et seq.*
170. See Murry, *op. cit.,* pp. 150 *et seq.* for comments.
171. Schlegel, *op. cit.,* p. 424.
172. Froissart, cap. ccxxxviii. *Vide* Bullough, *op. cit.,* p. 429.
173. Stauffer, *Shakespeare's World of Images* (Bloomington and London: Indian University Press, 1966), pp. 88 *et seq.*
174. R.F. Hill, 'Dramatic Techniques and Interpretation in *Richard I* (eds.), J.R. Brown and B. Harris, *Early Shakespeare,* Stratford-Upon-Avon Studies 3 (London: Edward Arnold, 1967), p. 114.
175. Sanders, *op. cit.,* p. 164.
176. Palmer, *op. cit.,* p. 173.
177. Reese, *The Cease of Majesty* (London, 1961), p. 244.
178. J. Winny, *op. cit.,* p. 68.

179. R.F. Hill notes the element of detachment in it to be unusual for a soliloquy in a tragedy, *op. cit.*, pp. 116 *et seq.*

180. W. Pater, *op. cit.*, p. 147—"And his grief becomes nothing less than a central expression of all that in the revolutions of fortune's wheel goes *down* in the world."

181. Yeats, *op. cit.*, p. 22.

Henry IV, Parts I and II

7

"None of Shakespeare's plays", said Dr. Johnson, "are more read than the first and second parts of *Henry the fourth*."[1] Perhaps no author has ever in two plays afforded so much delight. The reason is that with these plays history becomes even more comprehensive than it had been in the earlier plays. Shakespeare is 'of all humours' now. We have observed that if we look at *Richard III* and *Richard II* from the point of view of Indian dramaturgy, we may classify them as plays of the *bibhatsa rasa* (Odious sentiment) and *Karuna rasa* (pathetic sentiment) respectively. *Henry IV, Parts I* and *II* defy all classifications. Theodore Weiss says that here we have 'a confluence of the historical and the comic'[2] and G.L. Evans uses the term, 'comical-tragical-historical' to describe the plays.[3] Viewing the plays in the light of the *rasas*, we may say that they provide a rich feast of the *hasya* (comic) as well as the *vira rasa* (heroic sentiment). The plays move simultaneously on two diagonally opposed planes—the serious and the comic. The synthesis achieved between the two is a measure of Shakespeare's genius. On both these planes, Prince Hal, who is usually accepted as the *nayaka* (protagonist), has to contend against formidable *pratinayakas* (counter-heroes),—against Hotspur on the serious-heroic plain and against Falstaff on the comic. The latter being a close companion of the Prince, may also be identified with the *Vidushaka* of the Indian drama.

Henry IV, Parts I and II are the triumph of Shakespeare's Histories. With these plays we reach 'the climax in Shakespeare's treatment of English history'.[4] The achievement in respect of matter and treatment is equally matched in language and style.

This can be noticed particularly in the forceful prose of Falstaff and the brilliant poetry of Hotspur. Stylistically, both Falstaff and Hotspur are descendants of the Bastard. As specimens of the new realistic and forceful style now at Shakespeare's command, one may pick up the Honour-soliloquy of Falstaff, or Hotspur's dramatic accounts of the dandy courtier and of Bolingbroke. It is characteristic that though Hotspur's speeches are not soliloquies, yet they are delivered in the same vein as Falstaff's soliloquy.[5] They are monologues in which the character is engaged in an imaginary conversation with someone. In Bharata's *Natya Sashtra*, we come across a description of this kind of speech. It is termed *akashbhasita* there. The best speech of Falstaff and Hotspur belong to this very class and are far superior to the soliloquies of Richard III and Richard II.

Unlike *Richard II*, there is plenty of action in the *Henry IV* plays, but here too the emphasis is more on the inner springs of action than on action itself. Conscience and the tension between the political and the humane, between time and eternity, continue to be the major concerns with the dramatist. The commonly accepted orthodox, order concept and the sin-retribution-theory prevent us from appreciating these elements in the plays. In the analysis which follows, it is hoped that some fresh light would be shed on the motives and actions of the principal characters as well as on the various themes of the plays—the theme of honour, of mundane materialistic life and of the redemption of time, for instance.

The question whether *Henry IV, Parts I* and *II* constitute a single play or are two independent plays is an old one. It goes back to Dr. Johnson and Malone. While the former regarded them as one work, the latter held that *Henry IV, Part II* was conceived after the roaring success of *Henry IV, Part I*.[6] In recent times the unity of the two parts has been proclaimed by Tillyard[7] and Dover Wilson,[8] but strongly disputed by Shaaber[9] and Richard David.[10] Harold Jenkins has nearly succeeded in reconciling the conflicting views with his plausible theory that the two parts were originally planned as one play, but in Act IV of *1 Henry IV* Shakespeare changed his mind and conceived a sequel.[11] Without going into the controversy regarding the planning of Part II, the only assumptions made here are: First, Part II is a sequel to Part I, historically as well as chronologically; second, both Parts I and II have the same central characters, Henry IV, Prince Hal and Falstaff. It follows that the two plays can profitably be discussed together.

Henry IV, Part I, opens with a reference to the intended crusade, the note on which *Richard II* ends. It is convenient to assert Edward Hall's moral scheme behind the plays. Henry usurped the throne, got the Lord's anointed murdered, disturbed the divine order. Retribution must follow. There are the prophecies of Carlisle[12] and of Richard[13] himself. "The business of the curse comes in the very first scene", observes Tillyard,

> and is sustained throughout each part till Henry's death. Henry opens the plays by lamenting the recent disturbances and proposing a new crusade. Though an affair of policy, the crusade was also a penance for Richard's death, carrying on Henry's last lines in *Richard II*:
>
> I'll make a voyage to the Holy Land
> To wash this blood off from my guilty hand.
>
> And whenever the crusade is mentioned, as it is several times in the course of both parts, it should recall Henry's unremitting efforts to expiate it."[14]

This is the commonly accepted reading of *Henry IV* plays. Bolingbroke, we are told, suffers from guilty conscience. He "has put his soul in jeopardy by the sin of usurpation and seeks to expiate it by undertaking a crusade to the Holy Land".[15] In support of the view, Dover Wilson also observes that Shakespeare deliberately reshapes the historical data derived from Holinshed to impress upon us "the reign's brevity and inquietude".[16]

In fact, far from enlarging the miseries of Bolingbroke, Shakespeare tones them down considerably. Holinshed records at least two abortive Welsh expeditions of the king against Glendower.[17] After the first of these, there is also an attempt on the king's life. It concludes thus:

> Oh what a suspected state therefore is that of a king holding his regiment with the hatred of his people, the

> heartgrudgings of his courtiers, and the peremptorie practices of both togither? Could he confidentlie compose or setle himselfe to sleepe for feare of strangling? Durst he boldly eat and drinke without dread of poisoning? Might he adventure to shew himselfe in great meetings or solemne assemblies without mistrust of mischiefe against his person intended? What pleasure or what felicitie could he take in his princelie pompe, which he knew by manifest and fearfull experience, to be envied and maligned to the verie death?[18]

Shakespeare omits an account of the Welsh expeditions of the king. Indeed, there is a mention of the proposed Welsh expedition by the king at the end of *1 Henry IV* (V. v. 39-40), but we hear no more of it in *2 Henry IV* except Falstaff's comic remark that the king has returned from Wales with apoplexy. In Act III. Sc. i Warwick informs the king—casually and as a piece of comforting news—that Glendower is dead. There is no mention of the attempted assassination of the king, nor of the hatred of people,[19] the 'peremptorie practises' and the lurking fear of the king. It is difficult, therefore, to subscribe the view[20] that the above passage lends its tone to the opening speech of *1 Henry IV:* 'So shaken as we are, so wan with care' (I. i. 1 ff.) words, which, according to Dover Wilson, must be taken as referring both to his realm and to himself, "a sick, careworn,... oldman throughout the play",[21] "a sick man in body and spirit".[22] Such descriptions are more justifiably applicable to the historical Bolingbroke than to Shakespeare's. Besides the Welsh expeditions and the attempted assassination, Holinshed also reports pestilence, ominous meteor, diabolic visitations, the battle with Scots at Nisbit and the threat of a French invasion.[23] Shakespeare omits all these omens and misfortunes, except the battle with Scots. The personal illness of Bolingbroke is reported thus in Holinshed:

> ...he was eftsoones taken with a sore sicknesse, which was not a leprosie, stricken by the hand of God (saith maister *Hall*) as foolish friers imagined; but a verie apoplexie, of the which he languished till his appointed houre....[24]

This apoplexy, as noted by Hall, deprived Bolingbroke of "felyng, speache & movyng".[25] Daniel describes it in greater detail:

> But now the King retires him to his peace,
> A peace much like a feeble sickmans sleepe,
> (Wherein his waking paines do never cease
> Though seeming rest his closed eyes doth keepe)
> For O no peace could ever so release
> His intricate turmoiles, and sorrowes deepe,
> But that his cares kept waking all his life
> Continue on till death conclude the strife.[26]

Shakespeare must have been familiar with the anti-Lancastrian tradition (hinted at by Holinshed), according to which Bolingbroke was struck with leprosy by the hand of God. It contains the grain for capital moralising. So does Holinshed's account, for even though rejecting the leprosy-diagnosis, it maintains that Bolingbroke fell sick right at the moment when earnest preparations for the Crusade were in full swing. He was, it seems, denied the chance of expiation by God. The summing up moral is: "What man ordeineth, God altereth at his good will and pleasure."[27] If the dramatist aims at a pattern of resolve followed by cruel interposition in these plays,[28] would he let such matter go abegging?

While transferring the intended crusade from the last to the first years of the reign, Shakespeare does not do so with the king's sickness. The first mention of the sickness occurs only in *2 Henry IV* and that too in a comic vein by Falstaff:

> *Ch. Just*—Sir John, I sent for you before your expedition to Shrewsbury.
>
> *Fal.* —An't please your lordship, I hear his majesty is returned with some discomfort from Wales.— (*2 Henry IV*. I. ii. 99 ff.).

The same pattern continues for quite some time—Falstaff evading the unpleasant questions of the Lord Chief Justice with a mention of the king's sickness. We have reason to believe that Falstaff's account of the king's malady is exaggerated, for it is not only comic, but also diplomatic. The Lord Chief Justice reminds Falstaff of his Gadshill robbery, which was punishable by hanging. Falstaff, on the other hand, reminds the Lord Chief Justice that the king is grievously sick and that his days are, therefore, numbered. This is an indirect way of telling the Justice that Falstaff's 'tender lambkin' (*2 Henry IV*, V. iii. 115), the Prince of Wales, is shortly to ascend the throne. Under the new reign 'the rusty curb of old father Antic the law' (*1 Henry IV. 59*), itself would go away. Falstaff is to become 'Fortune's steward'. The laws of England are to be at his command. On that to-morrow, blessed will be those who have been Falstaff's friends and cursed will be those who have been unfriendly to him.[29] It is, therefore, in the interest of the Lord Chief Justice himself to come to terms with Falstaff. The King's sickness is thus used by Falstaff as a signpost to indicate the forthcoming danger to the Lord Chief Justice.

Much later in Act III, we notice the king afflicted with insomnia (III. i. 4 ff.). Then, towards the end of Act IV, we find him sinking:

> And now my sight fails, and my brain is giddy.
> O me! come near me, now I am much ill.
>
> (IV. iv. 110-11)

The symptoms are the same which were earlier exaggerated and possibly anticipated by Falstaff. A few lines after the swooning, follows the diagnosis—again reminiscent of Falstaff's—by Clarence:

> Th' incessant care and labour of his mind
> Hath wrought the mure that should confine it in
> So thin that life looks through, and will break out.
>
> (IV. iv. 118-20)

Two things become clear: the sickness is reserved for the closing years of the reign and the stress is on the cares involved in the king's office, unlike Holinshed, where it is on a lurking fear of assassination and unlike Daniel, where it is on a guilty conscience at death-bed:

> And lying on his last afflicted bed
> Where death and conscience both before him stand.[30]

Bolingbroke's sleep-soliloquy (*2 Henry IV*. III. i. 4 ff.) is much nearer in spirit to Henry VI's soliloquy on pastoral life (*3 Henry VI*. II. v.) than to Macbeth's 'Sleep no more' (*Macbeth*. II. ii. 35 ff.). No, Bolingbroke does not suffer from the guilty conscience of an usurper; he suffers from the disillusionment of an ambitious politician, suffers because of the poor compensation for the heavy price he had to pay as king:

> O God! that one might read the book of fate,...
> ...O, if this were seen,
> The happiest youth, viewing his progress through,
> What perils past, what crosses to ensue,
> Would shut the book and sit him down and die.
>
> (*2 Henry IV*. III. i. 45 ff.)

The moral, if any, that *Henry IV* plays draw is the simple and commonplace one with which the king concludes his sleep-soliloquy: "Uneasy lies the head that wears a crown" (*2 Henry IV*, III, i. 31). The same point is reiterated by Hal in his address to the crown:

> so troublesome a bed fellow?
> O polished perturbation! golden care!
>
> (*2 Henry IV*. IV. v. 22-23).

It is this 'golden care' which in fact, lies at the bottom of the king's sickness, both of body and mind. But the weight of this 'golden care' can hardly be felt by the usurper, when he sets it upon his head. The realisation, like the realisation of Richard II regarding the emptiness of his faith in the Divine Right, comes to him gradually and painfully through actual experience. Of course, one may trace Bolingbroke's cares back to the last Act of *Richard II*—the abbots' conspiracy and the thrifty son[31]—but the former had been nipped in the bud by Bolingbroke and in the latter he saw, "some sparks of better hope, which elder years/May happily bring forth," (*Richard II*. V. iii. 21-22). It is, therefore, a piece of dramatic exaggeration and rhetoric on the part of the speaker to say 'shaken' and 'wan with care'. The opening speech, though warmly appreciated as an instance of Shakespeare's mature style,[32] is in fact a set speech—artificial, insincere and full of contradictions. The verse is exquisitely light and lyrical, the metaphors are captivatingly beautiful. Such verse is, however, singularly inapt to express the idea of recently ended civil wars and the intended crusade. Bolingbroke is another 'popinjay', using 'holiday and lady terms' to describe wars (*1 Henry IV*. I. iii. 45-49). L.C. Knights[33] has rightly drawn attention to 'the violence of the negative' in the following lines:

> No more the thirsty entrance of this soil,
> Shall daub her lips with her own children's blood:
> No more shall trenching war channel her fields,
> Nor bruise her flowerets with the armed hoofs
> Of hostile paces. (*1 Henry IV*. I. i. 5-8)

This is not—what Ifor Evans takes it to be—a picture of "mother earth satiated with her children's blood, her soil, or entrance, normally thirsty now having no blood to daub on her lips."[34] As a matter of fact, it means just the opposite. The word "thirsty" rather implies that the thirst of the earth is yet unquenched. This and the prophecy of peace in 'the lisping line': "Shall now in mutual well-beseeming ranks" (I. i. 14), suggest "that Henry is actually describing what is to come."[35]

Besides, it cannot be presumed that the king is ignorant of the two actions, the Scottish and the Welsh, that his men are engaged in. In fact, as the dialogue proceeds, we learn that the king is better informed than his courtiers. He has already had a closed-door meeting with Sir Walter Blunt, lately arrived from Holmedon and while Westmoreland is still uncertain about the Scottish expedition, the king knows that Douglas is discomfitted. This ought to have given him joy and peace of mind. It, however, does nothing of the kind, for Hotspur has denied the Scottish prisoners. Although he mentions the prisoners issue only towards the close of the scene, it has been haunting him for some time. When the play opens it is this which is uppermost in his mind, not the guilty-conscience and the need for expiation. The crusade-motif is merely a cover to conceal his inner purpose of seeking an excuse to cut off[36] his erstwhile allies. This is brought out subtly through the emphasis that Shakespeare makes his Bolingbroke lay on the names of the prisoners captured by Hotspur:

> Of prisoners Hotspur took
> Mordake, Earl of Fife and eldest son
> To beaten Douglas, and the Earl of Athol,
> Of Murray, Angus, and Menteith
> (*1 Henry IV*. I. i. 70-73)

The list is of course taken almost verbatim from Holinshed,[37] but whereas in Holinshed it forms a part of the narrative, Shakespeare by putting it in the mouth of Bolingbroke, entirely changes the perspective. What further reflects the envious concern of the king for the prisoners is the emphatic use of the interrogative:

> And is not this an *honorable* spoil?
> A *gallant* prize? ha, cousin, is it not? (I. i. 74-75)
> What think ye coz,
> Of this young Percy's *pride*? (I. i. 90-91)

The prisoners stand for the honour, the gallantry and the pride of Hotspur, which accounts for the king's anxiety. From amongst the prisoners, Hotspur has agreed to deliver only Mordake, the Earl of Fife. This too is a historical fact taken from Holinshed, but again Shakespeare has entirely changed the perspective and the meaning. Holinshed reports the issue thus:

> and especiallie they (Percies) were greeved, because the king demanded of the earl and his sonne such Scotish prisoners as were taken at Holmedon and Nesbit: for of all the captives which were taken in the conflicts foughten in those two places, there were delivered to the king's possession onelie Mordake earle of Fife....[38]

It should be noted that although Holinshed does not offer any opinion directly on the moral question as to who was entitled to keep the prisoners, by calling the Percies "greeved", he appears indirectly to endorse the conventional feudal law of arms: "The Ransome of a Prisoner belongs to him who took him, unless he be a person of very eminent quality, and then the Prince, the State, or their General seizeth on him, giving some gratuity to those who took him."[39] On the basis of this, as noted by Humphreys, Hotspur could retain the prisoners except for the

Earl of Fife.[40] Shakespeare on the other hand, not only ignores the moral question, but also makes the king the aggrieved party. The Percies do not, as in Holinshed, come to vent their grievances, they are sent for by the king: "But I have sent for him to answer this" (*1 Henry IV*. I. i. 99). The initiative is thus transferred to Bolingbroke. It is he, who, just as in *Richard II*, precipitates the crisis. He makes of the prisoners-issue an excuse to crack down on the Percies, and though he talks sonorously of 'new broils', of chasing the Pagans from the Holy Land and enquires of Westmoreland regarding 'this dear expedience', in truth he has already postponed it for a more pressing expedience. The beautiful account of the proposed crusade is followed by the ambiguous: "Therefore, we meet not now" (*1 Henry IV*. I. i. 30). It comes as a severe jolt[41] on the heels of the preceding description and as a prefix to the enquiries regarding the actual preparation. The truth, as he discloses towards the close of the scene, is that he has already sent for the Percies and is planning how to cut them off:

> And for this cause awhile we must neglect
> Our holy purpose to Jerusalem. (I. i. 100-01)

Thus, examined closely, the opening speech of the play, turns out to be a superb example of dramatic irony, almost every line meaning the opposite of what it says apparently.

Various critics have noted the difference between the Bolingbroke of *Richard II* and that of *Henry IV*. According to Dover Wilson, Bolingbroke, 'a crafty politician' in *Richard II*, becomes a sickman, physically as well as spiritually, in *Henry IV*. Similarly Reese discerns a "decline from efficiency and decisiveness to the haggard uncertainty", but adds that this man, though less competent than Bolingbroke of *Richard II*, has been 'ennobled by office' and is more sympathetic.[43] On the other hand, James Winny holds that the Bolingbroke of *Henry IV* is 'a cynically adept politician'[44] who has dispossessed the rightful king by guile. He is sharply unlike his counter-part in *Richard II*. The latter displays no hint of the 'hypocritical charm' of this new figure. Harold Goddard also, who calls Henry IV the arch-hypocrite, says that this trait develops in him only after Richard's deposition. "On the day when Henry deposed Richard, he became a double man, one thing to the world, another to his own conscience."[45]

In fact, as observed by Schlegel, Bolingbroke's character is "admirably sustained throughout the three pieces in which he appears".[46] Incapable of 'noble ebullitions', the usurper King or *Henry IV* remains as much an actor and as crafty a politician as the usurping noble in *Richard II.* Whatever doubts one may have regarding his motives, they are finally dispelled by his death-bed confession to his heir:

God knows, my son,
By what by-paths and indirect crookt ways
I met this crown,...
It seem'd in me
But as an honour snatched with boist 'rous hand,
And I had many living to upbraid
My gain of it by their assistances,
Which daily grew to quarrel and to bloodshed,
Wounding supposed peace: all these bold fears
Thou see'st with peril I have answered:
For all my reign hath been but as a scene
Acting that argument. (*2 Henry IV*. IV. v. 183-98)

Part of the argument, thus acted was:

To lead out many to the Holy Land,
Lest rest and lying still might make them look
Too near unto my state. (*2 Henry IV*. IV. v. 210-12)

In this way, as L.C. Knights observes, the character provides "a sombre demonstration of what is involved in getting and keeping power".[47] The ironic political moral is the same that one comes across in Marvell's *Horation Ode*:

The same Arts that did gain
A power must it maintain.[48]

The peace of which Bolingbroke talks in the opening speech of *1 Henry IV* is at best only a painted peace and no one knows it better than he himself. Just as in *Richard II*, the king under the heavy obligations of Mowbray cannot trust him, so Henry-Bolingbroke cannot trust those who have assisted him to his fortune. He did well to banish Exton for his labours, but many—chiefly the Percies—who set him on the throne are still living and are still powerful. How to liquidate them? That is the question. Richard had predicted the mutual hatred and fear of the usurper and his helpers (*Richard II.* V. i. 55-68). The prediction comes true. The inevitable happens. And lest we forget, Shakespeare constantly reminds us of the prophecy. In *2 Henry IV*, Bolingbroke, reflecting on the inscrutable ways of fate and the changeable nature of human affections, remembers the invaluable service rendered to him by Northumberland, 'the man nearest my soul', who 'toiled in my affairs' like a brother: and 'laid his love and life (also honour and conscience) under my foot' (III. i. 61-63). But Bolingbroke remembers not only this, he also recollects the above-mentioned words of Richard and acknowledges their prophetic truth.

> But which of you was by—
> You, cousin Nevil, as I may remember—(to Warwick)
> When Richard, with his eye brim ful of tears,
> Then checked and rated by Northumberland,
> Did speak these words, now proved a prophecy?
> 'Northumberland, thou ladder by the which
> My cousin Bolingbroke ascends my throne'.
>
> (*2 Henry IV.* III. i. 65-71)

Incidentally, when Richard spoke those words neither Warwick nor Bolingbroke was by. Shakespeare is so much concerned with the dramatic effect of the words that he forgets the actual context or prefers deliberately to ignore it. On the rebels' side, the moral of Richard's prophecy is echoed twice by Worcester. First, he makes it the chief justification of the rebellion. They must raise a head in self-defence, for howsoever they bear themselves, they would always be suspects in the eyes of the king (*1 Henry IV.* I. iii. 280-87). On the second occasion, he makes it the excuse for not disclosing the king's offer to Hotspur. Worcester refuses to believe that the king would keep his word ('It is not possible, it cannot be', *1 Henry IV.* V. ii. 4.),

> For treason is but trusted like the fox,
> Who ne'er so tame, so cherished and locked up,
> Will have a wild trick of his ancestors. (II, 10-12)

Whatever one may say about the private character of Worcester,[49] he is a shrewd political observer. His diagnosis of the inevitable malady of mistrust is above question. It is difficult to see how the rebels could have acted otherwise than they did. Similarly, it is difficult to imagine how the usurper could have acted in any other way than he did. He attained the throne largely with the help of the Percies and he cannot brook to be reminded of this fact. In the process of usurpation, he not only deposed Richard, but also superseded the claim of Richard's rightful heir, Edmund Mortimer: "Let me not hear you speak of Mortimer" (*1 Henry IV*. I. iii. 119).[50] The ghost of Richard haunts Bolingbroke in the form of Mortimer.[51]

Richard's ghost also haunts him in the person of his own son and heir, Prince Hal. And what is all the more disturbing, this ghost is accompanied by another, the ghost of Bolingbroke's own youth, the young Hotspur. By making Hal and Hotspur coeval after Daniel's *Civil Wars*. Shakespeare succeeds in adding human dimensions to history and takes us deep into the psychology of the usurper-king-father. In deposing Richard, Bolingbroke commits himself to the 'best-man' or 'strong-man' theory of kingship. He was better and stronger than Richard. But now he appears to be 'caught in his own trap'.[52] Between Hotspur, 'the theme of honour's: tongue' (*1 Henry IV*. I. i. 80) and his own 'unthrifty son' (*Richard II*. V. iii. 1), there seems to be no question of relative merit. History appears to repeat itself. Hotspur becomes "a touchstone of the Prince's quality",[53] but he also becomes a mirror of Bolingbroke's past. Apparently, he is what Bolingbroke had been, while Hal is what Richard had been:

> For all the world
> As thou art to this hour was Richard then
> When I from France set foot at Ravenspurgh
> And even as I was then is Percy now.
>
> (*1 Henry IV*. III. ii. 93-97)

It is this disturbingly remarkable likeness of the two situations that weighs heavy on Bolingbroke, not the guilt of usurpation and the blood of the anointed.

Instead of working out a solution of the political question of usurpation, Shakespeare simply presents the situation as it is and deliberately sets it "in the widest possible human context".[54] The man who has devoted his life to sheer political expediency is made here and increasingly hereafter, to realise personal questions. In *Richard II*, when Bolingbroke enquires about his "unthrifty son" it is Hotspur who gives the news.[55] Now it is the news of Hotspur's glorious victory that reminds the king of the dissolute Prince. To the king's emphatic interrogative[56] regarding the worth of Hotspur's Scottish achievement, Westmoreland adds the affirmative appendix:

"In faith,/
It is a conquest for *a prince* to boast of"
(*1 Henry IV*. I. i. 75-76)

To the king, the observation, with the inadvertent use of *a prince* sounds ironic. Through a psychological association of ideas, he is instantaneously reminded of the Prince. If only Westmoreland and all the nation could have substituted *the Prince* for *a prince*, what a world of difference it would have made to the father: It is this inner desire of the desperate father which finds expression in the speech that follows:

Yea, there thou mak'st *me* sad, and mak'st *me* sin
In envy that *my* Lord Northumberland
Should be the father to so blest a son...
A son who is the theme of honour's tongue,
Amongst a grove the very straightest plant,
Who is sweet Fortune's minion and her pride,
Whilst *I* by looking on the praise of him
See riot and dishonour stain the brow
Of *my* young Harry... O that it could be prov'd
That some night-tripping fairy had exchang'd
In craddle-clothes our children where they lay
And call'd *mine* Percy, his Plantagenet!
Then would I have his Harry, and he *mine*:
(I. i. 78-89) (Italics Mine)

Placed beside the rhetoric of the opening speech, it makes a study in sharp contrast. Unlike the former, the feelings here are genuine and deeply personal. Note the change in the rhythm and the dropping out of the official 'we' in favour of 'I'. Whereas in the first speech of thirty-three lines, the first person singular occurs only twice in the objective and the possessive case,[57] in the present speech of only seventeen lines, it appears no less than ten times and there is no trace of the formal 'we'. In the next speech, after the first line, "But *I* have sent for him to answer this", the king is back again to his formal rhetoric. It is as if Bolingbroke, not yet prepared for the personal, is suddenly carried off his feet and off his guard. He utters genuine personal emotions which normally he would rather keep to himself. This throws into greater relief the artifice of the political world. The desperate wish of the father for a change of sons takes gross liberty with history, but it is not merely a picturesque piece of poetry; it forms a part of the central theme of usurpation and its ironies. It reflects the wish of the political usurper for human usurpation. The man who has usurped the 'Divine' throne forcibly through human agency, desires here to usurp the parenthood of Northumberland through Divine agency. The ghosts again! If only they could have changed places.

The parallel between Bolingbroke and the Rebels[58] is too significant to be missed. His description of the Rebels is instinct with irony. At Shrewsbury, he charges Worcester with betrayal of trust and, implores him to return to the 'obedient orb' (V. i. 9 ff.). Worcester is the man, who in Richard's time broke his staff of stewardship, forsook the court ('the obedient orb') and offered his service to Bolingbroke.[59] And he is quick to remind Bolingbroke of this.[60] Should he now return to the 'obedient orb', it would not to be to support Bolingbroke's cause, but rather the cause of Richard's appointed heir, Mortimer. To Worcester's genuine complaints, Bolingbroke replies with a general observation on rebellions:

> To face the garment of rebellion
> With some fine colour that may please the eye
> Of fickle changelings and poor discontents,
> Which gape and rub the elbow at the news
> Of hurlyburly innovation.
> And never yet did insurrection want
> Such water-colours to impaint his cause,
>
> (*1 Henry IV*. V. i. 74-80)

The truth of the statement cannot be challenged. In *2 Henry IV* again similar observations are repeated. The lead given by the Archbishop to the rebellion turns into religion.[61] Water-colours indeed! But what about Bolingbroke's own protestations in *Richard II*? And what is more, the truth of the observation applies not only to insurrection, but to all wars. What about the proposed crusades? And what about Henry V's French campaign?

Both the rebellions during the reign of Henry IV are replicas of Bolingbroke's revolt against Richard. The rebels attempt to emulate Bolingbroke's seizing of power.[62] His cunning is renewed in Worcester, his duplicity in Northumberland. The brighter side of his character is, on the other hand, renewed in Hotspur.[63] The same sense of injured merit which finds expression in Bolingbroke's complaint against Bushy and Greene (*Richard II*. III. i. 16-19), lives again in Hotspur.[64] The first introduction to Hotspur by Bolingbroke himself is as 'the theme of honour's tongue', 'sweet Fortune's minion and her pride' (*1 Henry IV*. I. i. 80 and 82). Yet in his first appearance, we find him at pains to exonerate himself of bad report. Concluding his damaging account of the courtier, he pleads:

> And I beseech you, let not his report
> Come current for an accusation
> Betwist my love and your high Majesty.
>
> (*1 Henry IV*. I. iii. 66-68)

This might well have been Bolingbroke's pleading in *Richard II* and is actually the pleading of Prince Hal, when he speaks of the harm done by 'smiling pickthanks' and 'base newsmongers' (*1 Henry IV*. III. ii. 25 and V. iv. 50). But the resemblance between Bolingbroke and Hotspur is more a resemblance of their situations than of their character. In fact, Hotspur represents that sympathetic image of the wronged noble which Bolingbroke projects for himself in *Richard II*. The Medieval concepts of honour and chivalry truly come to life in him.[65] As Helen Morris observes, Honour is a key word in the Histories.[66] It appears particularly so in the *Henry IV* plays. "Here", says Mahood, "Shakespeare's flying thoughts on language all settle round the notion of Honour, a Good Name."[67] The word provides the meeting ground for different moral worlds—the worlds of Rule, Riot and Rebellion.[68] Almost all characters participate in developing the theme of honour, but "Hotspur by his devotion to 'bright Honour'" (I. iii. 202)[69] represents the theme itself. It is a commonplace of criticism to suspect the honour of Hotspur. That he has 'blunt honesty' admits Goddard, but "his very honesty is based on a lie, a degenerate form of the medieval conception of 'honour'. The fact that Hotspur talks so incessantly and extravagantly about 'honour' shows that he distrusts his own faith in it".[70] In order to substantiate the view, Goddard points to the disturbed sleep of Hotspur caused, according to him, by 'fear begotten by falsehood' and goes on to remark that Hotspur "rationalizes his inborn pugnacity into a creed". The 'pugnacious Hotspur' like 'the sentimental Richard' is a victim of words.[71] The last of the remarks aptly diagnoses the flaw in Hotspur. In *Richard II,* Shakespeare explores the possibilities of the Tudor Jacobean concept of Divine Right of Kings. In *Henry IV*, he explores the possibilities of Honour and Hotspur is the principal medium for this. It is this that lies behind the extravagant protestations of Honour by Hotspur, not his lack of genuine faith in it.

It is singularly erroneous to confuse Hotspur's true honour with the counterfeit honour of Bolingbroke's.[72] Below the superficial likeness of the two, emerges their essential dissimilarity. While Bolingbroke is Shakespeare's portrayal of the consummate politician, Hotspur is his portrayal of the non-politician.[73] Both are "superbly drawn", says Marriott, "Bolingbroke the shrewd politician, the crafty diplomatist; Hotspur, the blunt impetuous, and hot-tempered soldier; courageous and generous to a fault; transparently honest, guileless and sincere".[74] Hotspur is "incapable of meanness of spirit".[75] He is, as described by Bolingbroke himself, "Amongst a grove the very straightest plant" (*1 Henry IV*. I. i. 81).

Whereas Bolingbroke "can always subdue the man to the official", Hotspur with his "human and manly instincts", "can never conduct himself as the unfailing official".[76] It is customary to compare Hotspur with the Bastard and Coriolanus.[77] In respect of his irresistible attractiveness, he has also been compared with Mercutio.[78] But there is another Shakespearean character, Mowbray, to whom he bears close resemblance. Let us hear the two challengers in *Richard II* amplifying their own concepts of Honour and the difference between Hotspur and Bolingbroke in the matter comes straight home to us. Refusing to give up Bolingbroke's challenge in two forceful replies to Richard, Mowbray builds up the Medieval concept of Honour:

> Myself I throw, dread severeign, at thy foot,
> My life thou shalt command, but not my shame,
> The one my duty owes, but my fair name,
> Despite of death that lives upon my grave,
> To dark dishonour's use thou shalt not have
>
> (I. i. 165-69)
>
> The purest treasure mortal times afford,
> Is spotless reputation—that away
> Men are but gilded loam, or painted clay...
>
> Mine honour is my life, both grow in one,
> Take honour from me, and my life is done: (ll. 177-81)

There is no ambition here, only an unflinching devotion to the principle of Honour, a passionate desire to exonerate oneself of slander. These are hymns to the Divinity Honour. For Mowbray as for Hotspur life itself derives meaning and significance from the ideal of Honour. In Bolingbroke's reply there are no such lofty sentiments.

> O God defend my soul from such deep sin!
> Shall I seem crest-fallen in my father's sight
> Or with pale beggar-fear impeach my height
> Before this out-dared dastard? Ere my tongue
> Shall wound my honour with such feeble wrong,
> Or sound so base a parle, my teeth shall tear
> The slavish motive of recanting fear,
> And spit it bleeding in his high disgrace,
> Where shame doth harbour, even in Mowbray's face.
>
> (ll. 187-95)

Commenting on this peremptory refusal of Bolingbroke, Herford remarks that Bolingbroke "disdains to argue; he opposes to the king's command no plausible generalities (such as ll. 177-81), merely his own invincible repugnance".[79] In fact, unlike Mowbray as unlike Hotspur, Bolingbroke is no votary of any such high ideal as Honour. The words 'Crest-fallen' and 'height' indicate his personal ambition. There are no generalities in his speech, because he does not recognise any general principles. The parley appears base to him not in respect of principles, but in respect of personalities. In his eyes, Mowbray is after all only an 'outdared dastard'. To come to peace with such a fellow would compromise the height of Bolingbroke and create an impression of fear.

That Shakespeare does not dismiss Mowray and his chivalrous honour lightly is evident from the highly complimentary reference to him in the most unexpected places. It is not for nothing that in the midst of acrimonious threats and counter-threats among the English Lords and just before the deposition of the anointed king, Shakespeare inserts a glowing tribute to the honourable knight by the righteous and upright Bishop of Carlisle:

> Many a time hath banished Norfolk fought
> For Jesu Christ in glorious Christian field,
> Steaming the ensign of the Christian cross
> Against black pagans, Turks, and Saracens,
> And toiled with works of war, retired himself
> To Italy, and there at Venice gave
> His body to that pleasant country's earth,
> And his pure soul unto his captain Christ
> Under whose colours he had fought so long.
>
> (*Richard II.* IV. i. 92-100)

In *2 Henry IV* again, we get a glimpse of Mowbray's spirit in his son. With his role much enlarged in the rebellion camp at Gaultree forest, the youthful Mowbray is the only figure who draws our sympathy. While the Archbishop and Hastings are only too willing to accept the offer of peace, it is he who with an intuitive feeling opposes it as long as he can. He is a miniature Hotspur. His vivid poetic description of the Coventry tournament resurrects the dead Mowbray, while at the same time it is a close parallel to Hotspur's account of Mortimer's fight with Glendower (I. iii. 97 ff.). To Westmoreland's reminder that the young Mowbray, has been restored to all signiories of "your noble and right well remembered father's", his impatient rejoinder is:

> What thing, in honour, had my father lost,
> That need to be revived and breathed in me?
>
> (*2 Henry IV*. IV. i. 113-14)

Like his father and like Hotspur, the only thing valued by him is Honour.

It is said that in Hotspur Honour becomes identical with 'personal glory', for he is incapable of thinking in terms of the state.[80] The division of the commonwealth at Bangor may be used as evidence to demonstrate this. The truth is that Hotspur is essentially a private man[81] and to him, as perhaps to his creator, Honour remains a private virtue. He believes in personal relationships and for him Honour forms the basis of these relationships. The unquestioned leader of the rebellion as he is, unlike Bolingbroke in *Richard II* and York in *Henry VI* plays, he never craves for the crown[82] and yet quarrels over a petty piece of land for the sake of honour. As he says after his emotional outburst:

> I do not care, I'll give thrice so much land
> To any well-deserving friend:
> But in the way of bargain, mark ye me,
> I'll cavil on the ninth part of a hair.
>
> (*1 Henry IV*. III. i. 131-34)

Where is the 'ill-weaved ambition' that could not be content with a whole kingdom? (*1 Henry IV*. V. iv. 88-90). Palmer comments, "There is no real ambition in Hotspur, but from Henry of Monmouth the charge was inevitable."[83] For Prince Hal as for his father, Honour remains a rationalisation of personal ambition. Bolingbroke speaks of the crown as 'an honour snatched with boist' rous hand' (*2 Henry IV*. IV. v. 192) and the Prince, putting the same on his head even before the king has passed away, remarks:

> Lo where it sits—
> Which God shall guard; and put the
> world's whole strength

Into one giant arm, it shall not force
This lineal honour from me: (2 *Henry IV*. IV. v. 43-46)

Chivalrous and honourable as the words are, they only serve to underline the personal ambition of the speaker. And this becomes plain when we place the speech beside the Bastard's famous: "Come the three corners of the world in arms" (*King John*. V. vii. 116). The Honour snatched with a boisterous hand becomes the lineal honour for the son. Hotspur's 'bright honour' on the other hand, is a stoic virtue, too abstract to take any concrete shape, too Romantic[84] and personal[85] to stand the test of actual experience. His whole case against Bolingbroke rests on the purely 'emotional ground'[86] that the latter has broken his oath taken at Doncaster. Bolingbroke is 'ingrate and cank' red (I. iii. 137), 'subtle' (l. 169) and 'proud' (l. 184),—'out upon this half-faced fellowship!' (l. 208). There ought to be some honesty even among rebels.[87] By betraying the trust of his allies, Bolingbroke has violated the honour of personal relationship.[88] His honour is open to the same charge which is laid at the doors of Brutus and other conspirators in the ironic use of the word 'honourable' by Antony.[89] The distinction between the other conspirators and Brutus is, as we know, of supreme importance:

All the conspirators save only he
Did that they did in envy of great Caesar;
He only in a general honest thought
And common good to all made one of them.
(*J. Caesar*. V. v. 69-72)

The distinction is the same which separates Hotspur from the other rebels as well as from the King and the Prince. Hotspur, "the very straightest plant" amongst a grove and Brutus, "the noblest Roman of them all", are both beyond any selfish ambition or personal envy. Both commit the same error of subduing human life to abstract thought. What Campbell says about Brutus can with equal force and justness be said about Hotspur: "His career is a history of the mistakes in which his rigid application of the stoical principles involve him."[90] Brutus sacrifices his best friend, Caesar, to what he thinks to be a higher political imperative,[91] Hotspur sacrifices himself to what he feels to be a higher ideal than Life itself. Unless compromised with expediency and geared to the times, Honour, like all other ideals, is suicidal. His uncle, Worcester has the wisdom to recognise this:

> He apprehends a world of figures here.
> But not the form of what he should attend.
>
> (*I Henry IV*. I. iii. 209-10)

Hal's superiority to Hotspur lies in the former being groomed to Time. He is aware of historical necessity and is capable of moulding his Honour as the times demand. Hotspur, on the other hand, rises above his immediate surroundings. His concept of Honour is too high and rigid to be affected by the temporal. However, like all such ideals, Honour is devoid of all meaning without Life. It becomes a mirage in the words of Falstaff:

> What is honour? a word./What is in that word honour?/ What is in that honour?/Air. A trim reckoning! Who hath it?/He that died a-Wednesday. Doth he feel it?/No. Doth he hear it? No..../But will it not live with the living?/Honour is a mere scutcheon (*1 Henry IV*. V. i. 133-40)

There could not have been a more devastating iconoclasm even from the pen of Bernard Shaw. This is "the extreme of verbal scepticism", as Mahood[92] puts it. "In a sense", she goes on, "Shakespeare means Falstaff to be right. Glorious war is strongly satirised when, after all Hotspur's rhodomontade about plucking honour from the pale-faced moon, Falstaff turns over the body of Sir William Blunt (*sic*)[93] to contemplate its grinning honour". Shakespeare does not stop even there. Falstaff, who stabs the dead Hotspur, is allowed to perform the final act of dishonour to "the theme of honour's tongue". What adds to the irony is Falstaff's laying claim to honour on the very basis of this most dishonourable deed. Dumping the cold Hotspur on the ground, he tells the Prince: "If your father will do me any honour, so; if not, let him kill the next Percy himself...I look to be either earl or duke, I can assure you." (V. iv. 139). Commenting on the mockery of Hotspur's 'bright honour' thus in words as well as deeds by the fat Knight, Grigori Koznitsev observes:

> There is much external beauty in the appearance of feudal honor, and the poet expresses the ideal of Hotspur in the full magnificence of its knightly imagery. But the gilt peels off quickly when fat jack becomes involved in the matter. Like a great adipose beast, he goes into the temple of the loftiest class ideals and, chuckling with satisfaction, tramples and pollutes the notions of warriors regarding knightly glory.
>
> Once humanity had dared—according to the famous words of Marx—it broke off with the past. It was a dark and fearful past, and jokes about it were anything but good-natured.[94]

With Falstaff on the scene, the gilt certainly peels off Hotspur's 'bright honour', yet it is as erroneous to take him as a class representative as to call him 'a northern provincial'[95] or continental and fascist.[96] To be sure, placed beside each other, Hotspur and Falstaff do appear like Don Quixote and Sancho Panza, but rather than Hotspur, it is Falstaff, introduced as a Knight, who is, in fact, a representative of the feudal class. "Falstaff", remarks William Empson, "is the first major joke by the English against their class system."[97]

Perhaps, there is more in the mutilation of Hotspur's corpse than meets the eye. When Falstaff ridicules Hotspur's Honour in his Bluntschli-like utterances earlier in the play, we feel convinced that Honour is a mere word. We thank the realist for the brainwashing he gives us. But when he stabs the lifeless Hotspur, we feel he 'goes a bit too far' and "the reason why we feel it so strongly is that the rebels have been made to look rather better than the royal family".[98] Even if this 'unnatural cruelty' does not 'evoke abhorrence of Falstaff',[99] it certainly evokes a fresh sympathy for the dead warrior and his 'bright honour'. It has been noted that Hotspur's honour-speech was 'a huffing part' for it is recited as an illustration of the same by Ralph in the *Knight of the Burning Pestle*.[100] True, but as Jorgensen[101] convincingly demonstrates, behind the speech lay "hortatory and gratulatory tracts" flourishing between 1589 and 1597. The subject of honour was undoubtedly a topic of the day. It had received expression in a literary jargon. "Hotspur and his 'bright Honour' were an anachronism in a military scene dominated by Falstaff, conscripts and gunpowder (not to mention the new ideal represented by Prince Hal)." Nevertheless, "to Elizabethans of 1597, the man who would pluck 'bright Honor' from the moon must have had an accent as familiar and as rich in connotation as that of the earth-bound warrior whom honour could not prick on".[102]

Despite his ultimate death and defeat, Hotspur retains his Honour. Who would not endorse the magnanimous words of his victor?

> This earth, that bears thee dead,
> Bears not alive so stout a gentlemen.
>
> (*1 Henry IV*. V. iv. 91-2)

The name remains a synonym for gallantry. Let us recall the absurd claim of Falstaff: I have killed Percy. If the king does not reward me adequately, well let him kill the next Percy himself.[103] By the way, this absurd claim of Falstaff's also exposes the hollowness of Hal's promise to his father, "I will redeem all this on Percy's head" (*1 Henry IV*. III. ii. 132 ff.) and makes fun of his confident words to Hotspur on the very eve of their fight:

> And all the budding honours on thy crest
> I'll crop, to make a garland for my head.
>
> (*1 Henry IV*. V. iv. 72 ff.)

But, it might be said, he keeps his word—*bēot he gatāeste*—and redeems himself. Indeed, he does, yet what a ludicrous way of laying claim to Honour: Falstaff's parody of Hal's achievement makes short-work of the glory the latter had all along been aiming at. If "the idea is that one who subdues a champion succeeds to all the honours he has won",[104] it is apparently absurd. Mere victory or defeat does not decide Honour. Sir Walter Blunt and many other decoys of the king slain by Douglas have gained immortal honour. There is a thing called "the chance of war".[105] We do not grudge Hal his victory over Hotspur, yet we feel sorry for the early passing away of the latter. And "we listen without grudging to his widow's rapturous eulogy in *2 Henry IV*".[106] By the simple ingenuity of making this eulogy a part of the indictment of Northumberland, Shakespeare adds to its dramatic effect and veractiy (*2 Henry IV*. II. iii. 9-45). The vivid imaginative reconstruction of Shrewsbury puts Hal's victory over Hotspur in correct perspective. It also brings to mind the desperate state of the rebels and the rashness of Hotspur on the one hand and the close call the battle proved to be on the other. Despite the odds heavily against them, how close to victory the rebels had come! It is in this context that, when a slight tilt in the balance would have given the day to Hotspur, Northumberland's absence gains added significance. So does the absence of Glendover and of the Archbishop, but while we do not resent their absence so much, we never can forgive Northumberland for his act of dishonour in lying 'crafty-sick' and allowing his son, brother and confederates to do or die. "After all", says Hazlitt, "notwithstanding the gallantry, generosity, good temper, and idle freaks of the mad-cap Prince of Wales, we should not have been sorry, if Northumberland's force had come up in time to decide the fate of the battle at Shrewsbury."[107] In fact, we are positively sorry and angry that the promised force of Northumberland does not arrive. Such feelings could not have been there if Hotspur's Honour had been a mere fiction and he had been unworthy of the succour.

And Shakespeare does the highest honour to Hotspur by making him the wisest philosopher of history even at the point of his death. For the most illuminating comment on his own career as well as on the whole process of history comes from the mouth of the dying Hotspur. Wounded mortally by the Prince, his initial reaction is "O, Harry, thou hast robbed me of my youth!" (V. iv. 77). It recalls to us the words of Falstaff, "honour pricks me on...but how if honour prick me off when I come on".[108] And yet, honour pricks Hotspur on once again to overcome his sense of loss of life:

> I better brook the loss of brittle life
> Than those proud titles thou hast won of me.
> They wound my thoughts worse than thy sword my flesh:
> (V. iv. 78-80)

This is the final attempt to subdue the human quantum to an abstract ideal. It is heroic and impressive. Nevertheless, it is removed from actual experience and, therefore, would not do. Hence, it is followed by a big 'But':

> But thoughts, the slaves of life, and life, time's fool,
> And time that takes survey of all the world,
> Must have a stop. O, I could prophesy,
> But that the earthy and cold hand of death
> Lies on my tongue: no, Percy, thou art dust,
> And food for—(Dies)
>
> (V. iv. 81-86)

Howsoever noble an ideal might be, it remains a slave of life. The pity that it is so and not the other way round! But life itself, however zestful or purposeful, remains a fool of time. The more the pity! The earlier lines become equivocal now. What is brittle—life, or honour, or both? Who has robbed Hotspur of his youth—Harry Monmouth or Harry Percy? What wounds his thoughts, the sword of Monmouth or his own abstract idealism which brought him to this blind alley and then forsook him? Indeed, as Branche tells us, "his view of historical necessity has matured only at the moment of death".[109] But this maturity could have come only through a painful experience. And it is not merely a view of 'historical necessity', it is much more besides. Historical time has its undoubted relevance. All men are subjects to it,[110] but when all is said, basic human virtues, noble ideals, nay, the very drudgery of day-to-day life, escape the tyranny of time.

It is in the light of this that Hotspur's 'honour', Bolingbroke's 'crusade', Hal's 'redeeming time', Falstaff's 'instinct' and the Gloucester-shire-tedium must be viewed. "Basic private virtues do not go out of date though their manifestations may."[111] Hotspur's 'bright (or 'brittle') honour' also does not go out of date, though it appears an anachronism in Bolingbroke's world of pretentious crusades. "Honour", says Robert Weimann, "could still be dramatically defined in terms of Hotspur's attitudes, but it was no longer possible to view it solely as 'bright honour'".[112] By the side of this figure of chivalry for ever lurks the fat knight and, as accompaniment to the apostrophe to 'bright honour', one always hears the scutcheon-catechism.

Falstaff has a 'tincture of the shaman' in him.[113] Morgann's admirable attempt to absolve Falstaff of the charge of cowardice[114] was based on a wrong premise: cowardice is contemptible and mean. Cowardice is a common human instinct, certainly more common than valour. It is shared by the unwilling soldiers as well as the victor of Agincourt. "Of all the thousand qualities", says Napoleon in Shaw's *The Man of Destiny*, "a man may have, the only one you will find as certainly in the youngest drummer boy in my army as in me, is fear. It is fear that makes men fight "it is indifference that makes them run away". Though Orwell may not agree (he believes that high sentiments always win in the end) yet he concedes that cowardice, dishonesty and such other human vices form the other element in man and can never be discounted. "When it comes to the pinch", he says

> human beings are heroic. Women face childbed and the scrubbing brush, revolutionaries keep their mouths shut in the torture chamber, battleships go down with their guns still firing when their decks are awash. It is only that the other element in man, the lazy, cowardly, debt-biking adulterer who is inside all of us, can never be suppressed altogether and needs a hearing occasionally.[115]

When it comes to the pinch even Richard II is heroic. Falstaff personifies the principle of libido[116] just as Hotspur personifies the principle of 'Honour'. He is a lump of the world,[117] as Edith Sitwell puts it, or 'a great symbol of common humanity' as Bryant labels him.[118] It is impossible to conceive of a Falstaff devoid of this prime human instinct of cowardice.

But Falstaff not only shams chivalry, he also shams remorse and reformation. Just as he does not believe in the Medieval concept of 'Honour', so he does not believe in Christian repentance and salvation. The lietmotif of repentance is also introduced in the very beginning of the play. Bolingbroke seems to repent that he deposed King Richard. To make amends, he resolves (or so he pretends) to lead a crusade to the Holy Land. The rebels, who are filled with shame and remorse for their ignominious part in Bolingbroke's usurpation, resolve to amend this by serving the usurper in his own coin. The Prince resolves to reform in public eye. Falstaff's remorse throws into relief the remorse of all these characters engaged in the political drama. In particular, it is a parody of Bolingbroke's sham religiosity. Bolingbroke speaks of the crusades, but in the same scene we find him actually preparing for a civil war. In the very next scene, we meet Falstaff in the posture[119] of Monsieur Remorse—a favourite posture of his. He is "the innocent beguiled by a wicked young heir apparent:"[120]

> thou hast done much harm upon me, Hal—God forgive thee for it: before I knew thee, Hall, I knew nothing, and now am I, if a man should speak truly, little better than one of the wicked...I must give over this life, and I will give it over: by the Lord, an I do not, I am a villain, I'll be damned for never a king's son in Christendom. (*1 Henry IV*. I. ii. 90-96).

This sanctimonious Puritan air is preceded by a protestation of melancholy: "I am as melancholy as a gib cat, or a lugged bear" (I. ii. 72-73). Empson has rightly drawn attention to the dramatic ambiguities in the play.[121] For all we know, Falstaff's melancholy and remorse might be genuine.[122] The Prince has all along been talking of the gallows, but to be sure, what piques Falstaff more than a reminder of the gallows or the buff-jerkin, is a reminder of the Moorditch. In Shakespeare's time, the Moor-fields used to be the haunt of beggars and cashiered soldiers and Hal manages to get in a cruel thrust by suggesting that Falstaff's future will be with the decayed and poverty-stricken soldiers.[123] Imagine Falstaff crawling and begging: The thought naturally upsets him. "Thou hast the most unsavoury similes", he complains. However, just as the king's resolve to wage Holy Wars is followed by preparations to punish his erstwhile allies, so Falstaff's melancholic remorse is followed by preparations for Gadshill. The robbery committed and the booty looted, we find him again pretending to become a pious Puritan:

> Ere I lead this life long, I'll sew netherstocks, and mend them, and foot them too.
>
> (II. iv. 112-13)

> I would I were a weaver; I could sing psalms, or anything.
>
> (II. iv. 130)

In Act III. Sc. iii. "when there is no Hal present to require entertaining",[124] he appears appalled at the idea of old age and is, as it were, prompted to repent before it gets too late:

> Well, I'll repent, and that suddenly, while I am in some liking. I shall be out of heart shortly, and then I shall have no strength to repent. An I have not forgotten what the inside of a church is made of, I am a peppercorn, a brewer's horse. The inside of a church! Company, villainous company, hath been the spoil of me.
>
> (III. iii. 4-10)

In *2 Henry IV*, however, when reminded of his old age by the Lord Chief Justice, he denies it firmly, protesting that he is young, while the Chief Justice is old. As for his broken voice, the explanation is, "I have lost it with hallooing and singing of anthems"(*2 Henry IV*. I. ii. 177). Perhaps this 'streak of Puritanism' in Falstaff, as noted by certain critics, has its origin in his Oldcastle-ancestry.[125] In any case it ill-agrees with his alleged role as Vice or tempter in the Prodigal Son-morality. Dover Wilson has suggested a number of reasons why the repentance of the Prince must be transferred to Falstaff. The Prince is not a real sinner. Shakespeare must guard his future Henry V against the breath of scandal. Dramatically the repentance of the Prince belongs to the last act of the play.[126] These explanations sound plausible enough. Nevertheless Falstaff's repentance has a much more significant dramatic function and Traversi is nearer the truth in linking it directly with Hal's conscious self-control and conversion. "When Falstaff describes himself", says Traversi:

> as 'little better than one of the wicked' and announces, ironically, his own conversion, he is at once ridiculing the idea of such conversion (which Hal will shortly

> assert, anticipating his own formal declaration, as a necessary public gesture) and admitting implicitly the existence of a background against which the limitations of his own dissolute vitality stand out.[127]

But, as noted above, Falstaff is a 'shaman' of the very idea of remorse and reformation and his mock-repentance exposes not only the promised amendment of the Prince, but also the crusades of Bolingbroke and the remorse of the rebels. The point that Shakespeare wishes to drive home is, perhaps, the genuine desire of the fat rogue to repent and renounce his past, notwithstanding his awareness that it cannot be unless God ordains. This is brought out cleverly in just one epigram of Falstaff's. In Act III. Scene iii of *1 Henry IV*, immediately after his resolve to repent and give up this life, he surprises Bardolph and surprises us with a complete volte-face:

> Do thou amend thy face, and I'll amend my life.
>
> (III. iii. 23)

Bardolph cannot change his face, nor can any man, except in the theatre with masks and paints. "Thou canst not make one hair white or black", says St. Matthew.[128] It ought to be easier for a man to change his face than to change his way of life. If one cannot amend the former, what hope is there for one's conscious moral regeneration? This makes a mockery of the projected crusade of the King as well as of the easy conversion of the Prince. Falstaff's own doubt in real inward amendment is certainly more honest than their belief in false, outward amendment. In *2 Henry IV*, he makes a mocking reference to Hal's repentance. Reminding the Lord Chief Justice of the box of ear, he remarks: "I have checked him for it, and the young lion repents—(aside) marry, not in ashes and sack-cloth, but in new silk and old sack" (*2 Henry IV*. I. ii. 190-94). The chances are that even if he had heard the much-debated soliloquy of the Prince, he would not have understood it.[129]

The final and the finest irony, however, is that with all his debunking of morals and mockery of remorse, it is Falstaff who repents in the end while the others do not. Even at his death-bed Bolingbroke is far from relenting. His last advice to his heir is a re-enactment of the same hypocritical piety that he himself has practised throughout his reign. Contrast this with the noble death of Falstaff (*Henry V*. III. ii.). Even by Shakespearean standards, it is undoubtedly one of the finest pieces. "The poet evidently expended", says Goddard, "every power at his command in this scene, and it is enough to say that the story does not suffer when put in comparison with the deaths of Hamlet and Othello, of King Lear and Cleopatra."[130] Middleton Murry goes further in his tribute to the Hostess's account of Falstaff's passing away:

> There are moments— and this is one of them—when I think that the most marvellous speech in all Shakespeare. It is wonderful. There is nothing remotely like this in all the literature of the wrold. How should there be? It is Shakespeare's requiem over the darling of his imagination. There is no death like Falstaff's: therefore there is no description of a death like his.[131]

Arthur Macnalty in an article, 'Shakespeare and Sir Thomas More',[132] draws a parallel between the description of Falstaffs death and More's description of death in *De Quatuor Novissimis* (1522), which was derived from Hippocrates. Dover Wilson, on the other hand, holds that the detail is drawn from the death of Socrates.[133] Referring to the latter parallel, Empson comments that its only possible implication would be that Falstaff, like Socrates, was a wise teacher killed by a false accusation of corrupting young men.[134] Certainly the death is unique because, whether due to censorship or the absence of Will Kempe the actor or sheer dramatic necessity, Shakespeare was forced to kill the character.[135] One may go even further and endorse Frank O'Connor's view that Falstaff's part in the third play had already been written and Shakespeare was compelled by the censor to cut it out.[136]

To contemplate Shakespeare's own feelings regarding the passing away of Falstaff on the basis of the very moving report by Mistress Quickly is rewarding. So are the scholarly attempts to excavate the possible sources that might well have helped the dramatist in his magnificent account of the death. The final justification of the description, however, would be its dramatic relevance. The old sinner dies an innocent child—'any Christian child'.—"Whosoever shall not receive the kingdom of God as a little child, he shall not enter therein."[137] He babbles of green fields.—"They can be seen along the road to Stratford—quiet fields of a tender green, the soft lines of low-lying hills, the peace of nature, like a park."[138] He has no monstrous visions. He has renounced his past and 'cried out of sack' as well as women.[139] At perfect peace with himself, he needs no music.[140] The only music heard is the babbling of green fields and 'God, God, God!' He dies a noble death with a vision of Paradise. Commenting on Bolingbroke's death, Goddard[141] draws attention to Tolstoy's story, *The Two Old Men.* Both the old men set out for Jerusalem and both arrive there, one literally but not spiritually, the other spiritually but not literally. In *Henry IV* too we come across a pair of old men. One sets out for Jerusalem, the other turns his back on Jerusalem. Ironically, the former never arrives there (or arrives there neither spiritually nor physically, only literally)[142] the latter, that is Falstaff, does. With no promises to keep, no words to honour, he yet redeems time in the true Biblical sense.

Much has been written on the famous soliloquy of Prince Hal and deservedly, for it brings to the fore certain fundamental issues regarding the play as well as regarding the character of the Prince. Broadly speaking, there are two schools of criticism. One, by treating the soliloquy as a dramatic convention, attempts to delink it from the character. Dr. Johnson, for instance, observes: "This speech is very artfully introduced to keep the Prince from appearing vile in the opinion of the audience: it prepares them for his future redemption."[143] Tillyard echoes Dr. Johnson, "The Prince in his choric self-comment is concerned first of all with justifying to an Elizabethan audience this apparent degradation of royalty."[144] The other school passes strong strictures on the Prince largely on the basis of the soliloquy. He is 'deliberately treacherous' in the words of Bernard Shaw.[145] He is ready "to use other people as a means to his own ends", says Bradley.[146] Both friends and foes are his instruments, he practises deliberate deception, observes Sen Gupta.[147] But as Lindabury puts it, "to surprise an enemy is usually considered good strategy, to surprise a friend goes by a harsher name."[148]

Comparatively little attention has, however, been given to the last words of Hal's soliloquy:

> Redeeming time when men think least I will.
> (1 *Henry IV*. I. ii. 212)

And yet, as Jorgensen observes, "The primary emphasis given to *time* in *Henry IV*, is the problem of its redemption."[149] The words 'redeeming time' echo St. Paul's exhortation to the *Ephesians*:

> See then that ye walk circumspectly, not as fools, but as wise, redeeming the time, because the days are evil.[150]

and to the *Colossians*:

> Walk in wisdom toward them that are without redeeming the time.[151]

That Shakespeare has the Biblical texts in mind while writing *Henry IV*, becomes clear when in *2 Henry IV*, replying to the Prince's query regarding Falstaff's company, the Page has this to say: "Ephesians, my lord, of the old church" (II. ii. 143). Ephesians were the people in need of regeneration, especially the old people, observes Bryant, adding further that it was probably Shakespeare who made Falstaff old, unlike Oldcastle or Jockey in *The Famous Victories*.[152] By making Falstaff old and sinful, Shakespeare underlines his need for redemption, but it is difficult to agree with Bryant that the Prince attempts to redeem the old man and failing in this, ultimately casts him off.[153]

When the Prince concludes his soliloquy with 'redeeming time', it apparently means 'making amends for wasted time'.[154] The Elizabethans, however, well familiar with the Biblical texts and religious tracts based on them,[155] could not have interpreted the words thus. To them, redeeming time meant taking full advantage of the present time (that man is given here on earth) for salvation.[156] Hal's sole concern is the public eye. He shows no awareness of the inward-seeing eye or the all-seeing eye. The Elizabethans could have easily discerned the emptiness and the limitations of his boisterous claim to redeem time. What he does redeem at Shrewsbury and elsewhere may at best be termed 'lost opinion' in the public eye.

> *King.*—Thou hast redeem'd thy lost opinion,
> (*1 Henry IV.* V. iv. 47)

By introducing the soliloquy, Shakespeare discounts the tradition of a miraculous sea-change in the Prince.[157] Perhaps, as Lindabury tells us, he wishes to make the conversion plausible.[158] In order to do so he opens a window in the mind of the Prince and thus succeeds in turning "the lack of verisimilitude in the theme into a psychological virtue".[159] The idea is that of an outward change along with inner constancy. The Prince's descent to the tavern world is never complete. Nightly exploits of Falstaff's grind do not make a Knight.[160] The clever Bishops also endorse this very view, when they reflect upon the change in retrospect. As the strawberry grows underneath the nettle, so the Prince obscured his contemplation under the veil of wildness, observes the Bishop of Ely. "It must be so", admits the Archbishop of Canterbury,

> for miracles are ceased
> And therefore we must needs admit the means
> How things are perfected. (*Henry V.* I. i. 60 ff.)

There is no spiritual regeneration of Hal, no redemption of time in the Biblical sense. 'Miracles are ceased'. And yet, so long as there is man, the sinner, and there is the idea of God, the merciful, miracles would always be there. The regeneration of St. Paul is a miracle, the redemption of the penitent thief, crucified with Christ, is a miracle. So is Falstaff's arrival at Jerusalem.

But a miracle is a miracle, because it is rare. Meanwhile life goes on with its mundane reality. People live, buy and sell, earn a name or a place (may be), sow wild oats in their youth and grow old and die.

> *Shallow* — Jesu, Jesu, the mad days that I have spent! and to see how many of my old acquaintance are dead!
>
> *Silence* — We shall all follow, cousin.

Shallow — Certain, 'tis certain, very sure. Death, as the psalmist saith, is certain to all, all shall die. How a good yoke of bullocks at Stamford fair?

Silence — By my troth, I was not there.

Shallow — Death is certain. Is old Double of your town living yet?

Silence — Dead, Sir.

Shallow — Jesu, Jesu, Dead! 'A drew a good bow; and dead! 'A shot a fine shoot.... How a score of ewes now?

Silence — Thereafter as they be—a score of good ewes may be worth ten pounds.

Shallow — And is old Double dead?

(*2 Henry IV*. III. ii. 34-54)

"Somewhere, to one side of everything", comments Kozintsev, "lives the man in the street. No matter what happens in the world, he senses the passing of time only by the changes in the price of live-stock."[161] Tillyard has very rightly drawn a parallel with Hardy's *In the Time of the Breaking of Nations*.[162] Shallow's enquiries about the price of bullocks and ewes remind us of another poem, Wordsworth's *The World Is Too Much With Us*. All the while aware of death with many of their acquaintances gone, old Double the arch-archer gone, the two cousins, both now at the end of their tether, sit contemplating the uncertainty of prices. They sit leisurely and Time appears to have stopped in their world.[163] They hear the bell tolling for old friends. There is still time to 'redeem time', but the world is too much with them. The Golucestershire scenes are not "a studied burlesque of provincial life and manners for the hilarious contempt of London spectators."[164] They are "firmly rooted in the actual".[165] With an 'unobtrusive art', little by little they build up the mundane every day life. Shallow is not "the protagonist of the provincial theme",[166] he is the protagonist of the day-to-day-life theme. He is Everyman. Like the characters of the political world, he has his own calculations and worries, but has no time or conscience to spare for God. As Tillyard observes, there is in the play, "the great contrast between the theme of civil war, the terrible vicissitudes of high politics and the theme of the perennial cycles of birth and death; and of the seasons with their appropriate tasks, without which man simply cannot exist".[167] But there is also the great constrast (and we must go beyond *Henry IV* in order to appreciate it) between the theme of mundane, materialistic life without redeeming the time, and the theme of spiritual regeneration through God's grace. The King's Jerusalem and the Prince's reform in the public eye are parts of the former theme.

NOTES

1. *Dr. Johnson on Shakespeare* (ed.), W. Raleigh (London: Oxford University Press, 1946), p. 124.
2. T. Weiss, *The Breath of Clowns and Kings* (London: Chatto & Windus, 1971), p. 295.
3. G.L. Evans, 'The Comical-Tragical-Historical method—*Henry IV*' *Early Shakespeare* (eds.), J.R. Brown and Harris (London: Edward Arnold, 1967), *passim.*
4. T. Weiss, *Loc. cit.*
5. The bastard's soliloquy on manners (*King John* I. i. 182 ff.) may also be mentioned in this context.
6. See H. Jenkins, 'The Structural Problem in *Henry IV*', R.J. Dorius (ed.), *Discussions of Shakespeare's Histories: Richard II to Henry V* (Boston: D.C. Heath, 1965), p. 42.
7. E.M.W. Tillyard, *Shakespeare's History Plays* (Penguin, 1962), p. 264.
8. J.D. Wilson, *Fortunes of Falstaff* (Cambridge University Press, 1953), *passim and Int. to 1 Henry IV* (Cambridge University Press, 1968), pp. ix *et seq.*
9. M.A. Shaaber, 'The Unity of *Henry IV*', *J.Q. Adams Memorial Studies* (Washington: The Folger Shakespeare Library, 1948), pp. 217 *et seq.*
10. R. David, 'Shakespeare's History Plays Epic or Drama?' *Shakespeare Survey* (1953), Vol. VI, pp. 137 *et seq.*
11. *Op. cit.*, pp. *51 et seq.*
12. *Richard II.* IV. i. 136 ff.
13. *Ibid.*, V. i. 55 ff.
14. Tillyard, *op. cit.*, p. 293.
15. J.D. Wilson (ed.), *1 Henry IV* (The New Shakespeare, Cambridge University Press, 1968), p. xx.
16. *Ibid.*, p. xxi.

17. Holinshed, *Chronicles* III. *Vide* G. Bullough (ed.), *Narrative and Dramatic Sources of Shakespeare,* IV, pp. 180 *et seq.*
18. *Ibid.,* p. 181.
19. The only exception is the account, given by the Archbishop of York, of the instability of common people's affection (*2 Henry IV.* I. iii. 87-108), but the Archbishop is after all a rebel-leader and his comment does not have the same validity as that of the Gardeners in *Richard II.*
20. Bullough, *op. cit.,* p. 181, *n.* 3. and A.R. Humphreys (ed.), *1 Henry IV* (London: Methuen, New Arden 1961), p. 3.
21. *Henry IV, Part I.* New Cambridge Shakespeare p. xxii.
22. *The Fortunes of Falstaff,* p. 61.

    Also J.H. Walter (ed.), *1 Henry IV* (Players Shakespeare Heinemann, 1961), Contemporary Thought, Politics and Events in the Play, p. 250.
23. *Chronicles* III. *Vide* Bullough *op. cit.,* pp. 180 *et seq.*
24. *Ibid.,* p. 277.
25. *The Union, vide ibid., n.* 4.
26. *Civil Wars,* Book III, 115. *Vide ibid.,* p. 282.
27. *Ibid.,* p. 277.
28. As discerned by critics, Tillyard for instance, *op. cit.,* pp. 293 *et seq.*
29. *2 Henry IV.* V. iv. 135-37.
30. *Civil Wars,* III Book. 118. *Vide* Bullough, *op. cit.,* p. 283.—The picture of stricken conscience and fearful apparitions that Daniel draws there may be seen in the death of Cardinal Beaufort in *2 Henry VI.* III. iii. 2 ff.
31. *Richard II.* V. iii. 3.
32. B.I. Evans, *The Language of Shakespeare's Plays* (London: Methuen Univ., Paperbacks 1965), p. 87.

    A.R. Humphreys (ed.), *op. cit.,* p. lxii.

    It is, however, not suggested that the style is immature. The artifice and the contradictions are purposely intended by the dramatist.
33. L.C. Knights, 'Notes on Comedy', *Scrutiny* (March 1933), Reprint Cambridge University Press, 1963), Vol. I, No. 4, p. 362.
34. B.I. Evans, *op. cit.,* p. 88.
35. Knights, *op. cit.,* p. 363.
36. *2 Henry IV.* IV. v. 209.
37. *Chronicles,* III. *Vide* Bullough, *op. cit.,* p. 183.
38. *Vide* Bullough, *op. cit.,* p. 184.
39. Sir J. Turner, *Pallas Armata,* pr. 1683, *vide* A.R. Humphreys, *op. cit.,* p. 8.

40. *Ibid.*, p. 8.
41. Knights, *op. cit.*, p. 363—This makes the account of the proposed crusade satiric.
42. *The Fotunes*, *op. cit.*, p. 61.
    See also R.W.S. Mendl, *Revelation in Shakespeare* (London: John Calder, 1964), p. 86.
43. M.M. Reese, *The Cease of Majesty* (London: Edward Arnold, 1961), pp. 286 *et seq.*
44. J. Winny, *The Player King* (London: Chatto and Windus, 1968), pp. 86 *et seq.*
45. H.C. Goddard, *The Meaning of Shakespeare,* Vol. 1 (Chicago and London: The University of Chicago Press, Phoenix Books, 1967), p. 162.
46. A.W. Schlegel, *Dramatic Art and Literature* (tr.), John Black (London: Henry G. Bohn, 1861), p. 424.
47. L.C. Knights, 'Shakespeare's Politics: With Some Reflections on the Nature of Tradition', *Further Explorations* (Chatto & Windus, 1965), pp. 13 *et seq.*
48. *Vide, ibid.*, p. 14.
49. Goddard calls him 'the liar', *op. cit.*, p. 166.
50. To quote the exchange:

    Wor—And that same greatness too which our own hands
    Have help to make so portly.
    North —My lord,
    King—Worcester get thee gone, for I do see
    Danger and disobedience in thine eye:
    O sir, your presence is too bold and peremptory.
    (*1 Henry IV*. I. iii. 12-17)

51. Goddard, *op. cit.*, p. 165.
    According to Goddard, Mortimer too is a ghostly character remaining mostly behind the scene.
52. *Ibid.*, p. 168.
53. J. Palmer, *Political and Comic Characters of Shakespeare* (London: Macmillan, 1962), p. 183.
54. L.C. Knights, *Further Explorations*, p. 14.
55. *Richard II*. V. iii.
56. Page 196 *supra*.
57. *1 Henry IV*. I. i. 30-31.—This should further cast doubt on the conventional sin-retribution-expiation theory and the sincerity of Bolingbroke's repentance.
58. J. Winny, *op. cit.*, pp. 96 *et seq.*
59. *Richard II*. II. ii. 58-61 and II. iii. 26-27.

60. *1 Henry IV*. V. i. 32-41.
61. *2 Henry IV*. I. i. Morton's words, 200-201 and in IV. i. Westmoreland's words, 32-41.
62. Winny, *op. cit.*, p. 151.
63. It is difficult to agree with Winny that in Hotspur the vices of Bolingbroke are renewed. *Ibid.*, p. 144.
64. Anthony La Branche, '"If Thou Wert Sensible of Courtesy". Private and Public Virtue in *Henry IV, Part One', SQ* Vol. XVII, Autumn 1966, No. 4, p. 376.
65. William B. Hunter, Jr. 'Prince Hal, Struggle Toward Moral Perfection', *South Atlantic Quarterly L.* (Jan. 1951), 86-95. Reprint in Sanderson (ed.), *op. cit.*, pp. 172-82. See especially p. 174.
66. H. Morris, 'The Histories', R. Gettings (ed.), *The Living Shakespeare* (London, Heinemann, 1962), p. 104.
67. M.M. Mahood, *Shakespeare's Wordplay* (London: Methuen, 1957), p. 178.
68. N. Coghill, *Shakespeare's Professional Skills* (Cambridge University Press, 1964), p. 65.
69. Paul A. Jorgensen, 'Hotspur's "bright Honour"', *Redeeming Shakespeare's Words* (Berkeley and Los Angeles: Univ. of California Press, 1962), p. 43.
70. Goddard, *op. cit.*, p. 166.
71. *Ibid.*, pp. 166 *et seq.*
72. As Winny does, *op. cit.*, pp. 139 *et seq.*
    Coghill remarks that King Henry's honour and Hal's honour and Hotspur's are all rooted in dishonour. Coghill, *op. cit*, pp. 66 *et seq.*
73. Reese, *op. cit.*, p. 305.
74. J.A.R. Marriott, *English History in Shakespeare* (New York: E.P. Dutton, 1918), p. 110.
75. A.A. Evans (ed.), *1 Henry IV* (University of London Press, 1962), Critical Commentary, p. 16.
76. H.B. Charlton, *Shakespeare, Politics, and Politicians* (The Eng. Association Pamphlet No. 72, April, 1929), pp. 14 *et seq.*
77. Middleton Murry tells us that the Bastard is split into Hotspur and Falstaff before his final avatar as Harry the King. See his *Shakespeare* (London: Jonathan Cape, 1965), p. 170.

    M.C. Bradbrook calls Hotspur an amplification of the Bastard and an anticipation of Coriolanus. *Shakespeare and Elizabethan Poetry* (London: Chatto & Windus, 1961), p. 205.

    Tillyard and Reese also compare him with the Bastard.

    Tillyard, *op. cit.*, p. 284. Reese, *op. cit.*, 306.
78. Murry, *ibid.*, p. 175.

79. *Vide* J.D. Wilson (ed.), *Richard II* (Cambridge University Press, 1968), p. 129.
80. D.A. Stauffer, *Shakespeare's World of Images. The Development of His Moral Images* (Bloomington: Indiana Univ. Press, 1966), p. 94.
81. "A rash private man", says Branche. See *op. cit.*, p. 379 & *passim.*
82. "He is not interested in political power", says W.H. Auden, 'The Fallen City', *Encounter* (Nov. 1959), XIII, No. 5, p. 24.
83. Palmer, *op. cit.*, p. 209.
84. A.C. Sprague, *Shakespeare's Histories: Plays for the Stage* (London: The Society for Theatre Research, 1964), p. 57.
85. Branche, *op. cit., passim.*
86. *Ibid.*, p. 373.
87. *Ibid.*, p. 374.
88. The story is repeated in Prince Hal's rejection of Falstaff.
89. *J. Caesar,* Mark Antony's Funeral Speech in III. ii.
90. O.J. Campbell, 'The Salvation of Lear', *ELH.* XV (1948), p. 95.
91. Bonjour, *The Structure of Julius Caesar,* p. 12.
92. Mahood, *op. cit.*, p. 178.
93. Or is it Sir Walter Blunt?
94. G. Kozintsev, *Shakespeare: Time and Conscience* (tr.), Joyce Vining (London: Dennis Dobson, 1967), p. 198.
95. Tillyard, *op. cit.*, p. 284.
96. G.W. Knight, *The Olive and the Sword* (London: Oxford University Press, 1944), p. 28.
97. W. Empson, 'Falstaff and Mr. Dover Wilson', *Kenyon Review* (Spring, 1953), Reprint in G.K. Hunter (ed.), *Shakespeare: Henry IV, Parts I and II* (London: Macmillan, Casebook Series, 1970), p. 145.
98. *Ibid.*, pp. 146 *et seq.*
99. Koznitsev, *op. cit.*, p. 197.
100. Tillyard, *op. cit.*, p. 283. and Reese, *op. cit.*, p. 307.
101. Jorgensen, *op. cit.*, especially pp. 44 *et seq.*
102. *Ibid.*, pp. 45 *et* 51.
103. Page 209 *supra.*
104. Kittredge, *vide* Humphreys, *op. cit.*, p. 107.
105. Hotspur's explanation of Mortimer's defeat at the hands of Glendower I. iii. 94.
106. Sprague, *op. cit.*, p. 57.
107. W. Hazlitt, *The Round Table Characters of Shakespeare* (London: J.M. Dent; N.York: E.P. Dutton, 1960), p. 284.
108. His Honour-speech, quoted on p. 209 *supra.*

109. Branche, *op. cit.,* p. 379.

110. Hastings in 2 *Henry IV*. I. iii. 110.

111. Branche, *op. cit.,* p. 377.

112. R. Weimann, 'The Soul of the Age: Towards a Historical Approach to Shakespeare', *Shakespeare in a Changing World* ed. A. Kettle (London: Lawrence and Wishart, 1964), p. 40.

113. Wyndham Lewis, *The Lion and the Fox* (London: Methuen, 1955), pp. 221 *et seq* esp. 221.

114. Maurice Morgann, *An Essay on the Dramatic Character of Sir John Falstaff* (1777), reprint in *Shakespeare Criticism A Selection 1623-1840* ed. D.N. Smith (London: Oxford University Press, 1961), pp. 153-89.

115. G. Orwell, 'Art of Donald McGill', *Horizon* (Sept. 1941), vide Tillyard, *op. cit.,* p. 290.

   Tillyard identifies Falstaff with this other element in man, that is, 'the unofficial self'.

116. Franz Alexander, 'A Note on Falstaff, *Psychoanalytic Qy. II* (Oct. 1933), reprint in Sanderson, *op. cit.,* p. 269.
   "He is symbolically like life itself" says Humpreys, *op. cit.,* p. xiv.

117. E. Sitwell, *A Notebook on Shakespeare* (London: Macmillan, 1962), Chap. I, 'The Hymn to Life', p. 1.

118. Bryant, *op.cit.,* p. 217.

119. C.L. Barber, 'Rule and Misrule' in Hunter (ed.), *op. cit.,* p. 218.

120. J.D. Wilson, *Fortunes, op. cit.,* p. 32.

121. W. Empson, *op. cit., passim.*

122. J.D. Wilson remarks: "Shakespeare makes it more interesting by persuading us that there is a strain of sincerity in it." *Loc. cit.*

123. B. Gellert, "The Melancholy of Moor Ditch A Gloss of *1 Henry IV.* I. ii. 77-80", *Shakespeare Quarterly* (Winter, 1967), Vol. XVIII, No. 1, p. 71.
   Also J.W. Draper's remarks on Elizabethan soldier's life and Falstaff as a typical representative of the class in 'Sir John Falstaff', *RES,* VII (Oct. 1932), 414-24.

124. Wilson, *Fortunes,* p. 33.

125. *Ibid.,* p. 16. Also D. Traversi, *Shakespeare from Richard II to Henry V* (London: Hollis and Carter, 1957), p. 57; and Reese, *op. cit.,* p. 294.

126. Wilson, *op. cit.,* pp. 33 *et seq.*

127. *Op. cit.,* p. 57.

128. *St. Matthew,* VI. 36. *Holy Bible.*

129. W.H. Auden's analysis of Falstaff's reactions to the play in his 'The Fallen City', *Encounter* XIII (1959), pp. 25 *et seq.*

130. Goddard, *op. cit.*, p. 232.
131. Murry, *op. cit.*, p. 179.
132. *Essays and Studies* (1959), p. 51.
133. *Fortunes of Falstaff*, p. 124. cf. Empson, *op. cit.*, p. 151.
134. *Ibid.*, p. 151.
135. Murry, *op. cit.*, p. 179. He thinks it is owing to the dramatic necessity.
136. F.O. Connor, *Shakespeare's Progress* (N. York) Collier Books, 1961), p. 96.
137. *St. Mark*. X. 15. *Holy Bible.*
138. Kozintsev, *op. cit.*, p. 207.
139. The Hostess's protest that he had not cried out of women is the protest of a professional woman.
140. James Winny has drawn a parallel between Bolingbroke's asking for music at death bed (*2 Henry IV*. IV. v. 1-3) and Falstaff's for a bawdy song (*1 Henry IV*. III. iii. 12), but ignores the fact that when Falstaff asks for the song, he is not on death-bed. *op. cit.*, p. 124.
141. *Op. cit.*, p. 198.
142. *Ibid.*, p. 198.—Goddard remarks: "Henry IV arrived neither literally nor spiritually". We can say, he arrives 'literally in the strict sense and not physically, if we keep in mind his last words: *2 Henry IV*. IV. v. 236-40.
143. Dr. Johnson, *op. cit.*, p. 114.
144. Tillyard, *op. cit.*, p. 271. Also D. Wilson, *Fortunes*, p. 41 and Sprague, *op. cit.*, pp. 55 *et seq.*
145. *Our Theatres in the Nineties* (London: Constable, 1932), II, p. 129.
146. A.C. Bradley, 'The Rejection of Falstaff', *Oxford Lectures on Poetry* (London: Macmillan, 1962), p. 257.
147. Sen Gupta, *op. cit.*, p. 128.
148. Lindabury, *Patriotism in Elizabethan Drama* (Princeton University Press, 1931), p. 22.
149. Jorgensen '"Redeeming Time" in Henry IV', *op. cit.*, p. 55.
150. *Ephesians* V, 15-16. *Ibid.*, p. 56 and J.A. Bryant. Jr. 'Prince Hal and the Ephesians.' *Sewanee Review*, Vol. 67 (1959), p. 204 and *passim.*
151. *Collossians* IV, 5.
152. *Op. cit.*, p. 213.
153. *Ibid., passim.*
154. Humphreys, *op. cit.*, p. 21 *n.*
155. Jorgensen refers to a number of these. *Op. cit., 56 et seq.*
156. *Ibid.*, p. 59.

157. Supported especially by *The Famous Victories* and Hall.
158. Lindabury, *op. cit.*, p. 23.
159. Traversi, *op. cit.*, pp. 6 *et* 58.
160. Elsa Sjoberg, 'From Madcap Prince to King', *Shakespeare Quarterly*, XX (Winter, 1969), No. 1, p. 14.
161. Kozintsev, *op. cit.*, p. 203.
162. Tillyard. *op. cit.*, p. 303.
163. Kozintsev, *op. cit.*, p. 205.
164. D. Wilson, *Fortunes*, p. 111.
165. L.C. Knights, 'Time's Subjects: *2 Henry IV*'. *Some Shakespearean Themes* (1959). Reprint in Hunter, *op. cit.*, p. 179.
166. Kozintsev, *op. cit.*, p. 204.
167. *Op. cit.*, p. 304.

Henry V

8

King Henry V, the victor of Agincourt, occupies the same venerable position in English history that King Chandragupta Maurya enjoys in Indian history. The former defeated the French and extended the English territory to France, the latter founded the famous Mauryan dynasty, vanquished the Greeks and extended his territory to the westernmost parts of India, including today's Pakistan and Afghanistan. Both possessed great qualities of leadership and are remembered as martial heroes par excellence. Chandragupta's victories are dramatised in Visakhadatta's *Mudraraksasa*, which is incidentally the only extant Sanskrit play with a wholly political character and a purely historical base. Strange as it might appear, what Visakhadatta places at the centre of the drama is, not the glorious victories of Chandragupta, but the reconciliation of Raksasa, the hostile minister of Nanda, with Chandragupta and his minister, the Brahmin Chanakya. The play depicts the machiavellian stratagems of Chanakya and both his and Chandragupta's magnanimity in granting pardon to Raksasa and appointing him a minister in their state. In Shakespeare's play on the other hand, the French campaign of Henry V, culminating in his victory at Agincourt, forms the main action. Apparently, it is a heroic epic, with the *vira rasa* (heroic sentiment) predominating from first to last. Apparently, Henry V is a paragon, a *dhirodatta nayaka*. This is how the play and its protagonist have generally been treated by the critics. This, however, is only one of the possible approaches to the meaning of the play. In the following pages, it is suggested that Shakespeare has deliberately worked on two different (in fact, contradictory) planes of meaning. On the surface level, he retains the exalted image of Henry V, but on a deeper level, he exposes the machiavellian side of his character. Though there are crafty bishops in the play, there is no equivalent to Chanakya in it and Henry himself has to combine the roles of the designing minister as well as the executing monarch. If we subscribe to the view that *Henry V* is a national epic, the play loses much of its artistic charm and moral significance. Besides, it appears to be an odd piece, coming on the heel of *Henry IV Parts I and II* and just preceding *Julius Caesar* and *Hamlet.* On the other hand, if we interpret it as a mock-heroic drama, it becomes an artistic triumph and exemplifies the spirit of moral questioning that one comes across in the earlier as well as the later works of Shakespeare.

In Chapter 3, we have noted that according to a section of critics, nationalism is the theme of Shakespeare's Histories. If so, *Henry V* ought to be his *magnum opus* among the History Plays, for as Marriott puts it, in *Henry V* Shakespeare reaches the climax of his patriotic drama.[1] From another point of view also—that of the Histories developing the image of the composite figure of the statesman-King[2]—*Henry V* marks the point of culmination. In all probability, it is the last of the English History Plays written by Shakespeare; and, coming just before the great tragedies, it occupies a unique position. However, bewildering as it might appear, the play has met with such severe condemnation from time to time as few if any of Shakespeare's works have ever been subjected to.[3] Peter Alexander traces this dislike to its predominantly nationalistic theme. "It is the most English of the Histories."[4] This may to some extent explain the reaction of a Hazlitt (an avowed lover of the French culture) as well as that of a Shaw or a Yeats, to the play, but it hardly offers any explanation for the unfavourable attitude of critics like Bradley, Masefield, Van Doran, Granville-Barker, Tillyard, etc.

Hazlitt, referring to Shakespeare's attempt to present Henry as 'the king of good fellows', observes:

> He scarcely deserves this honour. He was fond of war and low company; we know little else of him. He was careless, dissolute, and ambitious;—idle, or doing

> mischief. In private, he seemed to have no idea of the common decencies of life, which he subjected to a kind of regal licence; in public affairs, he seemed to have no idea of any rule of right or wrong, but brute force, glossed over with a little religious hypocrisy and archi-episcopal advice.[5]

Shaw considers Henry V an outright jingoist and has his dig at Shakespeare for trying to "thrust such a jingo hero... down our throats".[6] Yeats calls him "the sailor or soldier hero of a romance in some boy's paper".[7] It may be argued that Shakespeare was writing for the intensely patriotic Elizabethans and gave his audience what they wished for. This, however, amounts to accepting Alfred Harbage's pronouncement on *Henry VI*, which is equally applicable to the present play. "No patriotic Frenchman of Elizabethan times", he remarked, "and no internationalist of our own could watch the performance of such a play as *Henry VI* without having his sense of justice grossly wounded."[8] On the other hand, it also implies that the play has an easy access to the English hearts. The protagonist, by virtue of being "perhaps the most distinctively English of all Shakespeare's men", becomes particularly favourite with English readers.[9] Sprague's account of the ebb and flow of the play's popularity on the stage confirms the view that it has been generally revived in times of crisis and has been looked upon as a manifesto of English chivalry.[10] In Chapter 3, we have already noted how the two great wars, which threatened the existence of England, influenced the critical attitude to the History Plays in general. It is but natural, therefore, that critical response to the most English of the Histories has in particular been affected by the two wars.

Marriott, writing at the time of the First World War thinks that in *Henry V*, "Shakespeare got his chance of depicting an ideal Christian Knight; a ruler who was at once popular and successful, a man whom we may both love and admire"[11] and that the play is "essentially and primarily the model for all time of patriotic poetry".[12] Marriott, however, is too good a critic to be blind to certain 'drawbacks' in the play and to the essential nature of Shakespeare's art. He draws attention to the loose 'dramatic cohesion', to the 'lack of chiaroscuro' in the play[13] and, while accepting the 'ideal hero' concept of Henry V, he reminds us that Shakespeare is 'no flaterring portrait painter', but a 'ruthless analyst of character' who reveals the character as he reads it, leaving others to draw inferences.[14]

The truth is that from his sources Shakespeare got the picture of Henry as a paragon. Holinshed's chronicles, based on Hall, who in turn had followed the tradition set by Polydore Vergil, describe him thus:

> This Henrie was a king of life without spot, a prince whome all men loved, and none disdained, a captaine against whome fortune never frowned, nor mischance once spurned, whose people him so severe a justicer both loved and obeied (and so humane with all) that he left no offense unpunished, nor freendship unrewarded; a terrour to rebels, and suppressour of sedition, his vertues notable, his qualities most praise-worthie.
>
> In strength and nimbleness of bodie from his youth few to him comparable, for in wrestling, leaping and running, no man well able to compare....
>
> He had such knowledge in ordering and guiding an armie, with such a gift to incourage his people, that the Frenchmen had constant opinion he could never be vanquished in battell. Such wit, such prudence, and such policie withall, that he never enterprised any thing, before he had fullie debated and forecast all the manie chances that might happen, which done with all diligence and courage he set his purpose forward....
>
> ...for conclusion, a majestie was he that both lived and died a paterne in princehood, a lode-starre in honour, and mirrour of magnificance: the more highlie exalted in his life, the more deeplie lamented at his death, and famous to the world alwaie.[15]

An anonymous poem, *The Battle of Agincourt*, printed in 1530, gives an idea of Henry's image in the popular legend of the time. The poem which begins with a praise of Henry goes on:

> Of Henry the fyfthe, noble man of warre,
> Thy dedes may never forgoten be.
> Of knyghthod thou wert the very lodestarre;
> In thy tyme Englande flowred in prosperyte.
> Thou mortall myrour of all chevalry.[16]

Samuel Daniel also in his historical poem *The First Four Books of the Civile Wars Between the Two Houses of Lancaster and Yorke,* celebrates the virtues of Henry V and uses such epithets for him as 'magnanimous king', 'mirror of vertue', 'mirracle of worth'.[17] The anonymous historical play, *The Famous Victories of Henry the Fifth,* registered in 1594 and printed in 1598, is another instance of the panegyrics written on Henry V. In short, in the chronicles as well as in popular literature of the time, Henry V had been depicted as the copy-book paragon of kingly virtues. There were also traditions of his miraculous change following his annexation as well as of his good fellowship, both of which found emphatic expression in the *Famous Victories.*

In the preceding chapter we have noted how Shakespeare, rejecting the last two traditions, gives his own reading of Prince Hal's character. The Prince does change on annexation, but the change was planned well in advance and only appeared much too sudden to distant onlookers. He does participate in Eastcheap revelries and humours even 'the drawers' of the tavern, but owes his heart to none.

Tillyard talks of the two obligations of Shakespeare, emanating from his sources, obligations of depicting Henry V as the ideal political hero and of accepting the traditions of his miraculous conversion and good mixing—'both impossible of worthy fulfilment'.[18] He diagnoses this as lying behind what he assumes to be the comparatively lesser quality of the play.

> Shakespeare came to terms with this hopeless situation by jettisoning the character he had created and substituting one which, though lacking all consistency, satisfied the requirements both of the chroniclers and of popular tradition. No wonder if the play constructed round him shows a great falling off in quality.[19]

It must be admitted that the chroniclers' accounts as well as the popular traditions do come in Shakespeare's way, but as always, he refuses to submit to them and does not oblige them by 'jettisoning' the highly interesting and successful character of Prince Hal already created in *Henry IV*. In fact, in *Henry V*, he again incorporates his own interpretation of history without causing any substantial change in the basic outlines. As a result, the portrait becomes double-edged. On one level, Henry V remains the paragon, the model Christian king, as Dover Wilson[20] and J.H. Walter[21] have so eloquently tried to argue. Seen on this level, Shakespeare's Henry V appears to conform to the norms of an ideal Christian king, not unlike the portrait found in the chronicles and popular legend. The Romantics are generally blamed for being antagonistic to this heroic figure, but the German Romantic critic, Schlegel, observes:

> King Henry the Fifth is manifestly Shakespeare's favourite hero in English history: he paints him as endowed with every chivalrous and kingly virtue; open, sincere, affable, yet as a sort of reminiscence of his youth, still disposed to innocent raillery, in the intervals between his perilous but glorious achievements.[22]

And one finds it difficult to disagree with Schlegel. Yet this is only one-sided view—a view of Henry's portrait on the surface level. That Schlegel himself was by no means blind to the other facets of the portrayal is evident from his subsequent remarks on the celebrated deeds of Henry.[23] It is not enough to say, as Reese says, that Shakespeare does not accept the legend about Henry 'without examining it'.[24] In fact, Shakespeare rejects the legend, but he can do so only in an oblique manner. The audience, too well familiar with the paragon, could hardly be expected to accept any other image of their favourite hero. Moreover, in a queer way, through his French victory, Henry V was linked with the Tudor state in general and with the Elizabethan in particular. Being the new national king, he must have appeared as 'the herald of Tudor monarchy'.[25] The 'daemonic' Shakespeare, however, always conscious of the Janus in all human beings and the artist, who could see through the conscience of Bolingbroke as well as the 'bright honour' of Hotspur, could hardly take such an idealised image for granted.

Even those critics who try to exonerate both the play and the character of Henry V, concede that there is a lack of dramatic conflict and of plot development. The usual explanation offered for such shortcomings is the epic structure adopted in the play. Stauffer, for instance, after pointing out the shabby treatment of Henry's foes and the sheer lack of dramatic conflict in the play, makes the following observation:

> But for one of the few times in his career, he is not writing a drama. He is composing a patriotic hymn. Rather than as a play, *Henry V* might be considered as the greatest advertisement in literature, with this one distinction between the dramatist and the average writer of advertising copy, that Shakespeare here seems to have believed every word that he put to paper.[26]

To this, we can only say that a work of advertisement, howsoever superb it might be, is, by its very nature time-bound and hardly capable of appealing to the next generation not to say the present one. Secondly, when the writer is as great as Shakespeare, not only 'here' but everywhere, he seems to have believed every (or seems not to have believed any) word that he put to paper. Like Stauffer, Reese also admits that there is no real conflict in the play. The official manner is never relaxed. But he holds the epic medium responsible for these limitations as well as for the lack of reality in the portrait of the protagonist, for the epic praises heroes and denounces villainy and Henry is 'an appointed symbol of majesty'. Real life is not so simple. Human virtue is 'always muddied', or it would not be human, but the epic is the art that on special occasions transforms it into the ideal.[27]

It must be admitted that the epic character of the play is almost the first thing that strikes one about it and even if one refuses to be convinced by the above explanations, one may perhaps agree with Evans that its 'interest is epic rather than dramatic and that it is 'the nearest approach on the part of the author to a national epic'.[28] That Shakespeare is experimenting here with a new type of dramatic genre—the 'epic drama'[29]—seems apparent, but why should he have chosen this unusual form? Stribrny suggests that the theme being the triumphal account of English victory at Agincourt and Shakespeare being 'anxious to marshal and display all the formal resources he had thus far mastered', the epic drama was the inevitable choice.[30] Ribner also holds a more or less similar view, but he stresses rather the individual portrait of Henry V. "For his eulogistic portrait of a conquering soldier-king," he says, "Shakespeare used the obvious dramatic vehicle which the English stage had evolved for such purposes: that of the heroic play as it had been shaped by Marlowe in his *Tamburlaine*".[31] The comparison with *Tamburlaine* only highlights the essential difference between Marlowe and Shakespeare. Whereas the former gives an epic treatment to a tyrannical figure of history, the latter gives a mock-heroic treatment to a paragon of history. It is by giving a superficially epic structure and displaying it with a calculated gusto that Shakespeare manages to provide a sort of umbrella to his own reading of *Henry V*'s character and of his victorious campaign. Ribner has called Henry V, 'Shakespeare's Christian Tamburlaine'.[32] But there can be no 'Christian Tamburlaine'. The fact is that Shakespeare looks below the model Christian king, the traditional paragon and discovers a Tamburlaine. He, however, cannot[33] and dare not[34] write an outright satire and, therefore, adopts the next best way open to him. While, on the surface level, retaining the traditional heroic image of his protagonist, he punctuates it with irony. The resultant form is not so much an epic drama, or dramatic epic, or national epic as commonly assumed, it is rather a near approach to the mock-heroic drama.

In *1 Henry IV*, Shakespeare has already given us a mock-heroic scene (Act II. Sc. iv) and there are clear echoes of that in the Prologue which opens the present play:

> O for a Muse of fire, that would ascend
> The brightest heaven of invention:
> *A kingdom for a stage, princes to act*
> *And monarchs to behold the swelling scene!*
> Then should the warlike Harry, like himself,

> Assume the port of Mars, and at his heels,
> Leashed in like *hounds*, should *Famine*, *Sword*, and *Fire*
> Crouch for employment. (I. i. 1-8).

In *1 Henry IV*, the make-belief was achieved thus:

> *Fal.*—This chair shall be my state, this dagger my sceptre and this cushion my crown.
>
> *Prince.*—Thy state is taken for a joined stool, thy golden sceptre for a leaden dagger, and thy precious rich crown for a pitiful bald crown. (II. iv. 336-40).

Anne Righter has drawn attention to the player king metaphor in Elízabethan literature and to its repeated effective use by Shakespeare.[35] While on the stage the poor player, however, inadequately, attempts an imitation of the king, the latter in his council-chamber or in the battlefield is no less a player. The French ambassador reacted thus to Queen Elizabeth I's tears for Alencon: "She is a princess who can act any part she pleases."[36] 'All the world's a stage', including the Royal court and all men are acting certain roles, including the king himself. In fact, as Righter remarks:

> At the point where the distance between the world and the stage might seem the greatest—between the king in his majesty and the poor player with his imitation crown—the play metaphor in fact operates most powerfully, bringing illusion and reality into a juxtaposition that is both poignant and enormously complex.[37]

It has been pointed out that one of the functions of the chorus is to offer an apology for the limitations of both the stage and the author.[38] The apology, however, is not merely for 'this wooden O', but also for 'The little O, the earth' (*Merchant of Venice*, I. iii. 7) and for the very act of acting itself. Shakespeare was a player playwright, who must always have been aware of the limitations of the stage. Notwithstanding such limitations, however, he went on presenting scenes which would appear absurd from the purely theatrical point of view. In *Richard III* for instance, when at Bosworth Richard cries, 'A horse: a horse:

my kingdom/for a horse!' we are supposed to imagine that he has lost his horse in the course of the battle and is now on foot. On the stage, however, all along the battle (both before and after this cry) Richard would remain on foot. Shakespeare does not mind such inconsistances. In the next play after *Henry V* he does not desist from depicting the battle of Philippi. The player playwright, who makes his Richard II say that the antic, sitting within the crown of a king, allows him 'a breath, a little scene, to monarchize' (III. ii. 164-65), can hardly be expected to be so emphatically apologetic about the limitations of the stage or of his own. He cannot but be aware of the double implication of the player-king or king-player metaphor. The apology, then, is as much for the 'warlike Harry', trying to be 'like himself' as for the poor player, who doubles him on the stage. At the same time it is also an apology—hardly genuine—for any possible damage that might be caused to the traditional image of the successful man of action and to the favourite theme of jingoism by Shakespeare's 'flat unraised spirits'. By the time Shakespeare takes up the writing of *Henry V* he has acquired full mastery over his medium and if we cast a glance at his progress through the early works, we find him moving constantly towards greater and deeper realism. Having already created about a dozen successful plays and such immortal characters as Richard II, Falstaff and Shylock, he need not have apologised for 'flat unraised spirits' unless by it he meant a realistic, unromantic approach to the subject at hand.

Tillyard speaks of what he calls unsuccessful 'efforts to inflate Henry to greatness'[39] by Shakespeare. It would be nearer the mark to say that Shakespeare endeavours rather to deflate Henry of his greatness. In some respects, the play and the character—despite what Shaw has to say about its jingoism[40]—anticipate Shaw's own *The Man of Destiny* and the treatment meted out to Napoleon therein. The task, however, was not easy, for the subject was very close to Elizabethan hearts as well as to the Tudor state and in this respect the play marked—to borrow a phrase from Granville-Barker—'the danger point of his career'.[41] He passes the danger point under the banner of an epic and ever since then the world has been taken in by the banner.

Richard Simpson who discovers Essex behind Shakespeare's Henry V, considers the play as "a poem of victory, a glorification of war, not as an agony of brutal passions, but as an agent of civilization".[42] All wars, especially modern wars, are fought in the name of some good cause—civilization, freedom, democracy, and all leave behind 'ragamuffins'. Shakespeare keeps this constantly in mind, and even in the Prologue, while manifestly glorifying the warlike Harry, gives us a fair warning of the three hounds of destruction approaching at his heels—famine, sword and fire.[43] The same dogs-of-war image is employed by Mark Antony when he incites the Roman mob against the conspirators:

> ...and let slip the dogs of war,
> That this foul deed shall smell above the earth
> With carrion men, groaning for burial.
>
> (*J. Caesar*, III. i. 274-76)

and by Talbot, when he threatens to sack Bordeaux:

> You tempt the fury of my three attendants,
> Lean Famine, quartering steel, and climbing fire
> Who in a moment even with the earth
> Shall lay your stately and air-braving towers,
>
> (*1 Henry VI*. IV. ii. 10-13)

There is a 'polarization', as Stříbrny remarks in Shakespeare's vision of war, reflecting the inherent contradiction between its glory and horror,[44] but the glory is the facade, the horror the reality. The Prologue to Act IV, while apologising once again for the inadequacies of the stage, asks us to see the truth through its mockery:

> O for pity!—we shall much disgrace,
> With four or five most vile and ragged foils,
> Right ill-disposed in brawl ridiculous,
> The name of Agincourt: Yet sit and see,
> Minding true things by what their mock'ries be.
>
> (Prologue IV. ll. 49-53)

The entire action of war is a gigantic mockery of glory and justice, enacted on the stage, that is, Agincourt or the whole world.[45]

How exactly and with what motives and justifications does Henry launch his French invasion? He is not, as Charlton thinks, 'trapped into declaration of war'.[46] That is an impression one may derive from Holinshed's account,[47] not from Shakespeare's. As Bradley points out, "when he adjures the Archbishop to satisfy him as to his right to the French throne, he knows very well that the Archbishop *wants* the war".[48] The consultation is a mere ceremony, a mockery of Henry's sense of justice and moral obligation. The elaborate and painful exposition of the Salic Law by the learned Archbishop is hardly relevant to the dramatic action (and perhaps on this account is generally omitted in the theatre), for Henry has already made up his mind. He has not forgotten the death-bed advice of his wise father:

> Be it thy course to busy giddy minds
> With foreign quarrels; that action hence borne out
> May waste the memory of the former days...
>
> (2 *Henry IV*. IV. v. 213-15)

and the resolve to wage the French war, is influenced by this purely political motive rather than by the reasonings advanced by his counsellors. The scene, however, is by no means superfluous. Lily B. Campbell, looking for topical allusions in the play, speaks of the especial interest of the Elizabethans in the Salic Law and reminds us of "the fact that upon the right of the woman to inherit depended also the right of Mary and Elizabeth Tudor to the throne, the right of the Tudors to rule, and the right of Mary and James of Scotland to inherit".[49] In the dramatic context, however, it is more likely that, as pointed out by Battenhouse, a deep irony underlies the insistence on inheritance through female line.[50] The Archbishop's arguments by insisting on it and striving at the same time to extend Henry's claim to the French crown, by implication undermine his claim to the English crown itself and justify the claim of Edmund Mortimer instead.

Moreover, although Henry solemnly charges the Archbishop "to proceed"

> And justly and religiously unfold
> Why the law Salique, that they have in France,

Or should, or should not, bar us in our claim:

(I. ii. 9 ff.)

he is hardly interested in the justness of the cause, as Ribner would have us believe[51] or in the intricacies of the Law itself. The question is, in fact, limited to international power politics and personal ambition; and, when the king fails to get a direct and clear answer to his heart's desire, he is compelled to interrupt the Archbishop with the plain query: "May I with right and conscience make this claim?" (I. ii. 96). And the Archbishop obliges him with exactly the kind of answer he has been looking forward to: "The sin upon my head, dread sovereign!" (l. 97). The responsibility for the war of conquest is thus shifted on the Holy Church.[52]

Such convenient shifting of personal responsibility, however, can hardly win uncritical approval of the dramatist who was to create in the coming years characters like Brutus and Hamlet. The question of the justness of the cause and of personal responsibility which Henry succeeds in evading here, confronts him again, therefore in Act IV. Scene i. To the incognito Henry's assertion: "his cause being just and his quarrel honourable", the reaction of the two soldiers is logical and replete with deep irony:

Williams — That's more than we know.

Bates — Ay, or more than we should seek after; for we know enough, if we know we are the king's subjects; if his cause be wrong, our obedience to the king wipes the crime of it out of us.

(IV. i. 128-32).

Williams and Bates are not realists like Falstaff, they are believers in the doctrine of passive obedience and their reasoning is the logical culmination of this belief. They echo the two murderers of Clarence in *Richard III*:

1 Murd —What we will do, we do upon command.

2 Murd—And he that hath commanded is our king.

(*R III*. I. iv. 189-90)

It is ironical that the evasive attitude of the king is duplicated by his soldiers. Exactly as Henry has tried to shift his own responsibility to the Church, they try to shift theirs to the king. The very questions which Henry tried to ignore, boomerang with greater intensity to him in the next speech of Williams:

> But if the cause be not good, the king himself hath a heavy reckoning to make, when all those legs and arms and heads, chopped off in a battle, shall join together at the latter day, and cry all, "we died at such a place"; some swearing; some crying for a surgeon, some upon their wives left poor behind them; some upon the debts they owe, some upon their children rawly left...I am afeard there are few die well that die in a battle: for how can they charitably dispose of any thing, when blood is their argument? Now, if these men do not die well it will be a black matter for the king that led them to it; whom to disobey were against all proportions of subjection. (*Henry V*. IV. i. 133-45)

Miss Campbell remarks that the argument here touches upon 'one of the most controversial questions of the day' and draws attention to the surrender of the town of Deventer to the Spanish by Sir William Stanley in 1587, which became a *cause celebre* and, to the ensuing debate on the question of the soldier's responsibility for the justice of the cause for which he fought. Cardinal Allen in his defence of Sir William Stanley held that a subject is not bound to obey his king in opposition to his God.[53]

To the pertinent questions raised by Williams, Henry delivers a long class-room lecture, based on the tenet: "Every subject's duty is the king's; but every subject's soul is his own" (IV. i. 174). It implies that the subject is duty-bound to the king but for his private sins morally bound to God. This, however, does not absolve the king of his personal responsibility for the cause in which he undertakes war and effects 'many now in health' to drop their blood. And, although Henry would not acknowledge it in public, it is evident that Williams has made his point, for as soon as left to himself, Henry returns to it:

> Upon the king; let us our lives, our souls,
> Our debts, our careful wives,
> Our children, and our sins, lay on the king!
> (IV. i. 226-28)

It might perhaps be argued that far from accepting the situation, he is mocking here the unreasonable reasoning of such soldiers as Williams. If so, he is mocking himself by implication, for he has laid everything, including sin, on the Church. The picture of the horror of war painted by Williams bears close resemblance to similar descriptions of it by the king himself in his adjuration to the Archbishop[54] and in his parley with the Governor of Harfluer, calling upon him to surrender:

> If not—why, in a moment look to see
> The blind and bloody soldier with foul hand
> Defile the locks of your shrill-shrieking daughters;
> Your fathers taken by the silver beards,
> And their most reverend heads dash'd to the walls:
> Your naked infants spitted upon pikes,
> Whiles the mad mothers with their howls confus'd
> Do break the clouds, as did the wives of Jewry
> At Herod's bloody-hunting slaughtermen.
> What say you? Will you yield, and this avoid?
> Or, guilty in defence, be thus destroy'd? (III. iii. 33-43)

The war-machine of which the individual soldier forms an indispensable part, operates in two directions. On the one side, it lets the 'blind and bloody' soldiers go on a hunting spree, on the other, it chops off their legs, arms and heads. The theme of the horrors of war is naturally and inseparably linked with the question of Henry's own responsibility[55] and, his own acute awareness of the former increases the gravity of the latter.

We have already noted above that in his deliberations with the Archbishop about the Salic Law and about his own claim to the French throne, he is finally satisfied only when the Church dignitary declares: "The *sin* upon my head" (I. ii. 97). This indirectly reflects upon Henry's consciousness of the possibility of sin in launching the war. The last lines of his adjuration to the Archbishop were:

> *in your conscience* wash'd
> As pure as *sin* with *baptism*.
>
> (I. ii. 31-32).
> *(Italics Mine)*

"A baptizing of sin is what is here desired", says Battenhouse.[56] In Christian theology, baptism follows belief and repentance and in turn washes away one's sins.

> He that believeth and is baptized shall be saved;[57]
>
> Repent, and be baptized every one of you in the name of Jesus Christ for the remission of sins,[58]

Henry, however, does not seem to be interested in the remission of sin, but rather in its justification. The wash-image as employed here does not suggest the Christian concept of baptism, it is reminiscent of similar imagery woven round the Pilate metaphor in *Richard II*,[59] Traversi stresses the relation between conscience and political necessity in the character of Henry. Though never 'deaf to the voice of conscience', Henry, according to Traversi, has the politically useful 'ability to direct his conscience into convenient channels'. There is in him an 'overriding of private feeling by the will to power'.[60] What we have witnessed so far of Henry's character, however, hardly agrees with this analysis. He has vision: telescopic, for he can look into distant future, as well as microscopic, for he can look through the motives of his men—but no conscience, at least not till the hour of battle. A voice which is constantly heard and not heeded to is not the voice of conscience; a feeling which may be directed into convenient channels again and again, is not conscience. Such shuffling stuff may go by any other name but conscience. What is conscience then? For an answer let us lend our ears to the Second Murderer of Clarence:

> it makes a man a coward: a man cannot steal, but it accuseth him; a man cannot swear, but it checks him; a man cannot lie with his neighbour's wife, but it detects him. 'Tis a blushing shame fac'd spirit that mutinies in a man's bosom...it beggars any man that keeps it. It is turn'd out of towns and cities for a dangerous thing; and every man that means to live well endeavours to trust to himself and live without it.
>
> (*Richard III*. I. iv. 134 ff.)

To an ambitious politician, to a Machiavellian public figure, it is even more dangerous than the 'fatal Cleopatra' or the charming fat old Knight. It is inseparably linked with the Christian concept of God's justice (note 'latter day' in Williams's speech,[61] a reminder of the Last Day of Judgement). "The justice of God", says Raleigh, "doth require none other accuser than our own conscience."[62]

Henry trusts to himself and lives without conscience. He is in this respect his father's son and Richard III's brother[63]—a truly Machiavellian character. Going back to Traversi's analysis (never 'deaf to the voice of conscience'), one may perhaps say that he is never blind to the significance of a show of conscience in public life and in this he follows the advice of Machiavelli:

> A prince must take great care that nothing goes out of his mouth which is not full of the above-named five qualities, and, to see and hear him, he should seem to be all mercy, faith, integrity, humanity, and religion. And nothing is more necessary than to seem to have this last quality, for men in general judge more by eyes than by the hands, for every one can see, but very few have to feel.[64]

What happens in him, therefore, is not what Traversi puts as, "an overriding of private feeling by a will to power", but rather a camouflaging of the political motive (which is the same as his private feeling) with a deliberate ostentation of moral and conscientious reflection. One who knows he is in the wrong must take particular care to build an image of his righteousness, justice, clemency and religiosity. Such is the case with Henry.

No wonder, therefore, that while laying claim to French territory, he declares to the French Ambassadors:

> We are no tyrant, but a Christian King;
> Unto whose grace our passion is as subject
> As is our wretches fettered in our prisons: (I. ii. 242-44)

The 'wretches fettered in...prisons', remind one of the Christian apostles. The image of a cold unfeeling gaoler meant to describe Christian grace is singularly inapt. The third line reverses the meaning of the first and the dividing line between the two is too thin to justify this. At Harfleur again, while threatening the citizens with dire consequences, he still maintains a show of mercy. The long speech[65], which ends with the queer self-contradictory expression: 'guilty in defence', begins with an offer of mercy, though even this offer is mixed up with proud threats:

> How yet resolves the governor of the town?
> This is the latest parle we will admit:
> Therefore to our best mercy give yourselves,
> Or, like to men *proud of destruction.*
> Defy us to our worst: for, as I am a soldier,
> A name that in my thoughts becomes me best,
> If I begin the battery once again,
> I will not leave the half-achieved Harfluer
> Till in her a shes she lie buried.
> The *gates of mercy* shall be all shut up.
>
> (III. iii. 1-10) (Italics Mine)

The mercy which Henry, thus, offers implies that if the citizens prefer an honourable end to abject surrender, they are 'proud of destruction' and 'guilty in defence' and, thereore, deserve rapine and genocide. Critics[66] have noted a link between Henry's speech and *Deuteronomy* XX, obviously with a view to justifying Henry's conduct as the ideal Christian king. At best, there is only a superficial resemblance between *Deuteronomy* XX and Henry's speech. The instructions in the former clearly lay down that only the menfolk are to be put to death, not the women and the children:

> And if it will make no peace with thee, but will make war against thee, then thou shalt besiege it: and when the Lord thy God hath delivered it into thine hands, thou shalt smite every male thereof with the edge of the sword: but the women, and the little ones, and the cattle, and all that is in the city, even all the spoil thereof, shalt thou take unto thyself,[67]

Henry, on the other hand, lays special emphasis on the defiling of 'fresh-fair virgins' and the killing of 'flowering infants'—'shrill-shrieking daughters' and 'naked infants spitted upon spikes'. By a natural association of ideas, the killing of infants leads to sad mothers and both in turn lead to 'Herod's bloody-hunting slaughtermen'. The development of the imagery is so natural that the underlying irony—the 'Christian king' identifying his men with Herod's and by implication himself with Herod, the arch-tyrant and enemy of Christ—is generally overlooked. It is strange that largely on the basis of Henry's conduct at Harfluer, critics[68] have tried to identify him with the ideal man of power, whose portrait is drawn by Shakespeare in Sonnet 94.

> They that have power to hurt, and will do none,
> That do not do the thing they most do show,
> Who moving others, are themselves as stone,
> Unmoved, cold, and to temptation slow
> They rightly do inherit heaven's graces.

The only Shakespearean character who comes close to this near-impossible ideal is Prospero, the philosopher-magician king. Henry V does possess some of the attributes of the ideal man of power. He has power, like the lion to hurt and cunning, like the fox to know when and how to do it. He is the ideal Machiavellian Prince, not the ideal Christian or the ideal Shakespearean Prince.[69] He has hurt Falstaff ('hath run bad humours on the knight') with the result that the latter's 'heart is fracted and corroborate' (II. i. 121 & 123). And if we are not prepared to accept the testimony of Nym and Pistol, let us hear Fluellen: "as Alexander killed his friend Cleitus being in his ales and his cups; so also Harry. Monmouth, being in his right wits and his good judgments, turned away the fat knight with the great-belly doublet:" (IV. vii. 47-50). The comic comparison clearly brings out the greater responsibility of Henry for his action. If we recall Hooker's observation[70] on human will and actions, we may see that what Alexander did, he did in 'alienation of mind'. On the other hand, what Henry did, he did in right wits and good judgment. What is more, by making the Welshman inadvertently use the word, 'big', in lieu of 'great' and mispronounce it as 'pig'. Shakespeare makes deliberate use of pun. Thus, 'Alexander the great' becomes 'Alexander the pig' and so does his replica, Henry of Monmouth. This ironical treatment of Henry is directly linked with Falstaff's tragic and noble end. Hapgood thinks that there is a double swift of our sympathies in the case of Falstaff and considers the rejection and the end of Falstaff as instances of what he calls 'Shakespeare's delayed reactions'.[71] In whichever way we interpret it, we must agree with Priestley that it is the end of Falstaff which largely determines our attitude of sympathy towards Falstaff and resentment against Henry.[72] At Agincourt when outnumbered by the enemy, Henry orders the slaughter of the prisoners without qualms of conscience, and although his own soldiers think that it is a retaliatory measure (IV. vii. 8-10), Shakespeare makes it clear that Henry's decision is anterior to the killing of the unprotected boys by the French (IV. vi. 36-38). Fluellen's critical remark on the French action ('tis expressly against the law of arms, 'a piece of knavery', IV. vii. 1 ff.), is therefore, equally applicable to Henry's. Even though there had been no Geneva Convention, yet such ruthless slaughter of defenceless prisoners can hardly be justified. In taking the decision, Henry appears to be guided by the practical need to establish a military reputation for cold-blooded cruelty. "When the prince is with his army and has a large number of soldiers under his control", says Machiavelli, "then it is extremely necessary that he should not mind being thought cruel, for without this reputation he could not keep an army united or disposed to any duty."[73] No wonder, the soldiers voice their instant approval of Henry's ruthless action exclaiming "O, 'tis a gallant king:" (IV. vii. 10).

One may, perhaps, agree with Charlton that in *Henry V* there is no substantial modification in Shakespeare's apprehension of the political life—the apprehension that what is good in the world of politics is entirely unrelated to and generally the opposite of what makes for goodness in the moral life, the appreciation of the essential distinction between Machiavelli's virtue and the moralist's virtue.[74] It is a part of the Machiavellian virtue to put on the robe of piety. This is what we repeatedly notice in Henry V and in this respect he is a more consummate actor than Richard III. The latter also uses the prelates for personal end, but he does this only once, whereas Henry makes repeated use of religion throughout his political career. No wonder that attempts have been made to relate his various actions to Biblical precepts[75] and to look upon him as the model of Christian kings. Battenhouse, however, reminds us that in Dante's *Purgatorio 32*, Christendom is a tattered realm to be signed over and compares the popular view of Henry's perfection with that of the Pharisees and pious pagans in Roman times, responsible for the death of Christ, St. Paul and others.[76] Shakespeare's Henry has no genuine Christianity, only its 'glistering semblances'.[77]

A classic example of the superficial piety of Henry is his famous prayer at Agincourt on the eve of the battle (IV. i. 285-301). Appreciating the spirit in which the prayer is uttered, Dover Wilson asks: "Is this bowed figure the 'warlike Harry' who 'assumes the port of Mars' and hurls himself upon France.

> In thunder and in earthquake, like a Jove?"

It is the same, he says, "seen no longer from without but from within."[78] But Henry is almost entirely devoid of an inner self, for as Ellis-Fermor puts it: "There is no Henry, only a king" and

> Neither we the readers nor Henry himself nor his God ever meets the individual that had once underlain the outer crust that covers a Tudor monarch for there is nothing beneath the crust; all has been converted into it; all desires, all impulses, all selfhood, all spirit. He is never alone even with his God—least of all when he prays for then he is more than ever in the council chamber driving an astute bargain, a piece of shrewd diplomacy, between one king and another.[79]

The very question regarding the genuineness of Henry's piety is, therefore, superfluous.[80] It is significant to note that the prayer is immediately preceded by the soliloquy in which Henry decries all ceremony (IV. i. 257-63). If ceremony is ineffective as a remedy for physical ills how much more ineffective and ridiculous it should be in the case of a deep spiritual malady? Nonetheless the same Henry, who has realised the deceptive nature of ceremony continues to practise an elaborate ceremony of religion in "an attempt to buy off supernatural vengeance for Richard's blood."[81] Critics[82] have very appropriately contrasted Henry's prayer with that of Claudius:

> But, O, what form of prayer
> Can serve my turn? 'Forgive me my foul murder'!

> That cannot be; since I am still possess'd
> Of those effects for which I did the murder—
> My crown, mine own ambition, and my queen.
> May one be pardon'd and retain th' offence?
>
> (*Hamlet* III. iii. 51-56)

It may be argued that the 'ritual of piety' evident in Henry's action is based on the chroniclers' accounts.[83] In history, as suggested by E.F. Jacob, the reburial may had been a mark of the friendship that sprang up between Richard II and Henry, as a result of the kind treatment meted out to the latter by the former during the banishment of Bolingbroke.[84] In Shakespeare, however, there is no such hint of any genuine friendship between the two. Moreover, it is only through Henry's prayer that we for the first time learn of his good turn towards Richard. The manner in which he uses the ceremony of religion as a trump card to strike a deal with God, reflects not so much the 'superstitious'[85] nature of his piety as the prostitution of piety, so widespread in the world. Henry's famous prayer on the eve of the battle is, therefore, not unlike the prayers of most of us—"mockeries indeed fit to be used towards a leaden, but not towards the everlasting God".[86]

"All Henry asks", says Dover Wilson, "is that courage be granted his soldiers to fight against overwhelming odds, and that the crime of his father, in compassing the throne by the deposition and death of Richard, be not weighed in the balance against them."[87] This, however, overlooks the dramatic context of the prayer and the essential nature of Christian piety. Only a short while ago, Bates has remarked: "we have French quarrels enow, if you could tell how to *reckon*" (IV. i. 228-30). It is this sense of reckoning that Henry wishes his soldiers to lose: "take from them now/The sense of reck'ning" (IV. i. 286-87). In the *Bible*, the word 'reckon' is closely associated with the idea of Lord's judgment.[88] That the same idea is uppermost in Henry's mind too is evident from the words that we hear next: "Not to-day, O Lord,/O not to-day,...." The prayer in effect is that not only the soldiers, but God too might lose His capacity for reckoning for a while.

More than anything else, it is the fear of death that reminds one of God's judgment. It is significant that the word 'reckoning' occurs in the grim vision of judgment presented by Williams.[89] Henry in reply had denied responsibility for 'irreconciled iniquities' of the soldiers and had advised them to be prepared for death: "Therefore, should every soldier in the wars do as every sick man in his bed, wash every mote out of his conscience" (IV. i. 175-77). And the fact that at Agincourt Henry and his men find themselves in a hopeless situation—comparable to Dunkirk—perilously close to would-be death and defeat, has been admitted by Henry himself: "Even as men wracked upon a sand, that look to be washed off the next tide." (IV. i. 97-98). 'The king is but a man' and when he sees reason for fears, as others do, his fears are not unlike those of others (IV. i. 101-10). It is quite natural therefore, for Henry, to turn to God in the face of possible death. Thus, he tries to implement the advice he has given to his soldiers only a moment ago, for what else are Richard's deposition and death if not 'irreconciled iniquities' of the Lancastrian family? Shakespeare makes it clear that Henry's religion has two faces, apparently irreconcilable, namely, a public face and a private one. The 'ritual of piety' that he has been practising and that he promises to go on practising ('More will I do', IV. i. 298), is the public face of his religion, which reminds us of the projected crusade of his father. It is only human on his part, however, to become conscious of the inadequacy of 'all that I can do' at the moment of crisis and to implore pardon when death appears so near. This, then, is the private face of his religion. Referring to people who ask forgiveness at the last moment, Raleigh remarks: "certainly, these wise wordlings have either found out a new God; or made one...."[90] It need not surprise us, therefore, that the very opening line of the prayer distorts both God's nature and His work. The Christian God is not of battles, but above battles and His work is to soften by grace, not to steel. Henry's petition is Turkish piety in the spirit of an Amurath.[91] In Christianity, the one sure way prescribed to win God's forgiveness is to forgive others:

> And forgive us our trespasses, as we forgive them that trespass against us.[92]

The treatment meted out to Scroop, Cambridge and Grey, despite their submission to Henry's mercy, has revealed the incapacity of Henry to fulfil this one condition of God's forgiveness. In an article, defending Henry's treatment of the conspirators and the unjustified long tirade against them, Robert Kelly refers to the various Scroops in the History Plays in general and observes: "They stand for Satanic evil under an appearance of piety."[93] So does Henry himself, "the ravisher of France".[94]

The next scene where the king reappears, confirms our notion about his alienation from the Christian God. In reply to Westmoreland's wish that more men from England could have joined them, he declares in the vein of Hotspur:

> The fewer men, the greater share of honour.
> God's will, I pray thee, wish not one man more.
> By Jove, I am not covetous for gold,
> Nor care I who doth feed upon my cost:
> It earns me not if men my garments wear:
> Such outward things dwell not in my desires.
> But if it be a sin to covet honour,
> I am the most offending soul alive. (IV. iii. 22-29)

The use of Jove's name is cryptic and Dr. Johnson notes that "The king prays like a Christian and swears like a heathen."[95] The fact though Henry himself may not realise it, is that his God is a queer amalgam of the Christian and the heathen. The kind of severence he tries to effect between honour and riches is impossible in the light of Christian theology. King David in his thanksgiving to the Lord, holds: "Both riches and honour come of thee"[96] and God's reply to Solomon's prayer for wisdom and knowledge is: "Because this was in thine heart, and thou hast not asked riches, wealth, or honour, nor the life of thine enemies, neither yet hast asked long life...."[97] This implies that in the eyes of God to covet honour is as great a sin as to covet riches.

This, however, is not to distract attention from the fine qualities of the speech itself. John Wain is perhaps right in calling it "the most celebrated patriotic speech in the English language"[98] and Dover Wilson has made a very apt comparison of it with Churchill's famous speech during the Second World War: "If history never repeats itself, the human spirit often does: Henry's words before Agincourt, and Churchill's after the Battle of Britain, come from the same national mint."[99] Obviously, the specific words that are reminiscent of 'we few, we happy few, we band of brothers', (l. 60) are these: "Never in the field of human conflict was so much owed by so many to so few."[100] The lines with the theme of everlasting honour—

> And Crispin Crispian shall ne'er go by,
> From this day to the ending of the world,
> But we in it shall be remembered; (ll. 57-59)

also bear close resemblance to the following in Churchill's speech of June 18, 1940:

> Let us therefore brace ourselves to our duty and so bear ourselves that if the British commonwealth and Empire last for a thousand years, men will still say "This was their finest hour."[101]

"Our failure to capitulate" before the Crispin Crispian-speech of Henry is not "due to the fact that we have lost our taste for the pageantry of war",[102] or that we have outgrown patriotic tub-thumping. We have not. This is partly because of the undertones of irony implicit in the speech and partly because "we see so little of Henry, the man, as against Henry the king".[103] Battenhouse draws attention to the subtle irony with which the Crispin allusion is surcharged.[104] Saints Crispin and Crispian were shoemaker-brothers martyred by Diocletian. In the background of the Crispin-speech lies, as suggested by John Wain,[105] the following encounter of King Henry with Williams during his night vigil:

> *K. Hen*—I myself heard the king say he
> would not be ransom'd.
> *Williams*—Ay, he said so, to make us fight
> cheerfully; but when our throats are cut,
> he may be ransom'd,
> and we ne'er the,
> wiser.

K. Hen—If I live to see it, I will never trust his word after.

Williams—You pay him then! That's a perilous shot of an elder-gun, that a poor and a private displeasure can do against a monarch! You may as well go about to turn the sun to ice with fanning in his face with a peacock's feather. You'll never trust his word after! Come, 'tis a foolish saying.

(IV. i. 188-200)

Emphasising national solidarity above all, Henry seeks to answer the misgivings of his soldiers on their being used as 'food for powder' by the king and the higher-ups:

We few, we happy few, we band of brothers;
For he to-day that sheds his blood with me
Shall be my brother; be he ne'er so vile,
This day shall gentle his condition; (IV. iii. 60-63)

Murry, referring to the speech, remarks, "It was a dream: it has never been fulfilled...'Nevertheless, the ideal is the real. Only in so far as a king does incorporate the brotherhood of a nation, is kingship justified at the bar of the imagination which is reason." He thinks that Henry in sincerely endeavouring to achieve the national brotherhood, embodies 'an organic and creative order'.[106] While on one level the speech and the play do lend themselves to this interpretation, we must not forget the specific dramatic context which has called forth the speech. Besides, on a deeper level, the irony woven round the speech warns against a naive acceptance of Henry's claim, 'we band of brothers'. His refusal to meet Williams's challenge (IV. vii. 133-34) is snobbish[107] and reminds us of Austria's refusal to fight the Bastard in *King John* on similar grounds. The fact that he is no coward like the former, only suggests that he continues to believe in the Medieval concept of a hierarchical society. In the next scene, the way he reads out the number of the English dead in the battle is equally significant:

Edward the Duke of York, the Earl of Suffolk,
Sir Richard Kikely, Davy Gam, esquire;
None else of name;

(IV. viii. 103-05) (Italics Mine)

The common soldiers who shed their blood with the dukes and the esquires were nameless creatures after all. What happens to the promise that he who sheds his blood 'with me shall be my brother' and what remains of the band of brothers? It was 'a lost brotherhood', not only historically in the context of the Sixteenth Century, as V.G. Kiernan observes,[108] but also dramatically in the context of *Henry V.*

"Instead of expressing gratitude to the Bateses and Courts and Williamses of his army of yeomen", remarks Goddard, "Henry characteristically attributes his triumph wholly to God."[109] Reiterating his gratitude to God for the victory, he orders that *Non nobis* and *Deum* be sung (Two chantries for Pomfret castle and two chants for Agincourt:). Henry's humility in victory and gratitude to God may be interpreted as further proofs of his Christian piety, but his reiteration of the same "becomes psychologically suspicious in the highest degree. It ends by looking less like giving thanks to God for the victory than like putting the responsibility on God".[110]

The Fifth Act, though considered an anticlimax by many, has still deeper ironies in store. It is here that Shakespeare seems to give us his final assessment of Henry's achievement. The opening of the Act with Pistol forced by Flaullen to eat the leek, is not meant to provide comic relief after Agincourt. It is a symbolic comment on Henry's French campaign and his ultimate fate. To look back to the Prologue to Act III, Henry had refused the French offer, which he now accepts. Pistol's eating the leek, is, therefore, a prophecy, through parody, of Henry's fate.[111] Indeed, "the administration of the dose is so disguised by sentiment and diplomacy, so sugared over with protestations of 'love' and exchanges of 'brother France' and 'brother England', that the leek to all appearances might have been a piece of wedding cake. But leek it is, nevertheless".[112]

There is some bawdy in Shakespeare's Kate. The language lesson she has learnt—hand, arm, neck, chin (III. iv.),—is definitely suggestive of the progress in love-making[113] and her non-virginal status is suggested in her kissing Henry after saying that 'maids' do not kiss (V. ii. 280). The leek symbolism also suggests the love of fleshpots of Egypt,[114] and its association with David suggests his winning of non-virginal Bathseba.[115] The wooing itself contains no spark of Romeo[116], it rather reminds us of Richard's wooing of Anne, though the circumstances are the opposite. How perilously opposite to true love is Henry's wooing becomes apparent in his reply to Kate's point that she may not love the enemy of France. He protests that he is rather the friend of France: "for I love France so well that I will not part with a village of it; I will have it all mine; and, Kate, when France is mine, and I am yours, then yours is France and you are mine" (V. ii. 175-78). "It is closer to a rapacity for land than it is to the love of woman", says Goddard.[117] "Henry's marriage is essentially political", remarks Strībrny.[118] To judge it by its political results, Henry despite his victory never becomes the King of France, his only reward being the title 'heir' and the fact that he inherits through the female by marrying her is an appropriate answer surely to his demand for the French territory in II. iv.[119] Whether Shakespeare wrote the *Henry VI* plays or not, he is definitely aware of the ironic results of Henry V's victory and marriage—the wars of the Roses and the weak infant king. As Schlegel puts it, "all that has reference to this (Henry's marriage) is intended for irony in the play. The fruit of this union, from which two nations promised to themselves such happiness in future, was the weak and feeble Henry VI, under whom everything was so miserably lost."[120] The final chorus is a sonnet. The first quartet again apologises for the playwright's as well as the theatre's short-comings:

> Thus far, with rough and all-unable pen,
> Our bending author hath pursu'd the story,
> In little room confining mighty men,
> Mangling by starts the full course of their glory.

The second glorifies Henry as the national hero:

> Small time: but in that small, most greatly lived
> This star of England. Fortune made his sword;

By which the world's best garden he achieved,
And of it left his son imperial lord.

The third by reminding us of the future events, deflates the epic stature of Henry and takes the wind out of his military success:

Henry the Sixth, in infant bands crown'd King
Of France and England, did this king succeed;
Whose state so many had the managing
That they lost France and made his England bleed;

Nothing could have better expressed the popular as well as the ironic view of Henry's life and death.

It must not be imagined that it was without the knowledge and will of the poet that a heroic drama turns out to be a comedy and ends in the manner of a farce with a marriage of convenience.[121] It could not have been so when we know who the poet was and particularly if we keep in mind that *Henry V* falls between *Henry IV* and *Julius Caesar*. Střibrny who calls Henry V 'the new national king', in his attempt to reconcile the glorification of Henry with his denigration, remarks: "It adds to Shakespeare's greatness that he can divine, at the very moment of reaching his historical synthesis, the destructive and ultimately self-destructive nature of the new men and their new ways."[122] He also observes that "In the very act of apotheosis Shakespeare tears down Henry's godlike aureole and shows that 'in his nakedness he appears but a man'."[123] In fact, Henry is hardly a new man. He descends directly from Richard III. The difference is that he succeeds during his life-time whereas Richard failed. The difference is also that the popular Tudor tradition eulogised Henry as the ideal king and painted Richard as black as the devil. In both the plays, as in the tragedies which follow, particularly in *Julius Caesar* and *Hamlet*, Shakespeare attempts an 'exposure of the hollowness and rottenness of power'.[124] The heroic structure and the apparent apotheosis of Henry are the concessions Shakespeare is compelled to make to the popular tradition. But to look below the surface is to note mock-heroic as the real pattern of the play.

NOTES

1. *English History in Shakespeare* (New York: E.P. Dutton, 1918), p. 136.
2. Una Ellis-Fermor, "Shakespeare's Political Plays", *The Frontiers of Drama* (London: Methuen, 1967), pp. 34-55.
3. Peter Alexander, *Shakespeare* (London: O.U.P., ELBS, 1965), p. 196.
4. *Ibid.*, p. 196.
5. *The Round Table Characters of Shakespeare's Plays* (London: J.M. Dent and New York: E.P. Dutton, 1960), p. 285.
6. *Our Theatres in the Nineties* (London: Constable, 1932), II, pp. 128 *et seq.*
7. 'At Stratford on Avon' in *Ideas of Good and Evil* (London, 1903), p. 156.
8. A. Harbage, *As They Liked It* (N.Y.: Harper Torchbooks, 1961), p. 152.
9. A.C. Bradley, 'The Rejection of Falstaff' in *Oxford Lectures on Poetry* (London: Macmillan, 1962), p. 256.
10. A.C. Sprague, *Shakespeare's Histories: Plays for the Stage* (London: Society for Theatre Research, 1964), Chap. VI, pp. 92-110. Sprague draws attention to its revival in the Eighteenth century against the background of the French wars and during the Victorian Age, against that of the South African war.
11. *Op. cit.*, p. 136.
12. *Ibid.*, p. 166.
13. *Ibid.*, p. 137.
14. *Ibid.*, p. 166.
15. *Chronicles* III (583/1/59), *vide* Bullough (ed.), *Narrative and Dramatic Sources of Shakespeare* (London and New York, 1962), IV, pp. 406 *et seq.*
16. *Vide ibid.*, p. 412.
17. *Vide ibid.*, p. 424.
18. *Shakespeare's History Plays* (Penguin, 1962), p. 305.
19. *Ibid.*, p. 306.
20. J.D. Wilson (ed.), *Henry V* (New Shakespeare Cambridge University Press, 1955), pp. xvii *et seq* esp. p. xxxii.
21. J.H. Walter (ed.), *Henry V* (New Arden, 1961), pp. xxiii *et seq.*
22. A.W. Schlegel, *Dramatic Art and Literature* (tr.), John Black (London: H.G. Bohn, 1861), p. 428.
23. *Ibid.*, p. 432.
24. M.M. Reese, *The Cease of Majesty* (London: Edward Arnold, 1961), p. 319.

25. Zdenek Stribrny, '*Henry V* and History' in A. Kettle (ed.), *Shakespeare in a Changing World* (London: Lawrence & Wishart, 1964), p. 101.
26. D.A. Stauffer, *Shakespeare's World of Images* (Bloomington & London: Indiana University Press, 1966), Chap. III, The Garden of Eden, p. 100.
    Note also the explanation advanced by D. Wilson: "If the greatest story in English history, as he and his contemporaries thought it, was ill-suited for normal dramatic treatment, then a new form of drama must be invented. Theme and hero clearly called for epic; and the problem was how to use the theatre for this purpose. It was solved by setting a series of heroic episodes or tableaux upon the stage,..." *op. cit.*, p. xii.
27. Reese, *op. cit.*, pp. 321 *et seq.*
28. H.A. Evans (ed.), *Henry V* (Arden, London: Methuen, 1917), p. xli.
29. Stribrny, *op. cit.*, p. 86.
30. *Ibid.*, pp. 86 *et seq.*
31. I. Ribner, *The Eng. History Play in the Age of Shakespeare* (Princeton, N. Jersey: Princeton University Press, 1957), p. 183.
32. *Ibid.*, p. 183.
33. Owing to the obsession of his audience with the established image of Henry V.
34. Owing to censor and the link between Henry V and the Tudors.
35. A. Righter, *Shakespeare and the Idea of the Play* (London: Chatto & Windus, 1964), Chapter V, pp. 113-38.
36. J.E. Neale, *Queen Elizabeth* (London: Jonathan Cape, 1934), p. 256.
37. *Op. cit.*, p. 113.
38. J. Munro, Int. to *Henry V* (London: Shakespeare, 1958), p. 1018.
39. Tillyard, *op. cit.*, p. 308.
40. The remark quoted on p. 233 *supra*.
41. He uses the phrase in an altogether different sense that of a spiritual crisis. See his 'From *Henry V* to *Hamlet*', in P. Alexander (ed.), *Studies in Shakespeare,* British Academy Lectures (London: Oxford University Press, 1964), pp. 71-102, esp., p. 79.
42. R. Simpson, 'The Politics of Shakespeare's History Plays', *New Shakespeare Society Transactions,* 1874, Chapter IV, p. 41.
43. Quotation on pp. 238-39 *supra*.
44. Stribrny, *op. cit.*, p. 98.
45. The comments by Roy. W. Battenhouse on the lines in his '*Henry V* As Heroic Comedy' in R. Hosley (ed.), *Essays on Shakespeare and Elizabethan Drama In Honour of Hardincraig* (London: Routledge and Kegan Paul, 1963), p. 182.
46. H.B. Charlton, *Shakespeare, Politics and Politicians* (English Association Pamphlet No. 72), p. 16.

47. Holinshed, *Chronicles* III (545/2/6) in Bullough (ed.), *op.cit.*, pp. 377 *et seq.* and Sen Gupta's exposition in his *Shakespeare's Historical Plays* (London: Oxford University Press, 1964), pp. 141 *et seq.*
48. Bradley, *op. cit.*, p. 257.

    Also Palmer, *Political and Comic Characters of Shakespeare* (London: Macmillan 1962), p. 221.

    Sprague, *op. cit.*, p. 100.
49. L.B. Campbell, *Shakespeare's 'Histories'* (San Marino, California: Huntington Lib., 1963), p. 261.
50. Battenhouse, *op. cit.*, p. 174.
51. Ribner, *op. cit.*, p. 189.
52. Palmer, *op. cit.*, p. 321.

    Traversi, *op. cit.*, p. 171—Henry's "willingness to shift the responsibility upon others to use their connivance to obtain the justification which he continually insistently requires."
53. Campbell, *op. cit.*, pp. 273 *et seq.*
54. Quoted on p. 242 *supra.*
55. Traversi, *op. cit.*, p. 170.
56. Battenhouse, *op. cit.*, p. 174.
57. *St. Mark,* 16: 16. *Holy Bible.*
58. *The Acts,* 3: 38. *Holy Bible.*
59. Chapter VI, *supra.*
60. Traversi, *op. cit.*, pp. 170 *et seq.*
61. Page 244 *supra.*
62. Sir W. Raleigh, *The History of the World* (ed.), G.E. Hadow, *Sir Walter Raleigh Selections from His Writings* (Oxford: Clarend Press, 1927), Preface, p. 41.
63. See Chapters IV and V above.
64. N. Machiavelli, *The Prince* (tr.), L. Ricci (rev.), E.R.P. Vincent, (London: Oxford University Press, 1949), p. 79.
65. Part of the speech quoted on p. 245 *supra.*
66. D. Wilson, *op. cit.*, p. 150.—the speech is "merely an elaboration of *Deuteronomy* 20: 10-14".
    J.H. Walter, *op. cit.*, p. 66—While not going as far as that Walter too admits the possibility of *Deuteronomy* 20 being a source.
67. *Deuteronomy* 20: 12-14. *Holy Bible.*
68. John Wain, *The Living World of Shakespeare* (London: Macmillan, 1964), p. 64.

    Traversi, *op. cit.*, p. 169.
69. Machiavelli, *op. cit.*, pp. 77 *et seq.*

70. Quotation from Hooker on pp. 6-7 *supra.*
71. R. Hapgood, 'Shakespeare's Delayed Reactions', *Essays in Criticism* (Jan., 1963), Vol. XIII, No. 1, pp. 14 *et seq.*
72. J.B. Priestley, *The English Comic Characters* (John Lane, The Bodley Head, 1928), p. 102.
73. Machiavelli, *op. cit.,* p. 75.
74. Charlton, *op. cit.,* p. 18.
75. Walter, *op. cit.,* pp. xvii *et seq.*
76. *Op. cit.,* p. 167.
77. *Ibid.,* p. 168.
78. D. Wilson, *op. cit.,* p. xli.
79. Una Ellis-Fermor, *op. cit.,* p. 46.
80. Though even critics like Bradley and Sen Gupta, otherwise critical of the character, and pointing out the short-comings in his piety, do not doubt its sincerity. Bradley, *op. cit.,* p. 257.

    Sen Gupta, *op. cit.,* p. 146.
81. Bradley, *loc. cit.*
82. Sen Gupta, *op. cit.,* pp. 146 *et seq.*
    & H.C. Goddard, *The Meaning of Shakespeare* (Chicago & London: University of Chicago Press, Phoenix, 1967), p. 245.
83. See Walter, *op. cit.,* p. 106.
84. *Vide ibid.*
85. Bradley, *op. cit.,* p. 257.
86. Raleigh, *op. cit.,* p. 52.
87. D. Wilson, *op. cit.,* p. XL.
88. The Parable of talents in *Matthew* 25, esp. verse 19—"the lord of those servants cometh and *reckoneth* with them." Also *Matthew,* 18: 21-35. *Holy Bible.*
89. IV. i. 133-45.
90. Raleigh, *op. cit.,* p. 52.
91. Battenhouse, *op. cit.,* p. 179.
92. The Parable of the king and his servant in *Mattew,* 18: 21-35, *Holy Bible,* referred to above.
93. R.L. Kelly, 'Shakespeare's Scroops and the "Spirit of Cain", *Shakespeare Quarterly* XX (Winter 1969), No. 1, p. 73.
94. See H.C. Goddard, *op. cit.,* pp. 230 *et seq.*
95. Dr. Johnson, *op. cit.,* p. 131.
96. *I Chronicles,* 29:12. *Holy Bible.*
97. *II Chronicles,* 1:11. *Holy Bible.*

98. John Wain, *The Living World of Shakespeare* (London: Macmillan, 1964), p. 67.
99. D. Wilson, *op. cit.*, p. xxxi.
100. See Walter, *op. cit.*, p. xxix.
101. L. Copeland and L. Lamm (eds.), *The World's Great Speeches* (N.Y. Dover Publications, 1958), p. 446.
102. M. Webster, *Shakespeare To-day* (London: J.M. Dent & Sons, 1957), p. 173.
103. *Ibid.*, p. 173.
104. *Op. cit.*, p. 178.
105. J. Wain, *op. cit.*, pp. 67 *et seq.*
106. M. Murry, *op. cit.*, pp. 184 *et seq.*
107. See Flaullen's words, IV, vii, 135 ff.
Also see Goddard's comments, *op. cit.*, p. 253.
108. V.G. Kiernan, 'Human Relationships in Shakespeare', A. Kettle (ed.), *Shakespeare in a Changing World* (London: Lawrence & Wishart, 1964), p. 50.
109. Goddard, *op. cit.*, p. 255.
110. *Ibid.*, p. 255.
Battenhouse draws particular attention to the ironic connection between Henry's killing of the prisoners and his eagerness to give God's arm the whole credit, *op.cit.*, p. 178.
111. *Ibid.*, p. 175.
112. Goddard, *op. cit.*, pp. 261 *et seq.*
113. See Battenhouse, *op. cit.*, p. 180.
114. *Numbers,* 11:6.
115. Battenhouse, *op. cit.*, p. 175.
116. Goddard, *op. cit.*, p. 263.
117. *Ibid.*, p. 264.
118. Střibrny, *op. cit.*, p. 97.
119. Battenhouse, *op. cit.*, p. 175.
120. Schlegel, *op. cit.*, p. 432.
121. *Ibid.*, p. 432 *et seq.*
122. *Op. cit.*, p. 101.
123. *Ibid.*, p. 97.
124. Goddard, *op. cit.*, p. 268.

Conclusion

The History plays had their limitations. The hard facts of history could not be altered. The personnel could not be hired or fired at will, nor could the personae be modified except for little hairdos and minor facelifts. The national sentiments could not be hurt nor could the sensitiveness of the powerul be overlooked. There could be no free play of the playwright's fancy. No wonder therefore that the only History Play outside of Shakespeare in the repertoire of Elizabethan and Jacobean Drama worth acclaim is Marlowe's *Edward II*. One may perhaps mention Greene's *James IV* too but as pointed out by Ashley Thorndyke, it is "only pseudo-history"[1]. Besides if Greene has earned immortality it is not on account of *James IV* nor even that of *Friar Bacon* and *Friar Bungay*, but the left-handed compliment paid by him to Shakespeare:

> Yet trust them not: for there is an upstart Crow, beautified with our feathers, that with his *Tygers hart wrapt in a Players hyde*, supposes he is as well able to bombast out a blanke verse as the best of you: and beeing an absolute *Iohannes fac totum*, is in his owne conceit the onely Shake-scene in a countrey.[2]

The very fact that Shakespeare chose to try his hand at the Histories during his formative years as a playwright reflects his natural genius as well as self-confidence. Initially he might have got his break as a very junior apprentice with established University Wits like Greene, Nashe, and Peele. In course of the *Henry VI*-project, this 'Small Latin and Less Greeke'-knowing rustic, might have rubbed them up the wrong way, and the trio must have regretted having condescended to the idea of letting the Stratford-lad-turned player share the script with them. However, the fact remains that Greene's infamous comment earned free publicity for himself as well as Shakespeare and, to this day remains so, the left-handed factor having been returned to Greene with interest.

But that is history. Nearer our times, occurred the First World War with Great Britain and the British Empire at the centre. In the aftermath of the devastation the British (American) genius produced *The Wasteland*. It also went back to the Histories of Shakespeare just as in time of crisis a family goes back to the *Holy Bible*. So the nation remembered the long neglected History Plays with a new-found nationalistic fervour and fire. The result was a revival of interest in the History Plays and the emergence of a nationalistic approach to them. Works like the historian J.A.R. Marriott's *English History in Shakespeare* (1918) and R.V. Lindabury's *A Study of Patriotism in Elizabethan England* (1931) illustrate the approach. This too is history.

However, it is said that history repeats itself and so it did rather too soon with the outbreak of the Second World War in 1939. Once again the nation remembered Shakespeare's Histories with pride and gratitude. But the menace of Hitler's war machine was much more threatening and the crisis much graver this time, so much so that poetry seems to have lost its voice. In the words of James Reeves:

> The Hitler war came as the most powerful and threatening shock to civilization and the individual life which has ever been experienced. Was it the spirit of the time or the state of poetry in England which was responsible for the comparative dearth of new war poets ? The period was not without its poetry, but this had little of the significance of Georgian war poetry. The latter sprang from illusion and disillusion: in the Hitler war there was neither. Its poetry, if there was any, went mainly into prose documentation.[3]

The inspiring war speeches of Churchill, often echoing patriotic passages from Shakespeare's Histories, are one example of such powerful prose document. But the all pervasive anarchy let loose by Nazi nihilism was too grave a crisis to be countered by nationalism alone. What was needed was a universal philosophy of life based on sound ethical parameters. This was exactly what the nation discovered in Arnold Toynbee's magnum opus, *A Study of History*, which provided a moralistic point of view. Consequently when the History Plays of Shakespeare were reread in the wake of the II World War and the overwhelming impact of Toynbee's philosophy during the forties and fifties, the glasses used were those of order, degree and harmony.

Undoubtedly such specific approaches to Shakespeare's Histories have thrown new light on them and helped in drawing attention to them afresh. Nevertheless by concentrating on tailor-made designs this has led to cutting the plays down to prefabricated brands. As a matter of fact, however, there can be neither a nationalistic interpretation of history nor a moral one. "The only legitimate interpretation (of history) is the historical one" says Nirad C. Chaudhary writing of Robert Clive's exploits in India.[4] The observation is equally applicable to the History Plays of Shakespeare with the added qualification that the interpretation must take into account the artistic angle as well.

As an artist Shakespeare's prime concerns were men and women, and of course, their emotions and passions, their thoughts and ideas. When Greene and others hired him—underestimating his creative genius—to get a few homilitic passages copied and (may be) transformed to dramatic speeches and assist them in monitored back-up writing, they committed a grave error. The attempts to put Shakespeare into such water tight compartments as pro-establishment or anti-establishment, nationalistic or orthodox Degree-Order-oriented, tantamount to similar error.

Political ideologies—including Degree-Order, Divine Right of Kingship, Feudal rights, civil rights, nationalism bordering on xenophobia—are all present in the Histories, and naturally, for they happen to be the staple stuff of history. What is more, being a genuine artist, Shakespeare had the amazing capacity of being sensitive and sympathetic to all points of view, even contradictory ones. Surely it was his negative capability which enabled him to breathe as much life to Hotspur's paean to honour as to the scathing tirade against honour by Falstaff. No wonder therefore that during his life time both royalists and anti-royalists laid claim on him and referred to him with like surety. In all probability it was the Queen herself who was able to appreciate and respect the great poetic objectivity of Shakespeare more than any other of his contemporaries. This is evident from the well-known event of her visit to the Tower, recorded by William Lombarde, the antiquary and keeper of records in the Tower. Narrating her historic visit to the Tower on August 4, 1601, Lombarde notes :

> .... her Majestie fell upon the reign of King Richard II, saying, 'I am Richard II. Know ye not that?'
>
> W.L.—'Such a wicked imagination was determined and attempted by a most unkind Gent. The most adorned creature that ever your Majestie made.'
>
> Her Majestie. 'He that will forget God, will also forget his benefactors; this tragedy was played forty times in open-streets and houses.'[5]

During the trial, Essex was accused of frequenting and patronizing the performances. We know the fate of Essex and also the fact that the play was censored, yet to the credit of the great Queen, no action was initiated against Shakespeare.

The Essex rebellion was a crisis, in fact, the gravest that the Queen had to face on the home front. The History Plays of Shakespeare abound with various such crises like civil strife, threats of invasion, foreign campaigns, political conspiracies and power struggles. And quite naturally, but on such basis to conclude that the heart of the Histories, lies either in the political ideologies or temporal upheavals, would be wrong. The heart lies elsewhere. A character, modelled on a historical figure may well have his beliefs and ideologies, his aspirations and ambitions, nevertheless Shakespeare refuses to waste his energy on any propaganda or counter-propaganda or even a critique of the same. Instead he puts the ideas and beliefs as well as the dreams and desires of the historical characters into the test-tubes of life experience, and demonstrates how under the stress of circumstances more often than not the initial belief may be belied, the dream may be betrayed. The History Plays keep reiterating the phenomenon that in the whirligig of Time the individual is an agent as well as a victim of the ceaseless process of change. The Bastard who mocks at commodity good-humouredly in the beginning of *King John*, very nearly becomes a prey to it himself towards the end of the play. On the other hand, John, the unquestioned king of commodity ends as a conscience-ridden mortal. Richard II as also old Gaunt lose their vociferously declared faith in the Divine Right of Kingship and, in doing so both become more human, allowing natural human sensitivity and instincts to surface at last and subdue abstract ideas and ideologies. York on the other hand, who in the first scenes makes concession for honest private sentiments, ends up as a wooden figure of a loyal no-father. With the working of the unseen historical process, the characters also change places, shifting and shuffling their thoughts and visions under the pressure of multifaceted experience.

In the words of George Bernard Shaw, "the histories of Shakespeare are chronicles dramatized".[6] Yes, they are, but this is only half the truth. By and large, Shakespeare does remain faithful to history, retaining the basic outlines provided by the sources, and takes only a few artistic liberties for the sake of dramatic effect. The best known and perhaps the most atrocious of such liberties is reducing the age of Harry Hotspur by nearly half, and making him contemporaneous with prince Harry. In the heat of the drama, however spellbound by the sharp rivalry between the two Harries, we hardly have time to take notice of the aberration. Yet another kind of liberty taken by Shakespeare is so subtle that it is likely to escape notice altogether. The noted historian, J.E. Neale narrates the corrupt practice prevalent during the Elizabethan Age in recruitment of soldiers and, illustrates how Shakespeare does not hesitate in transporting one such incident to Henry IV's regime, substituting Deputy Lieutenant Trevor with Sir John Falstaff.

> Then came the repeated pressing of men for Essex's expeditions and the Irish wars offering opportunities to

those in the ascendant to line their pockets and vent their spite on dependants of their enemies. As Deputy-Lieutenant Trevor had prime responsibility for these levies, and when at last the downfall of his patron, the Earl of Essex, exposed him to retribution, he was prosecuted in the Star Chamber for various offences—extorting coat and conduct money from the county and diverting it to his and his friends' use, and levying men either through malice or to extract the price of their release. The occasions ranged from the Cadiz expedition of 1596 to reinforcements for Ireland in August 1600; and the documents in the case would serve as admirable illustrative pieces for muster scene in Shakespeare's *Henry IV*.

Whether Trevor pleaded 'not guilty' or tamely confessed the crime during the trial is not known. However, Shakespeare makes capital of the situation by letting Falstaff indulge in braggadocio at its best.

> If I be not ashamed of my soldiers, I am a soused gurnet; I have misused the King's press damnably. I have got in exchange of a hundred and fifty soldiers three hundred and odd pounds. I press me none but good householders, yeomen's sons, inquire me out contracted bachelors, such as had been asked twice on the banns, such a commodity of warm slaves as had as lief hear the devil as a drum, such as fear the report of a caliver worse than a struck fowl or a hurt wild duck. I pressed me none but such toasts-and-butter, with hearts in their bellies no bigger than pins' heads, and they have bought out their services; and now my whole charge consists of ancients, corporals, lieutenants, gentlemen of companies—slaves as ragged as Lazarus in the painted cloth, where the glutton's dogs licked his sores: and such a indeed were never soldiers, but discarded unjust serving-men, younger sons to younger brothers, revolted tapsters, and ostlers trade-fallen, the cankers of a calm world and a long peace, ten times note dis-honourable-ragged than an old fazed ancient; and

> such have I to fill up the rooms of them as have bought out their services, that you would the ink that I had a hundred and fifty tattered prodigals lately come from swine-keeping, from eating draff and husks. A mad fellow met me on the way, and told me I had unloaded all the gibbets and pressed the dead bodies. No eye hath seen such scarecrows. (*I Henry IV*. IV. II. 11-38)

This obviously amounts to distortion of a historical fact, and yet, it only reflects how Shakespeare succeeds in metamorphosing a factual information into universal truth, for such misuse of power to fleece and fill one's coffers with easy money, widespread all over the world and in all times, becomes specially pronounced in times of emergency. While butressing the character of the fat unscrupulous knight, based on the Morality Play figure of Vice, he must have considered the Trevor-trial incident to be exceptionally useful and handy. The outcome is a brilliant mockery of war as well as a travesty of confession.

As a matter of fact, at the heart of Shakespeare's Histories—just as that of his comedies and tragedies—lies the truth of art, i.e. the universal and eternal truth, not the trivial truth of facts and figures. And yet there are instances where he miraculously succeeds in transforming the latter into the universal and thereby into the truly poetic. The seemingly meaningless drunken exchange between Justice Shallow and Silence in *2 Henry IV* provides an example.

> Shal..... Jesu, Jesu, the mad days that
> I have spent! And to see how many of my
> old acquaintance are dead!
> Sil. We shal all follow cousin.
> Shal. Certain, 'tis certain; very sure, very sure.
> Death, as the Psalmist saith, is
> Certain all; all shall die. How a good
> yoke of bullocks at Stamford fair?
> Sil. By my troth, I was not there.
> Shal. Death is certain. Is old Double of
> your town living yet?

Sil. Dead, sir.
Shal. Jesu, Jesu, dead! 'A drew a good
bow; and dead! 'A shot a fine shoot.
John a Gaunt loved him well, and betted
much money on his head. Dead!' A would
have clapp'd I' th' clout at twelve score,
and carried you a forehand shaft a fourteen
and fourteen, and a half, that it would have
done a man's heart good to see. How a
score of ewes now?
Sil. Thereafter as they be-a score of
good ewes may be worth ten pounds.
Shal. And is old Double dead? (2 *Henry IV*. III. ii. 31-51)

Justice Shallow and Silence may not find any place in Tudor history, not even in the footnotes, just as the Gardeners of *Richard* II would not, nor Fluellens and Gowers of *Henry V*, nonetheless in his imaginative recapitulation of history, Shakespeare finds scope for them and makes poetic use of such universal figures in an astonishing manner.

In *English Social History*, Trevelyan makes the following telling observation :

> There is nothing that more divides civilized from semi-savage man than to be conscious of our forefathers as they really were, and bit by bit to reconstruct the mosaic of the long-forgotten past. To weigh the stars, or to make ships sail in the air or below the sea, is not a more astonishing and ennobling performance on the part of the human race in these latter days, than to know the course of events that had been long forgotten, and the true nature of men and women who were here before us.
>
> Truth is the criterion of historical study; but its impelling motive is poetic. Its poetry consists in its being true. There we find the synthesis of the scientific and literary views of history.[8]

Not all historical studies would pass this acid test. In fact, very few would. Among literary works based on history, the number of works which may qualify would be still fewer.

Shakespeare's Histories do, so do the novels of Scott, and of course, Tolstoy's *War and Peace*. To label these works therefore, as simply 'chronicles dramatized' is rather unfair. It amounts to nailing them down to the specific times and places, showcased in them, whereas their true greatness lies not so much in factual recapitulation of such and such times and places, but in tentative groping after Time and Truth.

"Vanity of vanities, all is vanity' (*Ecclesiastes* l. i)

Declares the preacher in the *Holy Bible*, and thus sums up the entire creation. In Indian metaphyiscs the word used for creation is *Leela*, i.e. play. It is astonishing to note that the metaphor chosen by Shakespeare for vanity—*stage*—is also taken from the play-world. Developing the metaphor fully this is how York describes the exit and entrance of Bolingbroke and Richard respectively in *Richard II*:

As in a theatre the eyes of men
After a well-grac'd actor leaves the stage
Are idly bent on him that enters next,
Thinking his prattle to be tedious;
Even so, or with much more contempt, men's eyes
did scowl on gentle Richard; (*Richard II*, V. ii. 23-28)

In the ultimate analysis therefore the historical characters too, though representing genuine personalities, turn out to be no better than players on the stage. As such the heroes or villains of history, though not fictitious and imaginary like Oberon and Titania, even the Moor or the Prince of Denmark, are no better/no worse than players with their exits and entrances. The only distinguishing feature is that in the Histories they strut and stumble on ths stage of genuine and known history. Besides, being the history of relatively recent times and familiar regions, the vicissitudes of life and vagaries of fortune must have had extra sharpness for the Elizabethan groundlings as well as the aristocracy.

The overriding spectrum that comes through the Histories of Shakespeare is summed up in the pathetic lamentation of *Richard II* on the eve of his ignonimous deposition :

For God's sake let us sit upon the ground
And tell sad stories of the death of kings:

How some have been depo'd, some slain in war,
Some haunted by the ghosts they have depos'd,
Some poison'd by their wives, some sleeping kill'd,
All murder'd—for within the hollow crown
That rounds the mortal temples of a king
Keeps Death his court; and there the antic sits,
Scoffing his state and grinning at his pomp
Allowing him a breath, a little scene,
To monarchize, be fear'd, and kill with looks;
Infusing him with self and vain conceit,
As if this flesh which walls about our life
Were brass impregnable; and, humour'd thus,
Comes at the last, and with a little pin
Bores through his castle wall, and farewell, king!
(*Richard II.* III. ii. 155-70)

It is in the fall of kingdoms, the turn of fortune with the movement of its wheel, and the undoing of once powerful monarchs that the subjugation of life as well as of times to Time, comes forth most pointedly. This underlying irony in the ceaseless march of history finds powerful expression in sonnet 64.

When I have seen by Time's fell hand defac'd
The rich-proud cost of outworn buried age;
When sometime lofty towers I see down-raz'd,
And brass eternal slave to mortal rage;
When I have seen the hungry ocean gain
Advantage on the kingdom of the shore,
And the firm soil win of the wat'ry main,
Increasing store with loss, and loss with store;
When I have seen such interchange of stage,
Or state itself confounded to decay;

Neither pomp nor power survives the onslaught of Time, only art does. The same vision of hisotry is presented in Shelley's 'Ozymandias of Egypt':

I MET a traveller from an antique land
Who said: Two vast and trunkless legs of stone
Stand in the desert. Near them on the sand,
Half sunk, a shatter'd visage lies, whose frown

And wrinkled lip and sneer of cold command
Tell that its sculptor well those passions read
Which yet survive, stamp'd on these lifeless things,
The hand that mock'd them and the heart that fed;
And on the pedestal these words appear:
'My name is Ozymandias, king of kings:
Look on my works, ye Mighty, and despair!'
Nothing beside remains. Round the decay
Of that colossal wreck, boundless and bare,
the lone and level sands stretch far away.

The History Plays of Shakespeare abound with trunkless legs and broken arms, 'food for powder', ultimately turned into 'food for worms', filing the pits. However, what transcend the actions as well as the flourishes, and survive, are the passions discerned and immortalized by the supreme sculptor of Stratford-upon-Avon.

If the History Plays of Shakespeare had simply reiterated the moral scheme of Hall and Holinshed, or preached the message of the Homilies, who apart from the academicians would be interested in them today? If they were meant just to glorify the *Res Publica*, what claim would they have on the imagination of peoples other than those of the British Isles? The reason why these plays not unlike his other works, have abiding interest for peoples of all times and all climes, lies partly in the realistic depiction of the rise and fall of states as well as individuals, caused by the continuous revolution of the Wheel of Fortune, partly in the dramatization of the tension between theory and practice of ideologies, but chiefly in the dramatic tension between the temporal and the eternal. To achieve all this while remaining faithful to the hard contours of history must have called for the kind of poetic genius and all embracing sympathetic understanding of life, time, and world, which only Shakespeare could be capable of. The well thought-out tribute by Ben Jonson:

He was not of an age, but for all time!
And all the Muses still were in their prime,
When like Apollo he came forth to warm
Our ears, or like a Mercury to charm!

—therefore befits the Histories no less aptly than it does his Comedies, Tragedies, and Romances.

NOTES

1. Ashley Thorndyke (ed.) *Minor Elizabethan Drama*, Vol. 2 (London: J.M. Dent, 1949). p. XIII.
2. F.E. Halliday, *A Shakespeare Companion* 1564-1964 (Penguin, 1964), p. 196.
3. James Reeves, *A Short History of English Poetry* (London: Mercury Books, 1964), p. 217.
4. Nirad. C. Chaudhuri, *Robert Clive of India* (Jaico Books, 1975). Introduction, p. XV.
5. Halliday, *op. cit.*, p. 271.
6. G.B. Shaw, *The Complete Prefaces* (London: Paul Hamlyn, 1965; p. 887.
7. J.E. Neale, *The Elizabethan House of Commons* (Penguin, 1963), p. 114.
8. G.M. Trevelyan, *English Social History* London: Longmans, Green & Co., 1947) Int. pp. IX-X.

Appendices

APPENDIX I

GENEALOGICAL TABLE ILLUSTRATING KING JOHN AND THE ENGLISH KINGS FROM HENRY II TO EDWARD III

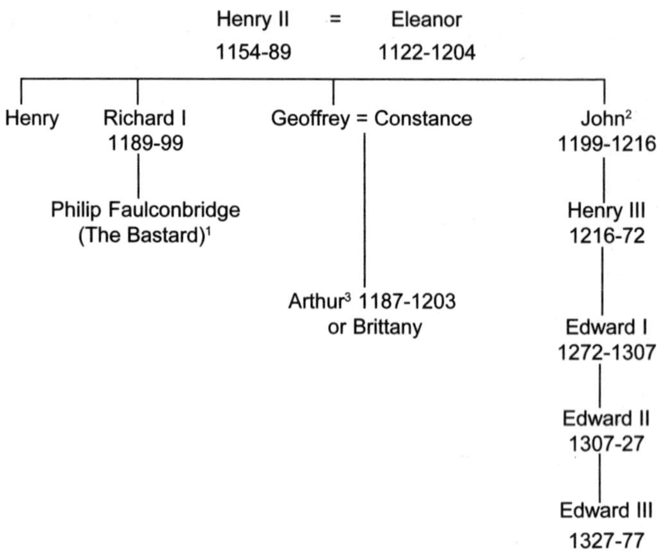

1. The Bastard son of Richard I.
2. Usurper; poisoned.
3. Imprisoned and an attempt to murder him; commits suicide.

APPENDIX II

GENEALOGICAL TABLE ILLUSTRATING THE OTHER 'HISTORIES' AND THE ENGLISH MONARCHS FROM EDWARD III TO ELIZABETH I

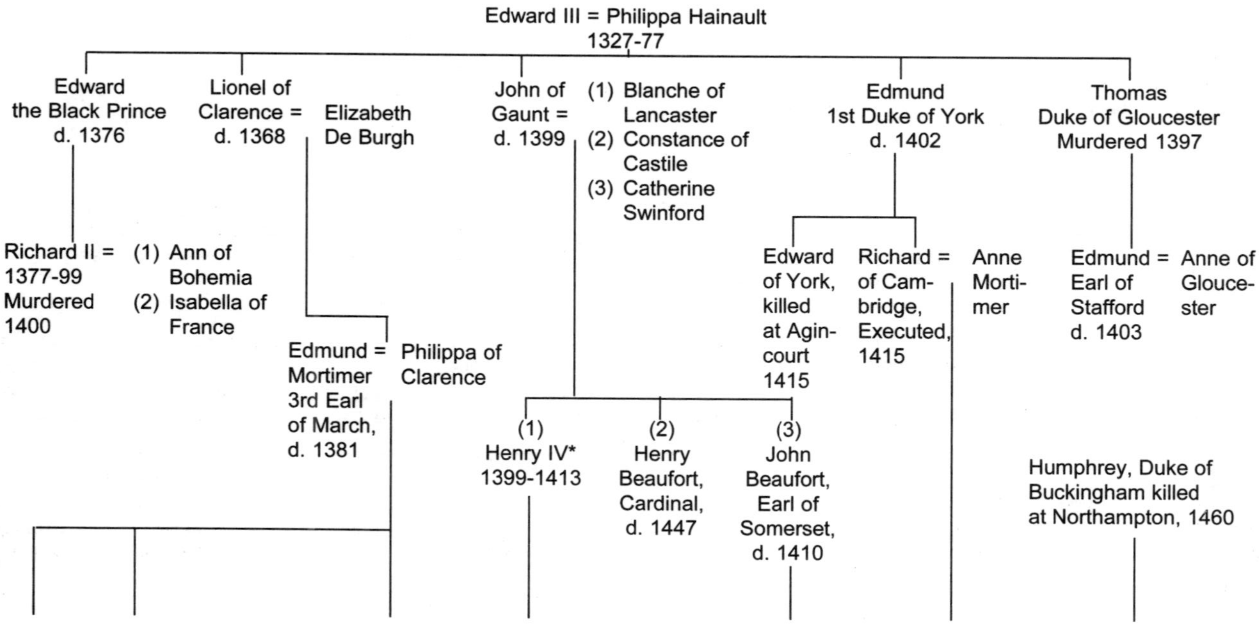

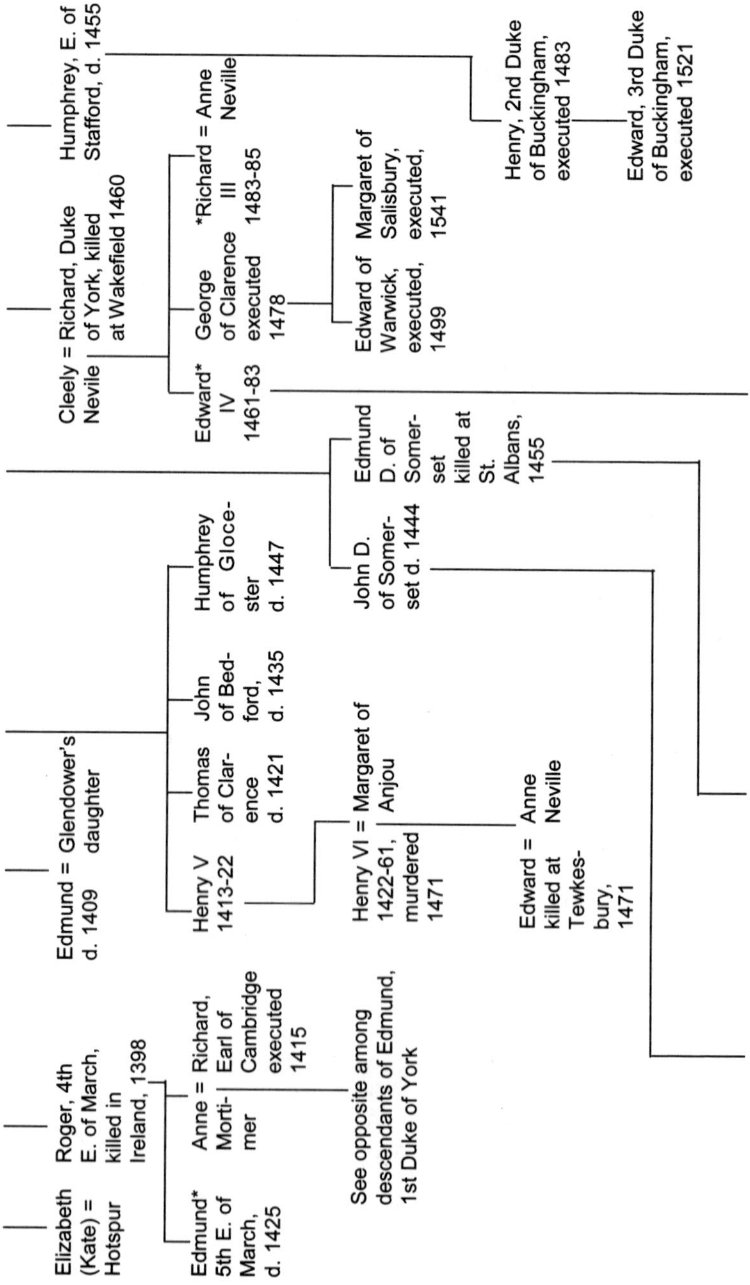
Elizabeth (Kate) = Hotspur
Roger, 4th E. of March, killed in Ireland, 1398
Edmund = Glendower's daughter
d. 1409
Cleely = Richard, Duke
Nevile of York, killed at Wakefield 1460
Humphrey, E. of Stafford, d. 1455
Edmund* 5th E. of March, d. 1425
Anne Mortimer = Richard, Earl of Cambridge executed 1415
Henry V 1413-22
Thomas of Clarence d. 1421
John of Bedford, d. 1435
Humphrey of Glocester d. 1447
Edward* IV 1461-83
George of Clarence executed 1478
*Richard III 1483-85 = Anne Neville
See opposite among descendants of Edmund, 1st Duke of York
Henry VI 1422-61, murdered 1471 = Margaret of Anjou
John D. of Somerset d. 1444
Edmund D. of Somerset killed at St. Albans, 1455
Edward of Warwick, executed, 1499
Margaret of Salisbury, executed, 1541
Edward killed at Tewkesbury, 1471 = Anne Neville
Henry, 2nd Duke of Buckingham, executed 1483
Edward, 3rd Duke of Buckingham, executed 1521

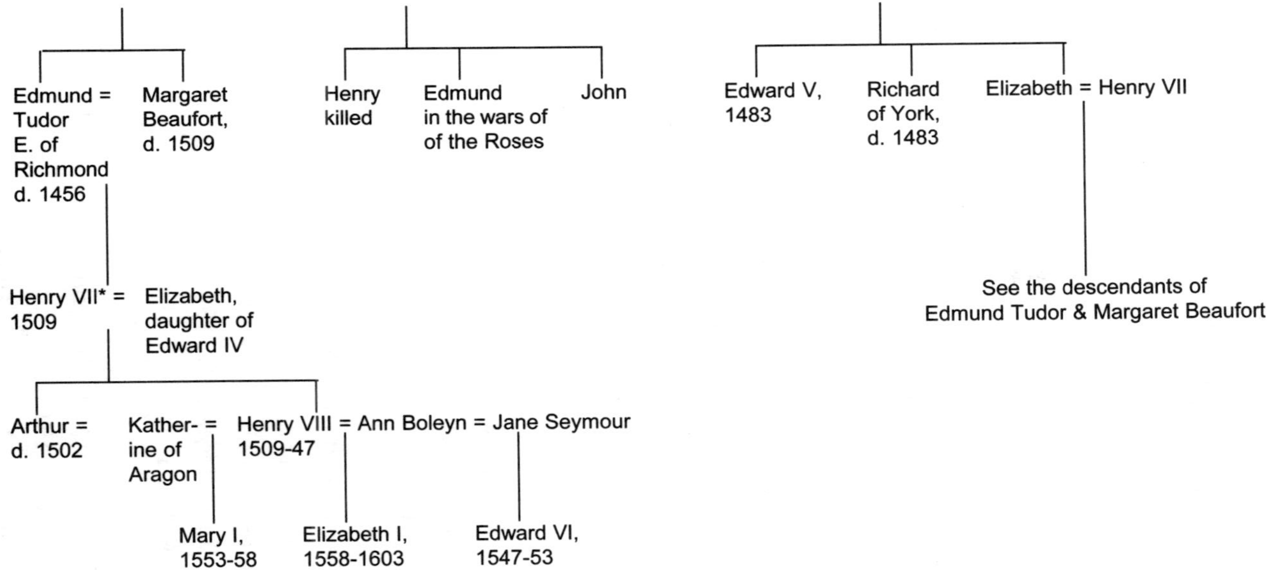

1. * Usurper.
2. ** Declared heir to the throne in 1398 by Richard II. In *1 Henry IV*, Shakespeare, following Holinshed and Daniel, confuses him with his uncle, Sir Edmund Mortimer.

Select Bibliography

I. MODERN EDITIONS OF THE PLAYS

(a) *Richard III*

W. Griggs, Facsimile (Q 1), Sh. Quartos xi, 1886.

W.W. Greg, Q Facsimile, Oxford, 1959.

A.H. Thomson, Arden, 1907.

H.H. Furness, New Variorum, 1908.

J.D. Wilson, Cambridge, 1954: 1968.

(b) *King John*

I.B. John, Arden, 1907.

H.H. Furness, Variorum, 1919.

M.R. Ridley, New Temple, 1933.

J.D. Wilson, Cambridge, 1936.

E.A.J. Honigmann, New Arden, 1954.

(c) *Richard II*

W. Griggs, Facsimile (Q 1), Sh. Quartos, 1890.

I.B. John, Arden, 1912.

H. Craig, Tudor, 1912.

J.D. Wilson, Cambridge, 1939, 1968.

P. Ure, New Arden, 1956.

(d) *Henry IV, Part I*

W. Griggs, Facsimile (Q 1), Sh. Quartos, viii, 1881.

A.E. Morgan, Arden, 1914.

S.B. Hemingway, New Variorum, 1936.

J.D. Wilson, Cambridge, 1946, 1968.

A.R. Humphreys, New Arden, 1960.

J.H. Walter, Players Shakespeare, 1961.

J.L. Sanderson, Norton, 1962.

A.E. Evans, University of London Press, 1962.

(e) *Henry IV, Part 2*

W. Griggs, Q Facsimile, Sh. Quartos, ix, 1882.

S.B. Hemingway, Yale, 1921.

R.P. Cowl, Arden, 1923.

M.A. Shaaber, New Variorum, 1940.

J.D. Wilson, Cambridge, 1946.

(f) *Henry V*

W.W. Greg, Q Facsimile, Oxford, 1957.

H.A. Evans, Arden, 1903.

J.D. Wilson, Cambridge, 1947, 1955.

J.H. Walter, New Arden, 1954.

(g) *Complete Works*

H. Kokeritz and C.T. Bouty, Facsimile of the First Folio, New Heaven, 1955.

H. Farjeon, Nonesuch Press, 1929-34, 7 vols., reprint 1953, 4 vols.

G.L. Kittredge, Boston, 1936, 1 vol.

H. Craig, Chicago, 1951, 1 vol.

J.J. Munro, London Shakespeare, 6 vols.

P. Alexander, *Collins & ELBS*, 1964, 1 vol.

II. THE PRINCIPAL SOURCES OF SHAKESPEARE'S HISTORY PLAYS

Places of publication are London, except where otherwise indicated. Modern usage is followed in titles. Modern editions of Historical Plays and poems are not mentioned separately.

(a) *Chronicles:*

(Brut) *Chronicles of England*, ed. W. Caxton, 1580.

Fabyan, Robert, *New Chronicles of England and France*, 1516, 1533, 1542, 1559.

Foxe, John, *Acts and Monuments of These Latter and Perilous Days:* 1563, 1570, 1575, 1583, 1596.

Froissart, Jean, *The Chronicle of Froissart* tr. Lord Berners, 1523, 1525, 1545.

Geoffrey of Monmouth, Bishop of St. Asaph, *Historia Regum Britanniae* Ed. Schulz, Halle, 1854; J.A. Giles, Caxton Society, 1844. Trans.

J.A. Thompson, 1718; J.A. Giles, Bohn's Library, 1847.

Grafton, Richard, *The Chronicle of John Harding in Metre... with a Continuation in Prose to this our Time* 1543.

Grafton, Richard, *An Abridgement of the Chronicles of England*, 1562, 1563, 1564, 1570, 1572.

——, *A Chronicle at Large,* 1568, 1569.

——, *A Manual of the Chronicles of England*, 1565.

Hall, Edward, *The Union of the Two Noble and Illustrious Families of York and Lancaster*, 1548, 1550, 1552.

Holinshed, Raphael, *Chronicles of England, Scotland and Ireland,* 1577, 1587.

More, Thomas, *The History of Richard III.*

Speed, John, *The History of Great Britain,* 1611, 1623, 1650, 1676.

Stow, John, *A Summary of English Chronicles,* 1565, 1567, 1573, 1587, 1580, 1590, 1598.

Vergil, Polydore, *Anglica Historia Libri,* XXVI Basle, 1534, 1546, 1555, 1556, 1570.

Vergil, Polydore, *An Abridgement of the Notable Work of Polydore Vergil.* Trans. by T. Langley, 1546, 1551, 1570.

(b) *Dramas*:

Kynge Johan (1530-36) By John Bale. Ed. J.S. Farmer, *Works*, 1907; J.H.P. Pafford, Malone Society Reprint, 1931.

The Troublesome Reign of King John I & II (1588-89) Sampson Clarke, 1591, Ed. J. Munro, 1913.

Richardus Tertius (1579) by Thomas Legge. Ed. W.C. Hazlitt, *Shakespeare's Library*, 1875.

Woodstock or 1 Richard II (1592) Ed. A.P. Rossiter, 1946.

The Famous Victories of Henry V (1588) Ed. J.Q. Adams, *Chief Pre-Shakespearean Dramas*. Boston, 1924.

(c) *Poems*:

Baldwin, William et al., *A Mirror for Magistrates*, 1559, 1563, 1571, 1574, 1575, 1578, 1587, 1610.

Ed. J. Haslewood, 1859; Lily B. Campbell, Cambridge, 1938, 1946.

Daniel, S., *The First Four Books of the Civil Wars Between the Two Houses of Lancaster and York*, ed. P. Short, 1595, ed. L. Michel; New Haven, 1958.

(d) *Modern Editions and Studies of the Chronicles*:

Boswell, Stone, W.G. *Shakespeare's Holinshed, The Chronicle and the Historical Plays Compared.* New York, 1896; 1907.

Bullough, G., *Narrative and Dramatic Sources of Shakespeare*, Vols. 3 and 4, 1960, 1962.

Hay, Denys, Polydore Vergil, *Anglica Historia*, Camden Society, 3rd ser., 1950.

Macaulay, G.C., *The Chronicles of Froissart* (tr.). Lord Berners, 1913.

Nicoll, A. and J. *Holinshed's Chronicle as Used in Shakespeare's Plays*, 1927.

Smith, R.M., *Froissart and His History*. Columbia, 1915.

III. BACKGROUND

Adams, G.B., *Constitutional History of England* (revised), Schuyler, R.L., London, 1960.

Akrigg, G.P.V., *Shakespeare and the Earl of Southampton*, London, 1968.

Allen, J.W., *History of Political Thought in Sixteenth Century*, New York, 1961.

Brown, J.R. and Harris, B. (eds.), *Elizabethan Theatre*, London, 1966.

Butterfield, H., *The Englishman and His History*, Cambridge, 1944.

Chambers, E.K., *The Elizabethan Stage*, 4 vols., Oxford, 1923.

Churchill, W., A *History of the English Speaking*, Vol. II, *The New World,* London, 1956.

Collingwood, R.G., *The Idea of History*, Oxford, 1963.

Craig, H., *The Enchanted Glass,* New York, 1936.

Cunningham, W., *The Growth of English Industry and Commerce During the Early and Middle Ages,* Cambridge, 1927.

Dunning, W.A., *A History of Political Theories from Luther to Montesquieu*, New York, 1947.

Durant, W., *The Renaissance,* New York, 1953.

Eliot, T.S., 'Shakespeare and the Stoicism of Seneca', *Shakespeare Criticism, 1919-35* (ed.), Ridler, Anne. London, New York, Toronto, 1951.

Elyot, Sir Thomas, *The Governour* (1531), London, 1907.

Evans, I. 'Shakespeare's World' in *Shakespeare's World* (ed.), Sutherland, J. and Hurstfield, J., London, 1964.

Figgis, J.N., *The Divine Right of Kings*, Cambridge, 1922 *From Gerson to Grotius*, Cambridge, 1931.

Hall, Vernon Jr., *Renaissance Literary Criticism,* Gloucester, Mass, 1959.

Hale, J.R. (ed.), *The Evolution of British Historiography*, *From Bacon to Namier,* London, 1967.

Harrison, G.B., 'Shakespeare's Topical Significances', *Shakespeare Criticism 1919-35* (ed.), Ridler, London, 1951.

——, (ed.), *Elizabethan Journals*, Vols. I and II, London, 1955, *England in Shakespeare's Day*, London, 1928.

Hart, A., *Shakespeare and the Homilies,* Melbourne, 1934.

Hooker, R., *The Laws of Ecclesiastical Polity* (ed.), Rev. John Keble, *The Works of Mr. Richard Hooker*, Vol. I (Oxford, 1888).

Hurstfield, J., 'The Elizabethan People in the Age of Shakespeare', *Shakespeare's World* (ed.), Sutherland, J. and Hurstfield, J. London, 1964.

Kingsford, C.L., *Prejudice and Promise in Fifteenth Century England*, London, 1962.

Laski, H.J. (ed.), *A Defence of Liberty Against Tyrants*, moded of *Vindiciae Contra Tyrannos* (1579), London, 1924.

Lovejoy, A., *The Great Chain of Being*, Mass., 1936.

Machiavelli, N., *The Prince*, tr. L. Ricci, rev. E.R.P. Vincent, London, 1949.

Meredith, H.O., *Economic History of England*, London, 1930.

Moore, Sir Thomas, *The Utopia* (trans.), Robinson, Ralph, London, 1952.

Montaigne, M., *The Essays of Montaigne* (trans.), E.J. Trechmann, London, 1942.

Nashe, T., *Pierce Pennilesse, The Works of Thomas Nashe*, Vol. I (ed.), Mekerrow, R.B., London, 1910.

Neale, J.E., *The Elizabethan House of Commons*, London, 1948.

——, *Queen Elizabeth I*, London, 1934.

Nicoll, A., *The Elizabethans*, Cambridge, 1957.

Pollard, A.F., *From the Accession of Edward VI to the Death of Elizabeth (1547-1603)*, W. Hunt and R.L. Poole (eds.) *The Political History of England*, VI, London, 1915.

Raleigh, Sir Walter, *History of the World*, G.E. Hadow (ed.), *Sir Walter Raleigh Selections from His Writings*, Oxford, 1927.

Sabine, G.H., A *History of Political Theory*, Part 3, London, 1963.

Strachey, L., *Elizabeth and Essex*, London, 1948.

Tawney, R.H. (ed.), *Studies in Economic History*, London, 1966.

Thomson, J.A.K., *Shakespeare and the Classics*, London, 1952.

Tillyard, E.M.W., *The Elizabethan World Picture*, London, 1943, 1967.

Unwin, George, 'Shakespeare's England' in *Studies in Economic History* (ed.), Tawney, R.H., London, 1966.

Wilson, C.H. 'Trade, Society and the State' in *The Cambridge Economic History of Europe* (eds.), E.E. Rich, and C.H. Wilson, Vol. IV, Chap. VIII, Cambridge, 1967.

IV. SOME ANTHOLOGIES OF SHAKESPEARE CRITICISM

Alexander, P., *Studies in Shakespeare,* London, 1964.

Duthie, G.I., *Papers Mainly Shakespeareian*, Edinburgh, 1964.

Gittings, R., *The Living Shakespeare,* London, 1960, 1962.

Granville—Barker, H. and Harrison G.B., *Companion to Shakespeare Studies.* Cambridge, 1934.

Halliday, F.E., *Shakespeare and His Critics,* London, 1949, 1963.

Hosley, R., *Essays on Shakespeare and Elizabethan Drama,* London, 1963.

Hurstfield, J. and Sutherland, J., *Shakespeare's World*, London, 1964.

Kettle, A., *Shakespeare in a Changing World,* London, 1964.

Le Winter, Oswald, *Shakespeare in Europe,* Penguin, 1970.

MacKail, J.W., *Aspects of Shakespeare,* Oxford, 1933.

McManaway, J. et al., *Joseph Quincy Adams Memorial Studies,* Washington, 1948.

Muir, K. and Schoenbaum, S., A *New Companion to Shakespeare,* Cambridge, 1971.

Ridler, A., *Shakespeare Criticism, 1919-35*, London, 1936. *Shakespeare Criticism, 1935-60.* London, 1963.

Smith, D.N., *Shakespeare Criticism: A Selection 1623-1840,* London, 1961.

Wagner, B., *The Appreciation of Shakespeare: A Collection of Criticism—Philosophic, Literary and Aesthetic—by Great Writers and Scholar—Critics of the Eighteenth, Nineteenth and Twentieth Centuries,* Georgetown, 1949.

Wright, L.B., *Shakespeare Celebrated,* Washington, 1966.

V. SHAKESPEARE SCHOLARSHIP AND CRITICISM (GENERAL)

Akrigg, G.P.V., *Shakespeare and the Earl of Southampton,* London, 1968.

Alexander, P., *Shakespeare's Life and Art,* London, 1939. *Shakespeare Primer,* London, 1951.

——, *Shakespeare,* London, 1964.

Baker, *The Development of Shakespeare as a Dramatist,* New York, 1923.

Barnard, E.A.B., *New Links with Shakespeare,* Cambridge, 1930.

Baton, A.M., *The Philosophy of Shakespeare,* Kingsport, Tennessee, 1937.

Bentley, G.E., *Shakespeare: A Biographical Handbook*, New Haven, 1961.

Bethell, S.L., *Shakespeare and the Popular Dramatic Tradition,* London, 1944.

Bonjour, A., *Structure of Julius Caesar*, Liverpool, 1958.

Bradbrook, M.C., *Shakespeare and Elizabethan Poetry,* London, 1951.

——, *Shakespeare, the Craftsman*, London, 1969.

Bradley, A.C., *Shakespearean Tragedy,* London, 1904.

Brooke, C.F.T., *Shakespeare Apocrypha,* London, 1918.

Brown, I., *Shakespeare,* London, 1949, new ed. 1957.

Campbell, L.B., *Shakespeare's Tragic Heroes*, New York, 1930.

Chambers, E.K., *William Shakespeare. A Study of Facts and Problems,* 2 vols., Oxford, 1930.

——, *Shakespearean Gleanings,* London, 1944.

Charlton, H.B., *Shakespearean Comedy*, London, 1938. *Shakespearean Tragedy,* Cambridge, 1948.

Clemen, W.H., *The Development of Shakespeare's Imagery,* London, 1951.

Coghill, N., *Shakespeare's Professional Skills*, Cambridge, 1964.

Coleridge, S.T., *Shakespearean Criticism*, ed. T.M. Raysor, 2 vols., London, 1930, revised edition, 1960.

Danby, J.F., *Shakespeare's Doctrine of Nature: A Study of King Lear,* London, 1949, paperback, 1961, 1965, 1968.

Doran, M. Van, *Shakespeare,* New York, 1931.

Dowden, E., *Shakespeare. His Mind and Art,* London, 1875, 1957.

Duthie, G.I., *Shakespeare,* London, 1951, revised ed. 1959.

Eagleton, T., *Shakespeare and Society,* London, 1967.

Ellis—Fermor, U., *Shakespeare the Dramatist,* London, 1961.

Evans, B.I., *The Language of Shakespeare's Plays,* London, 1960.

Fluchere, H., *Shakespeare.* London, 1953, paperback, 1961.

Fraser, R.A., *Shakespeare's Poetics in Relation to King Lear,* London, 1962.

Frye, R.M., *Shakespeare and Christian Doctrine*, Princeton, 1963.

Gervinus, G.C., *Shakespeare Commentaries*, (tr.), F.E. Bunnett, London, 1875.

Goddard, H.C., *The Meaning of Shakespeare*, 2 Vols., Chicago, 1951.

Greg, W.W., *The Shakespeare First Folio*, Oxford, 1955.

——, *The Editorial Problem in Shakespeare*, Oxford, 1962.

Haines, C., *William Shakespeare and His Plays*, London, 1968.

Halliday, F.E., *Shakespeare in His Age*, London, 1956.

——, *Shakespeare Companion: 1564: 1964*, Penguin, 1964.

——, *Poetry of Shakespeare's Plays*, London, 1954.

Harbage, *As They Liked It. An Essay on Shakespeare and Morality*, New York, 1947, 1961.

Harrison, G.B., *Shakespeare's Tragedies*, London, 1951.

——, *Introducing Shakespeare,* Penguin, 1954.

Hart, A., *Shakespeare and the Homilies*, Melbourne, 1934.

Hathway, M. (ed.), *Cambridge Companion to Shakespeare's History Plays*, Cambridge University Press, 2002.

Hazlitt, W., *The Round Table Characters of Shakespeare's Plays (1871)*, London and New York: EL, 1960.

Herford, C.H., *A Sketch of Recent Shakespearean Investigation 1893-1923*, London, 1923.

Holderness, G. (ed.), *Shakespeare's History Plays R II to H V*, Macmillan, 1992.

Holloway, J., *The Story of the Night,* London, 1961.

Hotson, L., *Shakespeare's Sonnets Dated and Other Essays*, London, 1959.

Hulme, H.M., *Explorations in Shakespeare's Language*, London, 1962.

Johnson, S., *Johnson on Shakespeare* (ed.), W. Raleigh, London, 1908.

Jorgensen, *Shakespeare's Military World*, Berkeley and Los Angeles, 1956.

Joseph, Sister Miriam, *Shakespeare's Use of the Art of Language*, New York, 1947, 1949.

Knight, G.W., *The Wheel of Fire,* London, 1930, 4th revised and enlarged ed. 1959, paperback, 1960.
——, *The Imperial Theme*, London, 1931.
——, *The Crown of Life*, London, 1948.
——, *The Shakespearean Tempest*, London, 1953.
——, *The Mutual Flame*, London, 1955.
——, *Shakespeare and Religion*, London, 1967.

Knights, L.C., *Some Shakespearean Themes*, London, 1959.
——, *Explorations*, London, 1946.
——, *Further Explorations*, London, 1965.

Kott, J., *Shakespeare Our Contemporary*, London, 1965, 1967.

Kozintsev, G., *Shakespeare: Time and Conscience*, London, 1967.

Lawlor, J., *The Tragic Sense in Shakespeare*, London, 1960.

Leishman, J.B., *Themes and Variations in Shakespeare Sonnets,* London, 1961, revised ed. 1963.

Lewis, P.W., *The Lion and the Fox: The Role of the Hero in the Plays of Shakespeare,* London, 1955.

Lings, M., *Shakespeare in the Light of Sacred Art*, London, 1966.

Ludowyk, *Understanding Shakespeare*, Cambridge, 1964.

Mahood, M.M., *Shakespeare's Wordplay*, London, 1957.

Masefield, J., *William Shakespeare*, London, 1911, revised ed. 1954.

Melchiori, G., *Shakespeare's Dramatic Meditations*, Oxford, 1976.

Mendl, R.W.S., *Revelation in Shakespeare*, London, 1964.

Moulton, R.G., *Shakespeare as a Dramatic Artist*, London, 1886.

Muir, K., *Shakespeare As Collaborator*, London, 1960.

——, *Shakespeare: The Great Tragedies*, London, 1963.

Murry, J.M., *Shakespeare*, London, 1936, paperback, 1965.

——, *Countries of the Mind*, London, 1922, 1931.

Nagler, A.M., *Shakespeare's Stage*, New Haven, 1953.

Nicoll, A., *Shakespeare*, London, 1955.

O'Connor, F., *Shakespeare's Progress*, New York, 1961.

Onions, C.T., *Shakespeare Glossary*, Oxford, 1953.

Parker, M.D.H., *The Slave of Life*, London, 1955.

Pater, W., *Appreciations*, London, 1889.

Pollard, A.W., *Shakespeare Folios and Quartos: A Study in the Bibliography of Shakespeare's Plays*, London, 1909.

——, *Shakespeare's Fight with the Pirates and the Problems of the Transmission of His Text*, Cambridge, 1920.

——, (ed.) *Shakespeare's Hand in the Play of Sir Thomas More*, London, 1923.

Quennell, P., *Shakespeare the Poet and His Background*, London, 1963.

Quiller-Couch, A., *Shakespeare's Workmanship*, Cambridge, 1918.

Raleigh, W., *Shakespeare*, London, 1907.

Ralli, A., *History of Shakespearean Criticism*, 2 vols., Oxford, 1932.

Reese, M.M., *Shakespeare: His World and His Work*, London, 1953.

Ribner, I., *Patterns in Shakespearean Tragedy*, London, 1960.

Ridley, M.R., *Shakespeare's Plays. A Commentary*, London, 1937.

Righter, A., *Shakespeare and the Idea of the Play*, London, 1964.

Robertson, J.M., *Montaigne and Shakespeare*, London, 1909.

Rowse, A.L., *William Shakespeare: A Biography*, London, 1963.

Sewell, A., *Character and Society in Shakespeare*, Oxford, 1951.

Sisson, C.J., *Shakespeare*, London, 1955, revised ed. 1965.

Sitwell, B., *A Notebook on Shakespeare*, London, 1948, 1962.

Smirnov, A.A., *Shakespeare: A Marxist Interpretation*, New York, 1936.

Spencer, T., *Shakespeare and the Nature of Man*, New York, 1942.

Spivack, B., *Shakespeare and the Allegory of Evil*, New York, 1958.

Sprague, A.C., *Shakespeare and the Actors*. Massachusetts, 1945.

Spurgeon, C., *Shakespeare's Imagery*, Cambridge, 1935, paperback, 1965.

Stauffer, D., *Shakespeare's World of Images*, Bloomington, 1949, 1966.

Stevenson, R., *Shakespeare's Religious Frontier*, The Hague, 1958.

Stewart, J.I.M., *Character and Motive in Shakespeare*, London, 1949.

Stirling, B., *The Populace in Shakespeare*, New York, 1949.

——, *Unity in Shakespearean Tragedy*, New York, 1956.

Stoll, E.E., *Shakespeare Studies*, New York, 1927, 1960.

Styan, J.L., *Shakespeare's Stagecraft*, London, 1967.

Swinburne, *A Study of Shakespeare*, London, 1879.

Traversi, D., *Approach to Shakespeare*, London, 1938, 1957.

Ulrici, H., *Shakespeare's Dramatic Art*, 2 vols., London, 1889.

Vyvyan, J., *The Shakespearean Ethic*, London, 1959.

Waine, J., *The Living World of Shakespeare*, London, 1964.

Watkins, W.B.C., *Shakespeare and Spenser*, Princeton, 1966.

Webster, M., *Shakespeare To-day*, London, 1957.

Whitaker, *Shakespeare's Use of Learning*, San Marino, 1953.

Wikham, G., *Shakespeare's Dramatic Heritage*, London, 1969.

Wilson, F.P., *Shakespearean Studies* (ed.), H. Gardner, Oxford, 1969.

——, *Shakespeare and the New Bibliography* (ed.), H. Gardner, Oxford, 1970.

Wilson, J.D., *The Essential Shakespeare*, Cambridge, 1932.

——, *Shakespeare's Sonnets*, Cambridge, 1963.

VI. CRITICISM (SHAKESPEARE'S HISTORY PLAYS)

Alexander, P., *Shakespeare's 'Henry VI' and 'Richard III'*, Cambridge, 1929.

Bevington, D., *Tudor Drama and Politics*, Cambridge, Massachusetts, 1968.

Bloom, Allan and Jaffa, H.V., *Shakespeare's Politics*, New York and London, 1964.

Briggs, W.D., *Introduction to Marlowe's Edward II*, London, 1914.

Brooke, N., *Shakespeare's Early Tragedies*, London, 1968.

Brooke, T., 'The History Play', Chap. IX in *The Tudor Drama*, London, 1911, 1964.

Brown, J.R., and Harris, B. (eds.), *Early Shakespeare*, London, 1967.

Campbell, L.B., *Shakespeare's 'Histories', Mirrors of Elizabethan Policy*, San Marine, 1947, 1963.

Charlton, H.B., *Shakespeare, Politics and Politicians*, English Association Pamphlet No. 72, 1929.

Churchill, G.B., *Richard III Upto Shakespeare*, Berlin, 1900.

Clemen, W.H., *A Commentary on Shakespeare's 'Richard III'* (tr.), J. Bonheim, London, 1968.

Craig, H., 'Shakespeare and the History Play' in *J.Q. Adams Memorial Studies* (ed.), J. McManaway, et al., Washington, 1948.

Dorius, R.J. (ed.), *Discussions of Shakespeare's Histories*, Boston, 1964.

Driver, T.F., *The Sense of History in Greek and Shakespearean Drama*, New York, 1961.

Ellis—Fermor, Una. 'Shakespeare's Political Plays' in *The Frontiers of Drama*, London, 1967.

Haeffner, D., A *Critical Commentary on Shakespeare's 'Richard III'*, London, 1966.

Jorgensen, P.A., 'Hotspur's "Bright Honour"', Chap. III in *Redeeming Shakespeare's Words*, Berkeley and Los Angeles, 1962.

——, "Redeeming time" in Henry IV, Chap. IV in *ibid.*

——, "My name is Pistol call'd", Chap. V in *ibid.*

Kingsford, C.L., 'Fifteenth Century History in Shakespeare's Plays' in *Prejudice and Promise in Fifteenth Century England*, London, 1925, 1962.

Knight, G.W., *The Olive and the Sword*, London, 1944.

Knights, L.C., 'Shakespeare's Politics' in *Further Explorations*, London, 1965.

Lindabury, R.V., *A Study of Patriotism in the Elizabethan Drama*, Princeton, 1931.

Leech, C., *Shakespeare, The Chronicles*, London, 1962.

Leggatt, A., *Shakespeare's Political Drama*, London and New York, 1988.

MacCallum, M.W., 'Shakespeare's Treatment of History', Chap. I in *Shakespeare's Roman Plays and Their Background*, London, 1935.

Marriott, J.A.R., *English History in Shakespeare*, New York, 1918.

Palmer, J., *Political Characters of Shakespeare*, London, 1862.

1945, reprint *Political and Comic Characters of Shakespeare*, 1962.

Partridge, A.C., *The Problem of 'Henry VIII' Reopened*, Cambridge, 1949.

Pater, W., 'Shakespeare's English Kings' in *Appreciations*. London, 1889, Calcutta, 1967.

Pitcher, S.M., *The Case for Shakespeare's Authorship of 'The Famous Victories'*, London, 1962.

Prouty, C.T., *'The Contention' and Shakespeare's Henry VI*, New Haven, 1954.

Reese, M.M., *The Cease of Magesty*, London, 1961.

Ribner, I., *The English History Play in the Age of Shakespeare*, Princeton, 1957.

Rossiter, A.P., *The Angel with Horns*, London, 1962.

Sanders, W., *The Dramatist and the Received Idea, Studies in the Plays of Marlowe & Shakespeare*, Cambridge, 1968.

Schelling, F., *The English Chronicle Play*, New York, 1902.

Sen Gupta, S.C., *Shakespeare's Historical Plays*, London, 1964.

Shuger, D.K., *Political Theologies in Shakespeare's England*, New York, 1988.

Sisson, C.J., *New Readings in Shakespeare*, Vol. II, London, 1961.

Sprague, A.C., *Shakespeare's Histories: Plays for the Stage*, London, 1964.

Tillyard, E.M.W., *Shakespeare's History Plays*, Penguin, 1962.

Traversi, D., *Shakespeare. From Richard II to Henry V*, London, 1957.

Waith, E.M. (eds.), *Shakespeare, the Histories Twentieth Century Views*. New Jersey, 1965.

Warner, B.E., *English History in Shakespeare's Plays*, New York, 1894.

Weiss, T., *The Breath of Kings and Clowns*, London, 1971.

Wilson, F.P., 'The English History Play'. Chap. I in Shakespearean and Other Studies (ed.), H. Gardner, Oxford, 1969.

Wilson, J.D., *The Fortunes of Falstaff*, Cambridge, 1953.

Winny, J., *The Player King: A Theme of Shakespeare's Histories*, London, 1968.

Yeats, W.B., *Ideas of Good and Evil,* London, 1903.

VII. GENERAL WORKS

Aristotle, *The Basic Works of Aristotle* (ed.), R. Mckeon, New York, 1941.

Aquinas, St. Thomas, *Works: Philosophical Texts* (ed.), Gilby, London, 1956.

Augustine, St., *The City of God* (tr.), J. Healey, London and New York, 1942.

Bharata-Muni, *Natyasastra* (the science of drama), Calcutta, 1967.

Carr, E.H., *What Is History*, London, 1962.

Chaudhuri, Nirad C., *Robert Clive of India,* Jaico Books, 1975.

Clemen, W.H., *English Tragedy Before Shakespeare*, London, 1961.

Croce, B., *Politics and Morals* (tr.), S.J. Castiglione, London, 1946.

Dhananjaya, *The Dasarupa* (tr.), G.C.O. Haas, Delhi, 1962.

Dryden, J., *Essay of Dramatic Poesy* (ed.), Arnold, Oxford, 1918.

Eliot, T.S., *Selected Essays*, London, 1951.

Elliott-Binns, *Jeremiah*, London, 1941.

Ellis-Fermor, U., *The Frontiers of Drama*, London, 1967.

Gardiner, P. (ed.), *Theories of History*, Illinois, 1960.

Johnson, A.H., *Whitehead's Philosophy of Civilization*, Washington, 1962.

Kane, P.V., *History of Sanskrit Poetics*, Delhi, 1961.

Keith, A.B., *Sanskrit Drama in its Origin. Development, Theory and Practice*, London, 1959.

Ker, W.P., *Form and Style in Poetry*, London, 1928.

Krishnamachariar, M., *History of Classical Sanskrit Literature*, Delhi, 1970.

Narasimhan, C.V., *The Mahabharata. An English Version based on Selected Verses*, Calcutta, 1965.

Neale, J.E., The Elizabethan House of Commons.

Raghavan, V., *Bhoja's S'rngara Prakasa*, Madras, 1963.

Raje, C.G., *Biography and History in Sanskrit Literature*, Bombay, 1958.

Reeves, J., *A Short History of English Poetry*, London, 1964.

Roston, M., *Biblical Drama in England*, London, 1968.

Rossiter, A.P., *English Drama From Early Times to the Elizabethans*, London, 1950.

Shaw, G.B., *Our Theatres in the Nineties*, 3 vols., London, 1932.

——, *The Complete Prefaces*, London, 1965.

Spengler, O., *The Decline of the West* (tr.), C.F. Atkinson, 2 vols., London, 1926.

Tolstoy, L., *War and Peace*, (tr.), Louise and Aylmer Maude, London, 1933.

Toynbee, A., *A Study of History*, Vols. I-X, London, 1954.

Trevelyan, G.M., *English Social Hostory*, London, 1947.

Viswanatha, *Sahityadarpana* (the mirror of literature) (tr.) and (ed.), P.V. Kane, Delhi, 1965.

Wells, H.G., *The Classical Drama of India*, Bombay, 1963.

Widgery, A.G., *Interpretations of History*, London, 1961.

VIII. JOURNALS

Abbreviations:

CJ	*Classical Journal.*
CQ	*Critical Quarterly.*
EC	*Essays in Criticism.*
EHR	*English Historical Review.*
ELH	*A Journal of English Literary History.*
ESMEA	*Essays and Studies by Members of the English Association.*

GM	*Gentleman's Magazine.*
MLN	*Modern Language Notes.*
MLR	*Modern Language Review.*
MLQ	*Modern Language Quarterly.*
NSST	*New Shakespeare Society Transactions.*
PMLA	*Publications of the Modern Language Association of America.*
RES	*Review of English Studies.*
SE	*Studies in English.*
SP	*Studies in Philology.*
Sh.Sy.	*Shakespeare Survey.*
SQ	*Shakespeare Quarterly.*
SR	*Sewanee Review.*
WUS	*Washington University Studies.*

Journals

Albright, E.M., 'Shakespeare's *Richard II* and the Essex Conspiracy', *PMLA*, XLII (1927), 686-720.

——, 'The Folio Version of *Henry V* in Relation to Shakespeare's Times', *PMLA*, XLIII (1928), 722-56.

——, 'Shakespeare's *Richard II*, Hayward's History of Henry IV and the Essex Conspiracy', PMLA, XLVI (1931), 694-719.

Alexander, P., 'Conjectural History, or Shakespeare's Henry VIII', *ESMEA*, XVI (1931), 85-120.

Armstrong, E., 'Political Theory of the Huguenots', *EHR*, IV, No. XIII (Jan. 1889, Reprint 1962), 16-30.

Armstrong, W.A., The Elizabethan Concept of the Tyrant', *RES*, XXII (1946), 161-81.

Auden, W.H., 'The Fallen City: Some Reflections on Shakespeare's Henry IV', *Encounter*, XIII (November, 1959), 21-31.

Bald, R.C., '*The Booke of Sir Thomas More* and its Problems', *Sh.Sy.* 2 (1949) 44-61.

Begg, E., 'Shakespeare's Debt to Hall and Holinshed in *Richard III*', *SP*, XXXII (1935), 189-96.

Beloff, Max., 'On Thinking About the Past', *Encounter*, XXXIII, No. 4 (Oct., 1969), 43-50.

Bonjour, A., 'The Road to Swinstead Abbey', *ELH*, XVIII (1951), 253-74.

Boughner, D.C., 'Vice, Braggart and Falstaff', *Anglia*, LXXII (1954), 35-61.

Bowling, W.G., 'The Wild Prince Hal in Legend and Literature', *WUS*, XIII (1925-26), 305-34.

Branche, A.L., 'If Thou Wert Sensible of Courtesy: Private and Public Virtue in *Henry IV*, *Part* U, *SQ*, XVII (Autumn, 1966), 371-82.

Brooke, N., 'Marlowe as Provocative Agent in Shakespeare's Early Plays', *Sh.Sy.* 14 (1961), 34-44.

Bryant, J.A. Jr., 'Prince Hal and the Ephesians', *SR*, LXVII (Spring, 1959), 204-19.

Cain, H.E., 'Further Light on the Relation of 1 and 2 Henry IV, *SQ*, III (1952), 21-38.

Chapman, R., 'The Wheel of Fortune in Shakespeare's History Plays, *RES*, new series, I (1950), 1-7.

Clemen, W.H., 'Anticipation and Foreboding in Shakespeare's Early Histories', *Sh.Sy.* 6 (1953), 25-35.

Cormican, L.A., "Medieval Idiom in Shakespeare", *Scrutiny*, XVII, No. 3 (Autumn, 1950), 186-202 and *ibid.*, No. 4 (March, 1951), 298-317.

Dabid, R., 'Shakespeare's History Plays—Epic or Drama?' *Sh. Sy.* 6 (1953), 129-39.

Doran, Madeleine, 'Imagery in *Richard II* and in *Henry IV*, *MLR*, XXXVII, No. 2 (April, 1942), 113-22.

Draper, J.W., 'Falstaff and the Plautine Parasite', *CJ*, XXXIII (April, 1938), 390-401.

Empson, W., 'Falstaff and Mr. Dover Wilson', *Kenyon Review* (Spring, 1953), reprint in G.K. Hunter (ed.), *King Henry IV, Parts 1 and 2* (1970), 135-54.

Fiehler, R., 'How Old Castle Became Falstaff', *MLQ*, XVI (1955), 16-28.

Friesner, D.N., 'William Shakespeare, Conservative', *SQ*, XX (Spring, 1969), 165-75.

Gellert, B., 'The Melancholy of Moor-Ditch', *SQ*, XVIII (Winter, 1967), 70-71.

Hapgood, R., 'Shakespeare's Delayed Reactions', *EC*, XIII (Jan. 1963), 9-16.

Hemingway, S.B., 'On Behalf of that Falstaff', *SQ*, III (October, 1952), 307-11.

Hunter, G.K., '*Henry IV* and the Elizabethan Two-Part Play', RES, new ser, V (August 1954), 236-48.

——, 'Shakespeare's Politics and the Rejection of Falstaff', *RES*. 3 (1959), 227-36.

Jenkins, H., 'Shakespeare's History Plays: 1900-1951', *Sh.Sy*. 6 (1953), 1-15.

Kelly, R.L., 'Shakespeare's Scroops and the "Spirit of Cain"', *SQ*, XX (Winter, 1969), 71-80.

King, Lucile, 'The Use of Hall's Chronicle in the Folio and Quarto Texts of *Henry VI*', *PQ*, XIII (1934), 321-32.

Kirschbaum, Leo, 'The Authorship of *1 Henry VI*', *PMLA*, LXVII (1952), 809-22.

Knights, L.C., 'Notes on Comedy', *Scrutiny* I (March 1933), 356-67.

——, 'Shakespeare and Political Wisdom', *SR*, LXI (1953), 43-55.

Kris, Ernst, 'Prince Hal's Conflict', *Psychoanalytic Q*, XVII (October 1948), 487-506.

Law, R.A., 'Structural Unity in the Two Parts of Henry IV', *SP*, XXIV (1927), 223-42.

——, 'Links Between Shakespeare's History Plays', *SP*, L (1953), 168-87.

Lee, Jane, 'On the Authorship of the Second and Third Parts of *Henry VI*, and their Originals', *NSST* (1876), 219-311.

McGuire, R.L., 'The Play-Within-the-Play in *1 Henry IV*, *SQ*, XVIII (Winter, 1967), 47-52.

McNamara, A.M., '*Henry IV:* the King as Protagonist', SQ, X (Summer, 1959), 423-31.

Monagham, J., 'Falstaff and His Forebears', *SP*, XVIII (1923), 353-61.

Mincoff, M., '*Henry VIII* and Fletcher', *SQ*, XII (Summer, 1961), 239-60.

Muir, K., 'A Reconsideration of *Edward III*', *Sh.Sy*, 6 (1953), 39-48.

Myers, A.R., 'Richard III and Historical Tradition', *History* LIII, No. 178 (June 1968), 181-202.

Nosworthy, J.M., "Shakespeare and *Sir Thomas More*", *RES*, new series, VI (1955), 12-25.

Pettet, E.G., 'Hot Irons and Fever: A Note on Some of the Imagery of *King John*', *EC, IV* (April 1954), 128-44.

Phialas, P.G., 'The Medieval in *Richard II*', *SQ, XII* (Summer, 1961), 305-10.

Reese, Gertrude, 'The Question of the Succession in Elizabethan Drama', *University of Texas, SE* (1942), 59-85.

Ribner, I., 'Bolingbroke, a True Machiavellian', *MLQ*, IX (June 1948), 177-84.

——, 'The Idea of History in Marlowe's *Tamburlaine*', *ELH*, XX (1853), 251-66.

——, 'Morality Roots of the Tudor History Play', *Tulane, SE*, IV (1954), 21-34.

Seng, P.J., 'Songs, Time and the Rejection of Falstaff', *Sh.Sy*, 15 (1962), 31-39.

Simpson, R., 'The Political Use of the Stage in Shakespeare's Time', *NSST* (1874), 371-95.

——, 'The Politics of Shakespeare's Historical Plays', *ibid.* (1874), 396-441.

Shapiro, A., 'The Significance of a Date', *Sh.Sy.* 8 (1955), 100-05.

Sjoberg, Elsa, 'From Madcap Prince to King, the Evolution of Prince Hal', *SQ* (Winter, 1969), 11-16.

Speeding, J., 'Who Wrote Shakespeare's *Henry VIII*?' *GM* new ser. XXXIV (August 1950), 115-23.

Tillyard, E.M.W., 'Shakespeare's Historical Cycle: Organism or Compilation?' *SP*, LI (1954), 34-39.

——,'Shakespeare's Historical Cycle: Rejoinder', *ibid.*, LI (1954), 40-41.

Van De Water, J.C. 'The Bastard in *King John*', *SQ*, XI (1960), 137-46.

Waldock, A.J.A., 'The Men in Buckram', *RES*, XXIII (January 1947), 16-23.

Watson, Sara R., '*Gorboduc* and the Theory Tyrannicide', *MLR*, XXXIV (1939), 355-66.

Williams, P. 'The Birth and Death of Falstaff Reconsidered', *SQ*, VIII (Summer 1957), 359-65.

Wilson, J.D. 'Shakespeare's *Richard III* and *The True Tragedy*', 1594, *SQ* III (1952), 299-306.

——,'Malone and the Upstart Crow', *Sh.Sy*. 4 (1951), 56-68.

Wright, L.B., 'Heywood and the Popularizing of History', *MLN*, XLIII (1928), 287-93.

——,'Some Social Aspects of Some Belated Moralities', *Anglia*, LIV (1930), 107-48.

Zeeveld, W.G. 'The Influence of Hall on Shakespeare's English Historical Plays', *ELH*, III (1936), 317-53.

——,"'Food for Powder'—'Food for Worms'", *SQ*, III (July 1952), 249-53.

Index